THE
FROG
PRINCE

THE FROG PRINCE

An Autobiography

By MAURICE GIRODIAS

CROWN PUBLISHERS, INC.   NEW YORK

To Laurette
To Lilla

I wish to express my gratitude to
Lilla Lyon, and to Goldian and Andre VandenBroeck,
without whose help and support this frog
would never have made it to prince.

French edition of *Une Journée Sur la Terre: Premiere Partie* Copyright © 1977
by Maurice Girodias
English translation (augmented) Copyright © 1980 by Crown Publishers, Inc.
Inquiries should be addressed to Crown Publishers,
Inc., One Park Avenue, New York, New York 10016
Printed in the United States of America
Published simultaneously in Canada
by General Publishing Company Limited
Library of Congress Cataloging in Publication Data
Girodias, Maurice.
The frog prince.
Translation of Une Journée sur la terre.
1. Girodias, Maurice.   2. France—Biography.
I. Title.
CT1018.G53A3513 1980   944'.009'94   80-11945
Design by Camilla Filancia
ISBN: 0-517-541955
10 9 8 7 6 5 4 3 2 1
First Edition

PROLOGUE

It has taken me all of a dozen years to confront at last this blank page which awaits my words. It was at the Frankfurt Book Fair, on a busy day, with hundreds of publishers scurrying around in Halle 7-A, and I had just managed to buttonhole my old friend John Calder at long last. Anyone who knows John is aware of the fact that you can't get a fiver out of the man even if your life depends on it. Well, my life depended on whether I could raise five thousand dollars somehow—within the next forty-eight hours—or my business would go under, once again. What a tragedy, you can't say no, please, John!

"Leave me alone," John was saying. "You and your money problems, you know . . . Listen, not only don't I have the money, but I never *lend* money. It's a sure way to lose friends, you know that, don't you? But money is easy to find here, why don't you ask the others?"

"Fat chance," I murmured somberly. John had been my last hope.

"Write your memoirs," he said. To get rid of me, quite obviously.

"Don't be an idiot, John!" I groaned. "I've got to get the money within two days maximum, otherwise it's all over. And it's only five thousand, it's really nothing, I'm sure you could—"

"Seriously," he cut me off, his pink face puckered in earnestness. "The autobiography of Maurice Girodias, that's a sure winner. Everyone will want it, the Americans especially; they're flashing their checkbooks all over the place. All you have to do is announce the project, that's all. You don't even have to write a line. Five thousand! It's chicken feed."

"You really think so?" I said, somewhat flattered by the implications. That Calder was a sly one, a Scotsman with a vengeance.

"Of course! They all respect you here. They know who you are . . . You've been had by some, you have swindled a few others, you have made and lost fortunes. People like a scoundrel who's down on his luck; they understand and sympathize . . . Plus all your escapades with the ladies . . . and that zany nightclub of yours, La Grande Séverine, hah, that's a whole story in itself! And, of course, I must admit, whether you knew what you were doing or not, you've discovered ten times more talent, as a publisher, than the three thousand noodles here. Think of it! Sam Beckett. *Lolita*. Miller. Genet. *Naked Lunch*. *Candy*. *Story of O*, goddamnit! And your crazy fight with Donleavy over the rights of *The Ginger Man*! And losing the rights of *Candy* to a bunch of American pirates . . . Well, the list is endless—Georges Bataille, Iris Owens, eh? And *Zorba the Greek,* de Sade, Alex Trocchi, Frank Harris! . . . You must tell me who wrote *Story of O* one of these days . . . And funny books like *The Sexual Life of Robinson Crusoe*. Akbar del Piombo! Who ever heard of someone like del Piombo? It takes lots of balls to market stuff like that to porno fans and not be gunned down by one of those maniacs. They have no humor."

"Well said," I opined.

"You know what you did?" asked friend John. "You disarmed the opposition. Just like that. All those prune-faced puritans in Britain and in the States, banned in London, banned in Boston; they've been silenced by the sheer ridicule of their position, just because of what you published. Just as if the emperor had clothes on after all. Your defense of real masterpieces, *Lolita*, *Naked Lunch*, even *Sexus* or *The Ginger Man*, this puts you in a class apart. No other publisher has ever done that. You are a liberator. I admire you." John's watery eyes belied his words, but, never mind, they were good words. Whatever I may have said about his tightness, he was generous when it came to fair praise.

"Well, John," I said, "that's all very kind of you but—"

"Let me finish!" John interrupted, very excited. "I know what I owe you. You practically forced me to publish *Tropic of Cancer* in England. I was terrified, but you convinced me to do it. That's really when I became a publisher. You've helped me, and you've helped dozens of those other characters around us. You changed the world, that's what you did. You made it safe for sex. You know what they call you in Tangiers? The Lenin of the Sexual Revolution. Hah! Single-handed you did what Churchill and Roosevelt together

couldn't have pulled off in a century: You destroyed Anglo-Saxon censorship, *blaaam*, all by yourself."

"Oh, John," I said weakly.

"That's right, my friend. You're a personage. All those punks here are not fit to shine your boots. All right now, you just make a book out of that. It will sell like hot cakes."

"But, John, I keep telling you that it will take *time* . . . Perhaps you could write it for me, you seem to know the story," I suggested.

"Don't be silly, you have to do it yourself. It may take twelve years or more, if you ask me, but never mind. For now all you have to do is simply to talk about it; you don't have to go to work on it. Stir them up, but be vague, tell them a few of your stories. If you're not a complete fool, you will have your money on time, five thousand dollars, and much more probably."

It was really tempting. And it sounded so simple, easy, and natural, the way he was describing the move.

"Okay, how do I begin?" I asked.

"Right now you don't have to do a thing. I'll do the groundwork for you. I have one hour before my next meeting, that's ample. But you, you mustn't make a move, understand?"

"Well, all right. But may I ask what you propose to do?"

"Simple. You know the best-seller mentality, eh? Well, all I have to do is to give them an image of your book as a potential best seller. You know—*By the Man Who Gave You* Lolita! Candy! Zorba the Greek! The King of Porn! That's the pitch. Easy. You know what maniacs they are with their million-dollar deals, bidding and outbidding one another to get the winner . . . a book nobody has had the time to read or even write . . . a name, a vague idea . . . and who cares if in the end it falls flat on its face, because by the time it comes out they forgot how much they paid for it in the first place . . . Ah yes, success, best sellers, miracles, millions of dollars, big reviews, that's the name of the game, that's why we're all in it, little boy gamblers, all of us . . . Yes, yes . . . So you see how simple it is, all I have to do is to drop on a few of them, the true believers, and ask them to lend me five thousand dollars. And just as I did when you asked me for money, they will say to me: Why do you need it, John? And I will answer: 'I just convinced Girodias he should write his autobiography, and I want to secure the British rights on the spot. He's broke, as usual, five thousand will do it, etc., etc.' You'll have your check within twenty-four hours, guaranteed."

"Johnny my boy, you're amazing! I do wonder why Her Majesty the Queen did not single you out, a man like you could have saved the empire."

"Oh, forget it, will you? What you have to do is simply to go to the Frankfurter Hof, sit in the bar, and look mysterious. But not a word to anyone about the book, eh?"

"I shall obey joyfully. God bless you, my precious friend." And I watched him fondly as he trotted off on his little Teddy bear legs into the gesticulating, negotiating populace.

It would be pointless to document the sordid details; suffice it to say that I was soon deluged with contracts, plus a pocketful of some fifteen thousand dollars in cash, which I fingered voluptuously through the tweed, feeling rather as if I had discovered a bundle of bank notes wrapped in an old newspaper, abandoned by some absentminded burglar under a bench.

That money came to me in a dream. When I woke up, the money was gone and I still had to write the book. I did a few pages, at least to give myself a clear conscience. I tore them up. I tried again. Worse still. That damned first page. . . . As we all know, the first page is the hardest one; that's where most people fail.

My story is not easy to write. It took me all those years and many tribulations to get close to it at last. Hard years, stark and punishing years; my life was turning against me for having treated it so badly. And in the end that's what saved me. I lost everything and I finally accepted my loss. Then I could start reconstructing myself. And write that first page! It may not be brilliant, but it has cost me a lot. And now I have a past and a future once again, and between the two a fulcrum—this book.

Born of a jest, this book has mysteriously developed inside me into a revolutionary event. I had to discover the mechanics of my inventions, the rules of my madness. The recent disasters of my life had reduced me to a tiny pile of ashes . . . destabilization by Henry Kissinger in '74, three years spent under the permanent threat of deportation, without money or papers, broke, broken, finished, virtually a political prisoner of the most undemocratic democracy in the world . . . what a fall! When I arrived in Manhattan in the mid-sixties, I was a hero of modern culture then; they saluted the event with a full-page interview in the *New York Times* book section, with a youthful picture of the hero himself complete with necktie and crew cut—the works. Ah! How I missed the boat. They offered me success, fame, easy money, but it all looked much too simple; I just disdained the naïve seduction. Of course the establishment doesn't like rejection. But I am not here to complain, only to explain what happened in the past, the distant past, and the more recent past. From the ashes in the crucible came this book—not written for any publisher, reviewer, or book trade member, but for you, reader, insofar as you are interested by the processes of life.

The facts are all there; the dates are reasonably accurate. The characters are not abstractions; I've tried to show them as I knew them, loved them, or endured them.

Of course, these images of the past are seen with today's eyes, the bifocal vision of someone who is waiting to be reborn. I regret nothing, except not to have gone far enough. I should never have stopped to think; it's only when I became reasonable that things went wrong. If I had my life to live over again—nothing would stop me; I've been through the fires, believe me.

You may also consider writing such a book as a money-saving exercise. All that big talk about psychoanalysis is bunk, of course; why waste ten years on the couch, plus a fortune? Write your autobiography and all will go well. I guarantee it.

I can even dream of extending that simple idea into an institution. Instead of paying taxes and giving the government money it always misuses, you open an author's account on Wall Street. You sign a contract with the government to publish your autobiography, in which it plays the role of a national vanity press. Right? Cost of publication to be paid by author. Just think of the advantages. So now we have an official excuse to write about the only thing that really matters: our own selves. Every ego gets a big boost; every cell of the social body comes alive again. The economy takes on a new meaning; the GNP becomes the Gross National Publisher. . . . All this is good for the moral fiber; the best education is self-education, and you practice nothing but that when you write your memoirs. Those with something to say will be heard by all; the others will be pulped. It will be an aristocratic society.

And the government will be in the business of selling books, paying royalties to authors, lying to them, lying to the public; well, it will be doing a publisher's job, which is bad enough, but less so than the armaments race. . . . That stupid threat of war under which we are made to live will be eliminated, and we will be free at last to sound our solidarity, not just in theory but in fact. Our total, ineluctable, biological, phenomenal solidarity. All the myriad egos, all the little ladies and gents who define themselves as "I" ten thousand times a day, they will have to define that mysterious "I"—since four billion "I's" is a contradiction in terms. Who—among the four billion of us alive today on this earth—can claim to be the center of the universe, with all the rest of us as bystanders? And yet that's what we do, an ancient ingrained error; this may be what they call the original sin, by the way.

When you sit down to write your autobiography, you will soon discover that this "I" of yours is no more than a pore in the elephant's hide. "I" am no more than the sum of what I receive and give out, what I exchange with other I's. "I" is an immaterial reference point, a center of gravity endowed with multiple functions like the center of the sun, which can be defined only in relation to other similar points. Whatever goes for suns goes for humans too. Yes? And that brings us to the erotic continuum.

This is a Buddhist-style term, of course, and I am using it not out of sheer perversity, but because Christianity has so well chewed up the issue of Good and Evil, of sin and holy water, that one must look for the truth in sources more profound than the papal encyclicals. When Buddha showed desire as forming the fabric of created life, he meant that desire is divine—a clear and simple position that surpasses all Christian ideas of sin and duality.

Let's look at Don Juan, if you will. He loved ten thousand women, so they say; or at least a great many. Each one of those amorous tilts altered irreversibly the psychic metabolism of the two contestants; or at least we want to assume that not one of the ten thousand was left untouched by the encounter, and that this also applies to the champion of love himself. In round-robin style he gave to each one a little of what he had received from the 9,999 others, and vice versa. Each one of the ten thousand, as you can see, served as an exchange center for that infinitely complex traffic. And so we can see that Don Juan is bound by this erotic link not only to those ten thousand women but also, through them, to one hundred thousand men he has never met, and again, through those men, to millions of other women. . . . And so on *ad infinitum*, not only in space but, of course, also in time.

It can thus be safely inferred that we have erotic cousins in each age of creation, from Atlantis to the birdmen of tomorrow, and from the conception of humankind to the time of its takeoff into the great intergalactic beyond. In other words, the human family can be depicted as a genetic continuum set in motion by an erotic continuum. You may look at the flow of generations as if it were the tunic of Nessos, a thick fabric impregnated with the heavy blood of human life, but alight with divine desire; by this erotic energy which fertilizes all the areas of the human presence.

It is understood that since we are all descended from that same source of desire, eroticism is to us the supreme science. But here we confront a semantic problem, which is not limited to a quibble over words.

For the middle-class ethics of the Western world, dominated by conventional Christian traditions, eroticism is necessarily perverse and corrupting; it is at the same time a poison that tarnishes the soul and the reputation, and a secret source of delicious remorse, of delightful tortures. Western eroticism was born in the confessional; from this covert dialogue between passion and repression our culture was born. How would your good father confessor make a living if it were not for Satan?

He makes sex a sin in order to extend his authority over all humanity, which needs sex to continue. By degrading the dialogue between Eros and Thanatos to a trite choice between lust and boredom, the church not only stifles our evolution, individual and collective: it insults Creation.

The divine Eros is the motor of the continuum, whether the Vatican likes it or not; and it's He who writes the story of our world, not the Holy Father. The tribulations of Eros in our time have occupied my entire life, and my father's life before mine. Our two stories therefore appear as only one in the continuum, my life being nothing but an intensified repetition of his own. Just as it took generations of mountain climbers to conquer Everest, it took a dedicated team of specialists, father and son, to trigger the sexual revolution.

This tale which I am about to start is therefore conceived as an episode in the erotic continuum. It is less my own personal story, which wouldn't rate all these pages, than the story of what happened to the mind of our time, of a transformation in consciousness. I see the changes I have undergone myself only as a reflection of the general movement.

My father and mother, and all those I have encountered on my way, are floating along with me down the continuum like tree trunks descending downstream. A few words, to start with, about my prehistory.

1

*Manchester in the 1890s.—Jackie and Freddie shake hands
over Miss Pennyfeather's supine body.—Ode to
a Nightingale.—La Belle Lantelme.—A musical war
and the real thing.—A French railway baron
and his daughters.—Spirits of the pampa.—Jackie as
a Bengal lancer...as a soldier in love...as D'Annunzio's
whipping boy...as my father.*

My father was born in 1887 in Manchester, England. His family was Jewish and had settled long ago in a handsome house across the street from the archbishop's palace. They had acquired their wealth in the ship-chandling business.

Manchester—and its neighbor, its rival sister, Liverpool—occupied the crossroads of traffic between England and her empire. A cosmopolitan city, always in ferment, she became a millionaire through commerce, and a billionaire thanks to the Industrial Revolution. Industry, chiefly the textile business, flourished along the foggy banks of the Mersey River.

Competition with London was fierce. This rivalry was a boon to the arts: bankers and shipowners aspired to be Medicis. Miss Horniman's famous theater and the Hallé Concerts had given the city an international reputation as a center of culture. The liberal *Manchester Guardian* was admired everywhere as a model of modern journalism.

Jackie came into the world in a family where money and religion had been cheerfully transmuted into music and letters. He was expected to become a scholar or an artist. Preferably an artist: His dreamy gaze and ash-blond locks would look well on a musician.

He was the eleventh of twelve children: first came nine sisters, starting with Emily, already married and a mother, and then the three boys, Louis, Jackie, and Freddie. It is therefore understandable that they should feel as a repressed minority. The wall of skirts was insurmountable, the male an endangered species. Louis reacted early by becoming an incorrigible scoundrel and took off after stealing his father's cuff links. He became a soldier of fortune and died, so it's said, during the Boer War. That left Jackie and Freddie alone against all.

Jackie was six when his father died and eight when his mother followed suit. She was a beautiful, generous woman, born in Bucharest. But his only vivid memory of her was of rosy plump pillows of flesh, the thighs he glimpsed beneath her skirts once when he was but a puling infant. . . .

Piano lessons were a royal pain. Miss Pennyfeather hid the soul of a metronome in the overblown body of an old maid. She flaunted an extensive décolletage that resembled a bed of pink cauliflowers. Jackie detested Miss Penny and her bosom and her aroma and the piano. Freddie, to avenge his brother, brought him a large green frog with muscular thighs. The creature was imprisoned beneath the piano lid to await the enemy. The outcome was uncertain; it was a matter of luck and ballistics. But this skirmish was a smashing success. The animal sprang headfirst into the mammary commissure. Miss Pennyfeather leaped to her feet and then slumped to the ground like a sack of potatoes. It was a fine moment. The two boys shook hands solemnly above the prostrate form of Miss Pennyfeather.

After the piano was abandoned, came the violin. Jackie had a good ear and a taste for music, but he would never make a great violinist. There is a faded photograph of him, dressed bizarrely as a girl, violin in hand, gazing at the lens with a quizzical eye. Not long after this picture was taken, he was spotted in the street, in ribbons and curls, playing a savage game of soccer with his brother and a ragged troop of hoodlums. From behind the high drawing-room window, the teacher showed Emily the scene with a prim look:

"Have you seen what they're using for a ball?" said he, tweaking his lapel.

"Heavens!" cried she. "My bustle!"

It must be noted here that after explorers drew the world's attention to the Hottentots, their protuberant bottoms exerted a subtle and unfortunate influence on fashion. Well-bred ladies equipped themselves with artificial buttocks made of rubber, a substance that itself came from Africa, and that made a good bustle eligible as a football.

"*Freddie! Jackie!* Stop this game immediately!"

Poor Emily had a hard time rearing her young brothers. Obscurely, they understood they could only preserve their future manhood by presenting a united front. Few boys had such good reason to assert a sacred brotherhood.

After the father's death, the family fortune had begun to melt away; clearly it would be impossible to send the sons to Oxford. Freddie quit school at fourteen, Jackie at seventeen. Forthwith Freddie entered the world of business by the back door, selling the *Guardian* at street corners.

Little was left of former glory—all that endured was devotion to the life of the mind. Systematically Jackie devoured not only the English classics but also Balzac and the Symbolists. He studied Chinese and knew Keats by heart. So far all that he knew of love was encompassed by the line of his favorite poet:

"*Forever shalt thou love and she be fair . . . ,*"

which made it seem something implacable and marvelous, hazily situated in the future.

"Look here, Jackie," scolded Emily, "where have you been all day?"

"I told you I was going cycling with Muriel. You know Muriel Bradford."

"But it's ten at night! Whatever will you do now? Will you marry her?"

Jackie was thunderstruck. Marry Muriel? At seventeen, on a salary of fifteen shillings a week! Was Emily crazy? Suddenly the appalling truth struck him. He thought of Muriel, of the wonderful afternoon they'd spent together . . . of course, he hadn't laid a finger on her . . . Muriel. . . . Under his sister's reproachful glare, he blushed furiously. Chaste Emily, showing him what a fool he'd been! A complete ass. No wonder Muriel seemed so irritated, so sullen on the way home, as he pedaled alongside her reciting the *Ode to a Nightingale*. He pulled the Keats from his pocket and hurled it out the window.

After this poor start, he managed to liberate himself from

his excessive naïveté. He soon discovered what interested him: business, for example. At twenty he started a company with a boy his own age to make and sell velvet. At one stroke he became the equal of the formidable Manchester merchants two or three times his age, who affirmed their virility by the number of whiskies they could gulp down without falling under the table.

Among these condottiere he carved out his own niche; he amassed an enviable fortune and enjoyed flaunting it conspicuously. He owned seven bulldogs, fifty pairs of trousers, and half a share in a racehorse named Algernon—Algie, for short.

His taste for Balzac, and especially his enthusiasm for *Une Femme de Trente Ans*, led him to fall for a woman of thirty, a lady of irreproachable breeding, whom he wooed with the most exalted literary fervor—until he discovered the devastating fact: she was scarcely twenty-four. This was a catastrophe from which he barely recovered, especially in the eyes of his cronies at the Swan Club. Here was the meeting place of the gilded youth of Manchester, which he had started with Gerald Cumberland, Walter Mudie, James Agate, Basil Dean, Lascelles Abercrombie, and Harold Brighouse, young lions all, who aspired to a life of letters or the theater. With or without bluestockings, life could be pleasant.

One spring morning Jackie set off to discover that Paris he had dreamed about for so long, that city of air and stone that gave birth to François Villon and Baudelaire. There at last real life rivaled the dream and even surpassed it. Reality as personified first of all by those nimble and stylish Parisian women who delighted in kindling a lusty leer in the men. It was a far cry from bluestockings. Did these lovely Parisians know how much they resembled their city?

In a fiacre he rode past the Tuileries, where a slight haze floated as in Watteau's *Embarkation for Cythera*. A sumptuous lunch under the arcades of the Palais-Royal: five courses plus wine for a shilling, that is, 1 franc 25. The Pont-Neuf, the Cluny Museum, the Luxembourg Gardens . . . the enchantment continues. The Comédie-Française. *Louise* at the Opéra-Comique. The Parisians in the audience were as decorative as those on stage; but they were most remarkable in cafés and restaurants, eating and holding forth vociferously, drinking and gesticulating, knowing eyes in florid faces, not to forget the artful moustache, and every single papilla on the alert . . . Voisin's, Maxim's, Henry's, all the high spots. At the American Bar he suddenly found himself face-to-face with an irresistible woman and fell in love with her the very instant they were introduced. By the time his lips grazed the back of her hand, he had completely lost his head. And when he looked up, he found his wishes instantly granted: The gay smile that greeted him opened up a delicious alcove and at the same time revealed to him the secrets of Parisian life. For the lady by whom he was smitten was Mlle Lantelme, one of the most famous actresses of the boulevards, and mistress, on top of that, of one of the most powerful men in Paris, M. Edwards, owner of the newspaper *Le Matin*. Her public adored her for being the *cocotte* who loves a good time, handsome men, and very young ones. Jackie had arrived right on schedule.

After those spring days in Paris, Manchester seemed leaden. People mistrusted the French, a frivolous lighthearted people who canonized their courtesans. The fogs of the Mersey inspired melancholy as much as those of Hamburg; the Germans felt at home in Manchester, as if they were among their kin. At the Club for German Waiters of Lancashire, the men took paramilitary courses and learned to handle weapons. And at the Hallé Concerts, the great German conductor Hans Richter stubbornly refused to play anything but Beethoven.

If the war brewing in Europe had erupted that very minute, the Entente Cordiale between France and Great Britain would probably have been reversed by London, if pushed, to the benefit of the Germans. Kaiser Wilhelm may have been mad, stupid, and intolerably vain, but he was Victoria's grandson, and family ties were still dominant. The three great powers had divided up Africa during the last quarter of the nineteenth century. To avoid open war there, the central portion, the Congo basin, had been entrusted to Leopold II, prince of German blood and king of the Belgians, and, also, uncle of Queen Victoria.

Leopold adopted the trappings of a humanitarian sovereign, but he was a gambler and unbridled opportunist; without even setting foot in Africa he had himself proclaimed king of the Congo and used it as his private domain, sending gangs of thugs there to put the blacks to work. With the invention of the automobile, rubber took on extraordinary value; blacks who refused to work at harvesting latex had their right hand cut off.

The Congo became the object of international dissension. As the empires of Russia, Turkey, Austro-Hungary and China foundered, Japan and the United States grew strong. In Ireland, the nationalist movement of John Redmond, who gently demanded home rule, was swamped by the radicals of Sinn Féin who called for the teaching of Gaelic in the schools.

Indeed Irish nationalism appeared to have breathed its last. Three centuries earlier British and Scottish settlers had been sent to Northern Ireland to create a colonial bridgehead there (as the French would do later in Algeria; indeed as Begin's government is doing today on the Right Bank of the Jordan). They proliferated; and, after Parnell, the last of the great Irish leaders, had been duly destabilized by the British secret service, it seemed obvious that Ireland would eventually become a second-rate British province, like Wales or Scotland. . . . However, at that point two maverick Conservative politicos from London decided to carve a new constituency for themselves in Northern Ireland, to further their personal ambitions, Edward Carson and Frederick Edwin Smith. F. E. Smith (also known as Galloper Smith) used tactics not unlike those which brought young Richard Nixon into the public eye, closer to us; he denounced a nonexistent conspiracy to stir up the loyalist feelings in Ulster. A militia was created in Belfast. Playing war, drilling and marching through the streets was a great game; the militia grew into an army, and the threat became so ominous to the South that the Sinn Féin in turn started to arm themselves.

Even in England, feminists threatened the conservative and patriarchal tradition. The stalwarts of the period—George Bernard Shaw, Annie Besant, H. G. Wells—launched revolutionary socialist theories by way of the Fabian Society.

Half a million unemployed roamed the countryside, spreading chaos and terror. Only a war could save the situation; no one has invented a better remedy for such grave threats to the social order. But would it be England and France against Germany, or England and Germany against France? Protected by her fleet, England risked little more than the loss of her surplus of Irish and unemployed; anyway, France and Germany would provide the cannon fodder. Everywhere, armed conflict was seen as a necessary evil. In France and Germany, young men went into training. Those who were about to die talked enthusiastically of war, as if it were a hunting-party.

Jackie had already embarked on his own war—a musical battle. To counteract the Teutonic dictatorship of Hans Richter, he and friends set up the Manchester Musical Society and successfully gave concerts devoted exclusively to English and French composers.

As secretary to the society he wrote a letter to the *Guardian*, protesting against the monolithic pro-Germanic stance of the Hallé Concerts. He then penned an answer under a pseudonym, denouncing his own letter with idiotic arguments. Under his own name again, he wrote a third letter to refute the second one. All Manchester society plunged into the fray. Assaulted on all sides, Richter could only vent himself with cries of impotent rage, hurling imprecations in which the name Debussy whistled like the crack of a whip. He sent his decorations back to the king and took the next boat for Germany.

Jackie was the man of the hour, the Robin Hood of Manchester. At that supreme moment, he fell in love. A hopeless passion, for she was a married woman. Nightly he lurked by her lighted window, his heart beating madly. He enjoyed his success in the afternoon; in the evening he was a hairbreadth from killing himself. Finally she offered a deal. He was to go away for six months; if at the end of this respite they were both still so inclined, she would leave her husband for Jackie.

The six months were long; he steeled himself for any outcome but what he found: She had left her husband for another man, and married him. Meanwhile her own sister, Nell, had married his own younger brother, Freddie.

A few days later Britain entered the war with France against Germany. That was his cue: He could die of love, but at the same time he would die for France, that beautiful country that he barely knew but had adopted forever. He went off to enlist. Thanks to his tailor, he was made an officer. Because he knew Balzac he was assigned to liaison. And because of his monocle he was assigned to the cavalry, although he scarcely knew how to ride a horse.

He was sent to Marseilles to be incorporated into a company of Bengal lancers that was expected to arrive from India. He soon found that its officers were centaurs of unparalleled snobbery.

Here his troubles began. The chestnut horse assigned to him was accustomed to leading parades, and in spite of all his efforts, Jackie was unable to stop it from trotting up to take its usual place at the head of the column. Hampered by his sword and his monocle, Jackie was desperately trying to master the beast, who felt his spurs and took off at a gallop, unleashing a volley of farts. The column halted. The cavalry, flabbergasted by this demonstration of equestrian skill, applauded as the horse finally came to a stubborn halt, facing toward the stable.

Despite these minor trials, the war seemed almost too mild under the sun of Provence. Marseilles was filling up with exotic troops. Galloper Smith, in a fantastic uniform, a Havana cigar clamped in his predator's beak, was seen coming in and out of the power centers, as were the maharajas from Kashmir and Kapurthala who paraded through the streets, riding at the head of their private armies.

An abundance of flowers, girls, aromas, café terrace melodramas, clanking streetcars, the frenetic crowd on the Canebière—all this made it hard to remember that one was there to die.

My mother, Marcelle Eugénie, was born in a troglodytic village not far from Almería on the southern coast of Spain. Her parents' house was the only stone house in the place; it was perched on a cliff whose flanks were pierced by the caves in which the locals resided.

Her father, Léon Girodias, was there to build a railway—his specialty after graduating from the Ecole des Arts et Métiers at twenty. His mother was a war widow, which gave him the privilege of abstaining from military service. Young people were supposed to serve seven years in those times, but the sons of the bourgeoisie could use many available loopholes to avoid wasting their best years so uselessly; they could even rent young peasants to replace them, and eventually die in their name.

Being very poor, my grandfather had to work at menial jobs to finance his own studies; and after graduation he looked for a post overseas because the best jobs in metropolitan France were reserved for the rich. He was sent to Algeria; and it is in Algiers, at a summer ball, that he met Marcelline Mangouin, daughter of a beautiful Spanish lady, the toast of the town, who was the widow of a *sous-préfet* of Constantine.

He made up his mind to marry her. He was hardly acceptable, socially, but this penniless young man appeared so hard-working, robust, and pleasant that the mother let herself be convinced. After that, winning over the daughter was easy. He was twenty and she was twenty-two. They began a life of wandering that kept them away from France for thirty years.

In those days France was committed to building a double empire, colonial and commercial, in competition against the British one. Léon belonged to the new race of intelligent and ambitious pioneers sent overseas to make their country's fortune, and their own. Once he had proved himself in North Africa, in Spain, and in Portugal, the Paris banks offered him nearly unlimited credit to undertake the creation of a railway network in Argentina.

Since the English explorer Sebastian Cabot had visited the Paraná River in the sixteenth century, and named the land Argentina because of the silver treasures he found there, the British had retained a special interest in it. To enlarge their influence, at the end of the nineteenth century, they had undertaken the construction of a vast railway system thanks to which the country would emerge from its primitive state at last and develop its resources. The French, however, had also managed to convince the local government to let them build their own rival system; the young engineer who had been picked for that job had a role to play that was therefore political as well as technical. And Léon made his fortune after he won the challenge; after a few years Wilson, his British counterpart, conceded defeat and resigned his post to become his assistant.

But all this had only been made possible thanks to his inexhaustible energy; he was personally supervising every phase of the construction. But he never had any trouble working fourteen hours a day, nor riding hundred of miles on horseback. To follow the progress more closely, he had bought a large hacienda in the pampa, in the middle of nowhere, and that is where the four children were brought up, in a world that was entirely their own. Indeed the last child, Maurice, was born there and without the help of a midwife, Léon himself having severed the umbilical cord with a kitchen knife.

Apart from the children's French governess, and the Italian immigrants who worked as house servants and gardeners in the orchard, the only other human presence was that of the gauchos, most of them Indians, herding their flocks and roaming the grassy plain by the rhythm of the seasons. There were no urban centers within a two-hundred-mile radius, no neighbors who could be reached in less than a day's ride. And so Mamita, as the young mother was now called, started building a French home for her family in that wasteland, as she had always done before, wherever Léon had pitched his tent. After a careful study of catalogs, a shipment of furniture in the latest style was ordered from Paris. She taught her underprivileged staff to clean, to sew, and even to cook; and the classical aromas of French cuisine permeated the house, lending authenticity to the Parisian decor. Hélène and Renée, the two older daughters, mooned over the illustrated monthlies and the fashionable novels of Gérard d'Houville, dreaming of *Paris.* . . .

Only Léon had been there, and then only as a student, but even for Mamita and her children, who had never even visited metropolitan France, Paris was the fulcrum of their lives. To be able to speak, dress, walk, dance, eat, laugh, and sing in exactly the way the Parisians did was for them a constant obsession. Having no roots in the motherland, those peripheral citizens of France were creating for themselves an image of it which far surpassed the known reality. The two little ones were relatively free of that collective mania; they had each other, and the pampas that stretched off into infinity, and their giant horse, which they loved to push into a thundering gallop, clinging to each other and shrieking with dizzy joy. Marcelle was nicknamed Trois-Pommes by her elders, due to her short size and plump figure.

The most recent craze in Paris was spiritualism. Ghost stories were very popular; some bore the seal of literary acceptance, such as Guy de Maupassant's *Le Horla*, which so impressed Mamita that she ordered Alan Cardec's famous treatise, *The Book of the Spirits*. The newspapers announced that several British scientists had initiated investigations in the field of parapsychology, which Professors Richet and Charcot were also pursuing in Paris; especially Charcot who was experimenting at his hospital, La Salpétrière, for the benefit of his students: A young Viennese doctor, Sigmund Freud, was one of them.

And gradually, in the evening, the whole family took the habit of assembling in the *grand salon* or the veranda to invoke the spirits. In addition to the family, "Mademoiselle," an impoverished young lady from Montpellier who served as teacher and governess for the children, took her place at the round table. Mademoiselle showed signs of being quite an exceptional medium, and she fell into a trance at the drop of a hat.

All the lamps were extinguished; shadowy night invaded the house, and only the cries of nocturnal predators pierced the silence. They soon attained a strange ecstasy; hands stretched out on the little table trembled with anguish and impatience. Léon's voice called the spirits, urging them to manifest themselves. The first knock, struck by an invisible finger, sounded out dry and hollow like a harsh tap of the knuckle on a gourd. Night after night the doors of the beyond opened to this French family, lost under the immensity of the southern sky.

The children found it an enthralling game, which gave them goose bumps and made their hair stand on end. The incredible dialogue that took place with the mysterious denizens of the table usually ended when Mademoiselle yielded to possession by some unknown entity with a frightful shriek. Hastily, lamps were relit and everyone bustled around the unfortunate woman who continued to cluck like a guinea hen in the grip of an eagle.

This was a serious matter. Léon's scientific training inclined him to skepticism and to a materialistic attitude; he could not believe in unexplained phenomena, and yet, night after night, they recurred. Mamita herself was a devout Catholic who at heart wanted to give her children a Christian education, but the spirits got the upper hand. And so when everyone was asleep she would creep out of bed to correct their catechisms in violet ink, substituting for church dogma the spiritualist precepts of Alan Cardec. Mademoiselle no longer knew what lessons to teach.

Léon, asking ceaselessly for proof from the spirits, received the message: "Know thyself." He was now determined to go further, and his quest led him to automatic writing and to long-distance reading. To his astonishment he discovered that he had the same predispositions as a medium as Mademoiselle's, which had so puzzled him at first; but at least he was able to approach that extraordinary experience in a detached, analytical manner. His engineering colleagues came from far and wide to verify his gift: He could read rows of numbers written in ledgers shut up under lock and key without making a single error. That his body could thus house an extrasensory apparatus of such precision, and which apparently defied all the laws of science, was a mystery too important to ignore and to reject; and yet he was quite unable to explain it.

Happily there were vacations during which they escaped the obsession with spirits and of the spirits. They used them to explore the continent in every possible way. They would travel south as far as they could and continue on horseback to explore the chaotic and denuded plateaus of Tierra del Fuego, down to the southernmost tip of the land. Or they would head north up to Iquaçu to discover waterfalls more majestic than Niagara, when one reached the frontier between Argentina, Brazil, and Paraguay. There you would discover an earthly paradise untouched by man: a garden created by nature and filled with a profusion of wild orchids, birds, and butterflies. Or they set off across the Andes toward Chile on a small railway whose terrifying route circled the unconquered mass of the Aconcagua. Inching its way along the base of those gigantic ramparts, outlined by eternal snows, the train looked like a microscopic toy.

When the Argentine project was successfully completed, Léon decided it was time to end the thirty years of voluntary exile. At the age of fifty he had accumulated a solid fortune. His successes had won him such a reputation in financial circles that he had but to appear, and all doors would be open. And he knew that for every franc he had made, the banks had made millions; it was time to change sides and become one of the owners.

First the children were sent home to school, the girls to convents where they languished of boredom, and Maurice to Jeanson-de-Sailly, to prepare for the entrance exams for Ecole Polytechnique. He was a smart fellow, a good sportsman, and he learned easily. He was more dashing and adventurous than the Paris boys, and the young ladies gazed at him admiringly as he sped past in his expensive racing car. His life was without a cloud.

Then two years later the parents rejoined their children in Paris and settled into a large apartment on the avenue du Bois, two steps from the Etoile.

The eldest daughter, Hélène, married a young officer, Edouard Laforgue, and followed him to Africa with their infant sons, Jacques and Mowgli. Renée was smitten by a young man-about-town, Jules Gastu, the scion of the illustrious

Montagu family, and they were discussing marriage. As for
Marcelle, she left the convent transformed into a model
young girl. The intrepid Trois-Pommes, tamer of wild horses
on the pampas, had turned into a slender and charming young
woman, but she was unable to get used to the ways of Parisian
society, where she felt awkward and out of place. When she
reencountered her brother, metamorphosed into a grown-up
young man, she realized how much she had missed him
during those years of separation. Maurice had his father's
nature; at nineteen he already looked mature, with the poise
of a man of the world, ready for the great responsibilities that
soon would be his. A picture of him taken at the time shows
him in morning coat and with a banker's pince-nez, but there
is a glint in his eye, and a warm heart beneath the starched
shirt. No one understood this as well as Marcelle.

As a student from the provinces, Léon had never had a
chance to familiarize himself with Paris as a whole; now that
he had decided to settle there for good, he set about becoming a Parisian by conducting a methodical exploration of the
town on foot, from the tollhouse of Neuilly to the Château of
Vincennes; from the kings' basilica of Saint-Denis to the market gardens that flourished beyond the southern gates of the
city; from the slaughterhouses of La Villette to the hills of
Saint-Cloud. At night, dressed in a workman's smock, he
played at being a porter and unloaded sides of beef at Les
Halles, or sat down to talk with bums on the heights of
Ménilmontant; it seemed best to learn how the Parisians
of all classes were living and thinking to really become
one of them. In the daytime he wandered along the quays of
the Seine or mingled with the poor people and the students
who thronged the narrow streets of the Latin Quarter. The
wide slashes made by Baron Haussmann in the living flesh of
old Paris had changed the looks and the spirit of the town;
Léon said to himself that one day the last traces of the ancient
city would probably vanish forever. Certainly neither the Bal
Bullier nor the new rectilinear boulevards, nor the nightly
illuminations provided by the electrified billboards, and all the
other wonderful contemporary novelties would ever make up
for the lost treasures of the past. The paradox was insoluble,
the march of progress was ruthlessly destructive. With time
everything will change, and the streets will never look the
same again. One day, for instance, the delivery wagons carrying on their sides the name of *Veuve Detourbe & Cie. Paint*

Manufacturers at number 7, rue Saint-Séverin, will no longer be harnessed to cumbersome Percheron horses. They will be replaced by trucks that will fill the city with nauseous fumes; the rich aroma of horse manure will be swept from the streets and the swallows with it; linden trees, plane trees, and lilacs will be asphyxiated, leaving only stone and concrete slabs for modern man to live in. . . . And yet nothing on earth could have persuaded Léon to give up his prize-winning automobile, his smart De Dion-Bouton, a slick masterpiece of modern engineering.

He was working then on grand international schemes, but the constant problems created by the German government made progress uneasy, each day adding a new reality to the threat of war. Léon foresaw that the year 1914 would be difficult, but the new Anglo-French Entente Cordiale remained firm. A quick war was indeed desirable; it would enable the Allies to get rid of the Kaiser and to roll back Germany's power, both industrial and colonial. As of 1915, the French and the English would be the sole leaders of the civilized world; that would be the time for him to make his move. To do it now would be courting disaster; and thus he would wait.

To make this wait both safe and pleasant, he decided to buy a house in the south of France, near Marseilles, in which to settle his family for the duration of the campaign. Marcelle was studying to become a nurse; Renée had just divorced Gastu and needed to recover her peace of mind in the bosom of the family. Hélène was due back from Dakar with her offspring, since her husband had been called back to France with his Senegalese regiment. Maurice still had a year to go before graduation.

The summer began with the assassination at Sarajevo; one month later all the countries of Europe were at war with one another.

After his initial experience with the Bengal lancers Jackie had spent four months in the company of the Royal Horse Artillery Corps, which had turned him at last into a competent horseman. He was awaiting impatiently his departure for the front; in a few days, in a few weeks at most his fate would be accomplished.

One afternoon, at siesta hour, three of His Majesty's officers strolled along the crest of a Marseilles cliff, on a path that led toward the little port of Cassis, seen in the distance, dozing at the end of the peaceful gulf. Two of them, familiar with France and all she had to offer, were talking about women, as usual. Jackie was the third man, and he was trying hard not to hear all that boasting and nonsense, which got on his nerves. From a high altitude they discovered, miniaturized by the distance, a sandy cove. Above it was a Provençal villa set in a handsome, lush garden dominated by the sprawling shapes of Mediterranean pines. A spot of color on the beach drew his eyes to a little bathing party far removed from the world of war. Two young women were seated in the shade of their parasols; a third one held the hands of two toddlers who staggered and shrieked with joy in the subsiding waves. A beam of sun glinted on Jackie's monocle. He grabbed the binoculars from one of his companions and feverishly adjusted them.

And here she was, suddenly so close, the one with the bare feet and sunlight in her hair, and he couldn't wait, he knew that he must go down that cliff and meet her. "Don't wait for me, go on if you want. I have to talk to that girl."

"You're *mad!* They're not that sort."

"I know," cried Jackie, hurling himself down the tumbled rocks. "Don't wait. They're not your type. Let me be." They followed him, however, laughing, stumbling on the steep slope. The three women stared at the alarming trio headed their way, but they were British officers. No need for panic; our Allies are well-bred.

Striking up a conversation was fairly easy thanks to the toddlers, who tried on their braid-festooned caps like connoisseurs.

"What did you call that one?" asked one of the officers. "Mowgli? Really? Like Kipling?"

"Yes," said Hélène, laughing, "because he looks as if he were born in the jungle. Don't you think so?"

Jackie managed to isolate himself, at a safe distance behind the parasols, with the barefoot girl. She knew only very few words of English, which suddenly she seemed unable to utter. As for Jackie, he realized with dismay that he would never manage to construct a sentence in French that would express —*what?* What words were there in any language to express the inexpressible?

The eyes of the young woman were asking disturbing questions. Fumbling in a side pocket of his military tunic, he pulled out a French-English dictionary and hastily leafed through it.

"Mademoiselle," he started after a moment, breathlessly, trying to pronounce the words distinctly, *"voulez-vous me marier?"*

"Oh!" said Marcelle, gazing with wonder at this elegant warrior with the monocle, so nice and obviously so crazy. "Marry you? *But to whom?"*

"My French is very bad today," said he humbly, recognizing his wrong use of the verb. "Marry *me* to *you*. Me marry you. . . . *You!* You . . ."

"Marcelle," she replied. "And you are . . . ?"

"Jackie."

"Very well, Jackie. As for marrying you, yes. Will that do, Jackie?"

At the beginning of 1915, Vauquois was the center of the eastern front at the very moment that Maurice, fresh from Ecole Polytechnique, was sent there. There his war ended, the very first day, with a bullet smack in the middle of the forehead. His parents received the official parchment stating, in the name of the nation, that Maurice Girodias had died *au champ d'honneur.*

Marcelle had difficulty recovering from the dull, suffocating pain, and Mamita began to rave in an alarming way. Jackie suggested putting off the wedding till he came back from the front, or till the war was over; he had wanted to die so badly that he had now become superstitious about his chances of survival. Far from being a perfunctory affair the war had turned into a savage contest of strength in the northeast of France, and the battle might well go on for years. Léon decided to take the family back to Paris. Mamita, her eyes red and tearful behind her mourning veils, spent her time trying to conjure the spirit of her son, beseeching the mediums and clairvoyants to help her, beseeching the powers of darkness to give her back her son.

At Ypres Jackie met at last with fear, which he had dismissed up to then as unworthy of a proud man. Fear was everywhere in that universal horror, in that blind struggle in mud and blood. First gassed, then blown up by an exploding shell, he wound up in the hospital in a pitiful state; but he was still more or less in one piece, and at least now he would be saved from front-line duty. He married in 1917, at the end of his convalescence, and soon after he received his new assignment: He was sent off to sunny Italy, far from the main war theater.

For a while he was in charge of the railroad traffic for the whole of Italy, a job to which he devoted such energy that the Italian officials, baffled, called him *"Il pazzo capitano"*—the mad captain. But his next adventure took him even closer to insanity. He was assigned to the contemporary Allied government in charge of the Croatian port of Fiume, on the Adriatic, which was then claimed by Italy.

Gabriele d'Annunzio—the Warrier Poet, as he called himself—was leading the nationalist party in that campaign. His supporters wore black shirts and formed themselves into legions, in the style of the Roman Empire.

It so happened that the city, nominally governed by an Anglo-Franco-American triumvirate, was in fact left in Jackie's hands, since his colleagues were all too busy enjoying life. He was thus faced with an unusual quandary when D'Annunzio appeared before the city at the head of his ruffians, and sent out a bombastic ultimatum. The Allies had practically no troops in Fiume, and no one wanted to risk a confrontation that could complicate the peace talks. The order came to give up; which is to say, to flee. Thus the victorious Allies were defeated by the Warrior Poet's histrionics, and their representatives forced to take to the sea in abject confusion. The Fiume victory was D'Annunzio's legacy to Mussolini himself, and it set the comic opera style of the Fascist era.

Instead of staying in Paris proper, the Girodias family had rented a house at Ligugé, near Poitiers, to await the end of hostilities. There all three sisters were struck down by the Spanish influenza that was raging through France. Jackie was in Venice when two successive telegrams announced the death first of Renée, then Hélène. Locked up in his hotel room, Jackie was sick with anxiety; if she died he knew that he wouldn't survive. After several hours, a third telegram arrived: His wife was safe.

After Germany surrendered, he could hardly wait to leave for Paris to be demobilized. There was delirious celebration everywhere he went, driving through the old medieval towns of Trevisa, Padua, Mantua, Cremona, Pisa, and Livorno, where he went aboard ship—everywhere there was dancing in the streets day and night. He arrived in France just in time for the birth of his first child, a boy who was named Maurice. Mamita had no doubt that this birth was the spirits' answer to her entreaties: Her son had been given back to her in the form of a grandson.

In Paris, peace engendered an extraordinary ferment. A million and a half men were being buried, men killed for reasons that already seemed dubious. Edouard, who had been wounded several days before the death of his wife, decided to start his life anew: He married the head nurse of the hospital in which he was recovering. Thadée, a tall, whinnying, gawky person, towered over him by half a head, but she was a forceful woman who would know how to make his two young rascals, Jacques and Mowgli, toe the line.

Paris was the center for all sorts of commerce and enterprises. Jackie plunged into the world of business. At the Chatham Bar, in the morning, this gentleman with a carnation in his buttonhole who sells a boatload of coal just leaving Cardiff, this is he. In the late evening, same day, same place, it is also he who buys it back at three times the price when his pile of saucers is up to his nose and the boat heaves into view at Cherbourg. The traffic in military surplus and securities was carried on by an exchange of witticisms, and its true beneficiaries were the bartenders and the lawyers.

Life viewed from the avenue du Bois was marvelously light and easy; they were close to Armenonville, Longchamps, the Pré-Catalan, and very far from Manchester. At night as he leaned over the crib draped in white percale, Jackie wondered briefly about the identity of its occupant, who babbled and gazed at him with such a dark stare.

Since his return he had often felt tired; Marcelle, whom he had rechristened Mars, insisted he should go to see a doctor. Finally, to reassure her, he went to a specialist and found out that he had tuberculosis in his one remaining lung. The doctors were noncommittal; mountain air was the only known cure, and few of the patients ever survived. The young couple went off to the sanatorium of Durtol, in Auvergne, for Mars insisted that she would never leave her husband. The grandparents would take care of the baby during their absence.

Nearly a year later, the two fragments of the family were reunited on the platform at the Gare de Lyon. Jackie was cured, through no medical miracle, certainly, but thanks to the devotion of one woman; he was still weak, puffy, older, profoundly changed.

Mars came up to her son whom Léon proudly held aloft; she barely recognized him.

"Maurice, it's your mother," the grandparents said. "Look, little one, it's your mummy!" But the child turned away from her. Why, kiss that stranger? No, he was only interested in the gleaming locomotive, which still exhaled a few plumes of white smoke.

2

Le Fond des Forêts.—Gliding up and down the breeze.
—The lurid gardener.—From Thomas à Becket
to The Browsing Goat.—Justice for a dead robin!
—Jacques and Mowgli.—The entire family dances the
French Cancan.—The devil in the square bottle.—Tango
fantastico.—Falling in love with Arlette and Clara.

Two men confront each other across a double ladder and struggle with billows of cloth as they hang swags. Light curtains waltz slowly in front of the high windows.

It's a big moment in my life. I'm two years old, and after lengthy preparations my parents have brought me by car to the large country house where we are going to live.

Perched on my little stool, I look up at my grandfather as he bosses everyone about. Hat askew, waistcoat unbuttoned, he commands the movers with sweeping gestures. I go and lean out the window and watch the men in the courtyard bustling around a great mountain of furniture, which disappears little by little into the house. Farther off I can see vast stretches of lush green lawn, ponds covered with floating, flowering plants, and many trees. It is difficult to take in all the details of this landscape still so new to me.

In my life my grandfather and grandmother come first, followed by a number of episodic, subordinate personages; and last come my mother and father. I know that my father is sick; he moves very little. My mother is someone who is constantly busy. Once or twice she carried me in her arms, and she must have felt that I did not enjoy it very much because she quickly put me down again. I feel better in the company of my grandfather, who is always singing and doing things that are interesting and sometimes even spectacular.

The seasons that follow this arrival at the house in Rozoy expand little by little my acquaintance with nature, which surrounds me in gardens and woods. Our house, large and high, is known in the neighborhood as le Château du Fond des Forêts—the Château of the Heart of the Forest. As for castles, I've seen better ones—in my picture books. Ours doesn't even have a dungeon or a machicolation, but it stands at the edge of a forest of tall trees, of massive timber, of unexplored jungles, and there I spend the better part of my days. Coming back from my peregrinations, I sometimes come across the recumbent form of my father, like a horizon of gray hillocks, languishing on one of the chaises-longues that are placed for his benefit all around the house. In the sharp autumn wind, buried under a mound of blankets, he dozes. In spring or summer, I see him propped up on pillows, reading. He must be extremely feeble. Sometimes our glances cross, but it's difficult to talk to him, for some reason that escapes us both.

The only ones to whom I talk a little are my grandparents, who arrive almost every Saturday from Paris in their car, laden with presents. For the rest, silence. I scarcely talk at all to the servants, but they are resigned to it and are kind to me. When unfamiliar visitors try to chat with me, my silence seems to make everyone nervous. Why even bother to say *bonjour?* Those people mean nothing to me; in fact, I'm not even sure their existence is desirable. I discover the power of silence, over myself as well as others. I discover that the muteness of a child in the midst of a group of chattering adults can trouble them greatly and finally reduce them, too, to silence. The woods crackle with a thousand noises; each square inch swarms with life; but trees grow silently, and though the wind may whistle, the clouds move by in silence. The grown-ups should take a leaf from nature's book.

It is difficult for me to paint the full majesty of my domain under the trees, my paths lost in the forest, a world that barred human speech and in which I could barely tell night from day.

I divided my time between life in the woods and the world of dreams, and could hardly tell them apart. My dreams were dominated by an unalterable thirst for mobility. Gliding at low altitude, I revisited all my familiar landscapes. Yes, the art of flying gave me a deeply satisfying sense of freedom; I was surprised to find myself the only one in possession of this talent, and I delighted in the astonished admiration of my family, ponderously seated around the dinner table, as I rose up, imperceptibly at first, above my chair and then took flight with a graceful arabesque, fluttered through the french windows into the garden, cleared a tall row of pine trees with a slight bound, and spun from there to the river, turning about on my bed of air like a feather graced with free will.

My nightmares, by contrast, were dominated by images of forced immobility. I was engulfed by earth, I was buried alive, I could neither flee nor stir, and I saw myself dying of terror. Such nightmares usually unfolded in a ravaged and livid landscape, while devilish battles in the sky pitted the most bizarre flying machines against one another, from armored trains to aerial battleships. Death marched forward from all sides. Death? It was death to be condemned to immobility.

The war had left many traces in the neighborhood. Several years earlier, in September 1914, the army of Marshal von Kluck had pushed its offensive right up to our house, which had briefly served as headquarters until the Germans were stopped at the nearby village of Varreddes. I could picture, standing in front of huge wall maps in our very living room, the German generals losing the historical battle of the Marne. One only had to scratch the soil to turn up mementos of those cursed times, rusting weapons, ragged remains of uniforms. As they ploughed the fields, the peasants would sometimes tumble across a skeleton whose helmet teemed with vermin. Ten springtimes had covered all this horror over with fertile humus, but it would take far longer to efface it from human memory. The god of war still haunted those hills and valleys; a hideous colossus gnawed by the winds and rains of the seasons, he exerted a lugubrious fascination whose grip I could not shake.

I confronted a troublesome dilemma. On the one hand, nature's melodramas proliferated in the fields and poultry-yards: Little animals were mutilated, chickens decapitated, and I felt a disgust that drew me quite naturally to a true-blue pacifism. On the other hand, looking at weapons and touching them aroused in me an irresistible sensual excitement. The revolver my father brought back from the war seemed at one and the same time both the most sinister and the most seductive object in the world. The weight of the metal, its deadly design, all the rites and mysteries that lent it power—the power to end life—all this stirred up in me a dangerously pleasant anguish that confounded my instincts and plunged me into great turmoil.

I was four when my sister Nicole was born, then came Sylvie a year later, and finally brother Eric, seven years my junior. Their presence barely disturbed my solitude, but it modified the family circle, and I spent more time in the chiaroscuro of the woods, *dans le fond des forêts*. Light as day, shadowy as dreams, I never fully knew if I was asleep or awake. Yet it was not in a dream that I visited the nocturnal glade where the rabbits were holding a conclave, gathered around their king, a large black male with gleaming fur and blood-red eyes. Nor was it a dream when I heard the rhododendrons, a mass of shadows glittering in the moonlight, swell with the music of the spheres. Those houses I built for myself in the tops of the handsomest trees in the forest, so thickly clustered that I could pass from one to the next without needing wings, don't tell me this was only the sorcery of dreams or false illusion, as I remember so well the time and effort, and the ingenuity it took to build them!

The most beautiful of all my trees, more impressive even than the tree with seven trunks whose giant arches crisscross in a flight of ogives, is no doubt the purple beech that rises near the house, a prodigy of nature that astonishes all the expert foresters. No one but I ventures to climb that colossal tree, a living city whose mazes I know well. Scaling it is slow and difficult because of the profusion of branches and coppery leaves, but I clamber bit by bit above the neighboring trees and look out, as if I were flying above them, over the irregular checkerboard of woods and cultivated fields. I reach the top and my outlook encompasses my immense empire: rivers and mountains, estuaries and islands, outlines of towns barely glimpsed on a horizon muffled by the mist rising from the seas.

To bring me down to earth, my parents asked the village schoolmistress to devote two hours a day to my instruction.

Every day at dawn a grand council was held in the kitchen as the servants exchanged spicy scuttlebutt before the masters awoke. The chief orator was the head gardener, Grossard, a long, lean, lanky lout, who was always running off at the mouth: "Yesterday I gave you a piece of my mind," he liked to say. "Well, today I'm going to give a piece of my———." And there came a word that made everyone bend in two with mirth, but that I could not grasp. When news reached the kitchen that the village schoolmistress had been engaged to teach me, Grossard got off a few choice sallies, for the poor woman was called Mme Labite, a name that lends itself to coarse jests.

It thus befell Mme Labite to teach me to read and write, add and multiply, and to slyly outwit society. She was a large, well-upholstered woman, stuffed into a dress of coarse weave whose orange hue clashed with the apoplectic violet of her complexion. She wheezed ceaselessly, climbing the stairs, walking, even sitting down. She was encumbered by enormous breasts that seemed to suffocate her, about which my grandfather had made some jocund remarks whose humor escaped me.

In front of her little band of jolly peasants in the village school Mme Labite could easily spread out her fleshly mass in the shelter of a high desk and crush them by her position. But when she came up to the château after school, it was quite different, having to practice in a boudoir instead of a classroom, with a spindly chair too small for her posterior; and one single, mute pupil. There was a certain poignancy to our daily exchange: She did her utmost to catch my attention, which was so entirely swamped by her physical presence that my spirit fled in order not to be suffocated. She gave up trying to get me to read aloud and soon gave up nearly everything. We then developed a very sweet and gentle interchange. She granted me responsibility for my lessons, because even at six, I was the boss; it was tacitly understood that she would not complain of me to my parents, and in return I would try not to unduly display my ignorance. And so we spent long hours together seated at the same table, each lost in his or her own dreams, gazing out blandly over the treetops.

That winter a drama erupted in the gardener's domicile. Ernestine, wife of Grossard, up and left him for a reason that astonished the villagers: After twenty years of marriage, lo and behold, she declared she could no longer bear her husband's vulgarity. Grossard the braggart and brawler turned melancholy and wild-eyed, cut to the quick by this unexpected betrayal. "As if a sow has the right to choose her pig," he would complain to whoever cared to listen. He became violent and dangerous, even to his plants. My grandfather came upon him one Sunday, dead drunk, blubbering into the wind and pissing on the strawberry plants in great sweeping arcs.

As spring came on, however, he cooled down; my grandfather said this meant that nature had done her job and the gardener had found another woman. He was right, but what he did not divine, because it was all too fantastic, was the identity of the chosen one. It was Mme Labite.

A widow for ten years, Mme Labite was slow to make up her mind. First of all, Ernestine's flight had not been forgotten, and gave her pause. Then for the schoolmistress, who was also responsible for the education of the scion of the château, to take up with a gardener, even a head gardener, it all looked devilishly morganatic.

Grossard had to tone down his talk, modulate his rustic manners, and sharpen up his appearance. Soon he was to be seen with his mop of hair slicked down with Gomina Argentina, which only emphasized his cauliflower ears. His scarecrow figure was studded with all sorts of protuberances that were somehow ironed out. All those combined efforts succeeded, finally, in vanquishing my teacher's inhibitions.

From that point on, all unfolded as in a natural history textbook. For me, it was a lesson in the nuptial mores of grown-ups. Mme Labite was dreamier than ever during the hours we shared, but her eyes sparkled and she yielded to her natural languor. One day she bustled in very late, with bits of hay emerging from her hastily skewered chignon, her broad face beaming. With the slightest encouragement, she would have taken me into her confidence. I was truly puzzled and tried to figure out how she could have found such happiness. And thanks to whom? Well, thanks to Grossard, who materialized in person at the end of our session at the door to my mother's boudoir where we were prettily ensconced. An unheard-of audacity! Yet he marched right in, cocksure, planted himself behind Mme Labite's chair, and plunked his grimy paw on her large breast to mark his sovereign rights. Her hue deepened from mauve to aubergine and she threw me an uneasy look, but could say nothing. What, indeed, was there to say?

The idyll of Grossard and Mme Labite furnished the village with much food for talk, and echoes reached our halls, both servants' and masters'. I was privy to all sorts of breathtaking tales whose point escaped me. According to Mathilde, Mme Labite had taught Grossard to undress completely to make love, a citified refinement that set tongues wagging.

Camille the cook vowed she had come upon them in full swing, naked as jaybirds, behind the raspberry bushes. Her husband, Paul Monfaucon, was sleeping off a drunk in the tool shed one day when they crept in for a session; he awoke with a start and gaped at the action. Another time they sowed panic in one of the village poultry-yards where they chased each other, stark naked and braying like donkeys. The hens fled in all directions, and their owner went to the constable to swear out a summons, but once the flock was reassembled the constable could not figure out how to word his charge. . . . Put yourself in his shoes, poor fellow!

In fact the only thing held against the two lovers was this mania for nudity, which struck people as a dangerous perversion. "It's never been done that way," grumbled the peasants. "Sure, everyone humps; but stark naked, no, that's going too far! What would the chicken coops look like if the hens and roosters took off their feathers for fucking, hein?"

Rozoy-en-Multien was a village ten centuries old, which comprised a hundred or so gray stone houses and a few farms scattered along a street of worn cobblestones. In the twelfth century, Thomas à Becket built the church that still stands there and made the town notorious—that very Thomas who, my father said, was an English saint who played politics. There seemed to be no clear difference between France and England in those days. . . . Nothing had happened since then, except, of course, the Great War; the village monument to the dead spoke little of the pain and terror it had sown. Not only had a score of village sons perished at the front lines, but when the *Boches* pushed their offensive to the plateau of Multien, all the able-bodied men fled. The very old men and the women stayed behind, to be terrorized by the troops who requisitioned everything; an entire harvest was lost the first year.

Our house lies a good mile beyond the village and can only be observed, from the road, through a large gate set in a semicircle of woods. We are thus not an integral part of the life of Rozoy, whose axis lies in the middle of the village between the Belloye farm, hidden behind its high blind walls, and l'Auberge de la Chèvre qui Broute, the Inn of the Browsing Goat, across the street.

The mayor, Amédée de Belloye, is extremely ugly. A crabby yellow face sticks out from hunched shoulders; when he stands up he looks, with his muddy leggings, exactly like a

praying mantis. He lives in squalor and meanness and thinks
he is mayor by divine right.

Cross the street and push open the jingling door of the
Browsing Goat—here's a jolly place! But before you step in,
just have a look above the door at the hanging signboard: It is
my mother who painted that white goat in a flowery field. The
owners, the Chamites, have been friends since we arrived in
Rozoy, and all sorts of favors are exchanged. Between André
and my father there is a special bond that is hard to explain,
unless it derives from the fact that they are both foreigners,
voluntary exiles. André and his wife, Marcelle, are archetypi-
cally Flemish; they both have fine features rarely found in this
part of the country. Even more astonishing is that André has
started a Communist cell in his back room. At first this just
makes everyone laugh. But in a few years, between one pint
and the next, André will succeed in turning his customers
around, never touching a drop himself or losing patience
with his listeners, or speaking ill of the pseudoaristocrat
de Belloye. (All this will lead, in a quarter century, to the
victory of Chamite over de Belloye in the municipal elections,
a victory that Karl Marx owes less to his meditations on the
class struggle than to the generous heart of his disciple. . . .
Half a century later André is no longer behind his counter,
since he has retired, but he is doing fine. As to the sign my
mother painted, it is still there, and the goat, although painted
over, is still recognizable.)

The class struggle has no place between André and my
father. They don't share the same ideas or speak the same
language, but this does not stop them from forming a solid
friendship. Based on what? What gestures, what feelings?

There was also Paul Gervais, who had sold us the château.
He himself occupied a large property in the center of the village, which descended in stairlike terraces to the banks of the
capricious Gergogne River and stretched beyond it into an
immense forest where stags and wild boar still roamed. It was
his passion for chess that drove Gervais to give up one of his
houses; after two matches with my father the deal was made.
From this grew another friendship just as solid and enduring,
and enchanting for me, because he was a man who liked to
invent things.

He had built himself an airplane and succeeded in making it
fly: months of fierce labor in order to be airborne for three

minutes and wind up in the hospital, that was his style. He had hunted wild game in Africa, taken part in the first automobile races, paid court to the most famous courtesans; but, first and foremost, he could make anything with his hands. He raised falcons for hunting and lived surrounded by countless dogs who ate at his table and slept in his bedroom, even shared his bed. His wife, a gracious old lady with snowy hair and a sharp tongue, was *la dame du manoir* straight out of a Gothic novel. The hunt was sacred to them; they had hunted for years, and it was no accident that their eldest son was christened Hubert in honor of the patron saint of huntsmen.

They had an arsenal at their house that so aroused my darker instincts that my father gave me, for my eighth birthday, the hunting rifle I had long yearned for. I was in ecstasy. The family assembled on the steps to watch me try out my first gun. I loaded it, raised it to my shoulder as I'd been taught, screwed one eye shut as I aimed at a cloud. Bang! A kick to the shoulder, a puff of smoke, a seductive smell of powder that went to my head. . . . I was in seventh heaven.

Later on, I found myself alone with my rifle and the truth struck me: This weapon was meant for killing. That was indeed its only function. So what? Of course, if you are a hunter, you have to kill wild animals; and so I decided to go out hunting. I filled my pockets with cartridges, borrowed a game bag from my grandfather, and set forth with the supple step of the New World woodsman to the nearby forest, a Fenimore Cooper hero. A trapper, the last of the Mohicans, on the prowl.

I proceed about a hundred yards, listening to the faintest echoes of creaking twigs, when suddenly, on the low branch of a linden tree that stretches across the path above my head, I see a bird with a red breast who contemplates me with his round eye. I raise the gun to my shoulder, take aim at this unfortunate robin, who is no doubt too fed up with life to consider flying away, and I squeeze the trigger. The kick knocks me flat on my behind, and the bird falls next to me, dead.

It's terrifying. Tears in my eyes, my head burning, I force myself to examine the perfect little being, whose plumage is barely ruffled by the entry of a single shot. Stretched out on his back, eyes glazed, its delicate feet like bent twigs . . . my friend. I have killed the most handsome, most innocent, most free being in all of creation. A robin redbreast cries out for justice.

Sobbing, I dig him a grave and improvise a modest funeral ceremony. I go home dragging my damnable weapon behind me. I shut myself up in my room and set to work; I have a hundred cartridges to empty of powder and buckshot. In an hour I've filled a tin can with powder, enough to kill a hundred birds as precious as my friend, my victim. I swear out loud never to kill again in my life. Then I strike a match and solemnly approach the tin. *Boom!* The conflagration is not at all what I expected. Blinded, my face roasted, I stumble, grope my way to the bathroom, plunge my face into cold water. The mixture of exaltation and terror is such that I feel nothing physical, but when the concentric flashes die down and I'm able to make out my face in the mirror, I'm overcome with horror. I no longer have eyebrows or eyelashes, and the auburn curls that my grandmother makes such a fuss over are charred. My skin is red and glistening, and burns horribly.

At that moment, I hear a rush of footsteps, and someone pounds on the door. I'll have to open up. When she catches sight of me, my mother cries out, grabs me in her arms, hugs me, then drags me over to the window and opens it. The smoke is unbearable; we're both coughing, with gasps that rasp the throat right down to the lungs. My mother takes me back into the room, she wants to understand: the burnt-out tin can, the large cloudlike stain on the ceiling, the buckshot scattered about. . . .

How to explain all this? But I discover to my surprise that she understands far better than I expected.

My mother amuses herself by illustrating a play, *Chantecler*, by Edmond Rostand. What I retain from the story is the idea that the sun shines specially for each of us. I start getting up very early to catch the sunrise.

It's a moment without equal. One particular day, I remember that I wandered for a long time through the rambling kitchen garden while waiting for the sun to appear. As I saw it first glowing through the trees and then rising powerfully into the morning's flawless blue, I felt as if I were carried away by an excess of glowing energies.

All the kingdoms of nature harmonize to celebrate the event; dew's minute mirrors sparkle on the hedges. The delight is contagious, I fill my lungs to bursting, it's joy I breathe in, stronger than oxygen. I take a path at random; this garden is inexhaustible, it produces enough to feed a whole town from the orchards to the greenhouses, which are filled with tropical plants.

As I ramble along with my hands in my pockets I discover that the right-hand one has a hole in it, and my surprised fingers encounter the body to which they belong, strangely unfamiliar, or is it rather familiarly familiar, intimately intimate? This contact awakens a feeling that fills my heart and my gut; I shiver as I head toward the sun, entirely in its sway. My breathing quickens, deepens, and waves of pleasure radiate from my right hand to the farthest limits of my body. I've had this feeling before, but never as strongly; it's both excruciating and delicious. The sun's rays work on my flesh through my clothes, they knead it and ripen it. Suddenly I gasp for breath, I am shaken by several spasms of sharp pleasure. And then I pull my hand out of my pocket and find it damp and curiously odoriferous.

So *that*'s what it is—Grossard and the schoolmistress? *That*'s what all the stories are about? But I can't quite imagine Grossard overcome by such subtle emotions; he's far too crude for that. How can people who are so ugly, so ridiculous, so repugnant possibly enjoy sensations as exquisite as those that just transported me? It's all very mysterious.

I have a question, then two, then fifteen, about sex, love, their relationship to the sun. So many questions; it will take me several lifetimes to answer them.

To tell the truth, I'm sick of Mme Labite, her strong smells, her orange dress, her monumental breast, and her gardener. She's taught me practically all that she knows, and I've substituted reading for daydreams. Of course, they're quite similar activities, but reading offers us somebody else's daydreams, to be digested in one's head and transformed into one's own stuff. It's supposed to be better. Maybe so. Most people, strangely, seem to prefer to use the dreams of another rather than their own. As for me, as I grow up the night's images vanish more quickly, they vaporize in the daytime. That's why I need to make them stick in my memory; I try to write stories. My father now spends his days writing with a severe look. He had a study fixed up for himself where no one is allowed to disturb him; he has shelves loaded with books, all kinds of pipes, a large armchair pulled up to the fireplace, even in summer, and he fills large notebooks with his tiny, tidy handwriting.

Two of his books have already come out in England, *Laugh*

and Grow Rich, and one called *The Browsing Goat*, which, I understand, is the story of the Chamites's pub. I myself haven't yet published anything; I'm waiting for a good offer.

On the other hand, I've become a great builder. Not tree houses anymore. I prefer true architecture, buildings that are both sturdy and interesting; I've just started building one behind the house that gives me a lot of satisfaction. In the beginning it was just a pile of battered old packing cases, but I made a solid hut out of them, strong enough to hold up a second story; then I realize that I can add a third. Of course, it's not easy, because there are no stairs. I have to hoist the boards while clambering up the outside, and I have to climb down again a hundred times to fetch nails, saw, or retrieve the hammer. But it works out, and now I can stand up on the third floor, nearly upright. Once I finish the roof, I climb up on it and it doesn't totter much. I am inspired to construct a loggia upon this roof. I am now the owner of a four-story house. It's true it still lacks a staircase, but my parents' house has only three stories, though it's much higher and full of stairs.

I'm extremely proud of my work. No one has yet admired it because my tower, situated behind the big house, rises out of their field of vision. Only my father might have noted my labors, since his study looks out on the back of the house, but I doubt that he ever looks out the window. I decide to have a public inauguration. Before sending out invitations, however, it seems wise to have a dress rehearsal with a select group. I invite my sisters and brother to tea. The girls are respectively three and four years old, but brother Eric, age one and a half, poses a special problem of transportation. Too bad the fine weather has turned to gray. However, if it rains we'll be well sheltered by the excellent roof of the loggia, which is nearly waterproof.

Nicole is uneasy, but Sylvie, sixteen months younger and less delicate, shames her into it. Clinging for dear life to the boards, they clamber up as best they can, hoisting the baby from one floor to the next like a parcel. Drooling and philosophical, he takes it with equanimity. The wind is rising and drops of rain begin to fall. *Zut!* But we've made it to a safe port. We are seated all in a row, for the fourth story is too low to stand up in, and our legs dangle out in the air. I pass around the Petits-Beurres Lu and strive to reassure my sisters by my relaxed manner. In fact, I'm in the soup, for the tower is oscillating in the wind like a maddened metronome. Only the baby remains unperturbed; if he began to cry it would be frightful. Everything creaks around us, the wind whistles ever more piercingly, I'm beginning to feel seasick, and my sisters start to sob. Suddenly I catch sight of my father at his window, three yards away from us, pipe in hand, gaping at me in astonishment and anguish as slowly, gracefully, and inexorably my tempest-wracked tower folds up and collapses in a din of breaking boards.

We emerge unscathed except for our fears and a few scratches, but that evening my parents decide to find me a boarding school where I can be with kids my own age.

The death of Paul Gervais, three or four years after our arrival in Rozoy, had deeply touched my father, who found himself thrust into greater isolation than ever, and he set about writing a few light novels in order to stave off boredom. There were also the altogether too rare visits of old friends from England and America; they came mainly out of curiosity, I suppose, in order to find out how my parents' romantic marriage had turned out.

There were the Jasserons, distant cousins who came from Algeria, and others who were Romanian, the offspring of one of my father's sisters. One of them, a boy named Teddy who was four years older than I, limped heavily. . . . There was also, thank heaven, a blessed month during the summer when my incomparable French cousins, Jacques and Mowgli, came to spend the beginning of their school vacation with us before going to the seashore with their parents. The arrival of these two genius rascals brought joy to the family and sowed terror in the village. During these four weeks I spent all my time assisting them in a subordinate role in the course of their hair-raising adventures. Those expeditions always ended in disaster; I was easily forgiven because I was the youngest, and after thinking it all over, my parents also forgave the cousins because they found them irresistible. When the two scamps surprised Grossard and Mme Labite *in flagrante delicto*, whereupon they made off with the *corpora delicti*—which is to say, their clothes—it was very difficult to make a tragedy out of it; when they slipped a dead screech owl into the bed of Tante Jeanne, my grandfather's sister (a hypocritical old maid whose annual visit drove the family to despair), it was hard to reproach them with all the sincerity the occasion may have

demanded; when they disguised themselves, both of them, as
M. de Belloye and, thus dressed, went through the village
doing the French cancan, my father had to present his excuses
to the mayor; but instead of reprimanding the cousins, he
shook Mowgli's hand and offered him a bottle of champagne.
Whereupon Jacques, the younger, remarked that if his
brother had the right to a bottle of champagne, he felt that he
had an equal right to one of his own. My father savored this
spirit of initiative, and the day ended in a general reveling
such as I had never before seen. It was very late when my
mother asked us to assist Tante Jeanne back to her room. The
old lady, however, with wig askew and corset unlaced, took it
into her head that she too could dance the French cancan.
Attempts to dissuade her proved futile. My father disappeared for a moment and returned dressed as a witch in a
costume he had improvised from Tante Jeanne's furbelows,
with blue spiders drawn with a fountain pen on his heron's
legs. Each one in turn wound up the trumpet-mouthed Gram-
ophone on which fox-trots alternated with the Volga Boat-
man. But it took my cousins' presence to trigger family festivities such as this.

Shortly afterward, I was invited by the Laforgues to spend
the rest of the vacation with them at Fouras-sur-Mer, a small
resort on the Atlantic coast, in the Charente-Maritime. My
parents agreed, my cousins yelped with joy, and I myself was
giddy with happiness.

I prepared myself for this voyage of discovery, which was to
begin with a long automobile trip with the Laforgue family.
The first night, we stopped at Ligugé where Jacques and
Mowgli's mother, my Aunt Hélène, was buried. Teddy had
admired his first wife as much as he had loved her, and after
her death the memory of her had turned into a cult. Was it in
order not to betray that memory that he had chosen as a second wife big Thadée, an excellent woman, but rather plain?
At any rate Thadée had herself become a willing servant of
the cult.

As soon as the door is closed on the hotel room I share
with my cousins, Mowgli brings a bottle of Cointreau and a
box of Havana cigars out of his suitcase. This trip is off to a
pretty good start. . . . And this syrupy liqueur that's inflaming
my throat and my brain so deliciously—well! I certainly
wouldn't mind taking another glass, what do you say, guys?
Sitting side by side on the bed, the cousins teach me how to

smoke a cigar. Mowgli is fourteen and has big hairy knees, and Jacques is twelve—a good age, perhaps, for smoking, but filling my mouth with these gulps of foul-stinking smoke doesn't seem to bring me any pleasure. Nevertheless, it's a matter of honor, and I have no choice but to persist. Still another glass of that delicious liqueur and the cigar's getting better. *Oh là là!* What a party! My head's spinning in all directions, and it is with deep pleasure that I contemplate these two men of the world, these two refined gentlemen, my cousins. How well they draw on their cigars, how elegantly they sip the stuff from the bathroom tumblers. Mowgli displays his skill at blowing smoke rings. But he's been smoking for years; he doesn't hide it because he looks older than his age. "In my thirties," he states without blinking—and no one contradicts him.

Three hours later and we're still there—for the very simple reason that we're unable to get up. The very thought of standing on my feet makes my head swim. Two drops of liqueur still remain in the bottle; no question of leaving it, these very two drops are the most important ones of the lot. Forgetting that I'm incapable of standing upright, I suddenly rise to reach for the square flagon and immediately collapse in a heap, horribly sick.

When Uncle Teddy comes to wake us up the next morning, he finds a scene of horror that draws from him a stream of military invective. He's a lively, compact, irritable little man who made his entire career in the colonial troops, and he can be quite terrifying with his waxed, turned-up moustache and bulldog's jaw; but that ferocious appearance cannot hide the fact that he has a heart of gold. He must have spent an exhausting night between his two women, the dead one and the all-too-alive one; in short, he isn't at the top of his form and the hideous smell in the room takes him by surprise. With a muffled groan he makes a beeline for the bathroom, leans over the zinc tub, and immediately lets go with a cataract that is also a salvo, punctuated with heartrending hiccups and abominable curses. His sons fly languidly to his rescue. I myself feel on the verge of giving up the ghost. . . . Ah, my first drinking bout, how well I'll remember it! As to you, Cointreau, damnable syrup, thanks a lot, never again! The mere sight of the squat square bottle, pretext and witness of our alcoholic orgy, will forever make me nauseated.

It takes a while to bring people and things back to order.

The colonel hesitates between military discipline and good humor, and finally, as always, he opts in favor of the sunny side, as, with unsteady gait and green face, we all pile up into the waiting car.

That same evening we reached Fouras, pearl of the province of Charentes-Maritimes, and moved forthwith into the villa Les Myosotis—"The Forget-Me-Nots." Here it is at last this seaside world I have heard so much about from my cousins! I am dazzled with what I see; our Bastille Day celebrations in Rozoy are chicken feed when compared to the perpetual festival that takes place on the esplanade in Fouras, each one of its carnival booths offering a captivating and unsolvable enigma to the gaping public.

In the evening, the façade of the "Mikado Palace—Grand Japanese Billiards" stood out with its swarm of Buddhas, masks, teapots, dragons, and dolls of every color, all illuminated from underneath and bathed in an eerie luminescence that gave them such a compelling quality. You would hardly recognize that place of miracles during the daytime, become an ordinary shack covered with flaky paint, a dilapidated decor behind which the carnival-hands lived their horizonless lives. Serves you right! Certain things are not to be seen in the glare of daylight and one had to wait for dusk to rediscover the Mikado Palace once again, hatching its harvest of mysteries, its displays of carbuncles, of Aladdin's lamps, and, perhaps, of sheer junk. Nearby were ghost trains with sneering skeletons, Italians stretching marshmallow, and there were also boa constrictors, strong men, toothless lion-tamers, and everything else needed to astonish, terrify, or jollify the not-too-demanding spectators.

My cousins' amusement at my stupefaction contained a touch of condescension. Their own pleasures were quite different, being essentially devoted to the pursuit of girls. Alas! The years that separated us hindered me from following their example, but I nevertheless went along with them to the local casino, which was no more than a large café in the middle of town, and where the gilded youth met and caroused at night.

Gilded, bronzed, coppered, high-vibrating, waltzing, tangoing, swept into a farandole that overflowed in the streets and awakened the good burghers at dawn. . . . Alas! Alas for me I beheld this spectacle as a bystander because I was too young to participate; nobody wanted me for a partner. My cousins themselves forgot my existence, and sitting in front of my lemonade, alone in the midst of the crowd, I prolonged the pleasure into a refined mood of sadness. So young; so lonely. . . . But, may I ask, what are you supposed to do at the age of eight, still in short pants?

I watched the couples going out of the casino into the night, and bunches of revelers cramming themselves into sports cars and spurting off crazily through the deserted streets. When the waiters started to pile the chairs on the tables of the casino and to sweep the floor, I sighed, asked for the check, and began to wend my way back slowly to "The Forget-Me-Nots," fancying myself in the role of an elegant desperado, perhaps some star-crossed man of the world leaving a Berlin brothel at dawn. . . . The smell of Gauloises smoked by others impregnated my jacket, lending quality to my fantasies, and I inhaled it with something like passion, trying hard to find it delicious. . . . But just wait and see: The day will come when I'll be the one to lead the dance. And then it will all be for me—the women, the wine, the cigarettes! For me the princely orgies! In the meantime, I certainly wish I could find some long pants; I'd look less like a kid.

Life on the beach runs parallel to that of the casino, while being at the same time its opposite. People show their skin instead of hiding it in finery, they adore the sun and forget the moon. The girls parade their charms, the boys strut on the diving board, and everybody wears the white duck cap made popular by the American navy.

For me, the ocean is a discovery of the greatest importance; it is, quite simply, the one element that was missing in my life. One morning, as I am plunging into the waves like a madman, I am suddenly turned upside down by the undertow and dragged toward the bottom in a tangle of arms and legs—most of which aren't mine. The wave passes, the tangle is unraveled, and I find myself, legs in the air, between two girls who are roaring with laughter as they get back on their feet and bound toward the beach. My heart leaps, and leaps again. . . . They are, how can I say it, *fantastic!* But what's the use of dreaming, they must be twice as old as I am. Well, perhaps not quite: One of them shows a hint of breasts in her bathing suit, the other not a trace. Twelve? Thirteen? Fourteen? Ah, if only I had long pants!

They belong to a wealthy family whose vast tent on the beach dwarfs all the surrounding ones; it stands proudly as a colorful canvas palace. I make inquiries of my cousins who question me in turn:

"Ah, so, you're in love, kid! Which one of the two is it? The one with tits or the other?"

Seeing me blush violently, they take pity and obligingly enlighten me. The parents live in the most beautiful villa in Fouras, they are very rich people, the girls aren't sisters but only friends, and both of them are aspirant ballet dancers at the Opera. Clara's the one with the chest, Arlette the one without.

"There you are, you know everything. But, really, they're out of your range, you fart higher than your ass, my good man. Find yourself a girl your own age; don't waste your time on Opera dancers, they are snobs, only interested in older men. And supposing they take interest in you, how are you going to manage with that two-bit whistle of yours? And two of them at the same time! You're just too greedy."

They were right all the way down the line, but I had discovered that rare, undefinable thing called grace. And once glimpsed, that wonderful and tragic secret, how could it be forgotten? Arlette, Clara. . . . My heart beats double for you! But what could I do without long pants? There was simply no solution to be found to this central problem, and so all I could do was to follow them when they went for a bicycle ride. Sometimes I picked up speed and passed them on top of a hill; then I would brake on the descent and let myself be slowly overtaken in turn, an extraordinarily voluptuous experience. As they were passing me they would burst out laughing, but would never address the least remark to me. What did I expect them to say, anyway? I don't know, but I was hoping to get my cue from them. And so I was leading an enchanted life, and I was plunged in despair.

At night, in the casino, I watched for their arrival; they were always in the midst of a stylish group, people who hardly ever mixed with the others. I sat watching them dance; light and exquisite, they were often followed by the beam of an admiring projector; people left the dance floor to give them a free field. Alone at my table, nursing a lemonade, I was eating my heart out, admiring them from afar, hoping against hope, panting with repressed emotion at the dizzying spectacle, strangled sobs pressing hard against my rib cage.

Jacques and Mowgli were already accomplished dancers,

but I wasn't at all good at it myself. At the Salaberry Dance Class where I went twice a week, the teacher told me that I should rather stick to sand castles. . . . It did look hopeless and yet I wouldn't give up, I persisted. I set myself a goal: I would become good enough to compete in the great tango competition that was to take place three weeks later, at the height of the season, and I gave myself two weeks to become the best tango dancer of the century. I was already picturing in my mind the result of my efforts, as I struck the pose in front of the bathroom mirror. The elegance of my style would be sure to dazzle the two belles. Of course I had to teach myself the other dances as well, the *Quadrille des Lanciers*, a complicated figure dance; the one-step, a simple one that consisted of walking straight ahead, then back; the Viennese waltz. . . . My head reels, better not get all those fancy steps mixed up!

Well, the organizers were quite undemanding, and I was admitted as a contestant simply by registering my name.

The big night arrives, and I try on a pair of long pants borrowed from Mowgli, adjusting them as well as I can to fit me. With my heart beating wildly enough to bring down the house, I await the beginning of the contest with my fellow classmates. At the last minute, disaster: My assigned partner, a ten-year-old girl, is struck by such stage fright that she pees in her pants, just at the moment of going on stage; she goes off in a faint. And this is when I suddenly feel the protective smile of Thadée upon me, and I realize that I'm trapped in a situation worse than death: My aunt has taken the same dance courses as myself, adult section, and I sense that she is going to impose herself on me as a partner, on the excuse that she wants to save my act. As a matter of fact, that's what happens. How can I refuse? We're already being pushed through the curtain and she holds me tightly by the arm. It's pathetic: My aunt is almost twice my size, with the arms of a policeman— all the gentlemen avoid her when she appears in the dancing class. My vision is befuddled and I can't see the audience, but I can clearly hear the racket my cousins are making at their table near the stage. Even the orchestra doesn't quite manage to drown out their howls of laughter. Get ready to go! *Go!* Like a feather I'm carried away by my aunt in a gyration borrowed from Swedish gymnastics—*Olé*—her own military conception—*Olé*—of the tango, *Olé!* At the last minute, considering my size, she has decided to reverse the roles, but without letting me know; and so it's two rival cavaliers who jostle each other rhythmically on the stage. The audience explodes with joy, the brass section explodes in decibels, the accordion contorts itself, and I stop fighting. My head reaches my aunt's chin; the few vigorous hairs to be found there grate against my forehead disturbingly during the dipping figures, and her lorgnette swings at the end of its gold chain like a murderous pendulum, hitting me where it hurts most. *Olé . . . Cooac . . .* Ouf. . .! And here we are: The orchestra was forced to stop before the end of the piece, vanquished by hilarity. My aunt forces me to greet the public with her. I do so, gracelessly, and she makes me start over again. It's a standing ovation that greets us and I sense that my aunt is on the verge of making a speech of thanks. I jump down from the stage while she descends the staircase with a firm step, and I suddenly find myself right in front of a table where, in the company of Jacques and Mowgli, the two beautiful friends, Arlette and Clara, are sitting, their eyes still weeping with delight. They kiss me right on the mouth. I am reeling with shock, delight, amazement. That's it! Right on the mouth, both of them! And so . . . so? And so, actually, I haven't accomplished a thing, since I've got to leave in two days. I've wasted all my vacation, lurking in the shadows, far away from them.

"What you did with your aunt really made us laugh," Clara says. *"You're marvelous!"*

"Yes," Arlette says. "Ah, what a woman, that aunt of yours! And to think we were wondering what they could possibly be doing in the Salaberry Dance Class! Do you live in Paris?"

"No, I . . ."

"You'll be coming back to Fouras next year?"

"Uh, I, well, I . . ."

"Of course he'll be coming back next year," Mowgli declares. "This is not a boy who gives up easily."

3

The very day I was born, my father enrolled me at Winchester, one of the poshest public schools in England. The idea was that I was destined to be a British gentleman. Eight years later, however, his aspirations had dwindled down to a much lower ebb. I was booked at the Collège de Meaux instead, a boarding school about twenty kilometers from our house in Rozoy. It was the only establishment of any repute in the vicinity, and my parents took me with them a few days before classes were due to start to register me, and also, I suppose, to give me a foretaste of what my new surroundings were going to be. Well, so I was going to become a French schoolboy after all.

It was a large, looming structure, a former convent of the order of the Ursulines, drowsing in a quiet corner of the sleepy little town. I noticed dandelions sprouting up from the pavement of the side streets.

Three austere buildings surrounded a cloister of massive square pillars, enclosing a courtyard planted with rows of dusty trees. Everything about the school seemed ancient and somewhat dilapidated; the playground, hallways, and classrooms were vast, and the refectory resembled a large medieval marketplace, divided by two rows of long marble tables. Obviously nothing had changed in the last three, four cen-

turies. The assistant headmaster greeted us. M. Cuche was a
snappy little man who could bark with the fury of a mongrel
or slide about on his rubber soles as silent as an eel. He took
us to see the chapel, which he obviously considered to be the
highlight of the establishment; then he ushered us into the
presence of the headmaster himself, M. Papillard, a grave
margrave in his florid beard.

Dusk was falling as we returned to the silent courtyard. We
stood there while my parents listened to M. Cuche holding
forth; an old gardener was raking up dead leaves in slow
sweeps to burn them. I gazed at the wisps of vegetal incense
dissolving in the air, which brought back a last time the fragrance of summer; I was lost in a daydream of what my new
life was going to be, of a world of boys and games and movement I was about to enter.

In the stillness of old age, the school seemed steeped in
tradition and old-fashioned learning. My parents were easily
taken in by this deceptive appearance, but the reality was
quite different. The place was in fact the dumping ground for
the most incorrigible hoodlums, kids who had been thrown
out repeatedly from Paris schools, or kids who had to be hidden away for one reason or another, children of scandal with
unmentionable daddies and jailbird mummies. The administration showed its democratic leanings by refusing to look too
closely into the private affairs of the parents or the academic
credentials of their brood, which were of the lowest. Let the
skeletons dance merrily in the cupboards—as long as the bills
are paid on time, *n'est-ce pas?* . . .

The big day came one week later; the entire household was
up at dawn to send me on my way. First a feverish bustle, then a silent drive through the early morning countryside.
My parents both seemed a little tense. They would only see
me every two weeks from now on.

The street, the steps leading to the high portal, were
jammed with a mob of families, kids yelling at one another,
buddyships being reconnected after the summer's interruption. As we pushed our way inside, the uproar took me by
surprise; the noise and the emotions were really too much,
especially for my father who obviously couldn't bear the turmoil. He shook my hand and filled it with the entire contents
of his pocket, a fortune in small change. Money! Before my
vacation in Fouras money had meant nothing to me, but now I

knew that it was meant to buy things. All of a sudden I found myself the owner of that heavy metal treasure, and I clutched it hard.

M. Cuche materialized from a mob, bowed to my mother, and, grabbing my suitcase, propelled us into a courtyard where a hundred boys, divested at last of their families, were tearing around like demons; our appearance with M. Cuche stopped them in their tracks. My mother squeezed my hand with a spasm of uneasiness, rare for her; but it was too late for regrets. She was about to lose to the world this boy she had never been able to talk to.

"Silence!" barked M. Cuche, raising his hand. "Here's a new boy for the class of M. Lebert. Show him what to do. Here, Genton, take him to the dormitory to unpack. Make it snappy, eh!"

The reason Genton was getting all the chores was simply that he was too slow and myopic to duck out of them. My mother went off with M. Cuche and I found myself surrounded by a circle of boys of my age who exuded a threatening hostility. Why? What had I done to them? Violent little faces already scarred by life, mangy alley-cat bodies, so these are to be my new companions? They were asking themselves a similar question, looking at my English cap perched on my auburn curls, my well-cut blue blazer, and my smartly polished patent leather boots. *All right, I was different, but was that a reason to hate me?*

Suddenly I had a flash . . . a picture from a tale came back to me, something from *The Arabian Nights*, illustrating "the Difference": A young prince surrounded by beggars throws the contents of his purse at them in a superb gesture, and they fall pell-mell at his feet in abject gratitude. Without thinking, I plunged my hand into my pocket and sent my whole fortune flying up in the air, as high as I could throw. *Slaughter!* The kids first tear at one another to grab the coins, and then turn on me. I find myself at the bottom of a pyramid of struggling, kicking bodies, shrieking, hissing, spitting devils; and all of a sudden I am blind with fury and start hitting back in all directions like a maniac, so blind, in fact, that I find myself punching and kicking the air as the human pyramid dissolves to reform elsewhere in a new scramble of fights and games. Wow! So that's human society, eh? I'm sitting on my rear end, my pretty clothes in shreds, my body battered but with my bones apparently intact. The only person near me now is Genton, leaning quietly against a tree, vaguely looking at me through his goggles like a fish in an aquarium.

"Grab your stuff," says Genton. "Let's go to the dorm. We've got to get back in twenty minutes for dinner. That crazy old Cuche, he's a real pain, you'll soon find out for yourself. C'mon on, let's go."

As for me, I didn't object to Papa Cuche for the simple reason that he had two daughters, Yvette and Nadine, who were allowed by special dispensation to attend all courses with us. They were enrolled in my class, which was taught by M. Lebert, a gentle and humorous man. Because of my fine clothes and pretty manners, Papa Cuche assigned me to act as *chevalier servant* to his daughters. He warned them not to play with the other young ruffians, and I was seated between them in the classroom. I had a slight preference for Yvette, who was sweet and pretty and had budding breasts; Nadine, the younger sister, had a sharp tongue and was flat-chested, but she was very funny. Once again, Fate, strangely insistent, was leading me down the garden path toward twin loves. But here the situation was reversed from that of last summer. This time I could no longer moon for the objects of my passion from afar, since I would be spending a good portion of my days sitting between the two of them. And so I acted like cock of the walk. Nadine was resigned to playing second fiddle to her sister, as she knew that the absence of a chest kept her out of the competition for the time being. But she was watching, and I didn't know how to express my attraction to Yvette— sharp-nosed Nadine was always in the way, hanging on. And so we functioned as an organic trio, spending our time in sober childish games, isolated in the midst of a crowd of boys who studiously ignored us. I knew full well that my peers hated me; such was the price I paid, and willingly, for my elevation to the higher role of gentleman-in-waiting to the Cuche girls.

In the hurly-burly of the playground, as I played a foolish game of hopscotch with my two companions, I would sneak a longing look at the fierce and fiery games of the other boys. They too, while acting supremely indifferent, spied assiduously on our *ménage à trois*. We were like three innocent explorers who had wandered unwittingly into cannibal country.

My debut as a scholar took place in this curious ambiance. M. Lebert himself treated me with special consideration because my mother had called on him, and their conversation had led to subjects in which they were both interested. He was the custodian of old manuscripts at the town library, particularly of a fine illuminated copy of the *Roman de la Rose*, one of the two or three in existence, which he had promised to show my mother. The friendship that developed between my mother and M. Lebert added to my infamy: I was teacher's pet. Because I was totally unused to the ways of society, I couldn't understand why the other kids wouldn't speak to me; I felt the loneliness acutely and I had no idea how to put an end to it.

Every two weeks, my father would pick me up on a Friday evening to drive me silently back to Rozoy, where I stayed till Sunday. What a transformation! The woods, the garden, even my own room seemed different. I felt like a war hero briefly on leave to his native village: At home they cannot possibly imagine what it's like at the front.

One Friday, Paul Monfaucon came to pick me up. This worthy drunkard, who worked for us both as valet and chauffeur, informed me that my father was gravely ill, that Paris specialists had been summoned by our local family doctor, and their arrival was imminent. When I got home the atmosphere was heavy anguish; my father was raving deliriously, grandfather addressed me in solemn tones. André Chamite was wandering around the house like a lost soul; he was nursing my father, and every day he shaved his dying friend, delicately cradling the delirious head in the crook of his arm. Two days later it was he who drove me back to Meaux, silent and solemn, and turned me over to M. Cuche, whom he took aside and briefed on the situation.

"What a tragedy!" said M. Cuche after André had left. "But you're a man; you must bear up. Keep a stiff upper lip!"

"Yes, M'sieur," I mechanically responded, thinking to myself that these premature condolences were in the worst possible taste.

"Poor little fellow!" he went on. "Madame Cuche was very sorry to hear about all this, and she suggests that you stay with us for a few days. Tomorrow instead of school, you can go to the Bossuet gardens with Yvette and Nadine."

The Cuche apartment overlooked the main courtyard of the school; my relocation was accompanied by the jeers of my colleagues. Ah, well! For the next few days I would not have to endure their presence, that was something. And I started dreaming about tomorrow's excursion in the mysterious gardens of Cardinal Bossuet. It seems that I had already accepted my father's demise; the thought barely bothered me.

The next morning I took off with the Cuche girls, all on our best behavior, with the family dog tagging along closely behind us. He was a stupid mongrel, mean, ugly, and yet so much a part of that interesting family that the kids had nicknamed him Cucuche. I tried to chase him away, but Nadine stopped me. I understood why soon after we got to the archbishop's gardens. An elaborate placard explained that in this charming bushy retreat the Eagle of Meaux, as Bossuet the great predicator was known, had composed his most pompous jeremiads. How very interesting, I forced myself to say, turning to my companions; and it is at that moment that I saw the scandalous scene. Cucuche, lolling on the gravel path, was grunting with delight while Nadine, a fiendish expression on her face, was masturbating him with a twig. It was a horrifying and fascinating spectacle—and so totally unexpected! Seated nearby on a stone bench, Yvette gazed off into the distance with a very red face while her sister, with that diabolical glint in her eye, methodically titillated her infatuated victim. Cucuche coughed, groaned, waggled his bottom in the dust, as his pointed, purplish penis visibly expanded. Suddenly he leaped up with a modulated, plaintive bark, signaling the end of the act. I found myself both excited and appalled. But Cucuche's ordeal was not over; in a lusty frenzy, Nadine grabbed him, pinned him to the ground, and began once again to manipulate him with zest in spite of the dog's desperate struggle. Nadine yelled for her sister:

"Hey, fathead! Give me a hand, will you? What are you waiting for, come and hold his paws!"

Yvette demurred. "But you are out of your mind! Leave him alone, Nadine, you're going to kill him!"

That evening, before we sat down to dinner in the Cuche household, the dog Cucuche began to vomit. His master picked him up gingerly to examine him, and as he palpated his belly, the mutt bit his hand viciously.

"In God's name! What's got into him, biting his daddy's hand?"

That night in my dreams, Cucuche and his master merged into one monster creature. . . .

Next morning, a phone call from Rozoy informed us that my father was out of danger. I was dispatched promptly back to the dorm.

Strange to say, it felt rather good to be back in my hard bed, surrounded by thirty other characters who had not been too friendly to me. Snoring and mumbling in their sleep, they were less offensive, more tolerable. In our midst stood the gray cubicle in which slept the assistant professor in charge of us and who was known as Miss Goose; he snored louder than anyone else. Above my head the tall window framed a rectangle of sky across which the moon wended its way through gossamer clouds. O moon in your wandering . . . how many hours I spent, craning my neck to see her, eyes glazed, submissive to her poetic whims, blocking out what was going on around me. . . . For the life of the dorm, it must be said, offered few amenities. We were supposed to relieve ourselves in a common *chaise percée*, always filled to overflowing. Washing was a very perfunctory affair: Icy water spouted, for only fifteen minutes each morning, from holes pierced in a pipe that ran above a zinc trough set against the wall. The picture would be incomplete if I failed to mention the fact that the denizens of that small preadolescent world were practically all cracked, demented, violent or catatonic, or both. There were many varieties of sexual obsession; in particular Bourleton, a mongoloid character who looked like a crazed Chinaman and pretended to be sleepwalking as he stumbled about at night, a phantom in white nightgown with outstretched arms and eyes rolled back—and always wound up his nocturnal perambulations in the bed of one of the little kids, who were always too terrified to complain.

At recess the next day, that strange, unexpected thing happened, an event of which I was the main actor and also the major victim. What was it about Yvette that troubled me so much? She was looking at me in that sad, funny way as if she expected me to guess something, to do something. Her look troubles me, stirs me, inflames me with the desire to cover her with kisses. I grab her and give her a resounding smooch. In an instant, the dozen or so boys playing nearby, who had pretended for weeks that we didn't even exist, all suddenly pounce on me as if I deserved to be lynched. I find myself engulfed by a seething mass of kicking, hitting, stamping devils. A second assault wave turns the carnage into slaughter; not knowing the reason for the battle, the newcomers tackle the first group. The bell rings, signaling the end of recess. I extricate myself from the scrimmage, thinking that I haven't done too badly. And then I see Yvette, hanging about at the edge of the battlefield, wild-eyed, twisting the hem of her smock. Seeing me emerge from the fray, bloody, bruised, and in tatters, she takes to her heels and flees.

Let her go! It's better that way; a choice had to be made, and I made it on the spot. If I wanted to be one of the boys, it's clear that I could no longer make a fool of myself with the Cuche girls, with their doggy trysts and their crepe-soled papa. I installed myself firmly at the other end of the classroom. During the next break, I cornered Genton and did my best to strike up a conversation with him. Crinking up his eyes behind his thick lenses, he greeted my advances with a sardonic smile: "Listen, dope! You've been beaten up twice already. If you don't watch your step, you'll wind up in the morgue."

"But it's not my fault—they always jump on me!"

"Tough shit! That's only a taste of what you're going to get if you don't watch out."

"What can I do about it?"

"You have to beat up somebody else. You can start with somebody smaller than you, or an easy mark, like me, or Lagrelée with his club foot. Then you go on to someone bigger for practice. But of course, if you go after one of the goons like Jaboure or Dugraveau, your number's up. Just go and lick two or three of the medium-size guys, everybody will leave you alone."

"Really?"

"Sure. Another thing—your clothes. You've got to dress like everyone else here. Look dirty!"

In principle he was right, but his method seemed despicable to me. I decided to consult Brothier, a fierce little peasant whom I had seen holding a dozen boys at bay, by himself, armed with a big ugly switchblade. Like Genton, Brothier was a loner; I had to bribe him with a box of caramels to gain his confidence. His advice was simple: "Get a blade, jerk. A mean guy who's good with a knife, he'll be left alone. Get it?"

It took me some time to digest that advice, and to hatch my plan. I went back to Brothier and rented his knife for the price of a bottle of violet-tinted ink and a packet of licorice. And now listen to what happened: Near the end of recess, I go up to a group of heavies.

Jaboure, who has Creole blood, looks me over with amused stupefaction and asks: "Where d'you think you are going, fella? Ya want me to soak your head in the shit hole?"

Dugraveau is more direct: "Come here, sweetheart, I like your looks. Show us your little pud so that we can have a good laugh."

He reaches for my fly. I pull my hand out of my pocket, armed with Brothier's knife, and in the same movement I manage to spring the catch; the blade snaps open with a mean professional *click!* Dugraveau's mouth is open in surprise, but it's too late to move—I lunge smoothly and stick the knife through his faded sweater. An excited crowd forms a circle around us. Dumbfounded, Dugraveau cranes his neck to examine the blood-stained gash in his belly. I close up the knife, punch him in the face, and, getting up steam, give him a solid kick in the balls. With a bellow, Dugraveau slumps to the ground like a sack of flour. He may be big, but he's slow and stupid; I did well not to attack Jaboure who's much more crafty. Dugraveau turns out to be a pushover—but it's impressive enough for our audience. If no one else takes me on, I'll be promoted to tough-guy status. I glance toward Jaboure and see him heading my way: "Well," says he. "Looks like you showed him, the big baboon! Didn't know you had it in you, champ!" He pinches admiratively my butterfly-size biceps, pretending fright. All right—let him make fun of me—he's admitted that I've won. Supertough, that's me! From now on even the big guys will have to be polite.

All this thanks to Brothier. In line with his advice, I gave up my clothes, my shirts, washing, studying, and went around dressed in rags worse than anyone else's. At recess the kids used to congregate behind the WC's to smoke cigarettes. Not to be outdone, I brought cigars filched from Mowgli (who had himself stolen them from his father, who had no doubt procured them from my grandfather) and I made it my business to smoke them in bed in the dorm, one or two centimeters a night. It made me horribly nauseated, but I stuck with it long enough to take three or four generous puffs, assaulting my neighbors with the stench as a way to establish my membership in the ruling class. I also cultivated other talents: With two or three strokes of chalk, I could caricature male and female genitalia on the walls in the most striking manner. I became the equal of Jaboure and Bourgarel, not to mention Dugraveau.

The little Cuche ladies vanished from my horizon; to replace them I chose several close buddies. First of all, Genton,
who had shown himself to be far more astute than he looked.
Another one was Jean Marcellin, a tough cookie who basked
in glory reflected from his brother, Raymond, then sixteen,
leader of the older boys as Jaboure was to us. Jean introduced
me to Raymond; his handshake confirmed my status. It was
good to be one of the killer elite.

All this politicking did not prevent me from toying with the
Muse, as the expression goes. I shall not dwell on the extent
and intensity of my outpourings—sonnets, odes, epic verse,
you name it—including a superb but incomplete drama in
halting Alexandrines, inspired collectively by all my idols:
Villon, Ronsard, du Bellay, Boileau, and, of course, Edmond
Rostand. I misplaced the manuscript one day and the oaf who
found it had the bad taste to deposit it on the desk of the new
French teacher, a young Parisian aesthete who had run
aground in Meaux, God knows how. As the class got under
way with the usual hubbub, de Richaud, as his name was, held
up the notebook that contained my work: "Someone has lost
this—"

"It's mine, M'sieur," I said, leaping forward, hoping he'd
hand it over without a closer look.

But of course he opened it and began to read, twisting a
strand of hair as he did so. All at once he clucked. I was furious, but powerless to stop him from reading, first in an indistinct murmur, then clearly declaiming my sorry verse. Thus
exposed, the faults of my prosody were downright embarrassing. He must have noticed my shame, for he finally stopped
and said: "Forgive me! I was indiscreet . . . but as one poet to
another . . . let me say, I'm astonished, really, it's very good!
Some day you'll succeed."

The class observed all this with rapt attention. I grabbed my
manuscript, and all I could find to say was the standard,
"Thank you, M'sieur." The minute class was over, I fled to the
professors' toilet—it was more dignified and better equipped
than ours. I locked myself in a stall, tore my manuscript to
shreds, pulled the chain. . . . Adieu, literature!

Les Che-va-liers de la Lu-une. . . . My grandfather had a curious
collection of old ditties that he hummed absentmindedly as he
drove through the night, between lines of poplars gliding by
on each side. The car was spacious and comfortable, equipped

with fur rugs and cushions to curl up on when one became drowsy. It was a luxurious caravan—my grandfather belonged to the race of nomads, only truly alive when in motion.

He would get bored during dinner, yawn, and take off into the night. Next morning he'd find himself breakfasting in Amsterdam; a few days later, we'd get a postcard from Budapest. Or Istanbul. He would probably have liked best to take off on his own, but all too often my grandmother contrived to go with him. Not for fun—these ceaseless journeys didn't amuse her—but the good woman had her own reasons for not letting her husband travel alone: humble jealousy. I was the prime beneficiary of this conjugal mistrust, as he took me with him on some of his rambles, and I served as his cover: I was my grandfather's duenna, a very instructive role! I learned to live as he did, in a perpetual movement that stirred up ideas and feelings. With his gaze fixed on the silver Venus that adorned the radiator cap, lost in a waking dream, he took in all the impressions the road evoked in him. It was his way to think and to exist. Our stops were festive and joyful, as the old man liked to eat, to drink, and, after he had packed me off to bed, to bandy with the ladies. We would stop at a sumptuous palace, or else, perched on a bare rock, looking out over mountains, dine on cheese and fruit. At every meal, my grandfather polished off two bottles of wine, the requisite fuel for his empire-builder's metabolism. Brief but perfect moments are still easily conjured by my memory—a lake glimpsed through pine trees; a Jura pass in the evening, calm, with cowbells faintly heard; the instant drama of dusk enveloping a village at the bottom of a gorge; arriving suddenly beneath the high gray walls of an ancient fortified town. . . . One night, I fell asleep in the car, and when we arrived at Pontorson, my grandfather carried me up to bed in his arms. The next morning, I was astonished to wake in this strange bed—whose sheets, said my grandfather, were woven from the moustaches of the notorious Connétable du Guesclin.

This was our last stop before reaching our goal, the Mont-Saint-Michel, which marks the dividing line between Normandy and Brittany. One of the most enigmatic examples of medieval architecture, part fortress, part monastery and basilica, the Mont rises on a lonely rock above the shallow waters of the bay of Avranches, which roll back as far as the line of horizon at low tide. When we set forth on the long causeway that parts the waves, I was struck by such a strong sensation of familiarity that I felt overcome by a light brain fever. All day, I felt that I was walking along a well-rehearsed dream, reliving something I knew intimately.

That evening, after we left the Mont, I turned back to stare at the lingering silhouette. I engraved that silver image on my memory and promised myself that I would solve its mystery one day. My grandfather's face shone red as flame in the setting sun.

Among my classmates was a character known as the Persian; clearly older than us, he already had to shave, and though he scraped his cheeks assiduously every morning, they soon glinted with a blue shadow—which disconcerted the rest of us downy-cheeked sixth-formers. He didn't care a hoot about being so different from his fellow students; in addition to which he never studied, never handed in a scrap of homework, and answered all questions with an exquisite smile, in what I took to be the Persian manner: the sidewise glance of a languorous gazelle. He had the look of a dreamer, a tale-spinner, a Scheherazade. The Persian had but one activity, in class, at recess, in the dorm: Wherever he encountered a large enough audience, he told endless and extraordinary tales, mingling events, digressions, and flashbacks. Those tales were freely associated to form an erotic saga that unfurled in a sumptuous bordello, with the Persian himself as the hero. The unlikelihood of his purported exploits bothered none of us; all that mattered was his art, his marvelous Oriental ability to clothe human frailty in fabulous costume.

Seated on a ledge above his public, his glance veiled like a seer's in a trance, he overwhelmed us with a flood of images. Listening to him, I felt as if I were witnessing the birth of literature. Homer himself must have started out like this. . . . At the same period I discovered the opposite extreme in literature as I read and reread *Voyage Autour de Ma Chambre*. That intimate travelogue by Xavier de Maistre creates such a sense of reality only thanks to the greatest economy of means: Nothing moves and everything lives. Between these two extremes one finds all of literature, methinks. Movement is the thing for us human machines.

I was lucky enough at Meaux to encounter two intelligent French teachers, as I was just starting to read and write, who taught me to respect the power of the word. Alas, we made poor use of it there. Most of the kids read nothing but war stories, with gory covers showing the heroic foot soldier in sky-blue tunic thrusting his bayonet into the breast of a dirty *Boche*, whose thuglike scowl clearly proved that he deserved his end. What troubled me more was the jingoistic nationalism of the state-approved textbooks destined to teach us the history of France. Clearly, kids were supposed to be idiots—or to become so after being steeped in these official confabulations; they were blinded by them from infancy and that clearly accounted for the French attitude of uninformed xenophobia.

Each time I opened a history text I was revolted by these lessons in imbecile chauvinism: *la perfide Albion*, the slap of the dey of Algiers, the unjust fate of Napoleon, and above all the incurable treachery of the Germans, who had succeeded the English in the role of hereditary enemies. From the time I was nine, I understood that all this was meant to condition us to become unthinking cannon fodder in the next war. What my history books showed most clearly was that kings and governments had ceaselessly waged useless wars, and from defeat to retaliation, that linkage of stupid vanity and bogus fatality would only stop if the victims revolted: the eternal victims, the humble warriors, the poor cretins who get wiped out with the first shot, like my uncle Maurice, with a bullet smack in the brow at age twenty.

The battle starts in the sixth form, when this madness is drummed into the kids, when they're told this is life, it's always been like this and you can't do a thing about it—your destiny is to obey without a peep.

Not mine, thanks. I will never forget my vow never to kill! And, quite clearly, it was my duty to launch political action. Like Jeanne d'Arc—I got the message. I soon found out how difficult it is to make others hear such clear and sane wisdom: Genton, Marcellin, and others to whom I tried to expound my thoughts looked at me as if I were the village idiot. At age nine they were already corrupted, reduced to robots. I found only two pals who would listen to me: Tricot and Lenglumé, not very brilliant individuals perhaps, but they seemed to catch on, in their own way. I exhorted them to state if they were ready to act, to found with me a secret society dedicated to fighting war propaganda. They stared at me, nonplussed.

"A *secret* society?" asked Lenglumé.

"Yes, secret!" I explained. "It will make our action even more impressive."

"Well, okay. And what would it do, this secret society?"

"To begin with," I proposed, "we'll confiscate all the history books, all the trashy novels about the Great War, we'll destroy them. I've drawn up a manifesto to explain our action. Since revolutionaries aren't thieves, every time we take a book we'll leave a sum equal to its price in its place."

"You don't say!" said Tricot with admiration. "You're not fooling around. And where are we going to get the dough to do that?"

"Each one of us will contribute what he can."

"Ya *nuts?*" cried Tricot, enraged, as if I'd insulted him. "I don't have money to pour down the drain like that!"

Lenglumé got to his feet to end our conference, but I grabbed his sleeve. "Look, pal, the money, that's secondary. To begin with, I'll give what I've got. Later, we'll see."

"Well, if that's the way you want it. . . . How much ya got?"

"Here," I said, solemnly. "Here's thirty-two francs."

"No kidding! *Thirty-two francs!*"

I won my point, by a woeful compromise—but to a true revolutionary, the end justifies the means. We dubbed our confederation the Thursday Society, choosing for our raids that day on which the classes visited one by one the newly installed footbath. There were no bathtubs or showers at the Collège de Meaux, but M. Papillard, in a gesture of modernity, had turned an unused amphitheater into the football hall. The desks were removed and in their stead rows of basins were set into the floor, from the upper to the lower tiers of the amphitheater. Somehow the elevation made it look even more ludicrous; one above the other you would see six rows of kids seated on their wooden benches, their feet soaking in tepid water, thirty minutes a session, till the dirt was demarcated sharply at midcalf; then each one slipped on stinking socks and redolent clodhoppers and took off. Some parents had protested against this devilish innovation, which threatened to give their little poppets a bad cold: an absurd complaint, since we were enveloped in suffocating heat, mingled with the malodorous reminders of the beans they stuffed us with at mealtime, and there was no question of opening a window. M. Papillard was forced, nevertheless, to reach a compromise with the rebellious parents, and he modified his edict to the extent that a student could, upon parental demand, be excused from the Thursday footdip. Thanks to apocryphal documents, Tricot, Lenglumé, and I obtained such

The Frog Prince

a dispensation, which caused Tricot to suggest that we dub ourselves the Footsoak Society. I blasted him with a crushing look.

"We have only thirty minutes per class, so cut it out! Let's go."

On the first Thursday, laden with mimeographed manifestos, masked with a kerchief that hid our features up to the eyes, we accomplished our mission without any trouble in the sixth forms, A and B, and the study hall of the fifth form. Our booty: twenty-two history textbooks by Mallet and Isaac, plus eighteen illustrated war novels. Outlay: 18 francs 65 centimes. *Fantastic!* And without a hitch. Not a soul spotted us. That night I savored my victory in bed as I tried to imagine what would happen next. Tomorrow the discovery of our deed would provoke a hell of an uproar! The local press would be informed and would give our manifesto the publicity it deserved; then the Paris papers would break the story. A great idea had been born: The most pacific revolution of all time had started, in the sixth form, Collège de Meaux.

The next day, strangely, nothing. Not a single shocked look, no exclamations of indignation. Those bastards! They were playing their cards close to the chest. It dawned on me that the thefts had probably not been reported by the victims, for fear of having to give up the money they had found in lieu of the books. I should have thought earlier of that possibility! One always tends to ignore the human factor.

Two days later, still nothing. Tricot and Lenglumé did not seem as surprised and disappointed as I was.

"So then, we'll get on with it next Thursday, eh?" asked Lenglumé.

"Of course. As long as our funds hold out."

Next Thursday, same maneuver, same success . . . *and same silence!* But now the purse was empty—the revolution had failed.

I could not fathom this disaster. Unless . . . but no, surely a dedicated militant would not stoop so low! Nevertheless, there was no other explanation. I had to put it to my fellow conspirators and if my suspicions were found to be correct, the guilty party would be sanctioned without pity, as behooves true revolutionaries.

"I expect you to tell the truth. After each raid, one of you went back to pocket the money and the manifestos, no? Which of you was it?"

"Ow, shut your trap, you don't know what you're talking about," Tricot shouted.

"You're bonkers," fumed Lenglumé. "Tricot and I are no fools, you're turning everything around! We saw you sneaking back into the classroom, *it's you who took the money.*"

"What?" I exploded, outraged by the cynicism of these ruffians.

"But of course it's your dough after all, you certainly have the right to take it back," Tricot suggested with a sinister leer.

"Anyway, that's enough, I'm fed up with this nonsense!" said Lenglumé. "We risk our necks for you, and instead of thanks we have to listen to your raving insults."

"A guy who steals his own loot, that's sick," concluded Tricot. "Let's beat it, Lenglumé, the president of the Footsoak Society has to pull himself together."

All right, bright guys, you win. Farewell, cannon fodder. . . .

M. Papillard was unlike other headmasters, for despite his luxuriant beard in an era dedicated to the clean-shaven look, he prided himself on being a modern man. Wishing to lend the Collège de Meaux a literary luster, he decided to rename it the Collège Georges Courteline in honor of the third-rate playwright who was its one and only alumnus of any distinction, freshly deceased.

The plan was clever but not without risks. Courteline had a rather racy reputation, and his lightweight comedies poked fun at the bureaucracy and the military. And so certain municipal officials, remembering his farcical *Follies of the Regiment*, balked. Papillard's party, however, insisted that Courteline was considered a national treasure, who had even been considered for burial in the Panthéon, where the famous men of France are interred. It will serve the prestige of the city itself, they further argued, because since the days of Cardinal Bossuet, it had owed whatever fame it enjoyed to its homemade brands of tasty mustard and mellow Brie rather than to the intellectual stature of its denizens.

So, it's settled. They're going to rechristen the dump. A bronze plaque is installed in the entrance hall, and the commemoration ceremony is announced to the far corners of the civilized world. Papillard hopes to attract the attention of the Paris newspapers; an idle dream of course, but he is entitled to it. As for us, his underlings, to assure our participation he bribes us with a day of revelry: no classes, and a feast to make the occasion memorable; second helpings, almond-stuffed pithiviers torte for dessert, and a beaker of bubbly besides. The quid pro quo: everybody in uniform, shoes well shined, and no monkey business, is that clear?

At mealtime things start going rapidly downhill. Papillard miscalculated. He should have scheduled the ceremony *before* the banquet, not *after*. The brats spend all morning raising a rumpus, scuffling and tearing one another to pieces. We crowd into the refectory, dirty and famished. We wolf down basins of beans, we swig liters of wine, and long before the bubbly is uncorked, our carousing is in full swing. It starts with a platter of sausages flung in the face of the unfortunate Gégène, our obese waiter. Next, without the slightest provocation, Brothier unsheaths his wicked blade, *click!* and jabs it savagely into Bourleton's plump buttocks. The latter leaps in the air with a soul-rending shriek and falls stiff as a corpse in the middle of all the crockery. Off with him to sick bay; that's one less to eat the pudding! No one is supervising us; all the masters are at the visitors' banquet being given in honor of the great man's widow. You can picture the chaos!

The first of our mentors to confront us is the ill-fated one we call Miss Goose, a myopic and incautious person. He's quickly routed with a fusillade of half-eaten rolls and other stuff. His colleagues then sneak in on us through the kitchen, outflank us, herd us into line, and threaten severe physical reprisals if we don't shut up instantly. Three or four cretins, all tanked up, climb on the table to protest. The masters grab them, cart them off by the scruff of the neck despite piteous protestations: "M'sieur, I didn't do it, it's him—"

"Shut your trap, you little creep!" Smack. *Ouch!* Bang. *Eeee!* I'm certainly glad to have escaped such humiliation.

The pupils are formed into a rough square on the parade ground, with the cleanest uniforms lined up in front. I'm not one of them. The scruffiest are secreted behind trees.

The notables advance, well-fed, glowing with self-esteem, chatting in little clusters. Their faces are suffused with a winy shine; they flutter and glitter under the sun in a grand array of lorgnettes, cocked hats, kepis, rosettes, and medals. The speechmaking is upon us. The subprefect, in full regalia, shoots his cuffs and pulls out a handful of papers that he unfolds, inspects, verifies, counts, and recounts. He clears his throat and launches himself on his peroration. We grasp only

an occasional phrase that rings out louder than the rest: ". . .
the genius of France . . . the golden pen . . . this historic
occasion. . . ." We miss little by losing the thread. The dignitaries, the mayor, Messrs. Prunette, Papillard and Cuche, the
profs, and the junior masters, arranged in concentric rows
around the orator, listen deferentially while sneaking appre-
ciative glances at the widow. Mme Courteline is a sparkling old
lady whose little straw boater is perched askew on her pretty
head. She looks as if she'd like to step out and execute a jig
after all that wining and dining. She wows us! "Boy, that
little old lady, she must be a good lay," comments Dugom-
mier, smacking his lips with the flair of a true connoisseur.

Across from us a third-floor dormitory window opens, and
the reporter-photographer of our local tabloid peers out. His
mug is entirely obliterated by a pair of dark glasses and a luxuriant handlebar moustache. At this sight our shaky formation
decomposes: Everyone wants to be seen tomorrow on the
front-page picture in the *Echo du Meldois*. Two hundred urchins outdo one another in ingenuity to catch his eye: Some
turn cartwheels, others form a human pyramid, and the more
nimble hang from the trees.

Cuche and Papillard dispatch a brigade of masters to take us
in hand. Crack, smack, thunk. *Ouch! Ouch!* Blows resound,
slaps ring out. What a brawl! What a ball! So now we have a
patron worthy of us. Yah! Courteline! Let other schools be
dedicated to the great—to Saint Louis, to Charlemagne, to the
Sacred Heart. For us, the modest ones, our own patron saint
will be the immortal master of bedroom comedies and boulevard farce, the inventor of Mister Soup. Speeches are cut
short, the massacre of the innocents proceeds. Before vanishing with her bedecked entourage, the widow grins and gives
us a little friendly wave of the hand. *She's with us!*

"Long live the widow!" the demented ones cry out. *"Vive la
Veuve! Ah-U, Ah-U, Ah Ursule, Viens ici que je t'enc—"* Slap.
Oof! Crack. Bang. *Ouch!*

Along with my political and other writings, I hoard in my
desk a treasure I have patiently collected, which consoles me
for many things: a notebook in which I paste photos of all the
movie actresses I admire. Brigitte Helm in profile, a marvel of
Teutonic purity. The green eyes of Louise Brooks sparkling
beneath her thick black bangs. Dita Parlo's small mouth,
which gives me such an intuition of perversity. . . . The

voluptuous body of Pola Negri . . . Raquel Meller . . . Lillian Harvey . . . Josephine Baker, whose thighs are *the* ultimate and threaten to make me lose my head!

Scissors in one hand, glue pot in the other, I collect women. I scrutinize their contours, compare them, divest them of their bathing suits, and dispose them, nude and languid, around the swimming pool. I stretch Josephine Baker out on a hammock that sets off her shiny dark flesh, I get Louise Brooks to dance one of her wonderful athletic jigs, I turn Pola Negri over to two strapping masseurs who, alas for her, are eunuchs. From time to time I take a dip in the pool to refresh myself, but the irresistible form of Raquel Meller swims toward me underwater and entwines me in a slow-motion pas de deux of such powerful sensuality that I nearly succumb, until Simone Simon dives to the rescue and snatches me gracefully away from the American vamp. Ginger Rogers displays her superb strawberry-blond body to perfection, as she dances, naked, with the black-and-white silhouette of Fred Astaire in a routine full of splits; all of it dedicated to me! Oh, the movies! What an invention, and how bleak my desk would be without this inexhaustible harem, swirling, cooing, begging for my attention, submissive to my whim. . . . The world's most beautiful women belong to me, and believe me, they *know* it.

How could they not feel in their innermost depths the ardent homage I pay them, night and day! My eyes squeezed tight shut, I embrace and possess them more intimately than I could possibly do in what is known as "the realm of reality." To me the movies are far more real than this so-called reality; I've always known that. I remember the first film I ever saw, long ago, when I was a little boy, once upon a time. . . . A film called *Jim le Harponneur*. In those days when we came up from Rozoy to spend a few days with my grandparents in Paris, some member of the family would take it upon himself to take me to the movies, and it so happened that on each occasion each one of them, not having consulted with the others, took me to see the same film about good old Harpoon Jim. But I didn't mind the ritual, since I had no idea that other films existed. The main features of the film were lush and bizarre—a giant whale, a mad captain whose leg was amputated with a cutlass and cauterized with a red-hot iron, a lady in a nightgown who walked across the sea to meet him. . . .

When it was his turn to take me to the movies, my father tsk'd and laughed in the darkness, and pronounced aloud a name I did not recognize: Moby Dick. What, *Moby Dick?* Who's that? I wondered vaguely. My father knows nothing about the cinema! Of course this is Harpoon Jim, what else could it be?

When he comes to fetch me, one Friday, my father is in a strange mood. We stop at every single pub between Meaux and Rozoy, and that's a fair number. I wait in the car while he pays his visit to the good people; he likes to recite Shelley to the peasants he meets, who understand not a word, but who appreciate the spirit in which it is delivered. After each stop, he has a little more trouble getting the car to start, staying on the right-hand side of the road, and avoiding the telegraph poles. Soon I'm filled with terror. He's possessed, he doesn't see at all where he's heading, we're just about to drive slam-bang into a wall—*ooof!* He saw it—just in time! Suddenly the car goes into a terrible skid, scales the bank, nearly pitches over, brusquely returns to the vertical, and so we unexpectedly resume our journey, zigzagging down the road as in a Laurel and Hardy scene. I'm in such a panic that I gird myself to leap from the moving car, but finally we pull up at our own gate; the car stops short with a mechanical hiccup that flings me to the floor. My mother has heard the uproar from the road and guessed everything; she lights the entryway lamp and I throw myself into her arms, sobbing. For the first time ever we find ourselves in the classical pose, mother and son. In a minute she pushes me away and says: "Now you go up to your bed like a big boy. I have to take care of your daddy, who is not well. We'll have a good long talk, you and I, in the morning."

The next day my father remains confined to his room; he must be in terrible shape. And now my mother undertakes to explain the situation, treating me as if I were a grown-up. I listen, wondering. . . . Two years earlier, consumed by a desire to go into publishing, my father had invested most of his money in a small house that was specializing in books on the arts, and that was run by Henry Babou, a rambunctious little man with a goatee I had met once or twice. Carried away by enthusiasm, Babou quickly ran through his own capital, and ours. Meanwhile, my grandfather had lost the better part of his own fortune as a result of the international depression. So we would have to sell the house, the estate, and settle in Paris. My father's health had sufficiently improved since his illness to allow him to function cautiously, and his one ruling desire was to go into publishing on his own with the funds that were left. The decision had been made for the whole family to leave for Paris immediately. All the tensions had, well, *depressed* my father a bit the day before, but he would be all right. And as to you, she added, we feel that you must stay in your school at Meaux till vacation time. In the fall you will go to a *lycée* in Paris, isn't that exciting? she asked. I was eleven, a big boy, I should be able to understand some of the difficulties of adult life. . . .

What a speech! The net result of all this is that in a few months I will be living in Paris and going to the movies every night. That will impress my buddies! So much for the Variety and *The Revenge of the Tekrites*. And there's a sense of justice about it; what was I doing buried in a dump like Meaux? I am a born Parisian and I am going back to Paris, my birthplace.

I spent the next two days taking stock of my past, revisiting my old haunts. My solitary adventures in the woods, they were a distant memory now, after my four years in boarding school. I found only broken-down remnants of my tree houses. A jungle of elder and mulberry trees had effaced all traces of the hut I had carved out of the underbrush; my aerial dwelling in the tree-with-seven-trunks had also vanished; only a few rotten boards and twists of wire were left. My poor bulldog, Poulbot, was gazing at me with the look of Socrates about to down the hemlock. His shining round eyes in the handsome black mug made it clear that he knew what fate awaited him: He would be given away to a neighboring farmer, and he would die of a broken heart. For more than a year we had kept only one old gardener, who did very little. The rose garden had reverted to nature. The sky was gray, the distant fields were hidden by mist.

Back at school, I told my buddies the good news: "I'm going back to Paris. I'll go to the movies every night!" I made quite an impression, in the fashion of a local dignitary who is summoned to assume high responsibilities in the central government.

It was the May-bug season, and to prevent their proliferation the town offered a bounty of one franc per kilo of bugs, dead or alive. The lust for cash went to our heads and we launched an all-out war against the world of bugs, harvesting enormous bagfuls of them during our Thursday afternoon marches into the countryside; which, incidentally, followed the weekly footbath and negated its dubious benefits. We lived in a cornucopia of May-bugs; in our effort to corner the market, we became obsessed by them, we became bugs ourselves. One popular sport was to harness ten or twenty of them to paper sleds and release them in the classroom. They would fly away shakily in unexpected directions, crisscross the air, and bang into the windows. The effect was very pretty, but that practice enraged the teachers.

At Easter, M. Papillard announced a prize for good fellowship to be awarded at the end of the school year by vote of the students themselves. Jaboure and Bourgarel presided over a meeting during which they swore their adherents to vote for me. This was done as a just tribute, on the eve of my departure, to one of the most creative pranksters, to one of the most uncompromising dunces in the entire history of this world-famous institution, the Collège Georges Courteline. After four years of loyal contributions to the cause of obfuscation, the time had come for me to reap the harvest of my unrelenting efforts.

I am now ready to receive this well-deserved homage. And when I think of the glorious Paris night life that is about to follow, I feel like a millionaire.

In the empty, dusty courtyard, carpenters have erected a monumental podium that is now being covered with red carpeting and bedecked with gilt chairs and green plants. A speaker's lectern is being installed from which, very soon now, my name will be called to accept the only prize I will have ever won in my academic life: a prize meant to recompense, not simple scholarship, but that which is so much more precious to me: friendship.

The anticipation mounts as we pupils are marched in, wearing our patched-up uniforms, class by class, and are made to sit quietly in rows on our refectory benches. Then the parents are admitted, a diversified throng that pours in and settles down on the sides. When everybody is seated, the notables, as well as our own faculty, make their dignified entrance and take their places on the podium, from which they look down on us.

Speeches are made, much pompous verbosity is allowed to flow. They celebrate the scientist and the poet, the farmer and the soldier, Vergil and Poincaré, and I don't know what other figures of mythology; this takes very long because each speech is constantly being interrupted by the din and clangor from trains entering or leaving the nearby depot. The air is hot, dusty, sunny, and punctuated with the erratic dance of the May-bugs.

Finally the great moment comes, and despite myself, I feel a hard knot in my throat. M. Cuche comes to the podium, calls my name in a loud voice, and announces that I have won the Grand Special Good Fellowship Prize. As I step forward, my buddies smack me on the lower back, and I feel myself to be, not walking, but majestically floating toward the dais, carried on the wings of fame. It is the mayor himself, M. Prunette, who hands the prize just as if it were the keys to the city. It's only *Quentin Durward*, a novel by Walter Scott I already read years ago, but who cares; M. Prunette and I, and all the others around us, and especially behind me, know the true meaning, the true value of The Prize.

And so I turn around solemnly toward my erstwhile companions, those dedicated knuckleheads, and I elevate *Quentin Durward* high above my head, like an Inca priest saluting the sun god from the top of a temple. M. Prunette, Cuche, Papillard, and the old codgers on the podium are all transfixed, baffled by this unwarranted addition to the traditional ceremony; so are the parents. But not so my buddies, who are prompt to capture the mood of the moment. Jaboure climbs up on a chair and intones a song from his native West Indies, in honor of both Josephine Baker—and me:

> *Adieu, foulards, adieu madras*
> *Adieu, pays cher à mon coeur. . . .*

Whereupon my classmates take up the chorus with great gusto:
> *Doudou à moi, lui qu'a parti*
> *Hélas! hélas! c'est pour toujours. . . .*

The worthies of Meaux are astonished but attentive. I see one elderly gent turn his ear trumpet to the choristers, with bright eyes and a smile on his wrinkled face. He marks the measure with his foot, lost in remembrance. I stay on the platform till the last verse is sung, clasping *Quentin Durward* to my chest. Applause breaks from the kids' ranks, then from the parents', and, timidly, from the podium itself. I can see

my own people in the crowd below; my mother looks embarrassed, but my father seems to relish the style of these *adieux*.
In his mind he translates the words of the pretty song:

> *Farewell, kerchiefs, farewell, Madras,*
> *Farewell, land dear to my heart . . .*
> *Dearest to me is he who's gone,*
> *Alack, alas, he'll not return.*

Does that tell him something about his son? Who is his
son? Well, I'm busy shaking dozens of hands, trading wise-
cracks and promises to write. Already kids are tearing down
the rue des Ursulines, headed toward the railroad station.
Others ensconce themselves in the family motorcar. Ours
awaits us, its roof laden with luggage, and off we go on the
road to Paris.

4

Moving to the big city.—Gregor Louchine.
—"How does it feel to be so damned ugly?"
—A Model-T and its eleven owners.
—The Delamare brothers.—The Theosophical Society
and Helena Petrovna Blavatsky, 250 pounds of Russian
spirituality.—Sylvia Beach and the public burning
of Ulysses.—D. H. Lawrence on the phone.—Birth of
The Obelisk Press.—Daddy's little girls.

It wasn't Paris where I finally ended up after the Collège Georges Courteline, but rather in the affluent suburb of Neuilly. At first my father had rented a very luxurious apartment in Auteuil, next to the Bois de Boulogne, but he was soon forced to realize that he had been aiming much too high, and the family retreated to less elegant quarters in Neuilly. A few months later, as funds kept dwindling, we found ourselves in an even more modest ground-floor apartment, but it was large and still in Neuilly. It was a five-minute walk to the Lycée Pasteur, the secondary school where I had been enrolled.

My grandparents had given up their place on the avenue du Bois, now known as avenue Foch, and they had come to live not far from us in a huge apartment house where they had finally been able to reassemble their furniture, which arrived from all directions. Uncle Pierre, my grandmother's brother, was boarding with them in a single room at the end of a corridor and spent his time in the company of Mme H. P. Blavatsky's *Secret Doctrine* and other monumental works of esoteric literature.

Uncle Pierre had spent his entire bachelor's existence in the shadow of his brother-in-law; in Argentina he had been his employee and now he was his tenant. At one time in the past, he had adopted my grandparents' taste for spiritualism, and then for theosophy, but he had gone much further in the study of the major texts, which had eventually become the complete dedication of his life. In order to read them in their original version he had started to learn Sanskrit and Hebrew when he was over sixty years old.

We got along very well, and I often went to visit him in his alchemist's den. He was a portly little man, swarthy of complexion, and you could easily take him for a Moor because of his coloring and features. The most singular event of his life occurred when, having been born with a club foot, he received as a child a providentially well-aimed kick from a horse, after which his brutally shattered bones began to grow normally. But none of the blows of life could have possibly reached that lonely and happy man; which caused some to call him selfish. In my view he was not. He was just fatalistic, methodical, and cautious, being a student of the inner man.

From my grandparents I had borrowed the books of Edouard Schuré, Annie Besant, Leadbeatter, and Blavatsky; I immersed myself in theosophical literature, which powerfully stimulated my imagination. This helped me to bear the Lycée Pasteur, which was hardly an amusing place. The kids were dressed to the teeth, almost all of them little gentlemen who came from wealthy families. Nothing like my bawdy buddies at Meaux! When I was still there, in that gutter of a school, waiting impatiently to leave at last for the big city, I would never have dreamed that one day I would be overcome by nostalgia at the memory of the old slave ship! And yet that's God's truth. I miss the smelly classrooms with the potbelly stoves, the medieval absurdity of the place, and the criminal nature of its denizens.

Weeks after my new school started, I had found no one I would have liked as a friend. One morning, however, as we were standing in the hall and waiting for the teacher's arrival, I spot this strange character for the first time, a tall and gawky fellow with a huge bedroom slipper on one foot. This seemed to indicate that he had been in an accident, which would have explained his absence during the first weeks of school. I look at him with growing interest. He is extraordinarily ugly, a horror, a fright. His wan complexion is embellished with purplish-blue pimples; two tiny yellow eyes like shoe buttons flank his wide, triangular, reddish nose, lending him the air of an intelligent dog. And then he has that long thin neck with a prominent Adam's apple that constantly jumps up and down.

And that frightful display is all the more haunting as he is a good head taller than most of the other pupils, and his face seems to hover above the common populace like a threat. He speaks to no one. Leaning against the wall with a dreamy air, he is holding an enormous satchel pressed against his belly, which gives him the silhouette of a pregnant woman. This guy must be a record-breaking bookworm; he stays at home and reads books, poor fellow, what else can he do? Anyway, he's a brain, you can see that right away.

Coming into the classroom, he heads straight for the back row and shoves away a kid who had the audacity to sit down next to him. He raises the lid of his desk to a vertical position and wedges it open with a ruler to shield his activities; but since I am also seated in the rear, it's easy for me to watch him. The English teacher, old man Delcour, who is easily given to anger, follows this routine in exasperated silence. The violence mounts. Is the old man going to blow his stack? He trembles with fury, but the strange fellow pays him no mind. After a few minutes, Delcour begins his course, beaten, vanquished by this freak.

This is serious! Let's put it in perspective: In my entire career as a schoolboy activist, I have never had occasion to witness a truly vicious teacher so masterfully reduced to impotence by a dunce! When the fellow opens his satchel, it appears that it is stuffed, not with books, but with enough food to fill a grocery store. I have to restrain myself not to break into applause when I see him extricate from his pouch, with grunts of satisfaction, half a loaf of bread, a bottle of white wine, a corkscrew, a can of sardines in oil with the appropriate can opener, a good-size sausage, three onions, a glass, a stick of butter, some potato salad, some beet salad, a plate, silverware, salt and pepper, an orange, a tin of Livarot cheese, and an apple tart wrapped in stained paper. He opens the bottle, lets out a cautionary belch, pours himself a glass, and swallows it greedily. And then he starts working on the can of sardines. . . . He doesn't spare his captive audience anything in terms of eating noises. I observe him masticating stolidly, methodically, his chin greasy, his gaze lost in the distance like a cow chewing its cud. His Adam's apple jiggles up and down, giving his ugliness something like pathetic intensity.

To me, a connoisseur, this is pure enchantment. I question my neighbor about the newcomer. "Oh, Gregor Louchine, he's Russian and completely daffy," he replies with a stupid snicker. . . . No, this person isn't crazy, I tell myself, watching him retrieve and gobble down some potato salad that had fallen onto his pants; he has the mind of a great artist and a sensitive heart. As to his table manners, that's another story, for sure.

The Russian has finished his meal. He takes out a copy of *Le Temps*, which has been folded four times in order to fit into his pocket; he opens it up and scans it absentmindedly, with the insouciance of a millionaire relaxing at his club, but from where I sit I can see that what he is so closely studying is only the obituaries. That's for the macabre touch. When class is over, there is the usual stampede toward the exit and I contrive to speak to him.

"Hey, is that you, Louchine?"

"Yes. And so what?" he snaps back, malevolently.

"Well, er," I hesitate. "Can you play chess? Are you a good player?"

"Not bad, kiddo, not bad," he answers, looking me over with a jaundiced eye. "So what's all this about? What do you want?"

"Well, er," I blurt uneasily, "I'm looking for someone who wants to play, in order to get some training, what, you see what I mean . . ."

"Chess, that's a pain in the ass," he announces. "I only play it at midnight when the moon is full, always against a naked witch, preferably black-skinned."

Obviously I could not keep up with that fellow's small-talk tactics, he is right out of my league. I don't really care about chess, and I may have come up instinctively with that approach as a metaphor substituting for the true-blue meaty question: *"How does it feel to be so damned ugly?"* But he pulls me out of my embarrassment by inviting me with great cordiality to come visit him on the following Thursday, in the afternoon. We are close neighbors: He lives on the street next to mine.

In the days that followed he was absent from school, but when Thursday came, I decided nevertheless to pay him a visit as had been arranged. His father, a gentleman with graying hair, let me in.

"Oh, are you Maurrrice?" he asked me in a very strong Russian accent, and repeated my name as if to commit it to memory. "Gregor hasn't been feeling very well for the past few days and so he preferred to stay in bed, but he's waiting for you. You know, I think he's bored in that school."

Well, that's not a bad father, I thought, at least he tries to understand. I wonder how he feels about having a son like that. . . . Here, in this apartment, I felt as if I had been transported to Samarkand, at the height of the sixteenth century. Everything was covered with old tapestries and silk hangings and displays of ancient arms and armor, icons all over the place, and lamps with fringed shades that projected more shadow than light. Gregor's room was also dark, somewhat oppressive, overloaded with samovars and Oriental miniatures, smothered under heavy bottle-green drapes, and with a large mahogany bed in an alcove on which he was presently sprawled out. His foot was turbaned with bandages and very much in evidence above the blankets.

Thank heaven there was no question of our chess game; I hardly played and it would have been a waste of time. And then there was so much to talk about! For the first time in my short existence, I was meeting with someone who expressed quite naturally by his attitude what I felt so strongly in myself, but was unable to formulate: a movement of total refusal and rejection of the false, cheap, and criminal society in which we were born. Alienation! Anarchy! Let fly the black flag! How good it was to find someone else who had that same special acid running in his system. And yet I was more of an idealist, whereas Gregor was cynical and desperate—more destructive than behooves a true anarchist, certainly. Any talk about reforming society gave him headaches. The only thing one could do about society, he advised me, is to avoid it, and that's why he preferred to spend his time in bed.

"As long as a fellow can play his own music to himself, why go out in the streets and catch your death of cold?" And this was no rhetorical question, because he immediately produced a violin and bow from under his sheets, and setting it in position, he whipped the air three times with the bow and attacked a jolly Beethoven dance tune. And then branched off into some wonderfully lachrymose gypsy serenade, sniffling lamentably all the while. He was quite good! Next, like a child showing all its toys to a new playmate, he reached over to his night table and took a large gleaming black revolver out of the drawer.

"What do you think of this?" he asked me gravely. "A formidable weapon. . . . It's with this that I shot myself in the foot."

"What?"

"My foot. I shot off the little toe. You've got to be a supermarksman to demolish only the one you've picked."

"Excuse me, but I don't understand! Why did you do that?"

"You ask me *why*? We've just spent an hour talking about it! Those bastards will never force me to kill. With this, I'll get rejected by the army."

"But you're only sixteen! You could have waited!"

"Why wait? Anyway, it was one of those days. . . . I was so down that I felt like blowing my brains out, and I made do with a toe. Now it's done, there's no sense harping on it, and I must ask you to desist. Really, where did you learn such manners?"

"Ah yes, manners now," I said defensively. "So that's what you have inside this big bandage? A foot with four toes?"

"That's right, kiddo," he said, beginning to remove the bandage. "D'you want to have a look?"

The truth of the matter is that it was damned good to have someone who shared my hatred for our common Neuilly environment, surely the quintessence of French unsmiling bourgeoisie.

Sundays were the worst. All the moral sores of the upper classes came out blatantly at the conclusion of the morning mass, around the church of Saint-Pierre, as the crowd preened itself and paraded in front of itself in preparation for the rituals of the Sunday family luncheon event. Gregor and I reveled in that sordid pleasure, listening to the absurd stereotypes being exchanged in the way of polite conversation. Not one real word, not one honest grin; and let's leave aside the clammy handshakes! The do-gooders' venom spouting out of those crabby faces was not to the credit of the religion they professed.

Neuilly was not ostentatious. The big fortunes were concealed behind high walls, inside conservative-looking turn-of-the-century villas; the less affluent lived in austere-looking apartment buildings such as our own, with a minimum of frills and thrills. The population was preponderantly Catholic; but there was a large Protestant community, and some wealthy

Jews who never advertised themselves as such. Artists, film directors, actors were very rare, and studiously ignored by the basic population. Glamour was consonant with bad taste.

Life inside those homes was not enviable. A prim sense of duty, economy and modesty dominated everyone's existence. As for enjoying life in any manner whatsoever, that would lead automatically to guilt, confession, and repentance; and the Catholic church frowned particularly upon the sexual act if it was not performed for the specific purpose of reproduction. Even then, the said act was to be conducted with a pure spirit. Any lewdness had to be avoided, and for that purpose special nightshirts with a frontal slit were made available to Catholic families when a well-tempered decision had been made to start a family.

The women suffered most from those conditions. As girls they were dressed up in ill-fitting garments designed to make them look dowdy and shapeless. Marriage came as a civic duty, an obligation whose only reward was the spawning of a large brood, so as to continue and expand the legion of the faithful. A woman of thirty always looked haggard and dried up as an old prune; always dressed herself in ugly chest-suppressing dresses. Quite often she wore thick cotton stockings meant to protect the leg against the cold, even in warm weather, rather than embellish it, and she was invariably shod in sensible shoes. Anything to help forget their sex! They were merely wives, that is to say, the assistants, companions, homemakers at the service of their husbands; or more simply, their domestics. . . . As to the husbands, they always pretended to work very hard, but that was a fraud. They were just cogs in a vast social structure that bestowed on them fees, salaries, profits, and honors that recompensed less their talents than their degree of compliance with the system. And since the very survival of the system had been dangerously threatened, in recent years, by the leftist dominance during the Front Populaire era, the zeal for conformity was now reaching new extremes. Neuilly, the wealthiest township of France, was answerable directly to the Good Lord of all the crimes committed by the leftists and the godless in modern times: the Bolshevik revolution, the surrealist movement, and the Front Populaire disaster. Things like Hitler and Mussolini tended to be dismissed as secondary ills, since, after all, those movements were not directed against private property. Neuil-

ly had been the launching pad for many of the Fascist movements that flourished in the thirties: the militant monarchists
of Action Française; the Croix-de-Feu, war veterans led by
Colonel de La Rocque; and Taittinger's Jeunesses Patriotes.
Each one was organized along paramilitary lines, and their
shock troops were quite vicious.

"What a pile of shit, that country of yours!" Gregor would
guffaw in his most sinister basso.

"But it's yours as well, you dope," I would retort.

"I'm proud to say that I have not one single drop of French
blood in my system. Yours ain't so pure, Mister demi-Jew,"
he would snigger.

Ah well, c'est la vie. . . . With the coming of the spring
season a strange idea cropped up in my head: Why not buy a
car and take trips to the country? I had made enough friends
by then, and I passed the word around: Who wants to be co-
owner of this dream limousine? Soon after I had ten subscrib-
ers, in addition to myself.

And so all eleven of us future co-owners, with ages ranging
from twelve to fifteen, plus the brother of one of us who was
twenty-one and had his driving license, went together to in-
spect the wares of the used-car dealers in Bezons, on the out-
skirts of Neuilly.

However, all we had was 550 francs, and we soon found
out that the Delahayes and Rolls-Royces were out of our
range. But we fell in love, all eleven of us, with a Model-T
Ford of most ancient vintage that was sitting with great gawky
dignity among the wreckage. *That's our baby!* And the price
was just right: 550 francs. *Oh boy, it's ours!*

It was ours, but without a battery, which the sly dealer told
us was never included for that sort of cheap-cheap price. He
was adamant. We had to borrow the money for a new battery
from the elder brother with the driving license, and he didn't
seem to find that funny in the least. No matter, we were now
all piled high in our superb vehicle, all eleven of us, honking
and shrieking like crazy, and zigzagging at high speed toward
automobile immortality. The gentleman with the driving license was terrified at his own driving, so we let him off.
We resumed our journey into the unknown with three pilots
at the wheel now, so as to compensate for the lack of experience, dammit. It was exhilarating, to say the least! The wind
blowing fast, all those buses and streetcars we missed by one

inch—or less—the gallant cops whistling away to salute the swift passage of our human pyramid on wheels, hooray! After the tobogganlike descent from the heights of La Défense we crossed the river with the speed of a bullet, then after some hesitations due to technical debates about changing gears, we gathered speed again to race along the central avenue de Neuilly with shouts of glee; then negotiated the complexities of the Porte Maillot traffic with nary a tangible hitch. And up the avenue de la Grande Armée! There was a heated argument among the drivers as we were approaching the Arc de Triomphe as to whether we would circumvent it—or drive straight under the immortal arch where the Unknown Soldier lies buried, with the flame of remembrance burning above him in memory of the dead of the First World War. There, reason prevailed, I regret to say: We circled the monument, and damaged the fenders and headlights of a few enemy vehicles in the process. Hooray! Down the Champs-Elysées now with open throttle, having considerable luck with traffic cops and other obstacles—the Grand Palais whizzes by on our right—and here's the well-known symbol from Luxor, Egypt, the obelisk on the place de la Concorde, a square middle finger pointing stonily at the sky—which grows out of the ground at full speed as we kick our mount, chugging and puffing, to ultimate exertions. More whistles! We veer to the right, follow the river toward the Trocadéro, and race uphill toward Passy. Two police cars are behind us, honking like crazy. But they stop at intersections and we don't; nevertheless it looks like the end of the trip is close. Some of us shout above the din: "They'll never get us! Let's go on!" But two of the little ones want to pee, or want to go home, and the tank seems to be close to empty. As we enter the Bois de Boulogne, with three police cars now in hot pursuit, a struggle for control develops at the wheel between those who want to go on speeding right around the lake and those who want to go left, back into the tricky safety of the woods. The final conclusion is found in a ditch, which stops our flight, but in such an artistic manner that no one is seriously hurt: We leave our short-lived automobile dreamboat lying topsy-turvy with its wheels still turning in the air, in a dying slow-motion rotation that is not devoid of a certain pathetic beauty. While we eleven co-conspirators scatter in all directions into the midafternoon tranquillity of the underwoods, laughing our heads off as we rush from one bush to the next, with the fat cops whistling and bellowing at us to surrender. "Surrender? Never! They'll never get us alive!"

A memorable outing.

In the august shadows of the Theosophical Society I had made new friends, Edouard and Claude Delamare Deboutteville, who were the eldest of five boys whose family also lived in Neuilly. They studied not at Pasteur but at Sainte-Croix, the rival institution, which was all-out Catholic, whereas my own *lycée* was considered a bit, well, shall we say trendy? A young philosophy professor, Jean-Paul Sartre, had just started his career at Pasteur, and he was reputed to be living with two women. That was a far cry from the degree of Jesuit respectability one had to achieve in order to teach at Sainte-Croix.

It was rather eerie meeting Neuilly people like the Delamare brothers in surroundings so alien to their home culture. And Sainte-Croix students at that! But I had noticed those two in my neighborhood before, and I had been struck by something rather intense and exotic about them. My surprise at meeting them again, face-to-face, was therefore modified by a sense of recognition; it soon proved that the déjà vu syndrome was mutual. We talked. We became friends instantly, easily. They were both whiz kids in the academic sense, and although they were not as rebellious as I was, my positions didn't seem to offend them. Strange! I asked them whether they were practicing Catholics, and they laughed. No, their choice of a school was determined by the quality of the teaching; the teachers themselves were a sorry lot outside of their ability to communicate knowledge, but as teachers they were tops.

Upon further acquaintance, the Delamares became even more interesting, steeped as they had been for several generations in various schools of occultism. The father was a small fellow with bulging blue eyes and a twitching moustache, an inventor and industrialist by day and a magus by night; even the three youngest brothers, aged four, six, and eight, were being brought up in the strictest occult orthodoxy. No playing cards were to be found in their home, but there was a wide choice of Tarot decks; at the dinner table a favorite game was to analyze one another's dreams. The least occurrence was immediately assimilated and interpreted according to esoteric doctrines, and when an argument broke out between the boys regarding the laws of Karma or other subjects of the same order, it was the father who settled the matter with supreme authority.

The Theosophical Society was for us an irresistible center of attraction. It was located in a tiny blind alley off avenue Rapp, on the Left Bank, where two buildings were facing each other, one a strange *fin-de-siècle* structure, its façade elaborately ornamented with patterned tiles; the other an edifice in pure "Occult-Renaissance" style, just as remarkable. Here was the seat of the Theosophical Society in France. The headquarters were in Benares, India.

The architecture was a blend of Oriental and Anglican, with lights descending from above and shadowy recesses below, from which the hypnotic geometry of the Master K. H.'s eyes would stare at you straight out of the infinite. Incense fumes to condition your soul, hushed conversations, old faces creased in smiles of overpowering benevolence, pseudo-Eastern costumes bejeweled with Tibetan amulets, and monkish-looking persons silently gliding past with enraptured expressions on their sallow faces. . . . Vegetarians all!

The Delamares liked to poke fun at this dedicated crowd; but they came back. And so did I. The obvious excuses were the library, which was extensive, and the lectures, some of them interesting, which were given in the adjoining theater; but the truth of the matter is that we were here, as all the others, in search of the miraculous. Yes—the great sudden voice out of the depth, the burning prophet, the star-crowned mahatma, the master whose one word will pull you forever out of the underworld darkness of your lives. We may snigger and denigrate the old fools, but aren't we young fools ourselves?

That is of course a subject that we studiously avoid in our exchanges, the two brothers and I, but it is nevertheless at the center of all our most private speculations. We talk a lot *around* it, though, as we are all fascinated by the idea of a Higher Estate, a community of beings more subtle and powerful than us, the products of a prior round of evolution, in whom all the faculties latent or underemployed at our present stage will have been fully revealed and awakened. We find many references to that inner circle in all mythologies and heroic romances, and even in popular fiction. I used to spend hours at the Musée Guimet, in a complete daze, absorbed by

the beautiful tankas in which the Buddhas or other high personages are always seated in the middle of a psychic theater
chock-full of lesser Buddhas, in an order and relation that appear as stringent and essential as that of the galaxies between
themselves.

Yes, this network existed—it couldn't be otherwise! We
couldn't even *live* otherwise! All the religions know that well,
with their legions of saints and angels. But the door to that
network, Where does it open? How can you get close to that
other reality and at least measure what it is, get a taste of it? Is
the Theosophical Society a place where you can hope to find
such a door?

Edouard tends to doubt it. Everyone shows great respect
for H. P. Blavatsky, the society's founder and famed author of *The Secret Doctrine*, but there is no denying the charla-
tan aspect of that inspired woman. Helena Petrovna, a two-
hundred and fifty-pound Russian peasant, an authentic seer
and mystic, has written, aside from her major works, some
truly low-class pulp about her otherworldly encounters in the
jungles of India; they would discredit her completely if her
followers were not so naïve and gullible. The tough lady who
followed her, Annie Besant, a British libertarian, a feminist,
and a staunch enemy of the establishment, used her organizational gifts to build up the society and give it a solid footing in
India. This had to be done so as to achieve full credibility in
the Western world among those people for whom there is no
true wisdom but of the East. To achieve that goal she used
politics and took command of the Indian liberation movement
against the British rule, and was made president of the first
National Congress after the independence as a result.

She is really the one who concocted the simplified philosophy that is fed to the rank and file; she wrote it out in rather
trite fashion, making central articles of faith out of the laws of
Karma and reincarnation. But that's what people want, simple
dogma. This ecumenical hodgepodge was adjustable to rough-
ly all religions, East and West, as well as to freemasons, businessmen, fakirs, nuns, masseuses: If you wanted a bit of a
mystical thrill in your life, you could subscribe to the Theosophical Society without renouncing your own basic religion.
And thus the society became big and rich, and prospered and
multiplied everywhere around the world, all this thanks to
that simple, businesslike approach.

It could rival now with the established religions, but it was still only a philosophical society, and it needed a person with truly prophetic gifts and charisma to make it fully competitive. Her search for a candidate led to the discovery of Jiddu Krishnamurti, a young Hindu boy, at the end of the twenties, and he was groomed to become the new Messiah. As he grew up, however, he started to develop his own independent views about the role he was meant to play. Until, in 1933, after Annie Besant's death, he announced to the world that he was no Messiah at all, just a dedicated student of theosophy. A reversed annunciation! And a rare act of humility, since Krishnamurti's later writings show that he had enough wisdom and power of expression to claim the highest role; but the philosophy he offers celebrates individual independence and ridicules the need for saints and prophets. And thus the vocation of the society to become the first great modern universal religion of the twentieth century was thwarted and turned around by its own would-be founder.

There were at the time in Paris many other more or less occult sects competing for the attention and subsidies of the thousands of stray individuals in search of a faith, old or young, male and female. And each one of those groups, most of them tiny, would brazenly offer you the only truth. Where was the truth in all this?

"It's an interesting point," said Claude. "Or perhaps even two points that you could make. First of all, this mass of people looking desperately for *the truth*. Whatever they mean by that. . . . And, second, the fact that those who claim to be in a position to offer you the truth are compulsive liars, by definition. Isn't that strange?"

"That's bizarre," Edouard agreed. "All great religions have that element of deceit and treachery about them. You have Judas, and Peter himself, at the root of Christianity. And now political parties have stolen the formula, also claiming that their truth, their model of society, is the only one. But what I'd like to ask is this—Isn't deceit itself a way of learning?"

"How's that?" I asked.

"Well, look at Zen techniques, for instance. They break down your illusory sense of reality by telling you point-blank that black is white. By denying the truth of things that are only true at our limited level of perception, they help us get to the major truth that lies behind the relative one."

"All right, I will accept that," said Claude. "But you must

look at it not just in moral terms of lying or telling the truth. Since I started to study biology and entomology, I've become very interested in the phenomenon of imitation, which is so widely spread at all levels of natural life. Evolution appears sometimes as the result of a process of imitation of idealized models. Couldn't you extrapolate and say that a religion always promotes a totally arbitrary model of the truth, and that it is up to the faithful to turn that model into a reality, simply by wanting to imitate it?"

"That's a fine idea," I said. "It makes me think of the *Imitation of Christ* in medieval times. . . . But assuming that you are right, where does that leave us with the Theosophical Society?"

"How do I know," Claude replied. "It's up for grabs. If there's any reality in what I've just said, then perhaps the original, unrevealed project in H. P. Blavatsky's mind, which she named 'theosophy,' has come to fruition in the life experience of those who were strong enough to penetrate the lies that followed, and find their own truth beyond them."

"Yes," added Edouard, "I am pretty sure that there are, inside or around the Theosophical Society, or close to it, some high-powered esoteric groups. In fact Claude and I had contacts with one of them."

"Oh yes? I'd like to learn more about that!" I said.

"You will, in due course," Edouard answered, rather primly. "But it's really up to them to decide if you are ready."

"Is that so? But how can they decide if they don't know me? Why all this secret stuff, anyway?" I asked, feeling pretty miffed.

"Well that's the way it is. Secrecy is the only protection against lies. And we're living in a time of lies, don't forget! Everything we touch is lies, we have reached the end of the Piscean era. . . . When we move into Aquarius, things will get better."

"Aquarius, when will that be?"

"Just wait a little half century, we're almost there," Edouard reassured me, in the tone of one who knows.

Those two fellows knew all those things because they spent their time reading, thinking, and talking about them, particularly with their father. It made me feel deprived and isolated, as discussions of that sort were impossible in my parents' home. My father was deeply irritated by any reference whatsoever to things spiritual; just as he could hardly bear having a son who was a total vegetarian, whereas he himself was such a dedicated meat-eater that he refused to touch vegetables. He had found me once or twice in the lotus position, in my room, and he had flown into a rage. An impotent rage, that is, because how can you forbid your son to meditate? It's not like stealing old ladies' purses. For sure there was nothing written down in the perfect gentleman's book of etiquette to ban the lotus position.

My mother had been very interested in theosophy in earlier times, but she was now hiding her game, since she wanted no conflict of any sort with her husband. As to my grandmother, Mamita, whose faith was particularly naïve, she was sure to come out with the silliest remarks during the family dinners. She saw me now, not just as her son's reincarnation, but, beyond that, as the avatar of some celestial personality.

"My son the Bodhisattva," my father would fulminate, overcome with exasperation. "The thirteenth sign of the zodiac! He's a dunce at Latin, mathematics, Greek—at everything. You don't find it extraordinary, Mamita, for a demigod to be the last of his class?"

My grandmother would then look at me inquiringly, uncertainly. Her need to believe was stronger than the flickering flame of her modest intelligence.

The only thing that would have given some hope to my father is that I was good at French, a language he was still unable to speak properly himself but which he greatly respected. Perhaps, later on, he could lure me into studying live-nature. . . . His taste for publishing had now taken a more concrete turn, and perhaps he was dreaming of a dynasty of publishers?

As we settled down in Paris, in 1931, the postwar agitation had crystallized in a number of new trends and situations. The Industrial Revolution had made continental Europe morally more decadent, especially France. At the same time, it had made the English-speaking countries morally more repressive than ever—even after the end of the Victorian era, and after a world war that had brought all nations in such close contact. This puritanical repression manifested itself mostly in the form of literary censorship: literature being only a metaphor for the freedom to think. . . . The most famous case had been the banning of James Joyce's *Ulysses* in America, and the actual *burning* of the book in England. Then Sylvia Beach, the American owner of a small bookstore in Paris, Shakespeare and Company, had sunk all her savings into this once-in-a-lifetime venture, the publication of *Ulysses* as an outlaw book in Paris. This had been followed by the appearance of illegal pirate editions of the book in America; then by Judge Woolsey's civilized verdict, which effectively ended the ban. *Ulysses* had made history; and Joyce, now famous, broke up with his plucky little Paris publisher to sign a big, fat contract with Random House.

There are many simple lessons to be drawn from that story! But Sylvia Beach, who had been a one-book publisher, set an example that inspired the creation of a number of small short-lived imprints in Paris by young expatriates, usually wealthy: Robert McAlmon, Edward Titus (who was Helena Rubinstein's husband—until she threw him out, thus causing him to go out of business), Nancy Cunard, Walter Lowenfels, and Gertrude Stein, who created her own press in order to publish her own works, when no one wanted them. And of course the Black Sun Press, Harry and Caresse Crosby's brainchild, the only one that nearly achieved full professional status.

All that activity had produced next to nothing in terms of literary discoveries, except perhaps for Djuna Barnes, and it had done very little that would really help defeat censorship.

In 1929, when my father was still in Rozoy, trying to extricate himself from his partnership with French publisher Henry Babou, he had received a long-distance call from D. H. Lawrence offering him the publishing rights of *Lady Chatterley's Lover*. The book was then the number-one scandal book and it would have been well worth starting a new imprint just to publish that one title on the Continent; but the complications involved with the Babou business were such that he did not feel he could take such a chance at that moment, and he had turned down Lawrence's offer.

About that same time Frank Harris had been forced to publish privately with his own money the first part of *My Life and Loves*, his pornographic memoirs, for lack of a publisher. He was then living in the south of France; the book had been printed there; but it had created such a scandal in England that the British government brought pressure on the French through its embassy to have Frank Harris prosecuted on account of his book's obscenity. There was no statute in France

to allow such an action, and besides, since the ill-fated prose-
cutions against Flaubert's *Madame Bovary* and Beaudelaire's
Les Fleurs du Mal, which had made the French judges look
like fools some fifty years earlier, no magistrate would have
dreamed of trying such a case—all the more since the book in
question was printed in English, and that made it practically
impossible for a French-speaking tribunal to pass judgment on
it. Nevertheless, to please His Majesty, a court in Nice had
arraigned Frank Harris, who had immediately undertaken
such a devastating campaign by writing thousands of letters
denouncing the complete illegality of the prosecution, that
the court had been forced to swallow its own indictment, and
had acquitted Frank Harris.

Putting all these elements together it was easy to imagine
what a clever publisher could do with them. No one had
thought of producing light erotica for the Anglo-Saxon tourist
visiting the Continent, spicy enough to attract those timid
souls, and yet not too much so as to avoid trouble with the
French authorities. The easy profits one could make in that
way could help finance a more speculative activity; for instance, each time an important book would be banned in the
United Kingdom or in America, it would be one more *cause
célèbre* to be added to the publisher's list. . . . And as to the
run-of-the-mill novels for the tourists, my father felt confident
that he could turn out one or two a year himself, and find
more elsewhere without too much trouble.

He had met in a bar an Englishman named Herbert Clarke,
a *bon vivant* who owned a printer's shop on the Right Bank.
He asked him if he would be interested in a fifty-fifty partnership to create such a business; Clarke said yes, but the day
before the contract was to be signed, he suddenly died. The
printer's foreman took over the business, and my father found
himself gradually forced into signing a partnership contract
with the man, Marcel Servant, but at terms such that he was
really working as a badly paid editor rather than as a partner;
the printer also had the right to veto any book that he would
consider too literary to be easily salable, and my father was
supposed to supply two books a year without royalties, as a
contribution to the partnership.

This was all extremely frustrating, but his financial situation
was such that he had no choice left. . . . The new firm was
named The Obelisk Press, and my mother designed a little
logo for it representing an obelisk sitting on a book, which

was probably meant to suggest a lingam and yoni as well. Under the pen name of Cecil Barr (which he had acquired as a result of frequent visits to a bar called The Cecil), my father contributed second-class masterpieces of light reading to the Obelisk list, such as *Suzy Falls Off*, *Bright Pink Youth*, and *Daffodil*, which ran into six printings, a huge success.

Servant was a difficult man, brooding and petty, who felt that he had waited much too long for his promotion from foreman to boss. He had a personal revenge to take against society, and fate had placed within easy reach the perfect sacrificial victim; it would be delicious to torture his gentlemanly hostage in every way possible. He never wasted a chance to do so.

When I went to visit my father, at his invitation, in the little cubicle he used as his office in the back of Servant's premises, I always felt terribly uncomfortable; the printer was sending ugly vibrations in all directions like a piece of stale Gorgonzola. But we did not linger long; my father would seize his hat and his cane, and off we went in search of a pleasurable haven, which is to say one of the elegant tearooms of the neighborhood where literary countesses held court.

The contrast between the printer's shop and this lovely birdcage filled to capacity with the most delightful creatures was rather unsettling. On one side, the somber world of hard work, the mixed smells of sweat and ink, the calloused, grime-encrusted hands; on the other, a world of pleasures and laughter, perfectly warm and seductive, although to me rather intimidating. In that particular tearoom where a very tall and lively and beautiful American woman called Hope was the reigning goddess, all the greatest families of France and Europe were represented, including a duchess who spoke with the nasal twang of Texas. How could I possibly describe that display of charm and beauty in this discreet, bookish environment, where the rites of the tea ceremony, Western style, were being carried out in accordance with the most charming étiquette? Scones and crumpets, majestic orange and chocolate cakes, mochas and pies galore, old family silver and the lightest china ever. I was covertly inhaling perfumes floating up to me from all sides, indiscreet body messages that made my head swim in guilty euphoria; my eyes were sensing rather than seeing, and I was doing my utmost to hide the glow of emotions that I was sure my face would betray.

How embarrassing to be fourteen, no longer a child and not

yet a man! My father would introduce me gently to one or two of his countesses, always a little anxious about my hand-kissing style, and over the chances of my dropping my *tarte-lette aux fraises* on the lady's illustrious lap. I was not expected to say much and I was soon left to my enjoyment, ostensibly of the pastry, *bien sûr*; but I was passionately feeding on the effluvia, on the mixed aroma of rare teas and precious skins, on the soft intensity of women speaking to one another, communing with one another over that secret they all share, whose existence I could sense vividly but whose nature no male creature will quite understand ever. Even the ugly ones and the ridiculous ones are part of the conspiracy, I thought; perhaps even more actively so.

And it sometimes happened that they would half turn their head in my direction and gaze at me from the corner of an eye with a faint smile. Pity the poor gawky boy! At least that is what I read in those brief looks of inspection, which made me inwardly stutter; but which may have meant something quite different, and possibly very down to earth for all we know.

On one of those occasions I was introduced to a lady my father admired, Susan Booth, an elegant divorcée, and her daughter Claudie, who was thirteen, overgrown, and had protruding elbows. Her presence was not purely due to chance; our progenitors had thought that they could thus engineer love at first sight, and be amused. I poured tea into Claudie's cup, and then a bit more onto her skirt. She looked at me in surprise, and then laughed at my anguished expression; yes, she was a friendly person, but why did she have to be so young and skinny? Her mother's *décolleté* was in full flower. Womanhood was like a vast sea caressing my soul under silent waves; my father was a lucky dog, and he knew it well. He seldom spoke to me, and the only education I ever received from him had to do exclusively with the appreciation of women, for which words are of no use—and indeed undesirable. "Don't overdress, there's never any need for that," he would say, or: "Always keep your nails short and well-trimmed." And it was clear that those small items of advice came straight from his lady-killer's fund of knowledge.

His other passion being music, he would sometimes take me to a matinée performance of the Concerts Pasdeloup, which I found not very entertaining, my musical ear being what it was. But to him those grand architectures of sound spoke a language he well understood, and his greatest pleasure seemed, not just to listen, but to find a beautiful music lover seated not too far in the audience, her profile lost in contemplation, and to drink in the drama of the sound through the flux of her own ecstasy. His eye would always discreetly rove from this faraway head of glorious chestnut hair to that bejeweled Nefertiti in the next row, or to a voluptuous blond nape nearby, in search of his musical companion for one hour of exquisite pleasures.

As to my mother. . . . My mother would never suffer from betrayal; she situated her relationship with her husband in a realm that was free of jealousy and other such forms of pettiness. She felt quite honestly that his worldly pursuits were more necessary and more natural to him than his function as *paterfamilias*. Since there was no one woman in the world who could entirely satisfy his need for womanhood, let him flower in the midst of diversity! She was dedicated by nature to construction and continuity, just as he was to his own frivolous quests; they had understood their differences and accepted each other with gratitude. They called each other by the names of textiles, she was Mademoiselle Finette and he was Prince Madapolam; which was a nice way to express their complicity. She knew that her husband's infidelities were indispensable to the equilibrium of their union and guaranteed its permanence. Naturally, there were difficult moments to go through, but the routine was well rehearsed.

Many a time I was present at scenes that took place as follows: An ebullient Jack comes home, an hour late for dinner, with a very elegant young woman of great beauty in tow. Mars puts down her book and greets the stranger with a friendly smile, giving the impression that we were awaiting her arrival in order to sit down to dinner. Furthermore the stranger's place is already set, a detail whose meaning the lady herself will quickly understand, assuming, as we will, that she is not deprived of imagination. Mars shows great interest in the visitor, making her say more things about herself than Jack would have dragged out of her in a hundred years of living together—she breaks the ground for him. The four children examine the creature, from their own points of view. Nicole is interested in her style and her clothes. The two little ones, Sylvie and Eric, exchange their observations excitedly in their secret code, which I have never broken. As for me, I stare at her discreetly, musing that soft jet-black hair with gray eyes is just what I've been dreaming about lately.

By the time dessert is served, the lady is conquered. By my mother, this time. They look at each other with understanding, with tenderness; I have even seen a tear or two shed at such moments, which mean: "Never will I take your husband away from you! I might borrow him a bit, for a few afternoons, but it won't go any further than that, I promise you."

Only on one occasion, to the best of my knowledge, did things almost take a serious turn. Venus herself came upon the scene, or rather Hope, the tearoom beauty, on whom my father had temporarily concentrated his powers of combustion. As the cliché goes, they are madly in love; Hope decides to leave her sculptor husband, Jack his tribe, in order to take off together the very same day. Jack comes back to the house to announce this thing to Mars and to pack a suitcase. They're standing face-to-face in the hallway, and he is talking. He is trying to explain to her the definitive nature of what he has been feeling so violently since the evening before. She doesn't say anything, but she doesn't discourage him in any way. After a long moment, he falls silent at last and looks at her. And he understands. Once again, Mars has vanquished Venus, which is as it should be.

It was after one of those Pasdeloup concerts that I met Nadejda de Bragança. It wasn't by chance; my father had a date with her in a shadowy bar, at a table located in a kind of alcove at the rear of the room. When we got there she was already waiting. From their first words I understood that she had asked him to bring me along; she was waiting for me, in short, as at a first rendezvous. My God, what a marvelous creature! I no longer knew how I had got to be there, in front of her, within the glow of her smile—it made my head turn! I was paralyzed, and instead of blushing, as was my habit, I looked at her, wide-eyed, unable to hide my mute admiration. No doubt she was used to being stared at in this voracious manner because, in the most natural way in the world, she continued talking to me while making me sit down next to her. From time to time she said a few words to my father, and then turned again toward me with her irresistible smile, offering herself to my eyes with obvious pleasure. The beauty of her face was heightened by a tawny blond mane that tumbled in light waves onto a cinnamon-colored velvet jacket, the same shade as her eyes. In rapid succession, I learned that Nadejda wrote poetry, which was not at all surprising; that she was an authentic princess of royal blood, which went without saying; and that my dad was head over heels in love with her, which was the inevitable consequence of the foregoing data. As for me, I had already reached the point of giving her my address in exchange for hers! Because, I should add, on the following week I was to go to England to spend my summer vacation in Sussex with my uncle Fred, my father's brother. Nadejda seemed fascinated, and talked to me about Sussex with great enthusiasm; and she made me repeat my promise to write her as soon as I got installed, in order to give her my impressions.

I scarcely dared look at my father, telling myself that he must be sick with jealousy. But then I realized that he was looking at her with the same appetite, the same wild admiration I felt for her and that, on top of it all, he was immensely enjoying our conversation. And quite suddenly, a silent spell fell upon us three, at the very moment when each one of the three was contemplating this rare and wonderful phenomenon, each one from his or her own angle: The father and the son had fallen in love with the same woman!

With the incomparable Nadejda.

5

*How many farthings in a guinea?—Two styles
of chauvinism. —King Harold as Uncle Fred.
—Sunsets and Sussex.—Nell. —Two or three letters
from Capri.—Annie, Lizzie, Fanny, not interested?
—Here she is, the golden one. —Parlez-moi d'amour.
—A heart in tatters. —Victoria, queen and railway station.*

It was my first trip to England. I was going to travel alone, at
least as far as Newhaven, where my English relatives, whom I
didn't know, were to meet me, having driven down from Sussex, where they lived.

To travel alone, how incredibly exciting! My father took me
to the train station, and upon saying good-bye he handed me a
fistful of British money. While the train was picking up speed
through the sad suburbs north of Paris, I spread out the
strange bills and coins on an open newspaper and began to
study them.

There are twelve pence in a shilling, two shillings in a flor-
in, but two and a half in a half-crown; as for the crown itself, it
doesn't materially exist anymore, no more than does the
paltry farthing. Then there's the pound, equal to twenty
shillings, and the guinea, which is worth twenty-one of them.
Although used for pricing goods displayed for sale, the guinea
isn't represented by a bill. There still remain to be considered
these big heavy coins of little value, the halfpenny, the penny,
and the double-penny, those three in bronze, and then the
threepenny piece, or *threp'pence*, which is hexagonal and yellow, and here is a silvery shilling, and the attractive silver six-
pence—which I like best of them all because it's compact,
practical money, well-contained in its tiny size. Last but not

least, let's not forget this secondary currency—a decimal accident—the ten-shilling bill. . . .

England didn't seem exactly simple. Why, for example, hadn't she adopted the decimal system? Was it in order not to concede an advantage to Cartesian logic, which would be like granting a moral victory to the French? Was it because they had rejected the French Revolution, and fought Napoleon, that the British were still refusing to adopt the decimal sytem, in a spirit of rivalry and revenge? How childish! And yet it is in England that the Industrial Revolution had been started: just think of the fantastic waste in man-hours, in transmissions, calculations, verifications. . . . The decimal system had made everything clear, easy, precise, and would have saved literally years of work spent on multiplying figures the hard way instead of just adding zeros. And what was the excuse for this wastefulness? "We want to protect our traditions," said the British; but what they were out to protect was their silly insular pride. What's more, since the British Empire embraced half of the world's population, and this complicated, imprecise, and onerous way of counting was imposed by 50 million Englishmen on half of the world population, which has just reached the 3 billion mark, and is still growing fast. . . . And thus more and more billions of human beings, yet unborn, will have to adopt the same accounting methods "because it is our tradition." . . . When one is fourteen, one still wonders about such things. One would like to understand.

But there is nothing to understand. It's the make-believe logic of adults, the logic of *Alice in Wonderland*—a book, be it said in passing, from which I had learned the little English I knew. I had been fortunate to begin my apprenticeship by means of this exemplary work: One must have read Lewis Carroll in order to appreciate, among other things, the British monetary system.

Next, I took two passports out of my pocket, one French, since I had been born in that country, and the other British because I had inherited that nationality from my father. English law left me free to live in this ambiguous situation. But between twenty and twenty-one, French law was going to force me to choose one of the two nationalities and to repudiate the other: Military service didn't exist in Great Britain, whereas it was obligatory in France. Thus the acid test for my citizenship was going to be *military service*. In other words, my belonging to the French fatherland demanded that I should be ready to die for it. Like my uncle, Maurice Girodias. Thus the only choice open to me was between two styles of chauvinism. What about being neither French nor English, but a free man?

I was alone in my compartment, and I decided to find some company. I soon found one to my liking, with a few other passengers elegantly seated on the pearl-gray banquettes, dressed in tweeds and smoking aromatic tobacco. How nice! I had no sooner left Paris than I was already in England, socially and linguistically; and I had come across a little group of pure representatives of the upper classes whose manner of speech struck me as truly amazing. What was the reason for these glossal contortions whose only result was to render the words incomprehensible? Was it done on purpose, to hide your true thinking, or your true designs? Language itself remained passive, conventional, and totally uninteresting; it is the manner of its use that gives it a sense, all those distorted sounds produced by the molars, the sinuses, the curve of the lips, the uvula, the tonsils, and even the collarbone and Adam's apple—everything except by what the French and other Latin peoples consider to be the usual organs of speech. The English I had heard spoken in Paris, I now realized, was only a kind of Esperanto, a form of pidgin English, to make oneself understood by the French thanks to a simplified language. The loutish ear of the "natives" evidently couldn't understand the Oxford accent whose acidulous and haughty whinny was the earmark of gentlemen of divine right.

The boat I boarded looked like a sort of floating bus. It wasn't William the Conqueror's ship, but it was going to allow me to make more or less the same voyage. Had the earth been flat, I was thinking, there wouldn't have been so many useless and murderous misunderstandings between England and the Continent, since one would have seen the others living on one side and the other of this narrow watery border; such a slight curvature sufficed to create isolation, and to transform the Channel into a political ocean.

There were enough waves and sea gulls to give one the illusion of the open sea; I even saw a tourist in golf knickers clutching the rail, having succeeded in giving himself the illusion of seasickness. The shores of France were disappearing from sight, the spray slapped me pleasantly in the face, and almost immediately after that, the line of chalky fortresses came into view, just as William had beheld it from his flagship with its load of horses, men, and its standards trailing in the wind.

On the pale cliffs, the numberless army of the Saxons was waiting for him with Harold at its head, the perjurer-prince, murderer of his brother, thief of thrones. The sailors were preparing for the landing while the knights mounted their palfreys, recommending their soul to God and lowering their visors. . . . While the tourists gathered their luggage together, their golf bags and souvenirs from the Riviera. . . .

Having cleared Customs, I find myself lost amid the motley crowd awaiting the travelers from the Continent, but I quickly spot, not King Harold, of course, but my uncle Fred. He's easy to identify, being a head or two taller than those around him, with curly yellow hair, a brick-red complexion, the shoulders of a furniture-mover, and he's dressed all in white, like a tennis-player. Standing at his side is a woman, older than he, who seems small by comparison: It's Aunt Nell, whose role in my father's past I know only vaguely. She is close to fifty and I am surprised by her silhouette, slim and lively, and by the clear light of her green eyes. Her face, which is hardly wrinkled, must have been very beautiful, but the fire has withdrawn from it. She hugs me, looking at me inquiringly, while Fred, who doesn't like to wait, takes my suitcase and hustles us toward his car. It's a rather old beige Rolls-Royce, which he drives offhandedly, like an expert, slouched in his seat, steering with one finger. Naturally, we drive on the left, which makes me faintly dizzy at first. We follow a labyrinth of little roads that enchant me and soon make me revise my first impression of the English before taking the boat: It's true their money is ridiculous, but that's the other side of the coin, the good side is their passionate love of nature. Sussex in its entirety is a garden full of verdant surprises, cascades of flowers, poetic vegetable plots in which I see countryfolk working in derbies. We pass an old man who looks like G. B. Shaw, sitting erect on his tricycle with a long beard falling vertically from his chin. We go through snug and musty villages where each house, each door, each tree contributes to a slowly ripening harmony. Modern life hasn't changed anything in the ancient hegemony of Nature, and one barely sees the automobiles that are modestly concealed behind flowering hedges and bouquets of trees. The cottages, pleated with age, seem like old furniture in a comfortable living room, and its thick carpet of lawn invites the beholder to take off his shoes and lie down in the shade.

During this lazy drive my aunt and uncle attempt to find out how much English I know—they don't speak a word of French themselves—and I answer them as best I can in the language of *Alice in Wonderland*, with mistakes in pronunciation which seem to amuse them greatly.

We enter through a gate and come to a halt in front of their house, which is the quintessence of everything I've seen along the way. A low rambling façade partly hidden beneath a Virginia creeper and the roof's thatched headdress. The foundations date back to medieval times, the walls to the sixteenth century, and the whole of it has been adapted without too much damage to the demands of the twentieth. But the low doors that force Uncle Fred to bend double whenever he moves around and the ancient woodwork are all intact. On a console table an army of cups and trophies testify to my uncle's great feats on the golf course.

Golf is his exclusive pastime. And if he chose this house, it is less for its charm and antiquity than because it is situated at the edge of a club where he can play whenever he likes. The golf links could have been designed by a landscape artist of Gainsborough's era; it is laid out in pleasant hills and valleys, with wide-open wooded perspectives.

With a light heart, I install myself on the first floor. A swallow dives into my room in a rush of wings, modulates a brief, acute salute, wheels around, and disappears. Perfect. The white walls are intersected at capricious intervals with handhewn beams. The window is framed with airy vines, wellsuited to the scenery one observes from it. First of all, a pond half concealed by weeping willows; and closer to the house, a lawn of deep green dotted with rosebushes. On the right a poplar shoots up lonely and superb out of the bushes, a feat of verticality with its rearing branches pointing straight to the center of the sky, a long pale body of gray and silver trembling in the breeze. Beyond, the last tiers of rocks and flowers in a stepped garden capriciously descending. To the left, the kitchen is almost completely invisible behind the shrubbery and the trees, which also conceal from us the only neighboring house, which serves as headquarters for the golf club. These two houses, along with Dr. Crawford's house, not far from here, as well as two or three cottages that appear to date back to Druidic times, constitute the whole of the hamlet of Ifield.

At nightfall, the golfers, having turned back into drinkers, celebrate their triumphs with whiskey and their defeats with beer. At this hour Nell usually takes a long stroll on the deserted golf course with Blotto, her amiable dachshund, nimbly trotting after her on his little legs. From the first day of my visit she invites me to accompany her and we start off, arm-in-arm, like two old friends. And this soon becomes a daily ritual.

Our conversations are wonderfully rambling, just like the romantic landscape within which they take place. Nell is married to Fred, but she is entirely her own person, and she will never let herself be dominated by his materialistic, success-seeking outlook—which she sees rather as a weakness. Like my father, he denies the existence of the spirit; he tries to reduce the entire universe to a business proposition, and the entirety of life to his own life. And so it becomes easy for Nell and me to find a basis for our complicity. We talk a lot about reincarnation, and I tell her what I've read in the theosophical literature on the subject. She has not read anything herself, but she comes out with simple, reasonable proposals, explaining it back to me in a way I had not yet conceived.

For instance, since all of nature is subjected to the law of repetition why should we, humans, be the only ones to escape from that universal rule? Could the uniqueness of each human person, the uniqueness of exceptional talent and of genius, be explained without an accumulation of prior experiences? Of course it is easy to deny this because we do not remember our prior experiences, our past lives; but memory is a thing of the ego, of the body, and its span is therefore limited to the life of the body. When the body dies, however, the forces that have first caused its conception, its life and growth, become crystallized in that subtle essence we call the spirit, that intemporal memory that absorbs the experience of a life and reinvests it in the next—so that each one of us may have been different persons at various times in the course of history, and yet remain blind to our multiple identification. Yes, why should we remember our past lives? A plant reduced to a seed becomes plant again without having to consult a textbook on botany. . . . It's just a matter of being able to distinguish between what lives, what dies, and what is transformed.

At sundown, then, every day of this miraculous summer, we continue our dialogue. My meeting with her was indeed miraculous, and the discovery of affinities rarely found between a boy of fourteen and a woman of fifty. But it was also miraculous because of the weather; no one could recall a summer so persistently sunny, and this abundance of light and warmth seemed to secrete an uncommon euphoria. A sort of happy torpor was overtaking those stalwart Englishmen, who were used to spending fortunes to flee their own drizzle and fog and get their ration of sunshine in the south of France, in Egypt, or India.

The spring had been very damp and the rain-soaked earth was being richly fecundated by the warmth; flowers glistened in the fields and in the rock gardens, reaching record-breaking height and splendor. Beneath a serenely radiant sky, the lawn exhaled iridescent vapors that suffused the great oaks in a halo of powdery light. During that entire season I never closed either my Persian blinds or my window even once, and the foliage soon started to invade my room, growing wildly along the white walls.

The topics of my conversations with my aunt were beamed back to me by the night sky, of a depth and brilliance that was also very unusual for southern England. A clear question was being asked of me, What about infinity? Yes, what about it? Thus I developed a taste for astronomy, and I tried to penetrate as best I could the solid enigmas it proposed. The physical rapport between my own private world and the world of galaxies was of course truly frightening: How could I, so small, possibly exist in a universe that constantly tends toward the infinite? However, I existed. I even existed to the point where I was able to ask myself why. I existed in fact as a point, as a focus, as a pure geometrical abstraction, a place without substance; as pure movement. Dimensions had nothing to do with the problem; only movement defined identity, for stars as well as people. The secret is inside. . . .

We were sitting one evening, my uncle Fred and I, on the golf club terrace, under the night sky, which was causing me to ask myself those questions. I felt that he had something difficult to say. Suddenly he attacked, highball in hand, in a confidential tone:

"You have absolutely no idea what one runs across in these bloody newspapers! As a professional man, sometimes I am ashamed; people will swallow just *anything*. Every summer it's the Loch Ness monster . . . but that's nothing. The other day, I read an article by some character who claims that the light of the stars takes *years* to reach us! *Even centuries!* Why write such silly stuff when all you have to do is look up and you can *see them*, those stars! That doesn't take years."

Fred obviously considered me a lost cause. Jack was a dreamer, a talented misfit who would never succeed in anything; I was my father's son, all right, but even worse. The vegetarianism I practiced, my cockeyed beliefs, by bizarre relationship with his wife, my taste for astronomy, all that made him very impatient. He would have liked to straighten me out, since my father seemed to have given up on me. But how to go about it? How could he make a breach in those high, thick walls? He had tried his luck with astronomy, and it hadn't worked very well.

Uncle Fred only spent three or four days a week at Ifield, he lived in London the rest of the time. He had a bachelor's apartment on Jermyn Street, of which even his wife didn't know the exact address, and he directed a small but flourishing advertising agency. Having started in life selling newspapers on the streets of Manchester, he was happy with the knowledge that it was now partly thanks to him that these same papers were still thriving. My uncle Fred's realm, like that of King Harold, was located on earth. But the stars had turned against Harold who had underestimated their power. It is said that the prodigious apparition of Halley's Comet in 1066 in the sky of Normandy had prophesied William's victory and Harold's sudden death: Harold had sneered at his astronomers, and meanwhile William, backed by his own, launched the invasion of England, confident that nothing could prevent its success. We find in that event the course of history being guided by a celestial phenomenon, and we may ask, Is this what some would call divine guidance? Or is it simply a self-fulfilling prophecy? Or is it, perhaps, that divine guidance itself works as a self-fulfilling prophecy?

The next day my father was to arrive from Paris for a weekend visit. As soon as he had settled down, the two brothers started discussing tourism. For some time now my father had been trying to obtain the backing of the French government to conduct an advertising campaign to help increase the volume of British tourism in France. The Americans, huddled up in one of their periodic bouts of isolationism, didn't want to hear about France. As for the English, they were going through a crisis of austerity due to the recent devaluation of the sterling, and the government discouraged trips to France, where life was more expensive. Italy and Germany were conducting an intensive publicity campaign to attract English tourists, financed by the State with huge means. Shouldn't France fight back her rivals? She had every reason, economic as well as political, to stimulate the inflow of tourism business from England thanks to the campaign Jack had mapped out with his brother's help. If the French government bought it, it would of course be Fred's agency that would be in charge of the program.

My father described for him his visits to the French administration. Those people were not easy! For instance, when he had seen Paganon, the minister of Public Works, Paganon had told him to his face that France had no need of foreigners, and English ones least of all. Others were more receptive, such as Raoul Dautry, who was reorganizing at that time the four independent railroad networks of France, all of them virtually bankrupt, into a state-owned company, the Société Nationale des Chemins de Fer Français, SNCF for short. Dautry was therefore in a good position to sponsor the project, and he did. Jack had obtained an appointment with the minister of Foreign Affairs, Edouard Daladier, thanks to his intervention. Having explained all this, my father asked Fred to come to Paris, when the time came, to go with him to see Daladier.

"What could I tell him, this Daladier? I don't speak a word of French!"

"It doesn't matter. I'll do the talking. Just your presence will count. It will amuse him to see an authentic golf-player in his office."

Fred didn't understand, but he promised to come and lend a hand. In three weeks. In order to hear Jackie speak French with the minister of Foreign Affairs, ha ha! Why not? Fred did not have much faith in his brother's grandiose scheme, but he did not mind the chance to spend a couple of days in Paris and investigate the pleasure spots and the watering places. And then—one never knows, if ever it worked out, it would be a damned good piece of business.

Later in the evening, my father and I found ourselves alone on the big chintz-covered couch, and he suddenly asked:

"What about Nadejda? Have you heard from her?"

"Yes," I said, blushing. "Two or three letters from Capri."

"Ah," replied my father, blushing in turn. "You're lucky. Do you write to her often?"

I would like not to have blushed. And I would have liked him not to ask me such questions. He, who didn't give a damn about the fact that I always got bad marks in school, inveterate dunce that I was—what right had he to mix in on my private life?

"Oh not too often. Only from time to time," I answered. "She asked me to write her some poetry, but it's years since I've written any. So I drew Blotto's portrait on the bottom of a letter. I suppose I'm not a poet . . ."

"Ah yes. Very nice," he mumbled.

We'd never had such a long conversation before. I was suffocating with emotion, indignation, and curiosity . . . but certainly not from jealousy, and that I wanted him to understand.

"You know, Dad," I said, "Nadejda is fantastic, but . . ."

I had no clear idea how to finish that sentence, so I stopped, but my father had understood. He looked at me, reassured and taken aback at the same time.

"I think I must say good-night," I said to him as I stood up, feeling it better to leave him to his thoughts.

How could I have confessed to him my own torments? They were as bad as his, but Nadejda had nothing to do with them.

The story was this. Upon my arrival, Aunt Nell had given me a list of names and telephone numbers.

"Here you go," she said to me, "these are young girls from the neighborhood, all from good families, all very nice, and they want to meet you. It's got around that my nephew is coming here to spend his vacation, a young Frenchman! Most of them don't know France, but the idea of seeing a French boy here, that's really got them jumping like fleas, and they've all got something to offer you. Fanny plays tennis very well . . ."

"Oh, you know, tennis, really . . ."

"Annie Forman could teach you to play golf . . ."

"No, thanks, golf, no, really, it's not for me."

"Lizzie is very cute, and a first-rate swimmer . . . Lizzie . . ."

"Listen," I say, "I've got a lot of stuff to read, I've got work to do, and frankly, I'm not interested in girls."

Upon which I blush violently.

"How's that?" cried my aunt, very disconcerted. "You prefer . . . something else?"

"No, no! Of course not!"

How could I explain to her? I didn't really mean that, about not being interested in girls, it's just that I felt that the girls on the list didn't sound very interesting.

"I prefer older people . . ."

"In what age group?"

"I was just joking," I said, trying to back out. "But if there's an astronomer on your list, with a good telescope, well . . ."

"With a telescope? No, that I don't have, my friend. You'll just have to get along by yourself. After all, you're big enough; I trust you."

In which she was quite wrong. If only she had insisted a little, if only she had told me about Lizzie Paxton, for example, whose Morris Minor broke down in front of the garden gate a few days later while I was walking on the road to Crawley in search of the Impossible, perhaps the entire course of my life would have changed. . . .

All that, be it said frankly, because of a few hairs that were sprouting on my chin! So intimidated was I by the necessity of purchasing my first razor that I had been putting it off for weeks. Soon after my arrival in England, however, it became evident that I had to come to grips with the matter. And so one morning, I set out for the little market town of Crawley, three miles from Ifield, and forced myself to enter a shop on the main street where cutlery was displayed in the window.

Once the door shuts behind me, there's no way to retreat and I must make my request of the clerk, a young girl my age, fresh and pert. She looks at my blushing face with a suspicious eye as if to assure herself that I'm legally authorized to become the proprietor of a razor. Do I even have a beard to shave? I see it coming—yet another one of those ridiculous scenes for which I seem to have a natural talent. The little hussy! I look pointedly at the two laughable tangerines that are pushing through her sweater as though I were going to ask if she had the permission to wear a brassiere.

She finally gives me the razor; I pay and rush out, reeling with shame and relief at the same time.

Razor in hand, I start walking around the village, furious at my shyness and my stupidity. . . . Suddenly, at the corner of a street, my path crosses that of a young girl whose image will remain with me for the rest of my life. My field of vision is invaded by this irresistible presence. Blue! In her blond hair, there's a blue ribbon; smiling with exuberance of her sixteen years, two lightning-blue eyes; her very simple blue dress brings out the golden freshness of her skin: It's a rainbow, blond, pink, and blue. She even has two black-and-blue marks, which embellish her bare legs. . . . I see all this in the space of a half second. I'm still registering the details, though she has already disappeared, borne off by her smile, ravished from my dream. . . . I try to remember her mouth. . . . Was she wearing sandals? It's really too stupid! I turn around and rush off in pursuit of her. It is She of whom I have always dreamed, the chosen one of my heart. . . . She's vanished, it's incredible, she has evaporated even faster than she appeared! Where did she go? I fling myself headlong into a narrow street. . . . No, this is a blind alley! I retrace my steps, I run like a madman.

Where has she gone? My God, my God, I've lost her. . . . But I can't stand around waiting for her to appear. What would people think? Sadly, I take the road back to the house and spend the rest of the day in torment.

The next morning, I return to Crawley, wander the same streets, and wait. I want her so hard to appear that she should hear me. But. . . . Nothing, of course. Nothing. I convince myself that the next day, or a day or two after that, I'll see her again. It's the law of probability. But nothing. One week, two, three, and still nothing. My aunt doesn't ask me anymore about my morning expeditions. I've never dared to confess the cause to her. One evening, however, she tells me that I read too much, I'm too serious; am I therefore not interested in young girls? "Annie? Fanny? Lizzie? . . . Maurice, really?"

My aunt was right. I had at my beck and call entire squads of those pink and blond nymphs who make for the glory of Sussex, just as butter and cream are the pride of Normandy. The whole neighborhood knew about the presence of the French boy, and the French boy alone was unaware that in England his compatriots had the reputation of being great lovers. For this reason alone, this idiotic and inaccurate reason, my aunt was getting innumerable telephone calls, pressing invitations, and visits from chirping young people in search of a partner for tennis, for a walk, or for a dance. But I wasn't available.

I had something completely different on my mind. My heart was taken and I lost interest in everything. Actually, I didn't remember too well what she looked like. In my mind, her image was continually appearing at that street corner, but upon it there had been superimposed other images of young girls my aunt had sought to interest me in, and they were all equally blond, pink, and blue. And yet there was nothing but Her in my heart. She alone was in my heart. The Unknown

One. Almost every morning during those three months, I religiously trudged the three miles going and the three miles back, and never again did I see her. Perhaps she had never existed. . . . Perhaps my faith in myself was not great enough to make her reappear?

On the other hand, the wife of the doctor who lived in the beautiful house next door, a large voluptuous woman of about thirty, took an interest in me that caused me great embarrassment. The romantic passion of this matron struck me as freakish, importunate, and completely misplaced. French boy or not, I was still nothing but an ignorant fourteen-year-old high-school student; what could I have possibly done with this blooming bourgeoise whose husband, moreover, was an ex-university heavyweight champion? It was idiotic. She would come over to our house at the most inopportune moments, and these confrontations were an almost unbearable test of my nerves. One day while I was reading H. P. Blavatsky's *Isis Unveiled*, installed in a deck chair I had ingeniously suspended in midair between the trees above the garden pond, she appeared so suddenly from behind a weeping willow that I started with surprise, destroying the precarious equilibrium of my installation. Whereupon the whole thing collapsed in slow motion, and I found myself standing in the mud, water up to the chest, holding up *Isis Unveiled* high above my head—I had at least succeeded in saving my book from drowning.

"Hello there," said Mrs. Crawford, "I wanted you to listen to a record my friends sent me from Paris. It's in French, modern songs . . ."

She was speaking to me from the bank of the pond, setting up her portable phonograph on the lawn while I clambered back onto dry land, hauling my deck chair out of the water. She wound up the machine and signaled me to listen to the words, which Lucienne Boyer seemed to sing for me alone:

> *Par-lez-moi d'amour,*
> *Re-di-tes-moi des cho-ses ten-dres . . .*

"Oh, you're all wet," said Mrs. Crawford suddenly, as an afterthought, as she watched me taking off my water-logged shoes. "Is it my fault you fell in? Oh, I'm really terribly sorry . . ."

> *Vô-tre beau dis-cours*
> *Mon coeur n'est pas las de l'en-ten-dre . . .*

The English are mad and English ladies even more so, be it in Sussex, in Brighton or London, two cities I had occasion to visit briefly; all these people are raving maniacs with unyieldingly fixed ideas, as deranged as their monetary system. (It's true that, seen from England, the French aren't so hot either, what with their politics, their Colonel de La Rocque, and the rest. . . . Well, madness is universal!) Mrs. Crawford finally gave up. With a look of defeat on her face, she closed up her phonograph and went away, rehearsing softly the song to herself, with her own accent.

Another three days and my visit will come to an end. The heat has abated and one sees sweaters appear at the club. For the last time, I take the road to Crawley. I rove the streets like a detective, I look into the shops, I go into the post office and even into the little church. I sit down on a bench in the middle of the main street. I wait. This village has become so familiar to me—every wall with its patina, every bush, it's all charged with memories, heavy with the emotions I felt in the course of this absurd quest. How many times did I think I had recognized her from afar? All it took was a blue dress, a ribbon. . . . Each time my heart was in tatters. . . .

I was almost relieved, that last day, not to see her. It would have been unbearable—finding her at last just on the eve of my departure! I took the road back to Ifield, stuffed into a cocoon of almost serene melancholy. If only I could convince myself that she *doesn't* exit, that I dreamed her. . . .

The next morning, the moment of departure has arrived. I see Uncle Fred getting his car out of the garage while I force myself to shut my window for the first time, which involves cutting the wildly growing vine, a real massacre; I take a somber pleasure in torturing this lush, rebellious virgin plant.

On the road, after a few minutes of silence, Uncle Fred smiles at me:

"Don't make such a face, old man. We're also sorry to see you go. But you didn't waste your summer, what with your drawings and your astronomy . . ."

"Oh!" Nell breaks in. "That looks like Lizzie Paxton's car."

She waves her hand joyously through the window and turns to me.

"You were really quite wrong not to want to speak to her. She's the prettiest girl around, you know, and so vivacious . . ."

And suddenly I see Lizzie, radiant and dazzlingly beautiful, driving her Morris Minor at breakneck speed with her left hand, and with the right, greeting us comically with a big wave of her hat. You have guessed correctly, of course! It was my transcendental blonde. Sitting beside her was a tanned, dark-haired young man who smiled at us with all his teeth.

"She's finally found a boyfriend," added Nell, inexorably. "They seem so happy together, it's really a pleasure to see them."

Before I left, Aunt Nell wanted me to visit London, which I had barely seen during a visit of a few hours with Uncle Fred, a month earlier. In a state of total stupor, I let myself be dragged from one taxi to another—those tall black boxes that turn on themselves with the practiced agility of whirling dervishes. They become a second home for me, a rolling mortuary, and I wonder dumbly about their shape, their size. Why so square, so high? These mechanical insects are hollowed out so that the high hairdos favored by the city's eminent men and women, duchesses and High Court Justices, can be transported with no damage done to the owners' dignity through the congestions of urban traffic.

My aunt explained to me that I was in the Tower of London, contemplating the Crown Jewels; in Westminster Abbey amid the famous dead; in Chelsea; and that this misty turmoil of a seascape was a Turner, and this couple of pomaded golfers, a Gainsborough. Two action-packed trips on top of a red bus woke me up a bit. Bovril, Piccadilly. We spent an hour in an Anglo-Indian cathedral made out of papier-mâché, in Russel Square, where the crowd was dressed in tweed in shades of sea green and pastels identical to those of the pastry at the Lyon's Corner-Houses. Buckingham Palace, with its scarlet soldiers of lead and feather, pulled me out of my lethargy once again. Ah, if only Gregor had been here, he would have enjoyed that scene! But alone with my aunt, I was defenseless: I kept waiting for the moment when my besotted mind would wake up and my misfortune would confront me in all its horror. I had lost Her . . . well, Lizzie. . . .

Finally, we go down Charing Cross Road, and then speed along the Thames in our mechanical box whose pilot is a cockney golem—all I'll ever see of him is his back and extended hand. . . . It'll take more to shake me out of my torpor than this smooth-skinned city with its lackluster rows of Victorian Gothic. . . . We finally enter the dizzying bustle of the train station. Like the mother of the English, it has been named Victoria; and like her, it wears vast petticoats, immense glass petticoats that contain people as under a bell jar; a museum of a railroad station, heart of the empire, a turntable whence the assembled crowds vanish into the steam, a colossal monument made of smoke and cast iron, of shrieks and whistles, of baubles and shining pendants. Nell sits down for a moment in the compartment where she has installed me. We have just spent an entire life together. Yet another one; Karmic curves beyond dimension have brought us together, and they separate us once again. For a brief moment, we have been more closely joined than any human couple ever was. Each of us knows that. I forget my unhappiness and bid farewell to my aunt. In taking leave of me, she, also, once again loses touch with an old dream.

6

*Studying the redheads.—Daffodil and The Obelisk Press
modestly flourishing.—A genius mountebank: Frank Harris.
—Another literary hobo in the Paris gutter, Henry Miller
by name.—The Tropic of Cancer contract.—Anaïs Nin
as seductress.—Doing Picasso's job.—The big woman
in the net.—A dog's cemetery.—Down the river
a tiny casket floats along.—The French Mussolini.
—A revolution, Gallic style.—Hitler only needs to appear.*

Traveling by boat train from England was like a return voyage
through the looking glass; I was slipping from one world to
another through a decompression chamber. With each revolution of the iron wheel, the fateful Sussex vacation was receding into the past; that entire summer was already appearing in
quite a different perspective.

What remained now of the twin Lizzies, the half-glimpsed
princess and the joyous tomboy person, was no longer a great
tragedy but an intensely erotic synthesis; that third Lizzie with
her handsome, smiling lover was all the more seductive as she
belonged not to me, but to another. Since I had lost access to
her reality, she had become all the more important to me, but
as a pure phantasm, as an image of the impossible. For many
months thereafter Lizzie Paxton recurred in my dreams as a
friendly succubus.

My school presented, by contrast to what I was coming
from, a gray, everyday autumnal image in which I found very
little nourishment. It seemed quite impossible for me not to
have any exchange whatsoever with my elegant young companions, except on the most frivolous level. Of course there
were little groups, networks, popular personalities, and so on;
what that social activity revealed, however, was simply the
driving will that possessed those youngsters to imitate their
parents, as closely as possible, in their life and their profes-

sion. What a bore! That environment was making me feel even more alienated, even more at odds with the system, with whatever it was that made those people tick. By contrast, I was therefore bound to act as the opposition; but the opposition to what? About what? It wasn't quite clear; but certainly one had to fight, to express dissent. And since the school was essentially impersonal, neither good nor really bad, we focused those negative feelings on certain teachers whose personality we found objectionable, for some futile reason. And I began to play the same function as gang leader and provocateur as had been mine at Meaux, finding myself once more involved in a permanent conspiracy to disrupt the school system.

It was rather startling to find, as the school term started, that one of the new assistant masters was no other than Raymond Marcellin, whose younger brother Jean had been my close companion in my first school. Raymond was studying law, and our reunion, although it was very friendly, left me with an uncomfortable feeling as I measured the scope of my friend's evolution in only two or three years. At Meaux he had been a tough leader of the anti-establishment underground, an expert in monkey business, a resourceful evildoer; here he was now, on his way to becoming *a lawyer!* And what's more, to subsidize his studies, here he was, doing a cop's job in this bourgeois school!

At about that time I made another acquaintance, through the Delamares—Sacha—who was the son of a famous couple of theater people, George and Ludmilla Pitoëff, Russian émigrés who had become a great and exceptional success in Paris. I soon found that, aside from being a dedicated chess player, Sacha had a remarkable characteristic: He had three sisters, each one a redhead. Three marvelously redheaded redheads!

I had first been forced to recognize the nature of redheadedness when I was confronted with Renoir's *Portrait de Mademoiselle Irène Cahen d'Anvers*—such a forceful statement you can hardly miss. But seeing three equally striking cases of redheadedness together, as sisters, that brought the point home even more eloquently.

So there weren't only blondes or brunettes? Redheads were not just a different hair color, but a different breed. I began to notice their many idiosyncrasies—not only as to skin-quality, those are obvious—but in terms of features, of the very structure of face and body. Among all redheads there were those points in common; truly beautiful redheads can easily be mistaken for sisters, and that has of course nothing to do with the color of their hair.

All this according to my observation! Because I have become an enthusiastic researcher of that one subject: redheads. Anywhere I glimpse a redhead I run, observe, spy. I turn around her, trying to get close enough to verify what they say about the scent. As a result I could boast that I know everything there is to know about the subtle design of a redhead's temple and cheekbone, of the brow's perfect arch, of the delicate ankles and wrists. I have fervently observed, from every angle (but also always from a safe distance!), the very presence of the redhead's body, at once lithe and heavy; flesh endowed with the cold sensuality of white marble, with its polished weightiness.

True-red redheads are indeed pretty rare, but one must also consider the countless hybrids, since the type tends to combine easily and to modify the ones it mixes with, usually in an interesting manner.

There are blond redheads, and redheads who started life as blondes; and russet redheads, as well as many shades of auburn determined by the measure of redheadedness involved. There are sometimes dark-haired people whose finely designed eyebrows reveal them as secret redheads. There are also redhead-redheads, of disturbing brilliance, whose fate is never easy. . . .

While I was busy with my redhead studies, my father was consolidating his fledgling publishing enterprise, which had been started in fact with his own book, *Daffodil*. It was far from easy in view of the restrictions imposed by Servant, whose veto power was invoked anytime he suspected that a book might have been chosen by my father because of its literary value.

Since the printer could not read a word of English, and since he was of a suspicious nature, the partnership grew more and more unpleasant. My father was restricted to three books a year, including the one he was supposed to write himself; that wasn't much to build up a list, but there were possible additions that the printer would tolerate because they meant easy money.

These were the novels published in England or in America that had been subjected to prosecution under the obscenity laws, and condemned. Each publisher not only had to pay a fine and court expenses, but also lost all the money he had already invested in the book. That is the point at which my father was usually able to get the publishing rights for very little money, and sometimes even to buy the printed sheets—which would then be bound with a new title page and an Obelisk Press cover. Each one of those books, having been subjected to intense publicity during the court hearings in New York or London, would be sure to attract the English-speaking tourists when visiting Paris. The sales were therefore always easy, and reasonably good, although on a very small scale, since each printing seldom exceeded one thousand copies, even for the most notorious titles. . . . Such were *Storm* by Peter Neagoe, a Romanian writing in English whose novel had been declared obscene by a U. S. court; Radclyffe Hall's *The Well of Loneliness*, a Lesbian saga of some repute; and Norah C. James's *Sleeveless Errand*, another Lesbian saga—both of them banned in Britain. In the rival department came James Hanley's *Boy* and *The Young and Evil*, the joint product of Parker Tyler and Charles-Henri Ford, in which was depicted the modern-style male homosexual life-forms in vogue among some young American expatriates with Bohemian leanings. Cyril Connolly's *The Rock Pool* was all about decadent modernism on the Riviera.

All those books had in common the fact that they had been originally selected for publication by a well-established firm, and also, of course, that they had offended the censor's sensibilities in some unforgivable manner. Each one had added a bit of prestige to the Obelisk imprint, and they had begun to mollify the printer's prejudices. My father felt confident that if he ever found the book of his life, even by a totally unknown author, even without any attending scandal—he would now be in a position to push it down Servant's throat.

In a class apart from the other books was Frank Harris's memoir, *My Life and Loves*. After his acquittal by the courts in Nice, Harris had decided to sell his rights to my father; the international ruckus caused by the prosecution had opened a large potential market for the book, and the printer had immediately agreed to back the deal. The first tome, privately printed in Nice, was redone in two volumes under a red-and-yellow cover with the Obelisk Press imprint, and two more volumes followed suit. Harris told my father that he had a fifth volume in the works, but no more was heard about it.

The business of the firm was easy to run. The market consisted in some twenty bookshops in all, a few of them in Nice, Cannes, Juan-les-Pins on the Riviera, and the majority in Paris—in Montmartre, Montparnasse, but essentially on the Right Bank, within spitting distance of the publisher's office. My father used to walk over to his bigger accounts, W. H. Smith or Galignani on the rue de Rivoli. Brentano's on avenue de l'Opéra, by far the biggest, absorbed all by itself nearly one third of the Obelisk Press production; every morning my father had coffee with his friend Davis, a pleasant, young-looking, white-haired chap who was top salesman at Brentano's, and business was transacted in a genteel, unpressured manner.

As the firm's reputation started to grow, so did the flow of manuscripts submitted to Obelisk. Most of them had already been rejected by a dozen or more publishers in London and New York, and for the author to send once again the torn and dismantled script to that crazy little publishing house in Paris, France, was a last desperate gesture in which he invested great hopes. Reading that sorry material, poring over the fantasies conceived by all possible varieties of misfits, and finally trying to pen a humane rejection letter, that was the one part of his operation that my father dreaded most. But he was compelled to give each manuscript an honest chance, in the hope that— one day—he would find the great work he had been waiting for since the beginning.

William Aspenwall Bradley was an old American gentleman of letters who had settled down in the Ile Saint-Louis, and started a literary agency there, which was devoted mostly to English-language authors. His business never amounted to much, but he didn't mind as profit was not the object anyhow. But it so happens that he was the only agent in a position to represent an American author in Paris, and so Henry Miller went to see him with the manuscript of *Tropic of Cancer*, which he had just completed. Bill Bradley had in turn sent it with his recommendation to my father, who happened to be the only publisher in the world who was in a position to print such a book. Simple.

At first he did not pay too much attention to Bradley's enthusiastic presentation, but as he started reading, he immedi-

ately fell under the spell. The writer's voice was totally authentic, and its brutal power was quite real. Who was the
fellow? A middle-aged American, unknown, stranded in Paris,
apparently living off the land, a sort of literary *clochard*. This
book, *Tropic of Cancer*, was not the work of a madman, and it
belonged to no school, to no category; it was the spontaneous
product of a man of genius, there was no doubt of that. But
above all, it was the work of a free man; it was more than a
masterpiece, it seemed to mark the birth of a new language in
literature.

The two of them, Henry Miller and my father, belonged to
worlds so foreign to each other that, despite their will to
communicate, misunderstandings were unavoidable. Miller
didn't know what to think of that curious British gentleman-
pornographer, and my father himself was quite disconcerted
by this great author's personality. Where had all the thunder
gone? That fellow from Brooklyn with his slow drawl and the
falsely self-confident manner, was he really the man behind
that great revolutionary book?

In spite of the reciprocal diffidence, they reached an
agreement on the spot about *Tropic of Cancer*, although my
father did realize, in the back of his mind, that he still had to
get the printer's approval of the deal, and that wouldn't be too
easy.

Indeed *Tropic of Cancer* infringed all the rules, notwithstanding its high sex content. To compare it to *Ulysses* would be no
help at all in trying to convince Servant, who held such idle
writings in absolute contempt. There had been no ban, no
prosecution, no prior scandal liable to inflate the book's selling value. . . . Unfortunately the meeting with Servant went as
badly as it could possibly have done.

"Why publish a book like that? It's an absurd risk," the
printer said.

"Well, look here," my father argued, "there's a minimum of
risks to be taken in order to discover a new author from time
to time! That man is a genius."

"Hah, a genius!" Servant countered. "You call *that* a genius,
a fellow who can't say a civil *bonjour* when he comes into
the office, and who can't even think to take off his hat when
he talks to you? Can a man like that become a best seller? No
sir! Never." M. Servant was deliberately playing the idiot to
make his partner's defeat even more painful.

There followed a series of wretched dialogues between the

publisher, my father, who wasn't really the publisher, and the author, Miller, who couldn't have found any other publisher in the entire world. Miller persisted in maintaining it was a fear of a prosecution that made my father delay publication of his book from season to season, but that he was too chicken to admit it. My father tried to explain to him his situation vis-à-vis his French partner, and the need for more time to convince him; but Miller refused to believe that a man as well-dressed as my father was could possibly depend on a character like Servant, whose existence he himself preferred to overlook. . . . The fact is that the chances of a legal action against *Tropic of Cancer* were real, but negligible. France was a liberated country. It was this sense of freedom, unique in the world, that had made France the center of fashion and of ideas; it had become the national hallmark, the main reason why people came to live there. Almost all modern painting ended up in the galleries of Paris because France was the natural home of exiles—as witness the encounter of my father and Henry Miller. But the prosecution against Frank Harris's memoirs, although it hadn't succeeded, was proof enough that the laws never afforded an absolute protection. There were in France many conservative, clerical, and military pressure groups, always busy infiltrating the government and trying to push bills through parliament to institute a strict system of moral censorship (or rather *sexual* censorship) on every book or periodical printed or sold in the country. When the most scandalous book of the thirties, Victor Margueritte's *La Garçonne*, had become the testing ground for the procensorship drive, the courts and the government had refused to yield to the conservative pressures, but the Order of the Legion of Honor—Marguerite was a member—threw him out in disgust. Surely the advent of Mussolini and Hitler was going to increase the power of the conservatives in the years to come.

Publishers themselves were not highly conscious of the lurking danger; for instance, Louis-Ferdinand Céline's *Journey to the End of the Night* had been subjected to a certain amount of self-censorship at the request of the publisher, Robert De-noël; and that seemed to indicate that there were certain uncharted borders one was no longer free to ignore. My father kept arguing with his partner that no such danger could ever threaten a book printed in English, since French law could only be concerned with works issued in the French language. But the printer only sneered at such arguments. The deadlock was final between them, and my father's bitterness was growing with each new setback. And each one of those crises was invariably followed by a disheartening session with Henry Miller.

The contract for *Tropic of Cancer* had been signed in 1932, and since then Miller, who already considered himself as a published, world-recognized author, was building up confidently his lifework as if the matter of publication had been settled once for all, and had become quite immaterial. That feeling of self-confidence derived to a large extent from the encouragements he was receiving from the growing number of his supporters, and singularly from the active friendship of one Anaïs Nin, a young American artist who had become his mistress and literary disciple. Anaïs was cosmopolitan, conspicuous, and she behaved with the generosity only a rich person could afford, although she didn't appear to have much money of her own. A mystery woman.

Henry felt that here was someone who should be able to solve his problem in a jiffy. That fellow Jack Kahane had an eye for women, everyone knew that, and someone like Anaïs could vamp him, and actually seduce him into publishing the book. In retrospect, my father was highly amused by the clever maneuvers Henry Miller had invented in order to surround him. First he had mobilized all of Anaïs Nin's powers of seduction to win over Bill Bradley, the agent from Ile Saint-Louis. He would then build up on the latter's prestige to impress and convince Jack Kahane, who had the reputation of being a snob. And since he was also known as a lady-killer, he sent to Kahane Anaïs in person, duly perfumed, and instructed her to go the whole way if called upon to do so. But all he could do was repeat once again, to Henry's unexpected envoy, what he had explained many times before to Henry himself. She did understand, however, better than Henry had ever done, that the situation was really just as described by Kahane. The only way to get *Cancer* published would be for someone to pick up the tab. The book had been stalled for nearly two years, and since there was no other way to unfreeze the situation, she would do it herself. . . . And this is how Anaïs Nin came to lend my father the money needed to pay Servant's printing bill.

By the time *Tropic of Cancer* came out, in 1934, Céline's *Journey* had already been acclaimed as the masterpiece of the day—or perhaps even of the century! It's probably no simple coincidence if those two books finally came out the same year, and in the same city.

At least that was for me the occasion for a double take, as my father gave me his copy of Céline's book to read, and I was duly enthralled by it; whereupon he gave me the galley proofs of *Tropic of Cancer* to read, only a few weeks later, and this too made a huge impression on me, although my understanding must have been somewhat incomplete.

Seeing me so deeply absorbed in those proofs, my father was suddenly tempted to do a very rash and unreasonable thing: He asked me to draw the cover of *Tropic of Cancer*, and told me that I would be paid the going rate for it.

It did not make much sense, quite obviously! My father knew me as a prolific doodler; but that could hardly be seen as an adequate qualification, all the more as they only were the doodles of a fourteen-year-old. But it goes without saying that I accepted the assignment without the slightest qualms. It would have been a sensible move for my father to ask a young Montparnasse artist, like Picasso or the others. They might even have done it for nothing, for all we know! But I was the chosen one, due to my father's sudden bout of paternal pride, and all I had to do was to sit down at my desk and fill the order.

Having the use of two colors only, black and green and gray paper, all I could come up with was an enormous black crab shape sprawled out over a terrestrial globe, and holding in its gigantic claws a human silhouette, prostrate. With smudges and bristles, and trails of snot to make it all really lifelike. Convinced that I had done a masterpiece, I handed it to my father, who looked tremendously impressed by it. Or was it flabbergasted? Anyway he handed me fifty francs, the agreed price, and the thing went straight into production.

Three weeks later my masterpiece was out, decorating the cover of Henry Miller's first published book, *Tropic of Cancer*; and I dragged Gregor to see it on display in Brentano's window, on avenue de l'Opéra. As soon as he saw it, he started barking like a dog, and then stalking it as a dog will do with respect to a lamppost, threatening to urinate maliciously in its direction against Brentano's window. I managed to drag him away from this incipient scandal situation, and sat him in front of a bowl of soup to calm him down a bit.

Gregor and I had become inseparable. My mother saw him

as something out of an animated cartoon, half elk and half mongrel; what amused her most was Gregor's freakish basso, which he seemed unable to keep under control. But what impressed her most in Gregor, more than the intensity of his ugliness, was the manner he had to play with it, to use it as a theatrical medium, perhaps as a disguise. In public places he amused himself by scaring people, just by looking at them. He could increase his ugliness, accentuate it and aggravate it to the point where it became quite unbearable. There were certain silences, charged with dread, when I knew that I had better not turn around and look at him. He would make any little kid break into tears on sight, especially the ugly ones.

Furthermore, he had developed a dismal taste for noise-making toys, which he was always prone to use in such a manner as to cause maximum embarrassment. He had a variety of them hidden in his clothes, at different places, thanks to which it was easy to sow panic in the subway, or create a scandal in front of Mona Lisa. As for the movie theaters they had a hard time with us, whenever Gregor felt in the mood, what with the cows, ducks, police sirens, donkeys, and clucking chicken. Would that be your idea of fun? After a whole afternoon of it, I would swear to myself that I would never see the fellow again.

. . . Only to creep back to the fold the very next day and, for instance, accompany Gregor to Luna Park, the vast amusement fair near Porte Maillot, where he said he had some pressing business. We entered the grounds and Gregor, without one look to right or left, made a beeline through the mobs of urchins to a booth inside which was displayed a large woman lying in a hammock. In a corner there was a target, which, when hit with a rag ball, triggered a mechanism, overturning the hammock and causing the fat girl to fall on the floor. It was impossible to get a word of explanation out of Gregor, who was literally foaming at the mouth, looking at the big woman hungrily as he was paying for a pyramid of cloth balls from the little old fellow standing behind the counter. The hefty beauty was hanging like a huge prey, in midair, as in a spider's web, and she was gazing down apprehensively at Gregor, the ugly spider.

Looking more and more excited, Gregor seized a ball, aimed fast, missed, took another ball, aimed, and struck right on target. Whereupon the mechanism did indeed overturn the fat beauty, letting her flop on the floor none too tenderly. After a short interval, she obediently climbed back into her bed of strings; whereupon Gregor, looking more and more crazed, picked up another ball, aimed, and there your are, once again, the big lady overturned with her derrière up in the air, and getting up fast, looking a bit shaken and sulky.

And thus it goes, on and on, faster and faster, the huge woman now puffing and aching, red and sweaty, and groaning audibly each time she must hoist herself, painfully, into her hammock, only to be brutally dislodged from same, again and again. A bovine nature, who likes to suffer!

The last time around, she bellows with rage and despair as she capsizes, and her bathing suit rips open right down the rear, revealing her rich behind. The flustered owner decides that it's time to call it a day, and starts closing his shop. But Gregor wants to hang around for his enamorata to appear; and indeed, after a long wait she does emerge, looking, in spite of her summer dress, like a third-class wrestler who just took the beating of his life. She starts with fear when she sees him, but Gregor, gallantly, suggests that we all sit and have a civilized drink at a nearby café terrace. She still looks frightened, but he holds her by an arm that is already covered with blue-and-black marks, and she doesn't dare disagree; she only complains that she needs something for her eye, for the cut on her cheek, the bruises on her knee, elbow, ankle. In his most unctuous manner Gregor invites us to sit down and order drinks while he runs an errand. Soon he comes back with a bagful of pharmaceutical presents for the lady of his dreams, and he showers her lovingly under bandages, bottles of iodine, and surgical plaster, just as if they were pearls and diamonds. He counts the bruises on her flesh; he finds her adorable with her blackened eyes. It soon transpires that my presence is no longer welcome; and I take my leave joyfully from this amorous young couple.

Another of his favorite places, which Gregor caused me to visit, was a dog's cemetery in a small island in a curve of the Seine, under the bridge that leads to Levallois-Perret. A dog's cemetery? Yes indeed, but it welcomes all other types of pets besides dogs. As you enter this strange place you are indeed confronted with a large sculpted horse, rearing high in salute. The cemetery occupies the tip of the island, and it is crisscrossed with sandy paths, along which you will find tombs and funeral monuments of all types, from the simple kennel built in shiny ceramics to the extensive dream palace of Oriental design. Some had bones and balls sculpted in high relief, and many had portraits of the departed beasts done in blue, sepia, or full color. All of them had lovely words attached, of praise, distress, infinite sadness, hurtful bereavement, adieu. . . .

A human cemetery must observe many proprieties that do not necessarily prevail in a pet's cemetery. Here you really can give yourself to the job and send off your beloved in magnificent fashion, in a tomb worthy of the Borgias. If you can afford the space, then you are welcome to build a pagoda, a Moorish palace, or a Hindu temple, the bigger the better.

The Seine was inflated with rainwater, and ready to spill over its banks. The rise had nibbled away the edges of island, absorbing gradually the contours of the necropolis and playing havoc with the tombs. Carried away in an eddy of the turbid waters, I saw a diminutive coffin slowly floating away toward the sea, surmounted, oh surprise! by a tiny Russian-style cross of Saint Andrew.

"Do you see what I see?" I asked Gregor.

"You could say it was a Russian dog," he conjectured.

"What a coincidence!" I remarked.

"Brilliant retort, old man!"

We were stretched out on the lawn of a little hillock, which I was thinking must be larded with defunct doggies. Gregor had decided to take a rest there, and who was I to question his right to do just that, and to sprawl out comfortably among the tombs? I was doing the same myself.

"*To kalon!*" Gregor declaimed, sweeping his gaze over the landscape of slimy water and broken-down factories, and, closer to us, on the little coffin made of precious wood that bravely continued its course toward the mouth of the Seine; and from there, God only knows toward what other destination.

"*To kalon,*" I replied gravely.

"And who do we have over there?" he asked, indicating with a toss of the hand a plump little Russian lady zigzagging between the tombs at full speed, and sobbing madly at the same time.

"From the general trend of the action, I might venture to guess that she is the mistress of the dog who's floating away. Do you understand what she's bawling about?"

"Come back, dushka! Come back, dulce, little soul, come back! or something of that order. Get up, goofy, we've got to go help this unfortunate creature. Come on, seriously."

He was already standing in the woman's path, addressing her in Russian with an overwhelming, exaggerated solicitude, and covering her piercing wails with his basso profundo. The Rasputin number, I thought, that's a bad sign. And I saw him pointing out to her a battered rowboat anchored to the bank with one hand while, with the other, he pointed to me.

"Can you row, fathead?" he yelled.

"Oh no, Gregor," I answered, terrified, "No, no, not that!"

But how could I reason with him? He's already in the boat. I can't help but to follow him; we assign roles to each other: He bails, I row.

The current was carrying us in the general direction of the coffin, which kept moving inexorably out of reach; but I managed to throw a few rather discerning strokes of the oar so that we began to gain ground on our objective. Everything would be swell if the damned boat was not leaking, and if Gregor was able to bail a bit more efficaciously. It's not his kind of work, that's clear, and our unforeseen expedition is taking a sinister turn: Are we doomed to perish, then, in order to save the corpse of an unknown dog?

"Do you know how to swim, old man?" Might as well ask him point-blank.

"I don't think so. And you?" he replied with a worried air.

"So you can't even swim, and possibly not even float," I said bitterly.

He was reclining there, doing nothing. Why should I exert myself with the oars, then, and be the only one to work? I let go of the oars and we started drifting slowly, and gradually sinking at the same time. Gregor was whistling a tune while waiting for the end. By now, there was a little crowd at our point of embarkation. Some fellow in an official-looking hat was shouting indistinct words at us, and blowing his lungs out on a whistle; meanwhile the coffin kept receding into the distance. . . . Bad, very bad.

"It looks like we are virtually under arrest," said Gregor. "We've got the police on our tail—you see that guy with the whistle? Get on with the oars, will you? It'll be your fault if we get caught this time."

Let's give it a final try, then. I strain with all my strength to get our wreck closer to the shore, and finally, instead of just sinking, we run aground in a foul cesspool at the foot of the river's steep bank. But it doesn't matter, we're saved! Gregor congratulates me with a hail of noisy slaps on the back. Once again, we have to make our getaway at full speed, or else we'll get collared by the owner of the whistle on the island of the dead dogs.

Those excursions with Gregor always ended up that way. We would set forth with a serious objective in mind, often of a cultural nature, and suddenly some incident would occur, and Gregor would immediately take his cue from it to plunge us into inscrutable complications. They, in turn, usually led us to a hairbreadth from jail.

These emotions stimulated Gregor's bulimic appetite. At seventeen he was lanky and cadaverous, seeming much older than his age, and he had a capacity for food absorption that verged on magic.

We would enter a restaurant only after long peregrinations during which Gregor methodically inspected a good half dozen of them: It was necessary to combine cheapness with abundance; next on the list was the look of the waitresses. And, of course, the general smell of the place was taken into consideration.

Once comfortably settled, Gregor chose his menu after long and tedious deliberation. He ate his food noisily, and once finished with dessert, he would order another portion of Saint-Honoré, with a side order of vanilla ice cream and chocolate sauce. Next he would order half a Reblochon cheese, a dish of fried potatoes, and then an Italian casserole, thus working his way backward through the courses of the meal and ending with a bowl of fish soup, and a piece of venison. His fantastic appetite evoked the admiration of the most blasé restaurateurs, and some of them even offered him a few additional courses free of charge, just to see him swallow. He would have polished off the dog's soup, given half a chance.

To kalon. . . . He himself never ceased to marvel at his frightful ugliness. Even after seventeen years with such a head on his shoulders, he wasn't used to it; he would never get used to it. And since he felt that the love of a fair woman would remain an unattainable dream forever, he was chasing skirts indiscriminately, thus compensating quality with quantity. The more so that he was built like a donkey.

"Of the two of us," he said, "I'm the most favored. What good does it do you to be a good-looking kid? It makes you stupid and pretentious, like Alcibiades. Monsieur doesn't wish to dunk his biscuit just anywhere, and so he dunks it nowhere. And me in the meanwhile, I'm making it with all the chambermaids in Neuilly, Le Vésinet, Kremlin-Bicêtre, Malakoff, Sceaux, Vanves, Garches, Colombes, and Bois-Colombes, ha ha! wherever I go. They're not very choosy and neither am I. We put a pillow over each other's face and off we go! Furthermore, and you can believe me or not, old fellow, but a really ugly type like me *excites* them. It does a special kind of thing to them. I know a cook from Brittany in Le Vésinet, when she sees me all naked, she faints dead away. It's not everybody who can say the same for himself, is it, my lad?"

The meeting my father was supposed to have with the minister of Foreign Affairs concerning his touristic campaign project was postponed until October, due to the current political upheavals.

Edouard Daladier, the strong man of France's Third Republic, had acted for a time not only as premier, but also as foreign secretary and war secretary. Daladier, chief of the middle-of-the-road radicals, had formerly represented the moderate element in the Front Populaire leftist coalition; whereupon he had turned himself into a semidictator. And then, suddenly, he had been ousted from the premiership, although he still retained the control of both War and Foreign Affairs ministries. Although down one peg, he was still the boss.

Uncle Fred had arrived, as agreed, the day before the meeting, all dressed up in sober businessman mufti, with a Londoner's bowler hat perched on his curly head.

Daladier, having grunted his welcome, gruffly motions his English visitors to chairs in front of his immense table. Next to him his *directeur de cabinet* sits gingerly on a small chair, like a fat hen on fragile eggs, an exquisitely pompous pompadoured person. Behind the French statesman there spreads out far and wide an immense Gobelin tapestry, in whose details my father is trying to find some inspiration for a suitable opening.

"*Monsieur le Ministre,*" he starts. And then stops as he sees the frown on the director's features; Daladier, who was in the process of lighting another Gauloise, interrupts his gesture in midair, with an impatient look on his face. Yes, of course, he should have called him by his former title, since, once premier, you keep the trappings forever.

"Monsieur le Président," he corrects himself. The director lifts a corner of his mouth in benign recognition. Daladier completes the act of lighting his Gauloise and draws a quick puff on it. He is a compact man, short and ruddy, with an aggressive nose and a craggy dome, mostly bald, and there is something vaguely Mussolinian about the heavy jaw; his demeanor, at once absent and garrulous, is meant to express an idea of power and concentration. Strong men need to look stronger than other men.

My father now launches for good into his speech, so well rehearsed that he hardly trips at all over the difficult words. He talks about publicity as a modern science, about its use on the national scale by the Italians and the Germans to promote their own tourist industry, about the moral and political issues at stake, about the great talents as a publicist of his brother, F. E. Kahane. Well, here we are, the project we are now submitting to you, Mr. President, is for the good of France. It is meant to protect your country against *"le concurrence—"*

"La concurrence," corrects the director.

"La concurrence," concludes my father, who always had difficulties with the sex of French words.

While talking, he had been able to observe that the numerous Gauloises Daladier chain-smoked, the way he puffed at them, stubbed them out, the angle at which he held them between his fingers, and the way they jutted from his tight jaws, all of those gestures constituted a secret language by which he was communicating with the director. To someone like Uncle Fred, all this smoking of Gauloise cigarettes, those billows of stinking smoke, were just another foul manifestation of French unhygienic, unsportsmanlike behavior. But to those subtle politicians on the other side of the Louis XV table, the signals of a Gauloise were not unlike those of a Morse alphabet spelling power. Yes, if you wanted to succeed in French political life, you had to understand the ways of the Gauloise. And so the director, having decoded his master's secret messages, was now expounding them in florid language to the visitors.

"Monsieur le Président wishes to thank you for your lucid presentation. He will soon dedicate his full attention to your report, but he would be most obliged for your informing him as to the budgetary requirements—"

"*The money—how much?*" rasped Daladier, impatiently breaking in for the first time. There was a short silence.

"Ten million," said my father.

A faint, almost dreamy smile passed over Daladier's face. *Monsieur le directeur* got to his feet, signaling the end of the audience. Daladier shook hands while lighting himself another Gauloise, and the two brothers descended the majestic staircase between lines of *Gardes Républicains* who were giving them the sword salute.

"So, are we in business?" asked Freddie.

"Let's find a place where we can have a drink," answered Jackie. "By Jove, I need a stiff one."

A few days later, Daladier had been called back to head the government, once again in order to save the country. He was now in a good mood.

Mostly thanks to Raoul Dautry's help, my father's brainchild seemed to be doing quite well indeed. Jack and Fred were summoned again at the Quai d'Orsay and serious discussions were begun, plans were drawn up, financial details examined. My father spent much of his time in the halls and corridors of the House of Representatives (known as le Palais-Bourbon, or more simply "La Chambre") or at the ministry of Foreign Affairs (known as le Quai d'Orsay), and in restaurants favored by politicos. He made friends among the chain-bedecked ushers and the supercilious shrews in the offices. In an obstinate and systematic manner, he furthered his project. And everything would have gone smoothly—if it hadn't been for that cursed game of politics!

Corruption under the Third Republic had reached legendary heights. When the last of a series of public scandals flared up, it promptly spread out in such a threatening manner that a right-wing coup seemed suddenly probable—were it only because it was on everyone's mind.

Alexandre Stavisky, a high-level international crook, was its main protagonist. His system was simple: He borrowed money from state institutions on nonexistent guarantees, paying off bureaucrats to cover his tracks. The payoffs had floated up the political hierarchy. And then Stavisky had been found out, networks of corruption were exposed within the government as well as inside the Radical party, which was in power. The agitation on the Right soon became quite hysterical, and Neuilly was now crisscrossed with bands of pimply activists swinging lead-weighted walking sticks. To keep the tension alive, monarchist and neo-Fascist leagues would ambush the Communists, who would retaliate in kind. Posters were put up and posters were torn down. In his Portuguese retreat, the pretender to the throne of France, Monseigneur le Comte de Paris, was licking his chops in anticipation, and furbishing his Edicts and Proclamations to the People of France.

Whooff—another explosion of headlines: Stavisky had committed suicide in a chalet in Mégève. Rumors started immediately, suggesting that someone had helped him pull the trigger of that gun; the newspapers actually printed pictures of the dead man's head showing the fatal wound, and all of France joined in the discussion of ballistic probabilities, and of paths of entry. This threw such suspicion on the undercover actions of the government that the conseiller prince, a high magistrate, was solemnly appointed soon after to investigate the circumstances of Stavisky's death—only to be found dead himself a few weeks later, decapitated by the wheels of a train.

Drastic!

In spite of such adverse conditions, my father's project had reached the point where it had successfully survived all the bureaucratic hurdles, and was merely awaiting the final blessing of the minister's signature and flourish. This was indeed a surprise to Jack, and even more to Fred; not to speak of my grandfather, who had never believed for one minute that his eccentric son-in-law had the least chance of succeeding, what with his ridiculous British accent and his general lack of know-how. He well knew what it meant to get any project approved by the French bureaucracy, with its political quicksands and its personality power plays: *im-pos-sible!* And Jack had done it? Even faced with the final proof, he wouldn't believe it.

On the morning of the appointed day, Jack dressed up for the ministerial encounter and hailed a cab to be driven to the ministry.

"Au Quai d'Orsay," he told the cabbie. The old fellow had a red nose and spoke with a heavy Russian accent.

"Impossible, Excellency," he said, looking at his passenger in the rearview mirror. "It is beeeg revolution in Champs-Elysées. Please to take *métro*, or walk on feet."

One hour later he finally arrived at the Quai d'Orsay, having observed on his way all the signs of an impending uprising. The Champs-Elysées was filled with rightist shock troopers, and the immense place de la Concorde was thick with people, chanting, shouting murderous slogans. The leagues were threatening the Palais-Bourbon, right across the river. A massive structure in the style of a Greek temple, it was defended by deep cordons of armed police and *gardes mobiles*, a particularly ferocious brand of antiriot troopers. The very center of France's democratic institutions was under siege; in fact, the French republic had only been able to survive that long simply because the parties on the right had no clear political alternative to offer, no leadership, no usable structures. The Right was already known as *"la droite la plus bête du monde"*—a well-earned reputation of conservative imbecility—but no French Hitler had yet arisen to take advantage of its gullibility and shortsightedness. And so the old Radical party and its tired machine—and all the other organs of the bureaucratic maze that all together constituted the French state—had never been seriously threatened, up to that point, by the rightist opposition. On the left, the Communist danger appeared as much more real. But the Radical party, which controlled the government, and therefore the army, felt that it could thus safely retain the balance of power between Left and Right.

Since the buildings of the Quai d'Orsay were contiguous with the Palais-Bourbon, Jack could observe from the high windows of the ministry the mounting agitation straight across the river on the Concorde. Next to him stood the man he had come to see, his main supporter within the Foreign Office hierarchy.

"Nothing is happening here anymore, my friend, everything is in suspense, and the cabinet is stepping down," the diplomat was saying. "Who knows what comes next? I certainly don't. Of course, I regret very much not to be able to compensate you for the loss of the time and work you have spent on this campaign project . . ."

"Believe me," Jack answered, "if I regret losing this business, it is not because of the money, but because the winner is our friend Hitler. It's us, the French and the English, who brought him to power. And we continue to give him the advantage on us by working against each other. The failure of my project is only a small example of what I'm saying."

"Yes, you are certainly right," answered the Foreign Office man. "There is so much we could do if France and England were genuine allies."

It was time to take leave of the good man, as Jack had promised to meet Nadejda for lunch, and she was living in the Hôtel Lotti, on the other side of the river, just behind the epicenter of the insurrection.

He shooks hands amicably with the Foreign Office man and they promised to see each other after the revolution. In the courtyard, a crowd of politicians, journalists and functionaries were bustling about in great disorder. Groups were forming around prominent men who seemed to have some announcement to make, but each time it was only another campaign speech delivered into a vacuum. Pushed around by the mob, Jack found himself in the arms of a big man reeking of *saucisson à l'ail*, and who was shaking his hand with emotion. Could that be President Edouard Herriot, mayor of Lyons, the most famous politician in France, and the moving spirit in centrist politics?

"Ah, dear friend!" Herriot said to him, "Thank you for coming, it's a testimony of your confidence that goes straight to my heart."

"Was that President Herriot?" Jack asked the man next to him, after escaping from the statesman's embrace. But that man turned out to be another radical deputy, who grabbed Jack by the arm and shrieked in his face:

"Only President Herriot can save the country! *And* the party! We must act, every moment counts!"

"Vive Herriot!" yelled the entourage of the famous man.

Elsewhere there were cries of *"Everybody with Daladier!"* or *"Power to Mandel!"* The reporters kept changing their headlines as they went from one group to the next.

An hour later, having succeeded in crossing the Seine to the Palais-Royal, and making his way through the throngs of excited people who surrounded the golden statue of Jeanne d'Arc, Jack finally reached the Lotti where Nadejda was waiting for him, looking ravishing in a hunting suit of tawny suede, his favorite color. She was feverish, as if impatient to fling herself into the fray. He managed to reason with her, steered her to the bar, and sat her down in front of a chateaubri-

and. She cleaved her steak asunder as if it were the enemy. She had never attempted to understand the complex parlor game of French politics, it was all so boring, and so she didn't really know who it was she was thus hacking at with her fork and knife, and she begged Jack to enlighten her. She was a niece of the pretender to a minor throne; who could be sure that someday, despite the morganatic laws, she wouldn't become a queen in some crumbling Lusitanian palace by the sea, full of parrots and sardine-fishermen wearing the uniform of the guard? . . . Nevertheless, in the depth of her soul, she felt herself a Communist. Yes, to share with everyone! Her heart was overflowing. "This little Clos-Vougeot isn't bad at all, Jack, you know. . . . Is this a Burgundy?"

After lunch, she still wanted to get into the action, but she felt a bit heavy. Jack had other ideas in mind to make this a historic day. Finally, they reached a compromise: They would go have a look at what was happening on place de la Concorde, but just a look, half an hour at most.

The atmosphere on la Concorde was combustible, violence was swelling in hundreds of apoplectic chests, the mob growled and seethed. Nadejda was already in the midst of a group of men, a superb lioness, miming a sort of warrior's ballet with them, yelling political slogans without any idea of what they meant. "Good Lord," Jack muttered, "I made her drink too much." He wanted to yank her away from her companions—might as well try to yank *la Marseillaise* from the Arc de Triomphe! In the end he managed to catch her eye, and with a dazzling smile, she let herself be dragged away; she was recapturing the memory of the Clos-Vougeot, and its promise.

At six o'clock, Jack left her in order to go to the Castiglione Bar where he met his friend, Snopko, who was to drive him back to Neuilly. But when he got in front of our house on rue Bertaux-Dumas, instead of returning to the corral, he hopped on the platform of a bus that was going back toward the center of town, which got him as far as l'Etoile; in the distance, on the place de la Concorde, another bus was burning. The rioters had pulled away the grilles from around the chestnut trees, to be broken down and used as missiles against the police, and fights were breaking out here and there at the foot of the avenue. The mob that was descending on the Concorde suddenly surged backward, cries of panic filled the air and everyone began to flee in front of a charge of *gardes mobiles* literally surging up from the pavement, and sweeping away everything in their path. Jack fled with the others as far as Fouquet's, where he saw the staff busily clearing the terrace and blocking the entranceways. A waiter recognized him, let him in, and shut the door behind him right in the face of a wheezing and breathless *paterfamilias* who begged and implored in the name of his six children, only to collapse against the door a quarter of a second later, struck down by the terrible lightning blow of a rifle butt. His disjointed, lifeless body was now lying on the sidewalk. Shots were crackling on all sides; the restaurant's clientele—filmmakers, their stars, and their financiers—were desperately hugging the flagstone floor.

Of course the violence had overshot its aim. Jack understood that this sixth of February 1934 had chased away the last shreds of reason from French political life. That type of politics could only lead to disunion, and open the way to Hitler, the great black magician. He wasn't yet visible; in Paris, his hysterical voice could barely be heard, and only from very far away. In fact, *no one wanted to hear it*. But the French were already divided among themselves, defeated in advance by their own dimness of heart and spirit. Hitler only needed to appear.

The day after the February 6 rightist manifestation, leftists came up from the suburbs and spilled all over the wealthy neighborhoods. Most store windows were broken on the rue de Rivoli, and some looting was reported. Fortunately, the *gardes mobiles* were exhausted and outnumbered, and the rightist insurgents of the day before were wise enough to stay quietly at home; thanks to which a civil war was avoided. But now everyone knew that such a possibility existed; France was a deeply divided country.

7

Rites of Spring in a budding grove.—Ingrid and Tarquin,
a genetic scandal.—Guy and Simone and the glory of
young love.—Boy-boys and boy-girls.—La Belle Rosine
and Gugusse the Clown.—Old Cossacks watching
from behind the drapes.—An evening in Montmartre
with the Goddesses of the Night.—One hundred
and seventy-five nightclubs to go.

With the return of the spring season, the sons and daughters
of the Neuilly bourgeoisie would resume their rites of court-
ship, and it was a joy to watch.

Pasteur was open only to male students but the Cours
Berthier, a secondary school for girls of the same milieu, was
installed conveniently close, in the next street. This allowed
future couples to preselect themselves under the chestnut
trees of boulevard d'Inkermann. The reciprocal choices were
guided essentially by considerations such as the parents' fortunes, numbers of servants, country houses, ambassador
uncles, and of course religion, a meticulous, painstaking
cross-examination, and it took years to reach the actual marriage ceremony. Before that welcome event, sex was strictly
forbidden, it goes without saying.

Surprise parties were organized by solicitous dowagers to
cause the young chrysalids to meet, mix, and compare merits.
Under the eye of the old ladies, deeply sunk into their
armchairs, the young couples would dance innocent slows,
clasped to each other at a chaste distance, protected against
sexual temptations by suitable barriers of acne, teeth in
braces, ill-fitting eyeglasses, and ridiculous clothes. Sex was the
enemy; the awakening of puberty was promptly channeled,
played down, medicalized. Masturbation was treated as a
disease. The more vivacious girls were soon broken in, their

surplus energy being diverted toward the sports or charity. Intellectual pursuits were discouraged, unless they served a purely professional purpose. It was dangerous to think; besides being too much of an effort.

However—there was that one memorable exception to the sexual grayness of our days. Every morning, as the crowd of young fops would mill around in front of the *lycée*, waiting for the classes to start, a breathless young person with bright blond hair would arrive, either running or walking very fast, holding by the hand an overdressed, rebellious urchin. She would deposit her charge in front of the main door and bound away with the grace of Diana's favorite deer. Someone grilled the urchin and we learned that she was an *au pair* Swedish girl, Ingrid, and also an art student.

Ingrid evoked and provoked. Her cheeks a bright pink, her pretty face animated, she would arrive rushing in the floating glory of her blond mane and push her way forcefully through the groups of passive boy bodies. Her intensity was a bit frightening, she was too beautiful, and also too unexpected, since we thought the Swedes should necessarily be cold, coming from such a climate. Ingrid left a trail of longing behind her, but no one ever dared make a pass at her, let alone speak to her. With her lightning appearance the boys' libido got its charge for the day; did she know, I wondered, that she was present in so many kids' torrid dreams? That must have been a nice fantasy, and she must have felt a keen pleasure, jostling those sheepish fellows out of her way in the morning. Perhaps that pretense of always being late was just an excuse to manhandle those silly creatures, immature and expectant, who stood so stupidly in her path?

It seems that Tarquin had never seen Ingrid or even suspected her existence, until that memorable day. Tarquin was an older boy, from the Antilles, a Caribbean mix with caramel skin, a slim waist, and an athlete's limbs. He belonged to a world different from ours, but we had never realized what this meant exactly until that particular morning.

A fateful movement in the crowd causes the sudden confrontation of Ingrid and Tarquin. There is a sudden hush in the crowd, and people move slowly away from the protagonists, as if it were a street fight. The two look at each other, fascinated, and then, in slow motion, Ingrid holds her hand to Tarquin's cheek and lightly caresses the amber skin. Tarquin lets his school books slip to the sidewalk and we see them walk away together, holding each other tightly, and they must be trembling with joy, with excitement.

Wow. We were all stunned! And it hadn't been a dream, since Ingrid had left a trace of her passage, namely the urchin, who was reminding us of that fact of life by raising hell:

"Hey, what about *me*? She didn't give me money for my snack, the bitch! Hey, guys, give me some dough or I'll go home and tell everything!"

Tarquin, Ingrid. Just imagine the conditions required to provoke such an encounter! Contemplate the genetic work of hundreds of centuries, of countless migrations, of inbreedings and crossbreedings, of historical landslides and virgin islands discovered, of slaves taken and slaves loved. Two time-genes at work, two genetic pyramids confronted, and at the tip of each, the most perfect evolutive product of those two genetic assemblages: Tarquin, the pearl of the Caribbeans, and Ingrid, the firebrand huntress from Scandinavia. Black Montagus, white Capulets, is this love's old tragedy, or is this the dawn of a new age?

The ways of seduction were impenetrable. They probably constituted the greatest single enigma of our lives, although certainly not one of us young cubs would have admitted to the fact. Many disguised that search into something else, usually some bookish pursuit. But not so my jolly *copain*, Guy Geoffroy, who never hesitated to use his dazzling charms to the best possible advantage. He looked as Nordic as Ingrid herself, because of a Swedish-American mother, but his natural good looks had been processed through the Parisian mold, and he dressed so as to present them in the best light, although never to the point of ostentation. Guy liked to be charming to all and to keep his friends amused, so his crushing superiority in terms of worldly charms was seldom resented by anyone.

And certainly not by the female sex! His range was wide, from fourteen to forty, anyone wearing a skirt was worth considering. Walking down a street with him was never a simple, functional exercise, but a complicated procedure that involved many starts and stops, following this stimulating backside or that, overtaking same and throwing a sidelong glance for verification and standard visual contact, turning around to check the address on a door where someone had just disappeared; and so on, and on. You might forget where you were headed for, in the end. . . . And once contact was established, and the profile of the wench had been found pleasing, only then was the full seduction routine triggered into action. It was easy enough—the lady could not refuse to turn her head and look at the person walking side by side with her. And she couldn't easily turn away after that, having taken in the striking young man, staring back at her with such an infectious grin, showing such a lot of healthy ivory, and the blue eye bright and merry; looking down at the prey, that eye would then fill with ineffable tenderness. Even the most austere housewife, on her way to the dentist, could not help being seized by the charm that irradiated from this fellow, so courteous, so well-dressed, so totally seductive. What he says may sound rather mad, but no matter. A little stroll to the Bois? It's not far, and it's such a beautiful day! And so is many a dentist's appointment broken; and so is my friend Guy thriving, his pockets filled with silky mementos, panties of all sizes and colors.

One day, however, I saw him for the first time with someone quite different. She must have been no more than fourteen, bright as the day, an elfin body and a quick tongue. Simone was very pretty—large gray eyes in a delicate face—and she was vivid, on the move, always talking with a passionate intensity and a very remote trace of a lisp that made everything she said sound awfully sensual and dramatic.

All this being said, I should add that Simone was not my type, whatever "my type" may have been; and that I was therefore able to enjoy her company and her friendship without any second thoughts. There was a big love affair going on between her and Guy, and since it was a somewhat erratic and tempestuous one, I was happy to serve in my role as a confidant and go-between for the two parties. It was my first adolescent friendship with a girl, and it was quite a new experience for me to approach a female person who was not an object of desire and dread. Or should I say dread and desire?

The other side of the coin is that, being the witness of that pretty idyll, I was feeling more and more left out in the cold, timid, and inadequate. And this was in sharp contrast with my secret life, nourished by an intense erotic imagination and a talent for self-seduction that turned me into the slave of my own needs. In fact I had been plunged into a nonstop sexual obsession since the earliest age, and since there were no outlets available, I was fast turning myself into an introverted sex maniac. But what can one do, considering that one cannot take a mistress at the age of eight? And that is how one turns into a dirty old man at the age of fifteen.

Other fellows were taking the classic shortcut to solve their problem. All around me I saw boy-girls and boy-boys with a lust for boy-girls form close friendships and special networks, as I had already seen happen at my first school, among the guttersnipes of Collège Georges Courteline. Well well, what about it, then? Some boy-girls were mighty peachy, and so close and available. That Pascalini for instance, who would always sit in front of me, letting me admire the curve of a suave nape, of a languorous cheek seen in three-quarter profile with a long silky lash for punctuation. No ugly hair on his girl's legs, long and perfect; they made him so proud that he would always display them to advantage by wearing very brief shorts. Yes, it would have been simple; I had but one gesture to make. I never did, although the temptation was at times rather insistent. It was the first time I was being vamped, and it had to be a boy! *Zut alors!* A boy with Josephine Baker's thighs; and yet a boy.

What was there to do, but to grind one's teeth?

If Gregor had lowered his ambitions to the level of housemaids, it was because he was a realist. Perhaps I should try to emulate him! When the fair came to Neuilly, I almost got my chance. . . . Almost.

For two weeks every summer, Neuilly's main boulevard was overrun by this cacophonic manifestation: La Fête de Neuilly, or for short, La Fête à Neu-Neu. The local population dreaded this annual invasion like a calamity comparable to a biblical plague, but the tradition was ancient and couldn't be uprooted. Despite vehement petitions from the solid middle-class residents, the mayor was helpless to prevent the return of the disgraceful purulence to our citadel of conservatism.

For over more than two kilometers, the booths of traveling shows from every corner of France and Europe offered their laughable wares. Every evening, a truculent and foulmouthed crowd would pour in from the suburbs and from the twenty arrondissements of Paris to party in Neuilly. The local bourgeoisie was not getting so much as a wink of sleep, while motorcycles enclosed in their metallic pits roared round and round ceaselessly. Gusts of horrified screams floated down from the tentacular swings and the dizzying roller coasters. The death trains with jumping skeletons, the wooden horses that revolved until everything reeled, hurdy-gurdies howling their valve-music, bumping-cars crunching into one

another in scrap-iron tournaments. . . . Barkers yelled themselves hoarse, monstrous loudspeakers competed for attention, firecrackers exploded right under your fanny. . . . Add to
that the shooting galleries and the bellowing street bands, and
it all made for a frightening racket. A perpetual crescendo, all
night long.

A disgrace, an outrage! Wave after wave of shrieking, sex-
crazed girls flanked by their bullies, out on a spree. And the
way they swayed from the hips, showing off in their Sunday
rags, that was something else! These were pimps you saw,
or *maquereaux* as they were called, sporting sideburns shaped
into exquisite points, all out chasing the neighborhood cooks
to seduce them, and turn those innocents into underpaid
courtesans.

The Magic Palace is certainly not the most spectacular of
the stalls, but one sees there an attraction singularly missing
elsewhere: La Belle Rosine. A barker made up as a clown
presents her to the public. From the foot of the platform, I
devour her with my eyes, a statue of flesh with a beautiful
enamel smile fixed under her makeup, and eyes like burning
coals set in bouquets of eyelashes. A life-size velvet doll!

"Step right up, step right up, let's see that change! Messieurs, Mesdames, a spectacle unique in the world! Mademoiselle Rosine, the most beautiful girl of five continents, in her
Famous Love-Magic Number! Ir-res-is-ti-ble! Come right in,
ladies and gentlemen, the show starts in five minutes! Step
right up, step right up, let's see that cash!"

As seen from the first row of the crowd, Mlle Rosine appears to me as a luscious symphony of breasts and thighs, her
curves exalted by a wasp waist. Her smile seems addressed to
me alone, it makes me shiver. Did I dream it? No! Kiddo,
your hour has struck.

"A volunteer, gentlemen! Come now, a volunteer up on the
platform! We're asking for a brave man, a fearless man to be
Mlle Rosine's partner. Who will know how to please her?
Come, gentlemen, which one of you is it going to be . . . ?"

And so it was that I found myself up on the platform, together with Gugusse the Clown and la Belle Rosine. With a
gracious bow, she accepts my candidacy; incredible as it may
seem, I don't feel any stage fright! Better still, I feel that
she didn't do so badly herself, considering the smooth elegance of my brand-new shantung suit. She takes me by the
hand and makes me greet the public with her. After which she

leads me into the wings while the audience pours inside and pays to see what's going to happen to me. Once they are all seated on wooden benches, the lights are dimmed. Music. I'm seated on a chair in the middle of the stage, separated from the public by a pane of glass, which is supposed to be invisible. Mlle Rosine then makes her entrance from the side in the charming costume of an erotic horsewoman. She starts doing a dance of seduction, whirling around my chair and rubbing up against me, multiplying her lascivious provocations.

During all this time—Gugusse the Clown had given me very strict instructions to that effect—I am to remain absolutely immobile and indifferent under her attacks. Well, that's not easy—because this dance has on me precisely the effect it is supposed to have. The invisible wall separating us from the public, as if we were in a hothouse, heightens the erotic tension; my nostrils capture an intimate perfume new to me, a spicy odor that goes to my head, makes my eyes flutter. I catch a glimpse of the spectators in the front rows—they are breaking up with laughter, and I realize that my anguished expression must look rather comical to them. . . . But that was nothing: Right now, to top it all off, Mlle Rosine sits on my lap, boldly spreading her anatomy upon mine, and she increases the intensity of her caresses in order to break my presumed indifference. What the public can't see—and neither can I, but I can feel it!—is that her round, muscular buttocks are subjecting me to a hair-raising erotic ordeal. I would never have imagined that anyone could do such extraordinary things, such *personal* things, *with their behind!*

The music changes and the Oriental pap is succeeded by Saint-Saëns's *Danse Macabre*, augmented by the sounds of chains and pots and pans. This is the high moment of the show! I've been told that at this very juncture, thanks to a very ingenious play of mirrors, the public will behold my metamorphosis into a hideous, grinning skeleton, on which Mlle Rosine will continue to ply her merciless project of seduction. . . . Ha ha, how deliciously macabre.

To help me resist Rosine's warm and sinuous body, I try to imagine what I must look like disguised as a skeleton. Sometimes I hear cries of horror or waves of laughter, and I can faintly make out some haggard faces suspended at the edge of the stage like Chinese lanterns. Seated upon me, Mlle Rosine bobs up and down more and more furiously, and I feel as if I were going to explode any minute. To the public, I may look like a repugnant skeleton, but to her I'm just a defenseless, enamored schoolboy with whom she amuses herself by bringing him thrice in a row to the heights of passion.

Thus it was that I became a carnival-actor during my spare time. After school, the next day and the days that followed, I rushed to the Magic Palace and took up my functions. First of all on the outside platform, where Gugusse the Clown used me as a dummy, bombarding my open mouth with a steady stream of Ping-Pong balls, which I appeared to swallow, much to the amusement of the astonished crowd. Next I found myself seated in the middle of the trick stage, ready to submit to Mlle Rosine's posterior manipulations.

This daily occupation was carefully concealed from my classmates and friends; not to mention my family. As a precaution I rigged myself out in a false moustache, a gift from Gugusse, which he himself pasted under my nose.

Every evening I spent an hour or two with Rosine and Gugusse; between acts, I was admitted to the intimacy of their nomadic house, their *roulotte*. They had taken a fancy to me because I represented a world as impenetrable to them as theirs to me. They asked me all kinds of questions, and heard my answers without understanding them very well. They had always lived on the road and the thought of big cities like Paris, with these thousands and millions of people immured in these huge stone and concrete apartment houses, masters and servants all mixed up together, struck them as unreal. Their own universe was their caravan, swaying along from place to place on county and country roads, harnessed to a wheezing tractor. "What can you do, that's the way of the Gypsies, always will be," wisely concluded Gugusse; whose real name was Bébert, by the way.

His was an inquiring, resourceful mind. He made me admire his installation of mirrors, cunningly adapted from a book on popular science, and which had become his breadwinner. Bébert also loved to show off his wife, to make of her a Venus offered to the eyes of other men, and she found thereby the means to satisfy the appetites of her voluptuous nature and yet to remain absolutely faithful, in a technical sense, to her husband. At each performance, she chose a man to her liking, a soldier, stevedore, or fireman, and made love to him furiously, in her own special way. It was a rare and sublime honor for me to be chosen by her as an everyday partner, and I was fully conscious of it; after a few days I was considered as one of the family, and the other carnival people began to accept me as a permanent fixture of Bébert's entourage, a freak like that other character on the easy chair. Facing the bed there lolled a dislocated skeleton topped with the black strawhat of a fandango dancer. Bébert was tinkering with its metacarpus, a Gauloise hanging from his lip, and a forelock over his eye, while Rosine, always in black tights under her kimono, sat at her dressing table with her liter of red wine close at hand, playing solitaire. Sometimes, when she would suddenly remember my existence, she would gently tease me. My sexual naïveté seemed almost to move her, and the thought of it deliciously tickled her avid derrière.

Rosine was learning how to tell fortunes, thus preparing for the future; one day the liters of red wine would take their toll, and she would then become a fortune-teller and Bébert a fakir. . . . He would do other tricks with his army of skeletons; he thought about it often, smoking Gauloises, and this perspective filled him with a somber enthusiasm. Bébert was a Cagliostro, a manipulator, and his dexterity was such that after three or four days, I still couldn't figure out by what boomerang effect the Celluloid balls I was supposed to be swallowing came back to his hand. The balls flew away dancingly from Bébert's fingers, forming an aerial bridge that seemed to end in the depths of my mouth—and then the maneuver was reversed, and the flock of balls went flying out of my nose to return to Bébert's hands. The effect on the public was hypnotic.

We were going through that routine, one night, when, in the back rows of the crowd pressing at our feet, I spot a tall familiar silhouette standing dark and forbidding like the statue of the Commander. My reflex is to bite on my Ping-Pong ball as it sails by. *It's my father!* Bébert loses control of the other balls in flight—panicked trajectories briefly streak across the stage, rebound in disorder. The crowd is shaken with a storm of laughter, they all think this is part of the act.

"Find yourself someone else, Bébert, I'm taking off," I told him hurriedly. "Here, take back your moustache."

Gregor's father had left Neuilly to settle permanently in his dacha at Le Vésinet. He had allocated a budget for his son that enabled Gregor to live on his own and pursue his studies or whatever else he might want to pursue. . . . Gregor had

rented a room in an anachronistic boardinghouse run by a
Viennese couple and frequented by a cosmopolitan clientele
of students, racketeers, and uprooted people of all kinds, a
Threepenny Opera bizarrely out of place in Neuilly.

I envied Gregor his independence, and the freedom it gave
to his existence. He no longer set foot in school; he read,
listened to music, played chess, and went after gross women;
sometimes he also gave himself up to orgies of *délectation
morose* so extreme that he had to spend the following
week in bed, in the dark. His cracked mirrors were draped
with black crepe because the sight of his own image gave him
funereal ideas. There were other times when he wasn't in one
of those macabre moods and then the spirit of enterprise returned to him, at the same time as did his peerless voracity.
He would dress carefully for the evening, black tie and all,
and would head toward some hospitable home.

His favorite target was the receptions given by aristocratic
Georgian and Russian émigrés, where the buffets were often
of great opulence. To pilfer these buffets wasn't an easy sport
because one had to deal with a numerous and organized competition; you had to get there early.

He would describe to me the way the old Cossacks posi-
tioned themselves ahead of time. They took up their posts
behind the drapes, faithful to the classic strategy of General
Denikin, and as soon as the way was clear, they all converged
together on the pyramids of zakuski, the displays of pastries,
mountains of pirojkis, platters of salmon, sturgeon, pelmenys.
Not to mention the caviar and the carafes of vodka: All
that disappeared before the rest. Wasn't this the very same
scorched-earth strategy that cost Napoleon his victory in Russia? When the Cossacks withdrew, with their pockets bulging
and their moustaches edged with sauce, their Imperial High-
nesses arrived in turn. Too late! Those elegant people would
only find mutilated blinis and disemboweled coulibiacs on the
battlefield.

At Gregor's urging, I had one of my father's old tuxedoes
altered to my frail size so that I might accompany him on
certain of his expeditions. The goal of our first outing was a
reception given by the Princess Romanoff, a former ballerina,
to announce the opening of a dancing school in Auteuil. Gregor told me to expect a display of food worthy of czarist extravagance, but, to his dismay, there wasn't even a buffet. A

terrible blow. Mastering his discontent, Gregor reacted with characteristic generosity.

"Come on," he said, "I'll take you out to dinner in a gorgeous place."

We soon found ourselves back in the streets of Auteuil. Gregor hailed a cab and said to the driver, who happened to be Russian himself:

"To Pigalle, Excellency! With all due respect."

Gregor is completely insane. A taxi! Well, it's his nature, there's nothing that can be done about it. I give myself up to this life of wealth. I sit back in comfort, pat the starch of my shirtfront, which is adorned with a false pearl of the finest water, and looking out at the electric festival of the Champs-Elysées, I strike a pose somewhere between roué and blasé. For my sole benefit, of course, as Gregor is glaring fiercely at the costumed crowd showing off on the broad sidewalks, the rich and the idle, the crooks and the actors, the paid women and their bankers. Quite a display!

Here's Montmartre, place Pigalle, place Blanche. The pickpockets steal past, slithering through the crowd, the whores squawk and yell lustily back and forth from one street corner to the other. Thousands of cars seem permanently immobilized, honking aimlessly at one another, with torrents of humanity streaming through the congealed traffic, in search of pleasure. We disembark from our permanently stalled taxicab and find ourselves carried along by the flow of gesticulating, sweating, and stinking bodies of pleasure-seekers until, in a steep street, Gregor calls me to stop. We're in front of an establishment whose discreet sign mysteriously says in electric-blue letters: SHEHERAZADE. A doorman in full uniform of the Imperial Guard opens the door for us as if we were famous millionaires, bowing deep, and we are greeted by the mellow strains of Gypsy music, amorous violins with a xylophone background.

Gregor crosses the threshold without hesitation and I fall into step, all the while trying to hold him back: "Gregor, don't go in, you blockhead, this is an expensive place . . ." A superb monocled aristocrat presents himself to us, bows his head respectfully, and murmurs: "A table for two, messieurs? This way, please."

The room is only half full, thanks to which we are given a central table that could have accommodated, in former times, the entire imperial family. A maître d'hôtel hands us two gigantic volumes bound in red leather and stamped in gold, telling us in a confidential tone, "You're lucky to arrive just in time for the floor show! At your service, messieurs! I'll be right back to take your order."

I look at Gregor. He is completely relaxed, peering right and left at the women in the room.

"Listen, Gregor, this is ridiculous! I've only got three francs!"

"So? Me, I've got twenty-two!"

Trying as best I can to keep a straight face, I half-open up the wine list, just enough to peek at the prices. Champagne at two hundred francs a bottle! I break into a cold sweat. I try to attract Gregor's attention, but he's only listening to the singer, carried away with delight. In the midst of this catastrophe, all this half-wit can think of is to fall in love! Each time the flunky approaches the table, he chases him away like an importune fly. Eventually, I get used to the routine. Next, there's a dizzying act of Kirghiz dances; and then more songs. Adding to my agony, I become aware of a rustling in the darkness as each of the two tables on either side of ours is being equipped with a pair of very pretty creatures. The subdued lighting, the source of which is hidden in the tables themselves, isolates them individually as in a corolla of shadows. Queens of the Night, casting sidelong glances at us.

The floor show ends in splendor, the lights come back and so does the maître d'hôtel, order book in hand, still obsequious but this time quite firm.

"Very well, gentlemen, which champagne will it be? I can recommend to you our *Cuvée Royale de* . . ."

"For me, maître, make it a lemonade," says Gregor, cutting him off with a gesture. "And for my comrade here, the same. So that will be two lemonades. As for the floor show, bravo! *Really* very good!"

"Excuse me, sir, but we don't serve lemonade."

The man with the monocle comes up to the table; three or four other flunkies are already hovering around. It's going to be terrible!

"In any case," adds the maître d'hôtel, "even if we *did* serve lemonade, the price would be the same."

The man with the monocle gives us a withering look.

"May I ask you, gentlemen, ahem, *who might you be?*"

"Oh," replies Gregor with a faint smile, "we are the schoolboys of the night, that's what we are. Again, congratulations for the show, but you really ought to post the prices outside. Really."

He beckons to me, and we get up in unison, first walking and soon after running toward the door, convulsed with panic and laughter.

"Catch those little bastards!" blusters the man with the monocle.

Our retreat is not very courteous and the four ladies of the night seem rather shaken by this scene: *"Well, how about that!"* each one declares in turn to the three others.

A bloodthirsty pack is at our heels and we're just about to be caught as we reach the front door when, miraculously, it opens from the outside and a grand duke staggers in. The pursuing team arrives just in time to fling themselves at his feet in abject fashion—the prospect of a ripe client makes them forget our existence—we slip away behind the back of this customer who's so much richer than we, and sprint toward freedom through the crowds like true maniacs, briefly pursued down rue Blanche, but only by the lilting melody of the Gypsies. In the far distance I hear the door of the cabaret slam shut, and we slow down. Gregor slaps me on the back repeatedly, hysterical with laughter.

"Ah, my duke, my prince, so we've shown you a good time, eh? What about that floor show?"

"You're totally insane, Gregor."

"Not at all! These nightclubs are horribly expensive, one must make them understand, see. It's doing them a favor, I think, really. And now, where do you want to go next?"

"What?"

"You've got a pretty large choice," he said complacently. "I've made a list of all the nightclubs in Paris that I'd like to visit, and there are one hundred and seventy-five. Not quite, perhaps, and there are only thirty-nine that really tempt me. And so at the rate of two a night every other night, a modest average, what, I'd need about six months to do them all. Yes, old bean, and all that without spending a kopek, ha ha."

"You're completely, totally—"

"Not at all. Here, have a look at my list. I've even got the phone numbers to reserve my table! Come on, schoolboy of the night, let's go have a look at Maxim's before the night wears off."

8

Krishnamurti turns down a god job.—The heavenly host in full array.—Vivian du Mas, the Red Magus.—Enters the beloved one: but why two of them?—Marcel Proust and frenchitude.—Anarchy and the fine art of killing kings.—The turn of the tide: Marx ousts Bakunin.

Krishnamurti was still considered schismatic by the old guard of the Theosophical Society, and he could not be officially invited to lecture at the Paris branch; but since the society owned the adjoining theater, the Salle Adyar, and often rented it to outsiders, an easy compromise was always within reach. I went to one of those famous lectures once, and I looked for my friends Edouard and Claude in the busy lobby.

The crowd around us represents mostly the avant-garde, progressive element among theosophists, as well as other types of occultists. There is, of course, a substantial contingent of elderly ladies decked out in mystic jewelry, their lips fixed in a smile of cosmic benevolence; but I can also see many young faces, for once, and there is a general feeling of expectancy, a certain exhilaration in the look of people, in their exchanges, which is unusual.

A commotion at the door signals the arrival of a large group of people, and the throng parts to give them passage. It is hard to believe, it is hard to describe the impact made by the arriving cohort! Most of them are dressed in long red capes, some with riding boots. Who are they: God's own storm troopers? Knights Templars reborn? In their midst are two rather remarkable personages. One is a man with Luciferian features, an eagle's profile, and silver hair worn in a sleek helmet; the other, a handsome, austere-looking woman, has the high forehead of inspiration. They stand out among their companions, some of whom are quite young, as the leaders of their community; there is a fervor, a militancy in that group that seems to make the conventional theosophists rather uneasy; and the presence of some very pretty faces among them, girls in particular, lends a slightly heretical air to the entire group. Whispered remarks are exchanged all around, and while surrounding people steal covert glances at the new arrivals, they stand well clear of them.

As we filter into the auditorium and take our seats, the group keeps together in the front of the audience, as if they had a special rapport with the speaker. Throughout the lecture and the question-and-answer period that follows, they remain perfectly quiet and decorous. Their enigmatic presence makes a disturbing contrast with the human environment; they nearly seem to sit in judgment of Krishnamurti's efforts to liberate his audience. Don't depend on outside help, he tells his public, but only on your own. But all the questions from that same public repeat the same eternal interrogation: Where is the Master? Aren't *you* the Master? No, *you* are your own master, he repeats over and over; don't look outside, search inside. Learn to meditate. Not to pray for favors, as so many do, but to meditate on your own essence, and open yourselves to the ever-present message inherent to your very existence. Create silence in yourselves if you want to reach wisdom, there's no other way. But—the old ladies questioned once again—"What about Jesus, the Buddha, don't we depend on the teachings of the Masters?" "No, *you* are your own master"—and so it went, on and on. Krishnamurti with his handsome dark face and all-knowing gaze appeared to his audience as the spitting image of a master, albeit a young and modern one; and there was, therefore, something wrong, or at least difficult to accept, in his lifelong campaign against comfortable religiosity, against the taste for acquiring psychic powers, and above all, against the fawning subservience to the myth of the Masters.

We spent the rest of the day, Edouard, Claude, and I, discussing the lecture and the strange people in the red cloaks. The brothers had approached them on one or two occasions; Edouard in particular was quite interested in them. The man with the silver hair was Vivian du Mas, he told me, and he had an obscure and adventurous past. There were episodes in Egypt, when his association with a certain Moslem secret society had caused him to be attacked and left for dead by some unknown assailants, presumably paid by the British Intelligence Service. . . . There had been various esoteric adventures after that, and the meeting with Jeanne Canudo, the woman with the noble forehead; she was the widow of an Italian writer, who had been a close friend of D'Annunzio. Together they had founded a community of young people at Le Vésinet, which had eventually been closed down after some parents had complained. Also a movement called the European Pioneers. Yes, European unity was one of the political goals they were working for, in close association with the best-known leaders of the federalist movement, German author Hermann von Keyserling especially, and Count Coudenhove-Kalergi, a diplomat of Austrian and Japanese parentage. Vivian's people apparently considered themselves as the heirs to great esoteric figures such as the Count of Saint-Germain, or Saint-Yves d'Alveydre. . . .

As Edouard filled in all those details, I became increasingly determined to find out more on my own. The group, he said, rented a suite of offices in the Sociétés Savantes building in the Latin Quarter, which served as center for their political activities, and a large apartment on boulevard Saint-Germain, overlooking the gardens of Cluny, where Vivian lived and taught, pretty much as an Indian swami in his ashram. Yes, Edouard said, he thought he could take me there with Claude, and obtain an interview for us with Vivian; or at the very least, a chance to hear him speak during one of the semipublic gatherings they held on Sundays.

Later that night, as I went to sleep, my brain kept conjuring up images of that exceptional, unheard-of collection of people as I had seen them earlier, and it became increasingly clear, as my memory merged with my dreams, that here was what I had been looking for since I was able to think. Here was, I knew it, an entrance to the path. . . . As to Krishnamurti's lesson, which had impressed me so strongly when I heard it, it had already lost much of its former meaningfulness, its power of persuasion. . . . I was perhaps even trying to forget it.

It's in a high state of anticipation and nervousness that I climb the stairs to Vivian's ashram, the following Sunday. Their carpeting, I dimly note, is threadbare, and the brutal smell of leek soup that reigned supreme in the lower levels is being gradually replaced by the penetrating fumes of incense, as we reach the fifth floor. The door is opened by a young woman in a blue uniform-type two-piece suit, who welcomes us pleasantly and ushers us through a door concealed by a heavy drape, into the room where the meeting is about to start. A dozen people, some of them in street clothes and others in red robes, are seated around that man Vivian, the silver-haired guru, who's himself sitting cross-legged at one end of a couch. Jeanne Canudo, dressed in a blue suit with silver buttons and a military belt, occupies the other end, a silent figure. Her gaze, fixed in midspace, gives a feeling of powerful inner concentration, on thoughts she does not care to share with us.

Costume seems important here, it plays an obvious role in the rites of communication. The guru is dressed in white Indian pajamas and a fiery tunic, very smart. He is shorter than I thought at first, but trim and wiry; I also notice that his hands are carefully manicured. He greets us with a smile and a few words of welcome that seem addressed to each one of us individually. His voice is warm, unaffected, and youthful; although he appears to be in his early fifties, he moves and speaks with the energy of a far younger man. His finely drawn features could have been painted by El Greco; the romantic, emaciated intensity of his profile is very Spanish. The eyes are light-brown, deep-set, and if he looks steadily into yours for only one second, you have no choice left but to obey.

In spite of all my efforts, I cannot concentrate on what he is saying, being caught in a dreamy state out of which I cannot shake myself. His face is turned toward the window, from which you have a plunging perspective of the wide boulevard, foreshortened into a trapeze mirror and reflecting the glare of the sun with blinding force. The incense contributes heavily to my stupor. Although I can no longer think, my mind perceives this experience on an altogether different level. There is a power at work here, but does it emanate from Vivian alone?

In a corner, two young girls are sitting next to each other like intimate friends, the youngest one a very vivid redhead, quite pretty, who I was told is Madame Canudo's daughter, Rolande. And then the curly brunette with the charming face and large thoughtful eyes must be her friend Laurette; Edouard had described both of them with undisguised enthusiasm. There is a tenderness between those two, a true intimacy that I find deliciously attractive. So these are the two vestals, the two virgin guardians of the temple.

After the session in Vivian's room, Rolande invites us, the Delamares and myself, to her own quarters to meet a few of the younger people. Who are they? A very handsome boy known as Oleg Karma; an older one with thick glasses who's called G.J.; the Billard brothers, who are identical twins with an identical lisp; and three or four others, which soon gives to the gathering the air of an authentic party. I am very much taken by the one called Laurette; she's eighteen—two years older than I—and it is with surprise that I learn Rolande's age: she's fourteen! They are both dressed in girlish fashion now, and I find them, well ravishing. Exciting! Lovely. Absolutely adorable! In fact no adjectives would qualify. I wonder if you can become friends with one, and not at the same time with the other? Rolande has the animal charm of the very young combined with the full maturity of womanhood. She is half Florentine, which must account for the early blooming, as well as for the delicate features and the voluptuous, slender-waisted Italian body. As compared to the girls of her age I've known in Neuilly, she seems mature, full-grown, and yet she's playful and wild as a newborn kitten. . . . I am fast falling in love. . . . But instead of talking to her I am now sitting alone with Laurette, looking at her lovely mouth speaking so wisely. Her charm is more demure, and there is music in her voice, and something very tender about the way she smiles at you.

In only a few minutes, I learn much from her about the group, and about its duality of interests. Vivian appears as a spiritualist utopian, who after many adventures and changes has crystallized his life's experience into an all-encompassing system. This provides both for the spiritual rebirth of mankind and for the creation of a universal structure of society, a redefinition of profession and social function in line with certain traditional teachings. It all sounds pretty spiffy! But I am certainly not laughing at her words. On the contrary, I am basking in the discovery of this new reality, finding in what she tells me many answers to old questions, and the confrontation of many intuitions. She tells me a bit about what Jeanne Canudo has undertaken. Kryia, as they call her, runs a number of activities of a directly political, and even commercial, nature from her own headquarters at the Sociétés Savantes. They complement Vivian's own creative drive, which is essentially of an intellectual and spiritual nature. He seems to consider that pure thought—meaning spiritual action exerted on the world by the directed will of a group of meditators—is the best instrument for the transformation of society, a perspective he describes as an absolute certainty.

Well, this certainly explains the somewhat demented dedication of my new friends. And yet their fanaticism does not bother me in the least, since it appears as a quality of youth, as an expression of enthusiasm and true generosity. Yes, this Laurette for instance, isn't she the very essence of goodness?

Coming down the same staircase a few hours later with my two companions, I come to grips with the old reality again. We follow the railings of the Cluny gardens, now enveloped in a haze of blue twilight; we run after a Neuilly-bound bus along the Saint-Michel quays and hurl ourselves onto the back platform, alighting in close succession like a flock of sparrows on a telephone wire. These old happy-go-lucky Paris buses are truly terrific, huge yellow-and-green tin boxes catapulted into the traffic by their satanical drivers. If you need some exercise, you can get plenty of that first by running after the bus, which seldom stops where it's supposed to; and, second, by standing on this rear platform and just trying to stay on it. In spite of the shaky conditions, I launch into an excited speech, explaining to the two brothers that I think that—well, *I've seen the light!* I've found the path, or at least the edges of the sacred forest—I've found! I've found! Thanks to them.

Claude, struggling to keep his balance, stares at me with concern. "Come on, old man," he says, "you mustn't take all that too seriously."

Edouard, holding himself as best he can to the rail, adds his own comment:

"Yes, Claude is right, you know. Vivian and his gang are interesting, but we took you along to show you one of the curiosities of modern life, not to corrupt your mind . . ."

The bus is stopping for an unforeseen traffic light with such wanton brutality that we are thrown together like billiard balls.

"Ouch!" Edouard complains. "Listen, the best part of this outfit, it's the girls. You know, the two pretty ones? Claude and I wanted you to have a look at Rolande in particular, and tell us what you think of her tits. Nice, eh? *Ooops—*"

I'm so indignant I could kick him real hard, but just at that moment he nearly sails overboard and I have to drag him back inside instead. Claude laughing his stupid head off—letting me save his brother's life without as much as lifting a finger.

"Which one of the two d'you like best?" he asks, still laughing.

As I look at him in anger and confusion, he adds: "You had better know this: Edouard has a crush on Laurette."

"Oh, come on now," Edouard counters, "it's true she's sexy with her innocent ways, but who's going to waste time on such a lost cause?"

The bus bounces on a pothole so hard that it looks like the end—but no, we have survived once more. My brain is in a muddle. . . . I thought they were better friends than that! I cannot understand why they are putting down something as serious, as valuable.

"We're being unfair," Edouard says. "Vivian is a terrific fellow, but to my own thinking, he's a psychic adventurer, not to be trusted. He holds his people together by forbidding them sex. He recruits mostly young, dedicated people as disciples, and they must take a vow of chastity: That's bound to make them pretty crazy, of course, and also to help him keep control of them. It's just like the Catholic system, you know—*My dear child, confess your sins, did you have unclean thoughts last week?*"

"Listen, Edouard," I say at last. "You're not fit to shine those people's boots . . . I mean . . . They are sincere, and there's nothing wrong about being *dedicated*, is there? You say those things about the girls only because of your big nose. You destroy what you can't get."

"Bhahh," Edouard spits at me. "Women know what a nose like this actually *means*. You're a complete dodo."

"So long, then, you two creeps," I shout at them, jumping off the platform as the bus slows down a bit to negotiate a turn. Running all the way to the Bois de Boulogne, the vast reservoir of green life that borders Neuilly, I sing to myself—*I've found! I've found!*

I walk excitedly along the deserted paths in the dusk, running deep into the woods between trees trembling with fresh spring foliage. My flowering head dances along with the budding branches, I am drunk with the earthy scents, with a happiness so intense that I feel tears running down my cheeks. I sit down at the edge of the lake, and a family of ducks converges toward me, eloquently quacking their welcome. I know they only expect breadcrumbs, and yet there is something so friendly about this ugly concert. . . .

My family is already having dessert by the time I take my place at the table. I had nearly forgotten their existence—pangs of hunger just reminded me of this table, and of the people sitting around it.

"There you are at last," my mother exclaims. *"Le poète maudit* has found his way back to his humble home. So, did you have a good time with your friends?"

How can I answer that? I do my best to patch up the incident, and I forage ravenously into the vegetarian delicacies prepared for me by my mother. She is such a good cook! The problem of feeding both of us—my father who is strictly carnivorous and myself who's the exact opposite—is one she always manages to solve in her own imaginative, exquisite manner. Will I ever find a way to explain to her what's happening to me? What would she think of Vivian? Of Rolande? At the thought of the pretty redhead, I blush profusely, up to the roots of my hair. Dammit! They're all peering at me with interest. Especially the two little ones, who always guess me out when I have a secret I want to hide.

Should I add that, by that time, I had made another overwhelming discovery, but of quite a different nature: I had started reading Marcel Proust, and as a result, a part of me was in the process of becoming quite Proustian. It had on my adolescent mind and sensibilities a wonderfully revealing effect.

For one thing it gave me the in-depth information I needed to understand the country where I was born, France. My father once said, in his broken-down pidgin French—"Just as Shakespeare is English, just as mothers and apple pies are American, Marcel Proust is frenchitude." Wow!

What about *frenchitude*, then?

Surely, I had seen displays of that quality in Rabelais, Montaigne, Racine, and Molière, some of the authors promoted by our educators, but they all gave us a rather heroic vision of it—even Rabelais and Molière—whereas Marcel Proust had only antiheroes to offer. Even his great artist types, Elstir, Vinteuil, Bergotte, owed their inspiration to a somewhat flawed or deviant vision of life. The great nobility of Palamède de Charlus is easily turned to ridicule by his lover's obscene talk. At the end of the cycle we see the concierge Jupien opening an all-male bordello to fulfill the secret needs of the good baron. One of the most ancient houses of the French aristocracy ends up giving birth to a house of prostitution. The entire horizon of French culture is invaded by adventurers, impersonators, and snobs, Morel, Bloch, the Verdurins—each one of them done to perfection!—while the chauffeurs, coachmen, cooks, and lackeys spend their time corrupting their masters. The young Duke of Chartres and his likes always fall prey to well-endowed butlers; a system of upward mobility is thus described thanks to which vulgarity and treachery always win, quite conspicuously with the promotion into the aristocracy of Odette Swan and Madame Verdurin; less visibly but most massively in the case of all those domestics who make it the goal of their lives to step into their masters' patent leather boots, and take over their dusty heirlooms.

This new France, emerging from two centuries of revolutions and counterrevolutions, is extraordinarily ratty, servile, and heartless; it is as vain as it is despicable, blind, frivolous. And we see that sordid material being used to create the most intensely poetic saga of human degradation ever conceived. Isn't that modern? Isn't that truly Jewish? The God of Israel was brutal and artless in blasting His people; Proust did a more effective job describing French society as carefully as he did.

Here's a great restless, fibrillating brain, encased in its very own cork-lined chamber, nourished by sickness; the Marcel Proust entity busily proliferates. It creates an enormous global narrative that is summed up by one single page, containing one long paragraph, itself reducible to only one sentence creating an image that becomes an idea, fragmented, detailed, disarticulated and, finally, recomposed in the form of a labyrinth whose entrance and exit are made somehow to coincide, canceling each other out, while at the same time they leave you the full benefit of this journey within four walls: the conquest of a cell, of a universal microcosm. For sure it's a cosmic job, as a perfect work of art should be; and thus nothing is sacred but the job itself. Our loves are treated like whale sperm, to be turned into fancy jewelry. Our vices are the fumes of human incense returning to the sun of creation.

All this to convince you that I take my Proust seriously! I read and read, forgetting sleep, meals, friends; not to speak of studies. And then I reread! All this started with *A l'Ombre des*

Jeunes Filles en Fleurs, of course, and my delighted discovery of a frieze of young girls against the background of the sea, wild horses of desire on a Normandy beach. Then I back-tracked and came up to the point where appears a little girl with reddish head and a golden skin, sparkling and rosy. Gilberte! When a little later I met Rolande, whose hair was not reddish but red, and whose skin was very white—besides which she was also twice Gilberte's age—I think I fell in love with her because I identified her so completely with Gilberte. I could only picture Gilberte's features as those of a war-rior-angel, which is the way I saw Rolande herself. When the two children lock into a playful erotic wrestling match under the very eyes of their assorted nurses and grannies, the identification became disturbingly evocative. I reread that particular scene many times, often bringing it to the same conclusion.

"Just read history, it's not so ancient," says Stepan. "Vera Zasulich was a little housewife like Ouliana when she shot at the chief of police in Saint Petersburg in 1877. She missed, but our Ouliana here, she wouldn't miss! Not even with a frying pan. . . . A few months later, one after another, there were two assassination attempts made against the Kaiser, that of Nobiling and that of Herder. Two solid men, real anar-chists. . . . And then Moncasi, a Spanish comrade, tried to shoot King Alfonso with a pistol, but he also missed. In Italy, an anarchist cook went after the king with his kitchen knife— that was a bit silly, of course. But meanwhile, back in Russia, it's a hecatomb! Within a few days, General Mezentsoff, ad-viser to the czar, gets shot right on a Saint Petersburg street; next, it's the head of the Kiev police, then the governor of Kharkof, and a few spies here and there. Everywhere. Finally, in 1879, Solovioff fires on the czar himself. He misses him. He empties his revolver on the emperor who zigzags away, miraculously escaping. But Alexander's a marked man, now; he lives in terror, he shoots at shadows, at his own aides, and he goes berserk at the slightest noise. . . . And in March of 1881, at the very moment he has finally decided to abolish serfdom, the anarchists of Saint Petersburg who fought so hard to obtain that result but who know nothing of Alexan-der's decision, ambush him as he returns from a parade. Rysa-koff flings a bomb under his armored carriage; the explosion kills all of his escort of Circassian cavalrymen, but Alexander isn't even injured. Rysakoff is arrested and the czar extricates himself from his damaged carriage in order to talk to him, to try to understand what this man believes, to find out what people have against him. At this moment, Grinevtsky, another comrade, approaches, takes a bomb from under his coat, and blows himself up with the czar. Everyone flees. . . . The emperor is mangled, mortally wounded, alone among the bodies of men and horses, his blood spreading on the snow. The death rattle in his throat is all that remains of his life. A third anarchist, Emelianoff, comes up with a bomb wrapped in a newspaper. But quite obviously, there's no need for that; the czar is dying, and his immediate reflex is not to flee but to call for help. He finds a group of cadets who were keeping their distance, brings them to the scene, and helps them to place the czar on a stretcher, still holding his bomb under his arm. . . . That's the Russians for you!"

"Ah, you're all very young," growls Gregor, who is hardly older. "Stepan, pass me the bottle instead of playing with it."

Kyrill and Stepan, two tall blond fellows, and Ouliana, a curly-haired, round-cheeked, spirited person, were true-blue anarchists, the children of Russian revolutionaries who had all been purged and killed under Stalin. They were kindergarten friends of Gregor's who had finally consented to organize this outing in the woods of Fontainebleau where we were spending the weekend camping under the natural shelter of the huge rocks. A campfire was burning high and clear in the night.

"And the Commune?" I ask. "That's really something, the Commune. The Russians don't have a monopoly on it, do they?"

"Everyone knows that the Commune was a put-up job," says Ouliana. "It was the result of a deliberate strategy by the French reactionaries. When the Communards lost, they were liquidated—thirty thousand of them, at least, including the women and children. An ideological genocide, and a fine page of history! France has missed all her revolutions and the Left is exhausted from its setbacks. As for Russia, our holy mother, just like France she betrayed her own revolution, her own children."

"Do you think the Marxist revolution in Russia could have turned out differently?" I asked.

"Of course!" Kyrill exclaimed. "There was a revolutionary tradition in Russia before Marxism was invented, and writers such as Turgenev and Tolstoy have left us a clear image of it. The nihilists were not out to destroy society, but on the contrary, to improve it, to educate the masses, and give them a chance to become individuals. The idea was that you can't improve society by force of law, through politics and state control, but only by helping people to be free agents, intellectually and socially. Many young students went to live with the peasants and the laborers to educate them; what use would it be to give freedom to the serfs if they were unable to cope with it? However, now we have Stalin."

"And so where did it go wrong?" I asked.

"Well, frankly," Kyrill answered after a little while, "there are two different sorts of explanations I can give you. First of all, Marxism, which is not at all Russian in essence, represented, at the time, the thinking of the German Left, and particularly Marx's ideas on scientific socialism. And of course, scientific socialism can only mean state socialism; that's a centralist ideology that was the exact opposite of what the Russian nihilists and the other revolutionaries were aiming at. Within the great labor movement at the end of the last century, especially the International Workingmen's Union, two tendencies were confronted, two completely opposite ideologies. On one side Marx and Engels, representing the Anglo-German bloc; and on the other side Bakunin, who represented the libertarian movements of Russia, the workers' unions of France and Italy, the Jura federation, the Spanish anarchists. . . . Well, Bakunin was eliminated, and all his followers in Russia and the Latin countries were reduced to silence. The take-over of Marxist ideology is the great disaster of modern times—"

"When do we eat?" Gregor asked.

"Shut up, Gregor," Stepan said. "The stew isn't ready yet, and we still have to hear about the Teutonic knights."

"Listen, Gregor, I'm talking to your friend here," Kyrill protested. "He asked me what we anarchists are good for in this day and age, and I'm giving him my own answer. So, go suck your thumb if you're hungry, I want to finish."

"Please, go ahead, Kyrill," I said. "What's that about the Teutonic knights?"

"Well, you know that the Roman church backed the Teutonic order at the end of the Middle Ages, and inspired the knights to conquer Russia and thus extend its own domination to the Slavs. Since then, the power struggle between Prussia and Russia has been constant. In fact it was the excuse for the rise of nationalism on both sides, and for the creation of the Russian Empire as well as of the German Reich. Well, my idea is really quite simple: I see the introduction of Marxism in Russia as a German victory. The Germans had failed to conquer Russia by the force of arms, and so they did something much smarter: They undermined the Russian Revolution, they used Marxism to corrupt and reverse its spirit. In other words, I see two parallel confrontations. One is a historical contest between Slavs and Germans. The other is an ideological one between freedom and organization, man and society. On the one side, you have the centralized, oppressive bureaucracy of the Marxist state; on the other, Bakunin's ideal of individual liberation, which is at the root of all anarchist thinking."

"I see your point," I said. "But it's a pretty gloomy picture. The bad guys always win."

"Well," Kyrill sighed, "of course there's something to that! That's the second point I wanted to make. *Our* kind of revolution is different, and it's not the easiest path. If you study the dynamics of revolutions, you will always find that they start with a generous, irresistible drive toward freedom. A few individuals take the lead; and that's where the trouble starts. Those leaders cannot resist playing politics. They've been underdogs for so long, and this new power they are now wielding goes to their heads, and they decide that they need more; their ego needs the nourishment—"

"Speaking of nourishment," Gregor whimpered; but he was not allowed to continue, as Ouliana, who was about half his size, kicked him in the derrière so hard that he nearly fell into the fire.

"On the other hand, just like Gregor," Kyrill resumed, "the people love their punishment. *We* are the ones who want to make them free and independent—it's not *their* own idea! In fact, they have *no* ideas, and they are allergic to any cerebral activity whatsoever. They are always ready to give up, to vote for the man who's sure to get them into the worst possible trouble. That's why democracy will remain an empty word— as long as democracy doesn't *teach* people how to be free, how to be themselves. . . . And who is ever going to give them that kind of knowledge? Not the political parties, not the state, not the press, not the state-subsidized educators! They can only learn to be free by hearing about other people who are free, free in the true sense of the word. And, in my opinion, this is the role of the anarchists. We are not a party, we are first of all individuals. And thus the best type of revolutionary action, for us, is the exemplary action that will shake people out of their lethargy, like blowing up a czar. Alexander's body lying in the snow, that was a forceful message to the Russian serfs, no? Here lies the tyrant, the master of your lives, and in spite of all his armies and his police, he was killed like a dog, by two young men."

"And now you have Stalin, instead," I reminded him.

"Yes, of course," Kyrill agreed. "But that's just what I was saying before. Stalin was the gift of Marxism, German-style, to Russia. . . . Of course the enemy won. It is winning everywhere. You have only to see the situation of the world today, dictators, prison camps, the armaments race, everything. Bakunin was defeated by Marx, and this is the result—"

"However," Stepan cut in, "the new generation will change all this. And meanwhile, dinner is served. Here, Gregor, hand me your plate, we're about to feed you again, although I'm sure I don't know why."

9

Cinderella and the Ogre.—I set my school on fire.
—I am being psychoanalyzed by Charles Laughton.
—Poor little lamb . . . so lovely, and nothing to drink!
—Vivian peers down into the night.—Amitié amoureuse.
—A mystical voyage through Brittany.—The manor
of the alchemist.—Romance in fairyland.
—Laurette and the higher path.

My mother had succeeded in making our ground-floor apartment on the rue Bertaux-Dumas, if not a palace, at least a perfectly habitable place, which certainly didn't at all reflect the level of penury we had reached. Thanks to her we lived indeed better than the solid bourgeois who surrounded us.

She had done everything herself. She had torn off the old wallpaper and done it over freshly, painted, cleaned, decorated, made the drapes, arranged the motley furniture with intelligence and style, performing in an absolutely professional manner the work of fifteen different specialists. Whistling all the while. Nothing could stop this little bulldozer housewife; she had a marvelously clear and organized mind, an iron will, and was fastidious in her honesty. But she was not a woman of the world, and that saddened my father, who was, in every other respect, always so proud of her. He did his best to coach her, to reassure her, but the demands of worldly life paralyzed her with anxiety. . . . One day, when they were still newlyweds, Jack had introduced her to one of his old war buddies, a gigantic lord of great elegance who she thought looked like an ogre. Tongue-tied, terror-striken, she let the grinning giant seize her hand while she felt, as in a nightmare, an elastic snap along her waist; and everyone had seen the little bloomers slide down to the floor. Never was she able to forget the aristocrat's petrified expression as he stared through his monocle at the little heap of white silk covering her feet. She still blushed when telling this story, which harked back to the romantic epoch of Finette and Madapolam.

No, my father's wife was not a woman of the world; and yet, without her, the world would have ceased to turn. Thanks to her, the four children were always nattily dressed, and he himself was able to sustain his reputation of unimpeachable elegance; thanks to his Cinderella, he was able to cut a fine figure in the company of duchesses. She sewed, hammered, scoured, brushed, cooked, washed, darned, ironed, shopped, kept accounts, directed her children's studies, made them repeat their lessons, organized games, brushed and combed, read, knitted, framed paintings, cut hair, fixed the plumbing, the radio, the electricity, broken pots and pans. And yet she remained eternally spotless and cheerful!

She was surely a perfect mother, and yet, to me at least, she was not a mother at all. The breach between us, which occurred shortly after my birth, when she left me in order to nurse my father back to health, had never been mended in all those years. She showed a diffidence in dealing with me that did not exist with respect to her other children. Did she have trouble placing me, identifying me as her child, her son? Of course she might still be secretly under my grandmother's influence, who saw in me the reincarnation of her son Maurice, a belief that was no longer mentioned but still prevalent; my grandfather himself treated me as such, and my mother's confusion must have been great. Since that belief had to be kept secret in order not to provoke my father's rage, this added mystery to it and, somehow, gave it even more credence. Could I really be her brother and her son at the same time? She was trapped between the past and the present, between her faith and her husband, between her son and her brother.

As I was entering my fourth year at Pasteur, the one that would lead to the *baccalauréat* graduation, I became again unruly and defiant. Of course my present school friends would never be dedicated iconoclasts like the kids in my first school; nevertheless, I had managed to bring together a pretty effective gang of troublemakers in my class. We were half-grown boys and these childish provocations were pretty ridiculous;

but what else could we do? In Spain they had bullfights insti-
tutionalized so as to rechannel society's potential for violence
against an innocent beast. Because bullfights were unauthor-
ized in France, we had to find a substitute for a bull, and our
choice fell on a physics and chemistry professor named Dubrocas.

He looked more like a wild boar than a bull, to be sure,
with his porcine eyes and the protuberant teeth sprouting out
unevenly from his mouth like tusks. That malformation was
the cause of a variety of speech defects; not only could he
never close his mouth completely, but his speech remained
incomprehensible, as, except for isolated words, only grunts
and whistles would emerge, in a spray of spittle. To top it all
off, he stuttered.

Why had this unfortunate fellow chosen this particular
calling? A bad choice indeed. All the more as he was an
inveterate poltroon, quite unable to cope with pressures,
emergencies, or confrontations. With his boar's head hunched
between his shoulders, standing on his hind legs in front of
his desk as the students filed in, shifty-eyed, his black coat
decorated with mementos of his last meal, he had the air of a
beast caught in its lair by a pack of hounds. He would have
liked to flee; but he was not a wild boar, and we were not
dogs. He was a humble professor, and he was supposed to
teach us chemistry. And so, in an incredible uproar, the class
was officially started. This daily martyrdom had gone on for
thirty years. The choice of the opening syllables was of prime
importance—he had to avoid those that whistled as well as
those that sputtered—but some evil spirit made him unfail-
ingly attack with words full of sibilants. The resulting slightly
sibilated postdental fricative, punctuated with pathetic ulula-
tions and gasping grunts for air, were received with savage
hilarity by the students. Dubrocas wouldn't have lasted long at
Meaux! But this was a different milieu, and since my colleagues concerned themselves exclusively with mediocre and
anonymous ragging, to me fell the task of throwing a bomb on
Dubrocas's desk. A bomb that didn't explode . . . because it
was only a good-sized turnip painted black, with a wick of
sputtering punk attached to its tail. Although the vegetable
did not explode, it smashed some beakers under the nose of
Dubrocas, who let out yelps of terror and fled from the classroom to the accompaniment of applause and whistles. He returned a little later with a crew of teachers' assistants who

laughingly defused my bomb, and the course was resumed as if nothing had happened.

There's no way out, I said to myself in despair, these kids are hopeless, I've had my fill of that. Seized by a sudden inspiration, I stuff the drawer of my laboratory table full of rags, douse them with all the inflammable substances within reach, toss in a lighted Bunsen burner, and close the drawer. Black smoke and sinister flashes immediately surge out from it. O wonder! My first successful chemistry experiment! Flames, billowing clouds, explosions, broken glass, stampedes—*wow!* As usual Dubrocas is looking for the exit, but this time he is so terrified that he keeps his eyes tightly closed and, for that reason, cannot find the door. He is seen feeling his way along the wall, repeating over and over, "The door . . . ! The door . . . !" just like a blind man. His hand finally encounters the knob of a door, which he pulls open and walks through, although it is only the door of the closet. He stays inside. Among the students, it's each man for himself; nobody seems to enjoy the show except me, the culprit. The brats literally walk on one another in their escape. Pyromaniac! Yes, that's me. I'm dazzled by this healthy agitation I've set off.

"Come on," calls Guy, pulling me by the sleeve. "You've done your thing, that's enough of that; now help me put out this goddamn fire, everything's going to burn!"

We smother the flames with whatever means we can find. A few pals also lend a hand; two minutes later and the fire's been mastered, with no help from the fire department, but there is black smoke filling an entire wing of the school. Flunkies, students, teachers, everybody's jostling on the stairs, in the hallways. The laboratory is blackened, devastated.

"Good job, my lad," says Guy, who's watching me attentively. "But next time, be a sport, warn your buddies!"

"Embarrassing as it is to tell you that, this thing wasn't premeditated. I swear! The only explanation is temporary insanity." And I look interrogatively at Guy.

"Temporary insanity? Probably not so temporary," he smiles complacently, tapping his forehead with the tip of an index.

The authorities arrive on the scene. They liberate Dubrocas from his closet. Spotting me, he points a trembling index finger at me, his eyes bulging, his buccal orifice sputtering, and barks in a rush of spittle:

"Madman! Mad student! This student is mad!"

I am taken to the doctor's office while the headmaster goes to telephone my family. A few minutes later, on the doctor's instruction, a squad of flunkies and male nurses conduct me under the chestnut trees of the boulevard d'Inkermann to escort me home. I am now grinning like an idiot, and they all seem surprised at my peaceful attitude. Am I pretending madness, or am I in fact the genuine article? A madman pretending madness, out of genuine madness, that would be pretty smart! After all, this destructive act was perfectly gratuitous, without any logic to it, political or otherwise, and so. . . .

My mother opens the door, looks at me with a questioning air and then at the characters around me. So, here's my mad son, she seems to think, looking hard at me. And then she briefly thanks my bodyguards, who depart, muttering indistinct words; indeed, what would be the proper thing to say in such bizarre circumstances? My mother herself doesn't know too well what to say to me. Her direct nature would prompt her to ask: "So, are you really crazy? Or is this just another one of your idiotic jokes?" Her experience with the males of the family, however, has made her cautious, and she simply says, "This is a very strange story, my son."

Strange! Always *le mot juste*. I notice the concentration in her features, which reflects an intense cerebral activity. Heads, Sherlock Holmes; tails, Einstein. . . . Once, some six months earlier, when I announced to her that I had been punished for some other act of cretinous misconduct, she had slapped me in the face for the first time in my life, and with enough force to knock out a bull. And yet she was a head shorter than I. . . . And now here we are once again, face-to-face! My cheeks are burning with apprehension. But she ends up by saying calmly, "Go to your room, read, do whatever you want. . . . We'll discuss this affair tonight with your father."

The matter was settled, oddly enough, in a general compromise. My parents didn't argue with the prima facie verdict of the school, according to which I was declared a madman fit to be tied; I was thus spared the dishonor of being officially expelled from school, not to speak of being brought to justice. My parents gave me the benefit of the doubt; I would never return to the *lycée*, but I would be allowed to present myself to the *baccalauréat* exam on my own. I had three months to cram in solitude. What a peaceful perspective!

Added provision to the treaty: I had to go see a psychiatrist my parents had heard highly praised, a Dr. Borel. Why not? After all, if I were really mad. . . .

"Pray be seated," gestures Dr. Borel, after moving away a pile of newspapers from an old chintz-covered armchair.

There are two windows, one opening on the Seine with a few barges slowly floating by in the distance, and the other on the rooftops of old Paris. From his comfortable chair, which is situated between the two, the doctor gives me a vague look with the gummy eyes of a big dog who hasn't quite managed to wake up. A languid breeze teases the papers on his desk, also stirring the doctor to drowsiness. His round face with its disheveled moustache reminds me a little of Charles Laughton. Assuming that Laughton were playing this role of a Paris psychiatrist, how would he dress? The doctor is wearing a black jacket, wide-striped trousers, and a vest festooned with a watchchain, which looks standard enough, but everything's all crumpled and twisted, as if he had slept fitfully, fully clothed, in a washing machine. . . . In a drowsy voice he inquires as to my age, poses inept routine questions, scratches his skull through the thinning hair with a pencil, and says:

"Now then, can you tell me what seems to be the matter?"

The question takes me by surprise. Let's see now, what is it that's wrong?

"The list would be too long," I tell him after a moment's reflection.

"Come on, now, I'm trying to help you, my young friend. Try to cooperate, it's for your own good."

He interrupts himself in order to yawn, cavernously, lengthily, copiously, and resumes:

"Talk to me a bit about the girls. What can you tell me about your girl friend, eh?"

How about that! I look at him, stupefied. Am I really supposed to answer such questions? To this sleepy creature?

"What?" I say. For want of something to say.

"Well, don't you understand me?" he inquires with the pained expression of a rudely awakened sleeper. *"Young girls . . ."* The words are accompanied with a vague gesture of his pudgy fingers, possibly meant to characterize the light nature of the breed.

"Excuse me," I finally say. "I'd like to leave."

Now it's his turn to have a surprised look on his face, and

he almost opens his eyes. But the effort is too great, and his plump body falls back voluptuously, irresistibly, into the soft cocoon of his armchair. He has just made too great an effort. Obviously, he's got only one thought in his mind, which is for me to run along so he can take a little snooze. Ah, what happiness! The young man has gone. . . .

I take the stairs four at a time and find myself out in the street, in a state of great fury and extraordinary exaltation. While crossing the parvis of Notre-Dame I curse my parents, particularly my father who dared to talk to this blusterer about my intimate feelings, of which he knows absolutely nothing. I wonder what he told the fellow? "My son is weird." Of course I'm weird! And proud of it! Even if I set fire to my school, he should understand that I had a reason for it, not so unlike the one that caused him to leave his own country forever, some twenty years ago. Why send me to that absurd man? We could have talked it over.

I cross the Seine and go into a café to telephone; I feel that I must absolutely talk to Laurette. Miracle, it's Vivian himself who answers the phone and puts her on the line. Laurette's fresh voice immediately sets off uncontrollable tremors in me.

"I must really see you, d'you have a few minutes? I've got a lot of things to tell you."

"Yes, of course," she says. "I'll be down in ten minutes. Where do we meet?"

"In the park around Saint-Julien-le-Pauvre, is that all right?"

I need an inspired place for this interview, and this is it. There are quite a few *clochards* around, and they look inspired too, although mostly thanks to their imbibing vast quantities of red wine. The sky of the day that's just ending is gradually losing its light, from the inside so to speak, and the branches of budding trees are perfectly delineated in dark gray against the lighter mass of Notre-Dame; my heart's beating very hard. What am I going to say to her? Nothing, of course, but I dream of what I would tell her, if I dared. . . . If such speech were possible. . . .

She arrives with the twilight, the light that suits her best. So, she did come out of Vivian's lair, just to meet me on a bench in a park! I am profoundly agitated at the thought that she cares for me enough to have interrupted whatever important thing she must have been doing, just to meet me alone. It's been some time since I last saw her, and so I tell her about the misfired fire, about my presumed madness, and about my visit of an hour ago to the sleepy doctor. Suddenly, I notice we're holding hands, just like lovers. For the bums who are surrounding us, there's no doubt that we're a romantic couple. There are a half dozen of them, good solid Paris *clochard* types, sitting or pottering around our bench, listening to us with interest and sympathy.

"You know, Laurette, I . . ."

"Hey, mister, here, have a swig. Here, be my guest."

A hand scaled with dirt offers me a half-empty wine bottle. Its proud owner has a hairy, bleary face beneath a huge straw-hat decorated with roses *à la* Renoir, and he's leaning on a baby carriage full of demented bric-à-brac. He is a proprietor, and even a collector; a leader in *clochard* society, one whose opinion is often heard. The other bums are standing around us, watching the proceedings with interest.

"Come on kid," he insists, "have a swig. It's good for the balls, you'll need it."

"No! Thanks."

"Allons mon p'tit gars," he cajoles. "For your own good, I swear. You look like you need it, you know that? Maybe you're one who drinks water! I know what I'm talking about. And the little lady too. . . . Hey *belle gosse,"* he addresses her tenderly, holding out his bottle of *vin ordinaire* to her. Obviously it's on her he has a crush, not on me.

Laurette smiles at him good-naturedly.

"I hate to refuse," she says. "But my mother has forbidden me to drink." This was intended as a feeble joke, but is not received as such.

"Arggh!" yells the bum. "Her *mother!* It's always the *mothers!* I'm really fed up with that refrain!" Passersby and *clochards* start assembling around us in the usual way, expecting some scandalous situation to develop.

But the fellow is really getting aggravated, he's dangerous, we had better leave on the run. I take Laurette by the hand and as we trot away from the little square I try to take up the thread of my speech. But she appears to be in a hurry to get back to Vivian, she hardly listens to me. I stammer out words without continuity, haltingly, trying to tell her that I love her, that I will always love her . . . and yet that I would never ask anything of her, *that I understand*. But our beflowered *clochard* is dogging our footsteps, dragging his carriage noisily behind him, and he harasses us, brandishing his bottle, fulminating against the mothers. Once again, we escape him and three minutes later, we reach the building next to the Cluny gardens, hand in hand, breathless, Laurette laughing, and me, stunned with emotion—it was all so brief, I didn't have a chance, and she's already slipped away. The heavy door slams after her with a sepulchral clang. Our *clochard* comes to help me in my predicament and kicks the door viciously.

"Her mother! *Her mother!* That bitch, fuck her, I'm going to have a talk with that woman, I know what I'm talking about. *Putain, fumier, conasse! Quelle femme dégueulasse!* Oh, poor little lamb. . . . So lovely. . . . And nothing to drink!"

I would have burst into tears right there on the sidewalk, out of sheer pain and frustration. But a fresh crowd is already gathering in a circle around us to hear this maniac who's squealing like a stuck pig. They don't understand the nature of the drama as yet, but they think it's going to be a juicy one. . . . And so it is! The spectators gape at a window opening high above their heads. Out comes a majestic figure, peering above the balcony, its silver hair in sharp contrast with fire-red robes, trying to make out the motley commotion down there on the sidewalk. This almost supernatural apparition, is that the young lady's mother? The public is not sure, but my *clochard* entertains no doubts on the subject.

"Madame," he yells at Vivian. "You're a whore, a slut! You should be ashamed of—"

The window closes abruptly. I run away, sobbing, stumbling between the milling crowds of students, unable to master the sobs and hiccups that rend my chest.

States of the heart: My heart was going in one direction, and my mind in another. My increasing participation, although still peripheral, in the activities of the group had turned me into a sort of neophyte, and as a result I had never as much as opened a school book to prepare for my *baccalauréat* exam. Who cares! Day after day I would see her, and the rare days I missed her were somber ones indeed.

As the reality of my condition became clearer, so did also my understanding that I had fallen for someone who was truly dedicated to the search, and who would probably never understand the nature of my feelings for her. But at the same time a warm friendship was growing between us, a climate of mutual acceptance and of mutual concern; an *amitié amoureuse* in which she was the friend, and I the lover. A most discreet lover! It was hopeless and it was delicious. She was two years and one day older than I, but sometimes I felt that the difference should rather be counted in thousands, or millions of years; such quiet radiance must be the end product of many lives.

And then it happened that my resourceful friends Claude and Edouard Delamare suggested that we all go spend the summer in their house in Brittany: that is, Laurette, Rolande, and myself, and G.J. some of the time. There would be other friends of theirs and it would be very jolly. I had heard a lot from the two brothers about their legendary summer house in Brittany, built by their occultist grandfather on a high cliff, on the side of an isolated fjord; and it all seemed too good to be quite true.

But parents met, arrangements were made. The matter of the *baccalauréat* was promptly disposed of: I passed the written exam easily, much to my surprise. And as this seemed really a bit too disturbing, I did my best to fail the oral exam. The examiner in geography, who was a kindly fellow, tried to help me with easy questions, but I turned him down by just not answering. "In what part of France is *le Massif Central?*" . . . Silence. . . . He seemed quite pained and baffled by this pigheaded and even rather suicidal attitude. But I was just as surprised and sorry myself; I didn't remember having really planned to fail.

At least my family took it philosophically, being well prepared for that additional disappointment. I would try again in the fall, perhaps; the truth of the matter being that I did secretly enjoy the failure. I felt a strong compulsion to break away from the bonds of society, tradition, routine. The *baccalauréat* was the one and only door, in our carefully centralized academic structure, to higher studies; you just could do nothing if you didn't have that degree. All of education was geared to this one focus, and it created a neat division between the haves and the have-nots; a protective wall around the entire bourgeois class. Setting my school afire was the first step, failing my terminal exam the second and definitive one; I was placing myself in a situation where I would have to be ten times more resourceful than the others merely to achieve equivalent results. . . . That geography examiner had probably interpreted my refusal to answer his questions as a purely self-destructive impulse?

But there was more to it than that! My suicidal and divergent postures were simply inspired by what I discovered of adult society as I was coming close to it. This world I could only reject; it's not me who's suicidal, it's that neurotic adult society, now facing me at such close distance. And I could only endorse Vivian's fiery condemnation of the modern world, and of the moral baseness of the common citizen. Of course he went on to include the family in his enemy list, and I could hardly consider my own as either oppressive or regressive; but I felt that he was surely quite right in a general sense, and that my parents, who had so carefully respected my freedom, may have failed me utterly in other less obvious but more elementary ways. In a sense my true family seemed now to be Vivian's ashram.

The plans for the summer included first one or two weeks in a little resort across from the island of Noirmoutiers, on the Vendée coastline. I would not stay in a hotel, but camp in the woods nearby, and leave from there to travel north to the Delamare's house in Brittany on my brand-new bicycle; all my friends would be waiting for me when I arrived, including Laurette.

Those nights I spent in the woods and sandy dunes of Vendée were devoted to her, to our impending reunion. I was going to rediscover her, this time as a holiday companion, as someone who sits with you on the beach, swims and laughs at silly jokes. . . . I tried to imagine her and Rolande in the middle of ten boys of various ages; through their eyes I could even conjure her grace, and share by anticipation the pleasure her presence would give them. It was really time to go.

I bid farewell to my hermitage, and before daybreak, I mount my bike and toil away on the uneven road, dragging with me a complex luggage, with the gleam of my flickering headlight surrounding me with an uncertain aura. This causes masses of reeds to loom up briefly here and there on the sides of the road.

My consciousness progressively attunes itself to the rhythm of the pedals, and the fresh breeze preceding sunrise dries the sweat on my brow. I tell myself that by leaving very early I'll be able to cover the three hundred-odd kilometers separating me from Prat-ar-Coum, the Delamare's village, in two long laps, provided I cross through the center of Brittany.

A muted luminosity now reveals the line of the shady groves and reflects itself in the tiny ponds that punctuate the watery land of Vendée. In the distance there is a diminutive bridge whose arched silhouette is neatly drawn against the blood-red background. By the time I reach it, the sun has emerged above the woods, turning everything ablaze in its rising glory—the sky, the Pays de Retz, and myself on my bike. After two hours on the road, my plans have already changed: Instead of making the trip in two days, I'm going to make it in four or five, going the long way, riding as close as I can to the coast. My gradual discovery of Brittany will provide a suitable preparation.

Thus my bike is directed to follow closely the capricious coast, and now decides, entirely on its own, in favor of little bumpy roads and deep-rutted paths; this is going to double the distance to be covered, but I will take all the time necessary. I refuse to rush.

Here we are, within sight of Saint-Michel-Chef-Chef (a name that invites etymological reveries); then I take the ferry that crosses the Loire to Saint-Nazaire, arriving on the soil of Brittany, whose salt marshes continue those of the Vendée. Behind me I leave the gray walls of Guérande, rising in the midst of fields of carnations, and I traverse Herbignac, Muzillac, and after skirting Vannes come into Auray, right in time for a great popular event. The fair of the Pardon de Sainte-Anne is in full swing. In the main square, which is teeming with peasants in antique Breton togs and red-cheeked women in tall white headdresses, people indulge in the innocent games of commerce. I stuff myself with crêpes and cider to the point where I have difficulty continuing on my way. The salty breeze, however, wakes me up as I rejoin the coast at Locmariaquer; where I settle down, in a field of dolmens, to spend the night under a sky that used to be familiar to the Celtic astronomers.

The next day, I take the road to Lorient and the morning air deliciously burns my lungs. I prolong the pleasure, pedaling straight into the sea winds, absorbing the spray through my skin; and when the evening sun goes down, and purple embers smolder in reflection in a universe of seaweed, I come to a halt at a farmhouse that overhangs a little stream. I rent for the night a whitewashed shack where a haystack serves me as a bed. I take off again at the crack of dawn, roll over the bumpy pavement of Concarneau, Bénodet, Pont-l'Abbé, and Pont-Croix, and also of Douarnenez, and spend the night in the cemetery of a church festooned with granite, eaten away by salt and time. On the fourth day, I progress around the peninsula of Camaret and then cross through Plougastel, pedaling between high walls of gorse, which lead me eventually into a forest of oak trees. I stop by a brook to refresh myself, sleep, and give free rein to my dreams. My conscious mind has given up the struggle, and I am only propelled now by an inspiration of the heart, by an intuition stronger than reason, covering the last remaining kilometers with a growing ardor. As I cross through the region of Brest and enter the land of Léon, I travel no longer on a bike but on a brilliant cloud, hallucinating, disembodied.

Saint-Renan, Ploudalmézeau. . . . My bike has trouble keeping up, groaning and creaking. At last I reach Lannilis toward the middle of the afternoon, and begin my search for a secluded estuary, or *aber* as they call them here, to find the hamlet of Prat-ar-Coum, no more than three houses at the end of a remote road. The bike races easily through fields of rye, moors of heather, my head hums beneath the blazing sun. Finally, from the top of a knoll, I discover the rooftop that had been described to me, and this gives me strength for the last lap. I push down on the pedals and my bike gobbles up the final slope as if it were going downhill; in one swoop I find myself on the other side of the top, propelled by the momentum of an invincible passion. The road plunges straight ahead toward a cove, and I suddenly catch a glimpse of my friends playing around in the water. They squeal with fright at the apocalyptic apparition—*but it's too late to brake!* The wind briefly whistles in my ears, the machine clears terra firma, and for a fraction of a second, my two wheels sparkle in the sun like a symbol of the infinite. And then my parabola curves into a diving arc, and still mounted on my vehicle, I plunge vertically beneath the surface with all my paraphernalia attached, traversing concentric layers of coolness, and when my feet touch bottom, I soar back to the surface, emerging like a Jack-in-the-box.

This brief immersion has refreshed my spirits enough for me to fully savor this unique moment. Unique! Splashing about among all these young swimmers is the one for whom I almost gave my life on the gravel path. . . . For whom I would give my life a thousand times! Her head is tightly encased in a discreet helmet of white rubber. Her skin is already tanned, her teeth are sparkling, and now, dripping with water, she embraces me tenderly amid the general commotion. Someone pulls me from behind; it's Rolande who's tearing me out of Laurette's arms, and I receive the embrace of a variety of people: Etiennette, Bernard, Jean-Loup, young folks of the neighborhood, who are splashing about together with the Delamare clan, and sometimes go boating with them. I can now clearly see, looming above us, the strange abode my friends' grandfather built for himself and his descendants.

Each of its four sides has many windows with jutting wooden balconies, each one opening over a different landscape; from the veranda that encircles the house, one has a view of most of the promontory, with its watery inlets.

After more or less drying off, the five brothers show me around the house. One of its attractions is the famous alchemical library on the ground floor; as I look around and re-emerge on the veranda I find myself confronted with the seated figure of the brothers' granny, a stout old woman in black with a face of white marble, handsome as a Roman emperor, her gaze lost in another horizon.

The boys are installed in a sort of dormitory and the two girls share a room under the eaves. A very proper arrangement, as could be expected. There are fourteen people at table for dinner, only four of whom are adults, and despite the vegetarian fare, it's all very heady and joyous. The glow of the setting sun is our illumination; in the distance, beyond the edge of the promontory, the sea appears far away, burning bright between somber rocks, and closer to us the deep landscape of steep cliffs and calm waters is slowly losing its contours in the descending darkness. The captive sea irrigates the garden on a lower level of the house and continues to travel inland for miles, pushing its long arm into a maze of nearly impenetrable vegetation, where it mingles in secret with the waters of the outflowing river. From the back of the house there is a landscape of receding dunes covered with heather, with solitary trees and dark groves. If you climb to the top floor and look down, you cannot escape a feeling of dizziness, as the house itself seems to float in midair like a toy lost in the wind.

Later, Laurette tells me about walks, about sunsets on the moors, about the influence of this landscape on her dreams, about the harmony of smells, shapes, and colors. Her voice is a whisper, for me alone, in the thickening twilight and I absorb gratefully the warmth of her hand in mine. I hardly breathe, or move, for fear of disturbing the perfect balance of this moment, when everything is blessed with the simplicity of love. Suddenly the lights are switched on in the house and the charm is broken; as she adjusts to the glare she has the enlarged pupils of someone coming out of a cinema.

After a few days life became very simplified; skins were sun-burned, noses peeled, and then it all turned to various shades of bronze. The two girls glittered in the midst of a collection of boys, and the resulting tension filled the house with crackling electricity. M. Delamare's gnomish moustache be-came ruffled with a nervous tic when he beheld his young female guests; that was a nice change to the constant company of his five boys, and he seemed quite ready for a display of scandalous behavior.

The days were perfectly full and happy, and my intimacy with Laurette developed more easily now thanks to the up-roarious company, the group life on the beach or in the boats. The beaches were of fine white sand, and entirely ours, since tourists were unknown in these remote parts, and the local people, who treated the sea as their livelihood, avoided to dip as much as a toe in it. It was a vigorous, agitated sea, and warmed to perfection by the passage of the Gulf Stream along the coast. The churches were full of ancient folks on Sunday mornings; the medieval fervor that overtook those old weather-incrusted Celtic faces was certainly more Druidic than Roman in inspiration. Next to me on the pew I saw Lau-rette in profile, lost in prayer; and I wondered about the uni-versal seduction of faith, which made her feel and respond so readily in unison with those souls of another age, another place.

The land of Brittany is everywhere mysterious at night; this is the well-known country of fairies, where bardic legends arise spontaneously after dark, between land and sea. The moors are reservoirs of darkness, they have been brushed right and left by the same salty breeze for millions of years. Our midnight perambulations lead us to rustic calvaries of pockmarked granite, and dark abandoned houses that all have a haunted look. Often we see small phosphorescent flames travel dancing through the darkness which the local people believe are those elemental spirits they called *farfadets*. And when, finally, after yet another one of those exhilarating days I collapse in bed, in the midst of my nine young male companions, her presence, which had been so close and tender all during the day, becomes overpowering as I lay in the gloom, thinking of her. My intense desire for her, which I had managed to push away and stifle when I was with her, now comes back with a vengeance, it erupts as an angry flower of flesh, and leaves me panting with remorse. This day-and-night torture, is this my own way to be happy?

My exalted state is so pure and complete only because I obey her unspoken wish. We must love each other with the innocence of kids, skin to skin, sharing the same warmth and the same thoughts, but no more. Her last two years of erratic studies were spent in a convent school, she tells me, and she became so attracted to the simple perfection of the sisters' life that she nearly became one of them. She was still thinking about it when she met Vivian—and now she is a vestal, a guardian of the temple. And yet the attraction she exercises on all the men and boys who approach her is such that she breaks more hearts, unwittingly, than a professional coquette ever will; my own included, alas.

All this being said, I am left with no alternative but to obey her will, and to follow this schizophrenic course. Let's not even try to think about the future! I can already feel that the hold of this growing thing can be broken no longer; when we are not together, if I suddenly think of her my body will shudder like a leaf in the wind. Sometimes I feel as if I had been given a potent drug, my mind reels and unravels, my body trembles uncontrollably as many other lives take over, as if reality were being decomposed through a prison. My old identity seems to be flying away in every possible direction fast as light. It sometimes takes several hours for me to come down. Can love make you *that* sick?

One morning we meet very early in front of the house to bathe together, the two of us, before the whole household awakes. She asks me to rub her back with oil—and soon she starts wondering why it takes me so long. And what can I answer to that? My fingers obey only very slowly to my brain and to her will; they caress in wonder that perfect skin instead of energetically rubbing; they do one small spot at a time instead of smearing the stuff in two or three strokes. . . . But does she *know* what she is doing to me? I can't go any faster, I am about to—

At this precise juncture the beautiful back suddenly leaves the tips of my fingers, she runs up a huge rock, plunges and frolics in the foamy wavelets, and turning back toward me, where I stand stupidly at the edge of the water, she shouts—

"Hey, what's the matter with you?"

"Nothing, nothing," I mutter inaudibly, greatly conscious of my absurd, of my humiliating state; and I suddenly run into the sea to hide my shame, my desire. She catches up with me in three strokes, and seizing me by the shoulders, she repeats—*"But what's the matter with you? Tell me!"*

We're standing, three-quarters submerged, face to face, clasped in each other's arms in the cool morning water, and now she well knows what's the matter with me. She cradles my head against hers, in sisterly compassion, and caresses me pensively as my body shakes madly against hers. Does that make us a married couple? No.

Later that same morning I find her sitting in the grass, in a secluded spot at the end of the garden, reading. It seems imperative to break the silence, to do away with that hypocrisy. Now she can no longer pretend . . . and *I* certainly can no longer pretend! She raises her eyes from her book and smiles at me. And that's enough to deflate all my brave questions; for a moment I had quite forgotten that I am still a child.

However, she does not refuse to talk—for the first time—about love. Yes, of course, she knows what it is. She had a great flame for an oldish actor, once, when she was fourteen, and then later she was actually engaged to be married to Robert. But she changed her mind, she could not, well, give herself, even to him. . . . It appears that now Robert has been ill for two years, and is in fact dying. Still hoping to marry her. His own sister even came to Paris to see her, and talk about it.

"If you married him, you'd save him," I say.

"No, that's really not true. And how would you expect me to play such a comedy? Once, perhaps, but since Vivian . . ."

And so we are once more back to Vivian; and bit by bit I get the story of their first encounter, when she was still in that convent school, in fact only about one year ago.

Her mother had taken her to a lecture in a certain occult outfit, The Cosmic Philosophers, of which she was herself an adept. . . . Yes, her mother too. . . . And there she had heard the speaker extoll, in a vibrant, raspy voice, the beings of higher stature who stand guard over mankind, and whom he called the Great Hierarchy, for one hour and a half; he was

himself of a small stature, disheveled, excited, probably mad
but strangely convincing. It was quite unlike her to pounce on
him at the end of the lecture, but she did, and he was very
friendly. His name was André Gauthier-Walter, he was essentially a poet, a surrealist turned occultist. Doesn't that make
sense? She wanted to know where and how in the world can
one enter in touch with the level of beings he had been describing. He asked her the reason for her question. Well, she
answered timidly, if I give my life to a cause, I would like to
be able to give it to the best one there is. . . . After thinking
for a moment he said: "I am giving another talk tomorrow on
the same subject, at the Sociétés Savantes—for a group of
people you should meet if you want to find out more . . ."

And so the next day she heard again about the Greater Beings, but the audience was on the whole much younger, and
they all seemed to know one another. There was a very pretty
redhead sitting just in front of Laurette; she was teasing the
boys instead of listening to the lecturer, who apparently knew
her and didn't mind. At one point Rolande, the girl, turned
around and looked at her: The two of them had smiled at each
other and they had become friends, yes, for life, she thought.
However, it is true that all the other people around her
looked interesting in one way or another. She was still listening to the lecture with half of her attention, while the other
half was becoming increasingly aware that something was
happening right here, now, in that room. She felt something
in the back of her, a tingling sensation on the nape of her
neck, as if someone were looking at her with great intensity.
She wanted to turn her head around, but she was unable to do
so, she felt paralyzed. Until suddenly her neck had obeyed of
its own movement, and her eyes met the strange, deep eyes of
the man who had been looking at her; he was standing with
his back against the wall, at the rear of the audience. There
was a faint smile playing on the man's lips as he was looking at
her, only at her. As if he knew who she was, and everything
else about her life; yes, those eyes knew everything. . . . The
rest was inevitable. And she did feel that it is at that very
minute that her life had really started.

I was both fascinated by her story and overwhelmed at the
thought of her belonging so completely to Vivian. Whatever
the nature of their relationship, her tender friendship for me
was a small thing in her life.

"There's a choice to be made," she repeated. "Some day

you, yourself, are going to have to make a choice, and I know it's not easy. Especially at first, it can be a torture. Asceticism is hard, the renunciation must be real, total. . . . But it is true also that it is like a mechanical process: the door is only opened to those who deserve it."

At that point she noticed that my face was covered with tears, and she held me tight against her.

"See here," she murmured. "You know that I love you a lot. . . . You know that, don't you? You're very important to me. . . . Come on, now, let's go swimming, you can shed your tears in the salt water. Come!"

Thus it was that, out of love, I denied myself love. Laurette's example was irresistible, and I couldn't renounce either her company or her esteem. Furthermore, hadn't my entire life, and all my aspirations, led me toward this one outcome? What they called *the path?*

I asked her to talk to Vivian about me and to let him know my desire to learn more concerning the work of the inner circle. . . . I thought about that vow of chastity with quite some misgivings; was it possible to renounce a thing, love, that I had in fact never known? It all looked so drastic and definitive. . . . But she was giving me her own example, and she should know.

10

From Arjuna to Jean Monnet.—From the lower chakra to the European federation.—Céline's pretty daughter. —Expo '37 in Gay Paree.—Our leftist government betrays the Spanish Republic; Franco wins.—A boring first job. —A passage to India, mostly on foot.—In Fascist land. —Mute in Nice, and pretty dumb as well.—A children's crusade.—The Foyer Pythagore.—Sunday meditations.

On my return to Paris, I was greeted with joy and surprise by my family. The sun had burned me deep brown and the Brittany fare had fattened me up: thirty-five pounds in two months! I was literally bursting out of my clothes.

"Could it be the effects of love?" my mother asked. "Did you perchance encounter a mermaid, my son?"

I turned crimson under my suntan.

"He's blushing! Look! He's blushing!"

Eric and Sylvie, the dirty brood! Scum of the earth.

"Which one is it?" asked one of them.

"The brunette with the curls, on the right," came the answer.

"You're crazy! It's the other one, there, in the boat—she isn't half bad!"

Youth must be treated with indulgence. As to my mother, how could I have spoken to her of my experiences, of the frothy state of my soul? It had become clear to her that I had fallen head over heels in love with a young spiritualist, a charming girl, moreover. And she hoped it would all soon go away.

Two days later, I made my way to the boulevard Saint-Germain and, my heart wildly beating, climbed the five fateful flights. Laurette herself opened the door; it was strange to find ourselves together once again, in city clothes, our tanned vacation faces beaming at each other.

"I spoke to Vivian. It would be best to see him right now."

She led me to his door, ushered me in, and left us alone.

"Sit down, dear one," he said in his youthful voice. "It seems that this vacation was a success for everyone; never have I seen so many happy faces!"

He went on:

"Laurette has told me already about your hesitations, about your problems. Perhaps I can help you? You know that we consider you already as being one of us? However—it's entirely up to you to decide what you want to do with your life. Do you have any clear idea about it?"

It wasn't fair: He was starting with the most definitive question. How could I reply, knowing that my answer would commit me forever? I was searching for words.

"I can understand the difficulty of defining one's aims with complete honesty, particularly at your age. You are unsure. Yet your presence here has a definite meaning. The interlocking patterns of human relationships lose themselves in the mists of time . . ."

The trite words were coming out effortlessly. He hardly knew me at all, and he was fishing for a way to make me trust him. Which caused suspicion instead. And then I remembered that two or three minutes earlier, when I had come in, his eyes were a pale blue; their color had turned much darker now, nearly brown.

Then he launched into a great tirade about Kryia's current master plan, which consisted in a sort of parliament open to young Europeans from all countries—les Etats Généraux de la Jeunesse Européenne.

"The young people are what counts, my dear friend, and they alone. Only the youth of Europe are capable of doing the work of unifying this continent. That's the first task to be tackled so that a constructive balance can be established in the world. We are undertaking this endeavor under Kryia's guidance, with the support of the higher powers. Kryia has made sure that we have the necessary political cooperation: Justin Godard in the Senate, Gaston Riou in the House, Anatole de Monzie in the government, Emile Roche from the Economic Council—the men who hold the real power in their hands. Abroad, we have Keyserling, of course, but especially

Coudenhove-Kalergi, and behind him, a good number of statesmen and diplomats who are sympathetic to our cause, or influential young economists such as Jean Monnet. But the breath of life must come from the young people. It's up to the youth of the Continent to lay the foundations of the new international democracy, United Europe! That is why, in a thousand different ways, you also are personally necessary to our movement. . . . But you must discover your natural vocation, which is that of Kshatriya, as I realized at first sight. In India, the Kshatriya are the caste of knights and of kings; their ethical views are well defined by Arjuna in the *Bhagavad-Gita*. . . . Just as an artisan has to perfect his *chef-d'oeuvre* in order to attain mastery in his craft, so the reincarnation in modern times of the Kshatriya must accomplish his spiritual destiny by devoting himself to the great political opus of the future, the first step of which is the creation of a United Europe. If you join us, you will also take part in the inner work, the secret work with which only a very small number of our friends are associated. You should also be aware of the fact that if you join us, the rule of silence will have to be respected rigorously and absolutely."

Then came a pause, giving the warning a chance to sink in. After which he continued:

"Furthermore, inner asceticism is possible only for those who have tamed their sexuality. Sexual purity is indispensable to complete realization. The vital power that emanates from the lower chakra is all too easily diverted from the needs of the higher being by sexual passion; yet it can be reoriented upward and directed level by level through the kundalini to the upper chakras where it will give birth to clairvoyance, to the powers that are called supernatural. This then leads to enlightenment, to the ranks of a superior humanity, to the Great Hierarchy that dominates the evolution of the world. . . . That is why asceticism implies Service and Renunciation. The Service is the gift of oneself to the ideal of the divine on earth; this is indispensable. Renunciation means giving up the fruits of one's actions, but in the first place, it is the sacrifice of sex."

The flow of his voice held me spellbound, but the meaning of his words remained floating in the air, in a suspension that refused to crystallize. An irresistible psychic force emanated from Vivian, from his face and from his presence as well as from his words, a force that swept away everything in its path, even the most recent past, even the most intimate feelings.

"The disciple must liberate himself from all ties," he continued. "Especially from the family, which is a psychological compost heap. All families without exception—the ones that seem the freest are often the most dangerous."

He fell silent; he was through. I had come to him expecting an exchange, a conversation, and I found myself taken aboard, adopted, integrated, set to rights, without having taken any decision whatsoever on my own. Vivian, bestowing a last magnetic look upon me, said with a smile, "Onward, dear one," and returned me to the lower worlds.

The feeling I was left with was gruesome but persistent: He did not like me a bit. A dreadful suspicion took hold of me: Could it be that he secretly condemned me because of my special friendship with Laurette? She was by far the closest of his disciples; there was a rumor afoot that he was working at developing in her the gift of clairvoyance, which she had manifested in a rudimentary way since her childhood. I suddenly realized, with a pang of horror, the gross absurdity of my situation. It had taken me all that time, and this last session with Vivian, to understand that my timid boy's love for her would never be a match for Vivian's authority over her—perhaps I could even say, his psychic possession of her. How could I have possibly thought that I could become the rival of my own guru?

She had been waiting for me outside of Vivian's room, and as we stood face-to-face on the landing, I tried to speak, but our difficult dialogue faded away immediately. What was the use of talking? The light in her eyes, the serenity of her face, her inner peace, this enigma. . . . And the sweetness of her mouth, the freshness of her skin, her shoulders, yielding and alive under the palm of my hands. . . . I melted into her, and abandoning myself to the limpid message of her gaze, I made her a gift of my eternal love, of my manly identity, and of my destiny.

The school year began, and with it came the oral part of my matriculation exam. I flunked it ruthlessly. Thus my academic career had come to an end right at its beginning, and I decided to let it go at that. Good riddance! The morose escalation that faced my successful and unfortunate buddies—a bachelor's degree, a master's degree, business, the factory, politics, the army—this was a thought that filled me with profound repugnance. . . . The examples of bourgeois marriages I was beginning to see sprouting here and there around me, starting from timid, half-baked love affairs—all that activity truly made me dizzy.

Jean Turpin, whom I had met at the Delamares' was, like them, a student at Sainte-Croix, which was run by the Jesuits, and where the Christian virtues were being dutifully instilled into the sons of the bourgeoisie. And they could draw pride from this product—a truly pleasant fellow, well-fed, well-scrubbed, well-dressed, well-spoken, complete with pink cheeks and honest blue eyes; he had recently consorted with an equally pleasant blonde who could have passed for his own sister. Edouard, when he introduced me to her, added with some pomposity that she was Céline's own daughter. *Wow!* Stupefied, I stared at this beautiful girl, and she was blushing with embarrassment.

"It's marvelous!" I said to her, clasping her hand with delight. "Do you know that I'm in love with your father?"

Extraordinaire! Would you believe it? Louis-Ferdinand Céline's very own daughter! Timidly, she drew back her hand and sat down next to Turpin, who had the look of a little enraged rooster.

"What a damned jerk you are," he snarled, very uncharacteristically. "If you think I married her because of her father's reputation, you're a fool. Have you even read it, his book?"

"And how! *Le Voyage!* After all! Anyone who can make use of the French language to—"

"Yeah," Turpin interrupted, his eyes throwing sparks, "anyone who uses the French language to turn it into *filth!*"

Everybody stared at him, wide-eyed with stupefaction.

"And as to his conduct as a . . . as a *father*, I must say that . . . well . . . hmmm . . . that . . ."

His words strayed, he had bungled it badly, he didn't finish his sentence; his pretty spouse was next to him, her head lowered, scarlet-faced, her eyes drowning in tears. It was a horrible scene, deeply disturbing. In Claude and Edouard's expressions, I read the reflection of the image that was forcing itself upon me: the outrageous Louis-Ferdinand abusing the innocence of this lovely child, his very own. And suddenly Knight

Turpin with drawn sword materializes on stage. . . . An extraordinary scenario!

Turpin got up, took his wife by the arm, and led her away
without another word, slamming the door behind them.

"Poor old Turpin has a problem," Edouard concluded with
a lecherous smirk. Then he began to tell us about the Ecole
Centrale, where he had just enrolled to study the engineering
sciences. His brother Claude was rather more attracted by the
natural sciences, biology in particular. They went on and on
about their plans for the future. Edouard wanted to build, to
organize. Having graduated from Centrale, he would automatically enter the army with an officer's commission and
would do his two years of military service. He would get as
much as he could from that experience. As for Claude, he
was, loosely speaking, a pacifist; a nature lover. I said that in
the event of war, I would refuse to fight, just like my friend
Gregor Louchine, and that I would never become a soldier.

"What, a defector?" Edouard was quite indignant. "Can you
imagine what that will cost you, for the rest of your life? Listen, kid, you already set fire to your school, you can't go on
like that. Your pacifist ideas, what good are they? It's pie
in the sky, but Hitler is not; he couldn't be more real. You
know that I'm not for the Front Populaire on the Left—but
I'm certainly not for those characters on the other side: Tar-
dieu, Daladier, and the other stick-in-the-muds. They mean
nothing, however. Beyond their stinking politics the fact is
that we are getting each day a bit closer to war. In a world
war, you'll have to take sides. The choice to make is for or
against freedom. Would you like to see all of Europe under
Hitler? Really! Tell me now, if *you* don't want to fight, why
should *I* fight for you?"

"That's up to you, dope," I said in disgust. "You're responding exactly as you're supposed to, you're walking right into
the trap. That's politics, that's the system for you. . . . The
Versailles treaty humiliated Germany and forced her to live
for her revenge. That was Hitler's chance. It's a vicious circle,
can't you see that? My dad, too, he wants to bash Hitler on the
head. But what's the good of that? As soon as that one is out,
you'll have to start again with Stalin. With the emperor of
Ethiopia, the mikado of Japan, the queen of Tonga. There's
no end to all that. For my own part, I find it healthier to
turn down all political systems. Ignore them! Laugh at them!

Expose them! For you, an idealist, a man of the spirit, I am amazed that you can even consider serving in the army. In the artillery too! Sending shells on the heads of those poor idiots. That's not very good for your Karma, my friend!"

It could have gone on like this forever. The thought stuck in my head that those very same exchanges, in almost the same terms, must have taken place a generation earlier, before the First World War. My own uncle Maurice, for instance, what could he have had to say about it? *Assuming that I was him*, why should I fall back into the same mistake and die a second time—like a reincarnation stooge? It became clear to me, suddenly, that it would take something as big as the great project of Vivian and Kryia to change the course of things: It was up to the young people to put an end to that war-and-retaliation rigamarole. They were right! The old people were hopeless; they had nothing to lose by sending the kids to the mortuary. I thought about next year—to coincide with the World Fair, the Expo-'37, to be held in Paris, we were to launch the first session of the Etats Généraux, and millions of young people would be there. Think of it! We could change the face of the world, just like that. . . . And indeed, the great year soon started in a noisy turmoil.

The Trocadéro neighborhood had already been turned into a permanent construction site, and dozens of pavilions, from the most exotic to the most solemn, were beginning to rise on the banks of the Seine, transforming the urban landscape, blotting it out. Germany and the USSR were erecting their naked bronze giants face-to-face; Arno Breker's massive pederasts were giving the Nazi salute to Stalin's thick-limbed proletariat, who were brandishing hammers and sickles back at them. Paris was pregnant with a prodigious internal proliferation: All the nations of the world were converging on a transfigured Champ-de-Mars, on a delirious Folies-Bergères, on unbridled circus nights from Montmartre to Montparnasse.

Under the Front Populaire, Paris had also become the city of the people; there was fraternizing in the factories and in the bistros in celebration of the new era. Capital of the Western world, it is the city of miracles from which all styles and inventions burst forth. Why would those hordes of goggle-eyed English tourists cross the Channel every week to spread out on the boulevards, the Latin Quarter, the banks of the Seine? By contrast few Parisians would ever travel to London, because, apart from a visit to Westminster (a cathedral far less flamboyant than Notre-Dame), there was nothing to do over there. Just nothing! And those Englishwomen with their funny clothes, poor things! Green tweeds and big feet. And of course the food was contemptible—and, just imagine: *no wine!* No, the French did not travel because France was the only place for food, wine, romance. That saved one the effort of having to study foreign languages. Three or four kids in a thousand would take German in school, and one in ten thousand Spanish. No one learned Italian. Of course everyone else was supposed to study English, but very few got far enough to read a Christmas card without help. Even bathtubs were seen as a foreign invention, liable to weaken the vigorous odors of a French body, and they were seen as signs of decadence; a good bidet was all you needed, really, because, quite apart from being useful to wash socks, it was also credited with an essential contraceptive function.

Of course, being the center of the world had its drawbacks, as you had to cope with those thousands of foreigners, and among those there were only very few American millionaires; indeed lots of them were suspicious-looking refugees, or artists without a franc to their name. Le Dôme and La Coupole were overflowing with that zany, restless, drunken populace, for which the peak of the season was the Quat'z'Arts ball, when the art students would paint their bodies and carouse all over the place dressed up as naked savages.

But the main thing was, French society was changing fast. The struggle of the classes was taking each day a more spectacular aspect, with great mass demonstrations, banners floating and slogans rising over oceans of human bodies during the great May Day and July 14 festivities. The proletariat was slowly becoming the dominant force under the joint guidance of Léon Blum, an effete, well-dressed, intellectual Socialist; the Communist overlord Maurice Thorez, a heavy-jawed Stalinist stooge; and Edouard Daladier, the boss of the center-left Radical party, which was the most numerous and the best-entrenched in the low-echelon bureaucracy and the provinces. Of course, as in any such alliance, those three were traitors—each one to the other two, as well as to himself, and to the people—but that was not visible from the lower ranks. The life of politics was throbbing in those mass celebrations, red-olent with red wine, sweat, and garlic, where Franco, Hitler, and Mussolini were defied, shouted out of existence, ridiculed as un-French, emasculated, and their effigies trampled in the gutter. The workers were winning, the bourgeoisie would soon loose their châteaux and their factories: Clearly the greatest revolution of all time was in the making.

Behind that ecstatic front, however, the facts of life looked pretty different. Grim, even. Franco was slowly winning in Spain against the disorderly, multiheaded Republic; Hitler and Mussolini were helping him, and testing their fast-growing air force, their tanks, their assault troops.

Italians and Germans, who did not like each other, were thus psychologically preparing their armies and their populations for political and military cooperation. At the same time the camp of the democracies was fast coming apart because of confused, conflicting ideologies and a lack of leadership. France was leading the democracies, and yet the major decision of the Léon Blum government was not to commit France on the side of Spain—an ominous decision that was dividing the anti-Fascist camp in Europe, and paving the way for Franco's victory.

The French government appeared absolutely secure in its confidence that the French army was able to cope with any challenge from Germany. As to the Italians, no one would take them seriously; their empire-building campaign against Ethiopia had been hopelessly bogged down in Eritrea. They were definitely better at *bel canto* than at fighting wars, even against such a moldy African empire as Ethiopia. There was no question that the French foot soldier was the best in the world. (Who said that? The French newspapers themselves, that's who!) As to England, France's ally, it was dependent on its navy and the surrounding seas as a sufficient line of defense. The British had no real feeling for war; they were seen, deep down, as sissies and hypocrites.

And so, where do I stand in all this, being half French, half English? The only thing I know for sure is that being one or the other is quite indifferent to me. I was born in France, but I do not feel that I really belong there. Being French, or British, or anything, what does that really mean? Nothing. My people, who are they?

Why, yes, I decided to take a lowly job, my first one. Every morning at eight-thirty, I board the *métro* at the Sablons station, and after two train-changes I reach Marcadet-Poisson-

niers, borne along by a tidal wave of workers. From there I go
to the I. Koch agency, Creative Publicity, where I have become an apprentice-designer with a salary of five hundred
francs a month, which is not enough to buy cigarettes; but of
course I don't smoke. Every day my mother prepares a vegetarian lunchbox for me, which I eat sitting alone in an empty
storeroom, reading the *Bhagavad-Gita*.

I am sometimes overtaken again by those attacks of split
personality that took hold of me during the summer in Brittany, but I am now used to them, and better able to control those wanderings in parallel layers of reality. Besides that,
I design toothbrushes all day long, or water pumps; and that's
a sobering activity. I have become a champ of the airbrush,
and I'm beginning to produce, in color, a section plan of a
giant pump ordered by the Guinard Company for Expo-'37;
it's extremely complicated and it will be a three-week job of
meticulous and drudging labor. I would a thousand times
rather lick stamps for the Etats Généraux, which are getting
organized in the rue Serpente headquarters, but I feel obliged
to earn a living, miserable as it may be. I see Laurette only on
Sundays, in the crowd, and I feel absolutely dejected. We are
far removed from Brittany and that summer full of promise.
Vivian has taken his vestal solidly back in hand.

The last day of the month, payday, I arrive at the office and
find my Guinard pump ravaged: The concierge's cat has tried
its claws on it during the night, the whole thing must be redone. It's the last straw, I decide to quit. To quit and leave for
good. To leave France, and the Western Hemisphere; and
that goes for Vivian, and his great projects. And for Laurette
as well! To see her express sorrow and concern, even for one
second, as I announce my departure, the thought fills my
heart with a great surge of perverse, maudlin bitterness. The
sweet evil of self-immolation grows on me as I write a note to
I. Koch, formally announcing that I resign my ludicrous position in his sordid enterprise, and another one to my parents
announcing that I am leaving for India. With my last paycheck, I buy a third-class ticket for Marseilles and Ventimiglia
on the Italian border. From there I'll go on foot in the general
direction of India—I've known for a long time that my destiny
awaits me there, the extrasuperlucid yogi who will show me
the true path.

A fever, a fervor, a dull exaltation seizes my body as I
climb, for the last time, the five flights of stairs to Vivian's

ashram. My spirit flies, I hardly feel my body anymore, and I am hardly conscious of the tattered carpet on the steps, of the usual pungent smells. I have hardly enough strength left to pull the bell. It is she who opens the door, and I drink in avidly the quiet beauty of her childish face, the tender lips, and the luminous wisdom of her eyes, the ivory skin of her bare arms, the lightness, the sensuality of her presence. Yes, it is she who opens the door, and her expression turns to puzzlement, to concern as she looks at me, at my catatonic expression, at the huge overcoat I carry over my arm, although the day is so unbearably hot outside, at the mangy suitcase hanging from the other arm, at the thick white wool turtleneck, at the jaunty night-blue felt hat on my head. A man on the run; or rather, a young gentleman on the run. . . . I kiss her lightly, on both cheeks, for the last time, and I am nearly overcome by the feel of her, by the female irradiation, hardly hearing my lips say, "Laurette, I came to say good-bye. I am leaving for . . . for India. By way of Marseilles. . . . Here, look at my ticket."

There is a dismay, astonishment in her expression, and I can't hear what she says. Instead of falling into my arms with a great sob, she opens the door to Vivian's room and once there I am forced to repeat my story in more sober fashion. He looks at me stonily when I speak of finding a guru in India: Isn't he good enough himself? He wishes me good-luck in a disgusted tone, and turns back to the great geometrical mandala on which he was working when I entered. She takes me to the door, muttering uncertainly, "Well, I hope that . . ." But I force myself not to turn back, and I leave her on the landing, peering down into the quadrangular spiral of the stairwell at the last traces of her vanishing knight-servant, now a knight-errant.

When I come out of my stupor, it is to find myself sitting on the hard wooden *banquette* of a third-class carriage in the train to Marseilles. My neighbors are already at their sausages and cheese, their caps cocked over one eye. . . . The next morning, arrival in the din and clamor of Marseilles, first lap of my trip. The radiant sun over the old Phoenician harbor wakes me up; if I can find a boat going to Greece, I'll get a refund on my ticket for the stretch between Marseilles and Ventimiglia. But I draw a blank, which means that I will have to sleep in the city and use the last portion of my ticket, to-morrow, to ride along the coast, to Italy. I am still in a daze, every bone in my body aching from last night's torture ride, letting myself be carried by a boisterous crowd of Provençals, I have no idea where to. In the midst of those jolly, sun-baked people in shirt sleeves and light frocks I realize that my getup is even more ludicrous than in Paris. The white sweater and the heavy greatcoat, an old ulster given me by my father, had been selected in anticipation of sleeping out under the stars, but in the devastating heat they look uncomfortably conspicuous, besides the discomfort itself. Also, just before leaving Paris for good and ever, I realized that a traveler without luggage would be suspect to the police and assorted customs officials, and so I provided myself with a small suitcase of imitation peccary. Empty, of course! All I'm taking is my train ticket, my passport, and my *Bhagavad-Gita*, plus fifty francs or so. Nothing more.

In Marseilles, I have misgivings that this empty suitcase could lead to embarrassing questions. Supposing someone were to pick it up and find out how very light it is? Since it's too small to encompass my overcoat, I purchase a kilo of sugar—that will be my entire food supply for the weeks to come—and complement the load with a few small rocks from an empty lot. I slouch somewhat aimlessly along the quays of the Vieux Port, drenched in sweat, my head buzzing, my bagful of stones pulling heavily at the end of my arm. Here I am on the first leg of my great spiritual adventure, my journey to the East.

The strangeness of my situation is such that it defies analysis. Did I really sever all bonds with the past? Will I perhaps forget, one day, even my own language? But is Marseilles so different from Calcutta? One should be able to live anywhere, really, and I am already very far from Paris. For instance, look at that fellow in his pajamas: He's reading his newspaper on a huge copper bedstead installed right in the middle of the sidewalk. No one pays any attention to this quiet family scene and the throng just walks around the group, the kids playing while the mother cooks up chow on a brazier. Life, here, is a public thing, and it requires loud expression, pungent drama, verbal delirium. Peals of laughter and vociferous quarrels, oil and garlic, bel canto galore. I feel so dizzy that I make up my mind to sacrifice a substantial part of my means to spend one last night under a roof. I take a room in the shabbiest little hotel I can find and collapse on the not-too-spotless bed. The semidarkness that surrounds me feels almost cool. Outside, night is falling and the sounds of cooking reach me from various directions, accompanied by the smell of things deep-fried in oil, which make me twist with pangs of hunger; I try to picture the horrid-looking squids dancing a death jig in the skillet, so as to fight off the stomach pains. This bed, really, brrr. . . . Clad in nothing but my shorts, I eat a few pieces of sugar. My dinner. No toothbrush, too bad. And so I settle down for some meditating. Nothing comes. I finally fall into a fitful slumber permeated with groans, pierced by the cursing and the cries of love that float up in the Marseilles night. I'm assaulted by dreams of such frightful obscenity that they wake me up at dawn, haggard and exhausted.

I take the train to Ventimiglia. I have trouble making out a few stanzas of the *Bhagavad-Gita*; my gaze is lost in the densities of blue, guillotined by lightning bolts of red rock. I try to adjust to the fact that India is drawing closer kilometer by kilometer. En route to India, I will have to cross Mussolini's Italy. I tried to make myself forget about that hair-raising prospect, since it couldn't be avoided anyway.

With my arrival in Ventimiglia, however, there's a partial return to reality. I present my British passport to a man in a uniform who inspects it with an air of suspicion, asking me a variety of questions before waving me on, almost with regret, I can sense it clearly. A customs official chalks across on my imitation peccary suitcase, without even bothering to open it. An incredible miracle! Indeed I have become too strange-looking for my strangeness to be questioned. I cross the border and reach a square where a bunch of fellows are revving up some heavy motorbikes; they're wearing riding breeches, shiny top boots, and black shirts. I leave the border town, suffocating with the heat.

As I start walking, I am tantalized by the thought of getting rid of my cement overcoat; yes, but what if I freeze to death during the night? And there are people everywhere, so that an action of that sort would be sure to be observed by someone, and they would start asking me questions—and then what? The road runs along past uninterrupted blocks of private properties neatly delineated by fences and high walls. People are watching me as I go by, and I hear them jabber among themselves. Their language is a mystery to me, which makes my isolation even more complete. The purpose of my being here, on this road, is now lost, and my consciousness is reduced to survival conditions. Fighting the heat. Awareness of being under constant watch. Every five minutes or so one of those thugs in black roars by on his motorbike, circles around me once or twice, and then roars back where he came from. I try to calm my hunger by sucking a piece of sugar; in keeping with my finances, I allow myself no more than one piece an hour. I walk through Bordighera and several other tiny resorts, separated from the sea by the continuous line of villas, each one with a private beach. At dusk I decide to go off the road in search of a secluded place; I discover a little path that winds down toward the seafront. Here's a lucky break! I spot a large bush that cannot possibly belong to anyone, I crawl under the lower branches, dragging my over- coat and my suitcase behind me, and I immediately plunge into a nightmare sleep. Traveling in the mystic India of H. P. Blavatsky, beating a path through the phantasmagorical jungles, the deep night crawling with deadly threats. . . .

My awakening is sudden and brutal, in an explosion of screams and blows. I find myself caught in a veritable marma- lade of kicking bodies, arms and legs flailing hysterically: As luck would have it, I had picked the secret nest of those two lovers—falling pell-mell on top of me and getting the shock of their lives. My panic is even worse than theirs! I disengage myself as best I can and I run like a ghoul under the peaceful starry sky, still clutching my precious suitcase, of course, as well as the overcoat and the blue sombrero.

The next evening, broken with fatigue, I decide once again to leave the highway, at a crossroads, and after walking uphill for a few hundred yards, I discover a small inn. The idea of a bed is overpowering, and I knock on the door. The owner asks for my papers, and I beat a hasty retreat, stammering some meaningless explanations. Things get better a little later, however, and I manage to spend the night sheltered by a thicket of small trees where no one disturbs me. Next morn- ing, back to the dusty highway, the well-entrenched villas, the mongrels that sniff at my ankles, people watching me with pursed lips from their doorsteps. Men in black keep storming past in clouds of dust, more and more frequently. . . . Could it be that there is only one of them? My brain's humming, my vision is all blurred, my lips are cracking with fever, I'm a starving zombie, notwithstanding my sugar cubes, a zombie with an unquenchable thirst despite the sparkling fountains that I pass. I am tempted to lap the water like a dog, but I fear that would reveal my desperado status, and get me arrested.

At last I enter a smallish town with a look of humanity about, a large square, and a small *trattorìa* with a terrace. I collapse on a chair, order *café au lait* and rolls, and gulp it all down like a maniac. When he brings my fifth cup of coffee the waiter starts talking to me, asking me questions in Italian that I don't understand. Is it by chance, or as the result of a subconscious calculation, that this terrace where I sit is located just across the street from the railroad station? I begin to hallucinate—I can clearly see a beautiful, gleaming black locomotive, *puff puff puff,* a pullman car with luxurious velvety pearl-gray seats. How much cash do I have left? Now, was I talking to myself? Who is that character sitting next to me? I did not even see him arrive—about thirty, gray suit and black shirt. He speaks to me in several languages, each of them incomprehensible to me.

He finally tries addressing me in broken French, and so I learn that he's intent on recruiting me for combat in Spain with the Italian volunteers. A war is going on there, let's not forget the fact, and to his beady eye, I look like cannon fodder.

"*Molto* mooney," he expostulates, "*bella uniforme.*"

That does it! I throw money to the waiter, without counting, and make a beeline for the station—with that damned fellow right behind me, breathing down my neck, talking, talking without interruption. Where to go? "Nice," I shout to the ticket man behind his window. Hooray, I have enough money, plus a few liras left after I pay for it. By another lucky break, a train is just pulling into the station—*and it's the right one for me!* I jump into a third-class carriage, pulling my paraphernalia after me. But the recruiting agent flashes a pass with red and green stripes at the controller and boards the same car, right after me. What do you think! After all the work he's done he is not going to let a recruit escape that easily. Sitting right across from me he continues his spiel. But as we get closer to France his voice takes on a tone that's almost plaintive, out of sheer desperation at my lack of comprehension. Furthermore, it's become impossible for me to answer him in any way—for I suddenly realize that I'm quite unable to speak: Something is blocking my throat, some psychosomatic dragon or other. At last the fellow gives up and gets off the train at Bordighera, after throwing me a last look of hurt, hate, and dismay.

Ah, back in France. What splendid, mellow, sloppy customs officials! Even the cops look reassuring, and the drabness, pettiness, and mediocrity associated with all the servants and monuments of official France look delicious after the evil pomposity on the Mussolini side.

I shut myself up in the lavatory to get some of the dirt off me. Looking into the mirror, I scarcely recognize myself; my tangled hair stands on end when I remove my hat, my face is deeply burnt by the sun, I look absolutely mad, insane. I get the rocks out of my suitcase and, one by one, plop them into the toilet bowl. If they can't explain how they got there, they can always call on Hercule Poirot to explain the mystery. After that, I go to the dining car and by means of signs and mimics, I order more *café au lait*.

Facing me, two tables away, I notice a group of overdressed Frenchmen observing me shamelessly and making ironic comments. The one in the middle remains silent, contemptuous of his fawning entourage. Who is he? Could it be— Yes! To my surprise I recognize the great Victor Francen, the famous star, the overlord, the hero of so many melodramas of the bourgeoisie. His beard is powdered with gold like Jupiter's, and his face covered with a foundation cream giving him a brick color, almost as intense as my own. He gazes at me with a studied expression, combining insolence and interest, and when I inadvertently return his gaze, he winks, wets his lips, and forms them into a kiss. The disgusting message hits me with all the power of its vulgarity. Victor Francen, the matinee idol, at once virile and fatherly in his admiral's uniforms or his well-cut surgeon's tunic, yes, *that's Victor Francen courting me!* Shock! I shudder at the memory of those maudlin love scenes—Francen face-to-face with his stumpy, morose-looking leading lady, Gaby Morlay. No wonder he went queer! But queers always disturb me, and being exposed to that obscene provocation, in such a public, obvious, degrading manner makes me want to throw up. I put all the money I have left on the table and flee with my cumbersome gear, bringing down pyramids of rolls on my way out; peals of laughter follow me in my retreat, Francen's minions are howling like sick dogs.

I stay locked in the lavatory until Nice; it's idiotic, but I can't stop trembling with the shock of it. That dirty old queen unsettled me, he found me out, pierced my paper-thin armor. I do have problems coping with the world; with the fact of being alive within a human shape, even. It's almost a week since I flung myself into this catastrophic adventure, and everything's giving out—nerves, head, the very skin inside which I'm frying. I'm totally undone by the realization of my incurable foolishness. Good God, won't I ever manage to do anything *normal?* Can't I even *run away* normally? Once again, the train rolls between the sun-drenched scarlet rocks, but now away from India, away from the great dream of wisdom; and yet, through the lavatory windows, the Mediterranean broadcasts an appeal to calm, to serenity, to a feeling of detached, supreme, ecstatic well-being. The sheer intensity of the blue, the myriad vibrations of light over water, the deep soothing message of the great mother, all-embracing, mellow waves, tender waves. . . .

We are coming into Nice; I have relatives here, my French military family. My little old uncle Teddy Laforgue settled down here, because of the climate, with his great warhorse of a wife, Thadée. I haven't seen them in years, but I know that I can depend on them to put me up for a short while and, well, negotiate my surrender to my parents—to society!—at reasonable terms. Hey—perhaps I will even find my cousins Jacques and Mowgli with their parents? Unlike me they are sane people, my cousins; as they realized they were not too brilliant at anything, they decided to make a career in the army, like their old man. The killing business, that's restful, well-paid, and most honorable. Mowgli got into the top-notch military school of Saint-Cyr, not without difficulty; but the handsome, carefree Jacques bungled everything to such an extent that nothing was left for him to do but to enlist in the school of noncommissioned officers at Saint-Maixent. Shame! What a first-rate idiot—my cousins aren't intellectuals, and they're the first to admit it. In fact, they're downright proud of it; they always thought school books were meant to be sold for pocket money.

I look feverishly for the Laforgue name in the phone book, and I draw a blank. The idea occurs to me to go over to the Cercle Militaire, the officers' club where my uncle is certain to be registered. The man at the desk looks up when I come in, and I can read in his expression that what he sees before him is nothing less than a desperate anarchist about to throw a bomb at him. He looks at my suitcase in terror, points at me with one hand, shouting for help. I try to say the words, *"I'm Colonel Laforgue's nephew!"*—but of course nothing comes out.

He gathers his courage as he sees me standing there, my mouth working spasmodically with no sound coming out; he pulls out a huge revolver from a drawer and points it at me. I flee—as I'm supposed to.

No voice. No money. No hope for the misfits. . . . I drag myself along a sunny side street that leads down to the famous Promenade des Anglais on the seafront. By chance, I lift my head and on the platform of a bus that's just pulling away, I catch sight of my good, my beautiful cousin Jacques! There he is, in the midst of a cluster of passengers, standing with his laughing black eyes plunging deep into the adoring blue eyes of his fiancée, Lilly, the two of them fastened to each other in a two-way smile of pure bliss. I cry out: *"Jacques!"* Alas, no sound comes out, and I almost pass out with anguish; the bus picks up speed and I chase after it, clutching my heavy ulster overcoat and feebly brandishing my empty suitcase. But my efforts are to no avail; my legs feel like rubber bands, the cinematic élan dissolves in slow motion, freezes into a useless lunge. It is so written: I shall expire on a Nice sidewalk, my mouth wide open in a noiseless call, in the midst of this festival of colors and songs. . . . I shall be snuffed out, suitcase in hand, before having really lived at all.

Sixty-two minutes later, at aperitif time, place Masséna is seething with people under its arches; nobody can perceive my presence any longer, as I zigzag aimlessly among groups of lively, gossipy, flirtatious people. Why am I here? The reason becomes clear when, *flash!*—on that terrace over there, I spot Jacques sitting with his back to me, with Lilly seen in profile. Next to them, three jabbering ladies of a certain age; from her family, no doubt. I tap on my cousin's shoulder and he turns halfway around, sticks his hand in his pocket, and hands me fifty centimes without looking at me. Every fiber in my body wants to shout—"Jacques!"—but my mouth cannot issue the sound. Should I let myself collapse at his feet? I tap him on the shoulder once again, all the while making a great effort to breathe out the sound of his name. But it is Lilly who finally looks up at me and screams:

"Mon Dieu! Jacques, look, it's . . . *it's Maurice!"*

Jacques took care of everything, and my uncle Teddy was very kind too. My family got a reassuring telegram, and I was invited to stay in Nice with the Laforgues until I felt able to cope with my defeat, with Paris, with my parents; a few days spent in Nice would lend my escapade a vaguely touristic air.

I spent my time up on the hills, high above the city and the sea, sitting under the gray olive trees, contemplating the vast spectacle of nature, and reading to myself the verses of the *Gita*—

> *Hear now of a time of light when Yogis go to eternal Life; and hear of a time of darkness when they return to death on earth.*
>
> *If they depart in the flames, the light, the day, the bright weeks of the moon and the months of increasing light of the sun, those who know Brahman go unto Brahman.*
>
> *But if they depart in the smoke, the night, the dark weeks of the moon and the months of decreasing days of the sun, they enter the lunar light, and return to the world of death. . . .*

On the day of my departure, I bought a little basket of pink carnations, and then took the train back to the old sheep-fold, not feeling too proud of myself. My parents' reception was intensely dignified, sober, and friendly. They treated me as an equal, an adult who had his problems, like themselves, and everyone else as well. I was stunned to learn that my father, as soon as he received my farewell letter, had gone over to see my friends on boulevard Saint-Germain and, even more extraordinary, that he had come away rather favorably impressed. My parents understood my need to live alone and offered to pay the rent on a studio in the Latin Quarter. They asked me politely what I had in mind for the future. After my adventure, my sole desire was to work with my friends: "Do whatever you want," said my father. "But at least make some attempt to earn your keep. For your own sake, you know, old bean." How could I ever bring myself to hate those people? And yet they were my family! And even Vivian had made friends with my dad! It was all very confusing.

"When your father came here," Laurette told me later, "he saw Vivian first, but it was Kryia who took him in hand. She was as successful with him as with her mighty politicos. She's *really* incredible! When he left—a true gentleman from head to toe—I could have sworn that he was about to ask Kryia out to dinner. As he opened the door to leave, he had a dreamy air about him, and he said, with his funny British accent: 'And he did not even take his *teeth*brush!' That's fatherly concern for you, I think. You are free to leave your home forever, but don't forget the teethbrush!"

Yes, that was my dad all right. But I was glad, as well as surprised, that he had made friends with Vivian and Kryia so easily. He had not breathed a word to me about them, of course, but at least he had been able to verify for himself that they were both superior people, notwithstanding their funny clothes. They were, intellectually, the enemy; but at least they were substantial adversaries, interesting people, literate—and who knows if I might not be able to learn something useful from them?

And learn I did, as many great projects were in the works by which Vivian and his followers were about to renovate human society.

Chief among them was the European federalist cause. Vivian's idea was as drastic as it was simple: Anyone above age twenty is merely repeating what he has learned and what he has been trained to do up to that point. There's nothing to be expected from the adults, especially in the field of politics; adults are merely children with wrinkles, plus a thirst for power. . . . How would the federation of Europe come about in a world so hopelessly divided by the power games of the adults? The answer is clear enough: *Call in the children!* That was Vivian's vision: a sort of Children's Crusade to turn Europe into a truly revolutionary society.

These were not to be ordinary children, of course. Vivian had in mind a vast plan providing for what he called children's republics, where the kids would organize themselves under their own responsibility, with little or no participation of the adults: Such a system had been in use for centuries among certain African tribes, and it did produce excellent results at their level. Why not provide the white European kids with all the instruments of learning, and let them discover their own approach to social life, to culture, and even to science? Adult brains were sclerotic, entrenched behind ready-made ideas, and concerned exclusively with results and so-called hard facts. Such as war, and factory work! Confronted with the basic problems of life, the children's answers and solutions would no doubt be much more genuinely creative. . . .

In an immediate and practical sense, the group was about to launch, during the following summer, the first session of what they called les Etats Généraux de la Jeunesse Européenne—a sort of young people's parliament to which would be invited kids from all European countries. Vivian's idea was now being turned into a major political project by the ubiquitous Kryia. Her personal influence over such key politicians as François de Menthon, Anatole de Monzie, Gaston Monnerville, and others, all of them leaders of the ruling Radical-Socialist party, made it possible to obtain government sponsorship—as well as subsidies—for that enterprise. This first yearly session of the Etats Généraux would open within the great popular turmoil Expo-'37 was bound to create in Paris, during the summer months, and the publicity would surely be tremendous. Young people from Africa would be invited to participate as well, so as to prepare for the next step beyond the unification of Europe, which Vivian termed "Eurafrica"—a global federation of the two continents.

Aside from this, Kryia was working on schemes that were more specifically her own. As a practical feminist, she had introduced the idea of a salary to be paid to mothers and housewives for the work they were doing at home; and this had been adopted, first by the Radicals, and soon after by the leftist alliance, the Front Populaire, as part of its revolutionary platform. Great changes had already been accomplished, since the Front Populaire was in power, in favor of the working classes—the forty-hour work week, the three weeks yearly vacation paid by the employer, the right to strike, to retire at a reasonable age, and that great novelty: social security. The salary for housewives would surely come next.

Another of her pet projects was to breathe new life into the French cooperative movement. It had been initiated at the beginning of the century (the brainchild of Louis Blanc, one of France's most practical revolutionary thinkers), but it had never developed beyond a certain point. All during the Middle Ages, cooperation was a deep-set practice in the life of peasants and townspeople in France, as elsewhere in most of Europe. It was perfectly feasible to adapt that principle of sharing to modern life, in terms of production, distribution, and consumption, and to agriculture as well as to industry. The idea of making the consumer the master of the game was truly French—assuming that the French are the individualists they claim to be! Cooperation was true-blue socialism in the Gallic tradition, the French response to Marxism *à la* Moscow, to Hitlerian autarchy, or to Yankee capitalism.

All this pleased me enormously, and because of my enthusiasm I was made second-in-command of a model cooperative recently founded by Kryia, the UJC—or Union of Young Cooperators. At first we would work as a travel agency, organizing the trips and sojourn in Paris of all the groups of young people who would congregate in Paris for the Etats-Généraux; and, in line with the cooperative principle, our clients would all become members of the UJC and be allocated a small share of the agency's profits.

Well and good! G.J. was twenty-nine and my only boss; a pleasant enough fellow, who was perpetually consumed by his taste for science and technology. He was one of Laurette's fervent admirers, and curiously enough, that made us friends rather than enemies. I became his assistant, his executive director, day-and-night buddy, and commissioner for external affairs. Which is to say, I was the one who would represent the UJC, by definition a leftist enterprise, in any dealings we might have with the various Front Populaire organizations. That function remained pretty much of an abstraction, but it gave me a taste of basic politics, and it confirmed me as a leftist.

And I was also earning a salary for the first time in my life. An extremely modest salary, since all this was done for the Cause, just enough to keep body and soul together. Just enough for me to afford the unbeatable prices of the Foyer Pythagore menu.

This was a seedy-looking vegetarian restaurant close to the church of Saint-Séverin, in the Latin Quarter. It served as a meeting place and refectory for an assortment of terminal oddballs, ancient occultists, and anarchists from a forgotten era—we were nearly the only young people among that clientele, G.J. and I, when we took our meals at the Foyer. This we did frequently, and it was not just to treat ourselves to "more grated carrots than you can possibly eat"—it was, in fact, to graze our eyes hypocritically on the charms of the local waitress, an explosive person known as Didi. And this, G.J. and I would never have admitted to each other!

At least G.J. was a bit more open about it. He would actually change his glasses for a more appropriate pair, wipe them carefully for better vision, and peer meditatively above the menu, as if he were in search of some elusive thought. Everything looked gray and old in that restaurant, the food, the clients, and the decor—and by contrast Didi appeared as a fleshy statement in favor of youth, color, vitality, and *joie de vivre*.

At her approach the old codgers, who pretended never to pay the least attention to Didi, would show signs of extreme nervousness, coughing, sniveling, scratching themselves, dropping their dentures, and some would even get a little color in their faces. The brief skirt would come frolicking between the tables and everybody would plunge their nose into a book, or a dish, looking severe, and guilty. As to myself I must humbly admit that I was responding no better; I would sit in front of G.J. with my back to the room, due to my excessive vulnerability when faced with sexual provocation. How else could you call her, that person? A flesh bomb! She could enslave you forever with one fiery glance.

Sure enough, G.J. and I, we were two famous hypocrites, and I was the worst of the two. At least G.J. had the advantage on me of having known the pleasures of the flesh, as it is known, before he became one of Vivian's disciples. But I had only my dream of such pleasures, magnified a hundredfold by the fact that they had never been gratified in any other way. Walking out of the Foyer Pythagore, I felt confused, seething, angry with myself to the point that I sometimes banged the door shut; two hundred yards away as the crow flies was Vivian's ashram, and I could easily picture, at the feet of the master, She for whom I had solemnly given up any hope whatsoever of knowing the manly joys of love with a beautiful woman. . . . When I looked at Laurette, at times, I would compare her—viciously—to Didi. The beautiful innocent! She would glance back at me with her charming smile, and I would, inwardly, apologize to her.

The more it went, the more holy she seemed to become. I admired her new personality as a full-time *clairvoyante* at Vivian's service—his seeing-eye dog, as she herself laughingly explained—since he appeared to be himself deprived of the inner vision due to some psychic drama of the past, as the story went. The memory of last summer's moments of pure and intense love were receding into the past. . . . Nevermore. All my life I would be her knight-servant, a soldier-monk. . . . But, oh that Didi!

Rahulla, our secret lodge, met on Sunday evenings in the boulevard Saint-Germain ashram. Sitting tailor-fashion in my corner, I would observe from afar the ease and familiarity of their exchange, of their wordless understanding. The room was soon thrown into darkness. The only traces of light that remained came from a few embers of incense, placed under portraits of the Masters of the Great Hierarchy, mysteriously revealing random profiles and features of disciples fixed in

their various meditation postures. G.J., our universal tech-
nolomagician had invented an apparatus that captured atmos-
pheric vibrations; during each of the five or six successive
meditations, this instrument gave off continuous sound at
variable pitch. Vivian gave the theme for each phase, which
was sometimes of a political nature. At the end of the phase,
the light would come back on; everyone blinked, and Laurette, her eyes still absent and strange, a reddish vertical
mark, rather like a birthmark, in the middle of her forehead,
would describe what she had seen, images or symbols. Then,
in his own manner, Vivian would make *tableaux* or stories out
of it, interpreting what she had seen with a freedom that was
always somewhat surprising. Laurette, although still not quite
back on earth, would sometimes struggle to express some
timid protest if she felt that he was going too far against what
she felt to be the meaning of what she had seen.

But he was the unquestioned guru, and no one would dare
question his word on any issue at all, whether mundane or
spiritual. Take, for instance, the 1936 presidential election.
One of the two contestants, Justin Godard, we considered as
our own candidate. He was speaker of the Senate and a leading figure of the Radical-Socialists, as well as one of Kryia's
devotees. The other man was the incumbent, Albert Lebrun
himself, a highly respected politician with the brain of a min-
now; which means that we did have our chance. For weeks,
the Rahulla lodge concentrated all of its metaphysical powers
in order to bolster Justin's rising star. On Election Day, a
special grand reunion was convened, hours of meditation
before the voting. The oracle was consulted. "Laurette, *are you
there?*" "Yes," she murmurs. "Yes, I can see a face . . . the
president's face . . . still very faint . . . but, yes, I see a white
moustache, but . . ."

"*It's Godard!*" proclaims Vivian in a vibrant voice, as the
light comes back. Incredible and yet true: our man in the
presidency, an event of extraordinary consequences! Everyone is tremendously excited, but Laurette is heard, pleading
to Vivian: "Wait a minute, I didn't actually see *Godard*—just
an old man with a moustache."

Nobody listens—and a few minutes later, in the midst of
the general delirium, when the radio announces that the pres-
ident-elect is Albert Lebrun, we are all floored and Vivian
leaves the room without a word. Lebrun also has a white
moustache, didn't you know?

11

*Tropic of Cancer slowly infiltrates America, England.
—Kurt Enoch.—Bogous and Dillie.—The liberation of
The Obelisk Press.—Stuffing Ginette into her corset.
—A spring shindig for Henry Miller.—The last
of our heroes leaves for the Spanish front.—Waiting for
Julius Caesar.—I become a big executive,
suddenly and not for long.*

Tropic of Cancer was a modest success, and this brought my
father great satisfaction. By the spring of 1937, within two
and a half years, some six hundred copies had been sold out
of a printing of one thousand, and Anaïs Nin's loan had been
partially paid back. *Daffodil* and *My Life and Loves* were selling
ten times better to the tourist trade, of course, but Miller's
reputation in the United State was slowly building up by word
of mouth. The Obelisk Press was receiving streams of tiny
orders from our single American trade client, the plucky
Frances Steloff, owner of New York's famous avant-garde
bookstore, the Gotham Book Mart. Sometimes for six copies
at a crack! We had to mail them one by one, wrapped in
anonymous brown paper with all kinds of moronic markings
in the hope of duping the U.S. Customs—which sometimes
worked, and often didn't.

The entire staff of the Obelisk Press consisted only of my
father and a shapely secretary, and he had appointed as his
sole foreign distributor a small firm with offices on place
Vendôme, Continenta, whose entire staff was made up of
German refugees. Its founder and boss was Kurt Enoch, formerly a publisher in Leipzig, a former Luftwaffe officer who
had received the Iron Cross for his conduct during World
War I. Although a patriotic gentleman, he was a Jew, and so
was his young wife, with whom he had fled to France after

Hitler's rise to power. And so it was Continenta's job to wrap
up that dynamite literature in a variety of deceptive ways and
airmail it from various post offices all around Paris so as to
further confuse the U.S. Customs bloodhounds. Enoch had
accepted his social and professional downfall with a stout
heart; having been a high-ranking publisher and being now
forced to eke out a living as a specialist in pitiful contraband
techniques did not offend or discourage him in the least. Indeed he drew great pride from the efficiency of his staff.

My father admired him for this gentlemanly fortitude, and
he was also grateful for the feeling of security he drew from
Enoch's cooperation. He was thus able to spend most of his
time in his favorite bars, engaging in his favorite study—the
object of which was the female sex. He trusted Kurt's business sense implicitly, and he started paying attention every
time he tried to show him why and how he should get rid of
his partner, M. Servant.

But he was also receiving the same kind of advice from
another solid friend of his, a Russian émigré, Michel Bogouslawsky. As a medical student in Moscow Michel had conspired against the régime, and he had been shipped off to a
Siberian prison-camp in due course. Fortunately for him his
family was influential enough to secure his liberation; in 1905
he had thus become an exile in Switzerland, a first stop for
most revolutionary exiles; and then in New York where Michel became a streetcar conductor. He felt the job was too
much for him, what with the zany traffic and people constantly throwing themselves under his wheels, or threatening to do
so. He was pining for a position as cabdriver in Paris instead,
and he finally managed to pay his passage back to Europe. The
war came soon after that and he enlisted in the French army,
and soon became an officer and a doctor. At some point
during the war he fell for a beautiful redhead, an Irish
girl with a sharp tongue called Dillie, who was just as ravishing as he was rough-looking, just as pale-skinned and refined
as he was craggy-faced and rambunctious. He had also met
Jack, and Marcelle, his French fiancée, at about that same
time, and they served as Michel and Dillie's witnesses at their
marriage; in turn Michel and Dillie were the witnesses when
my parents got married in 1917. . . . After the war Michel
Bogouslawsky had started on his own a small foreign books
import business in Paris. The all-powerful house of Hachette
had offered to integrate his tiny enterprise within their na-

tionwide organization, with the status of partner. From that point on, his life had become remarkably stable.

Bogous (as we called him) was therefore in a position to help his old friend conquer his freedom from the evil Servant. He did his best, and my father was able to negotiate a friendly separation from Servant in the spring of 1937. He would have to borrow money to buy back the stocks of books from him and his emancipation was to cost him dearly, but everything would be in order by autumn. To celebrate this new beginning, my parents threw a grand spring cocktail shindig, at which Henry Miller would be guest of honor.

Our parties, be they literary or otherwise, generally got off to a good start but often ended up in somewhat of a chaos. The beginning was characterized by superb logistic arrangements, thanks to my mother's organizational prowess. On these occasions we were all proud to behold the spectacle of her maneuvers in the kitchen, whipping up twenty different dishes at a time, flawlessly, at hallucinating speed, and without ever breaking a thing. And when everything was ready, Ginette had to be laced into her corset before the guests arrived.

Our household staff has been reduced by stages to this affable round-faced peasant girl of sixteen who maintains that she has never sinned. Nevertheless, in the three months since she has been with us, she has almost doubled in weight; this, we all agree, is becoming increasingly suspicious. With one foot planted on the lower back of her Rabelaisian housemaid, my tiny mother pulls on the corset strings. Ginette, bracing herself with both hands against the kitchen table, squirms and screams with laughter, saying that it tickles. Everybody lends a hand. Next, she must be helped into her black dress and this isn't easy either, a bit like trying to stuff an oversize jellyfish into a sock. Then the final touch: a pretty white lace-trimmed apron. She is set down on a chair. My mother arranges her hair while my sisters try to wedge her feet into high-heeled pumps, but her feet are too fat, too round, and I am called to the rescue. I do what I can.

Finally, the maid is dressed in an adequate fashion. She can barely move, but she'll at least be able to open the door and serve the buffet. Just now the bell rings. Ginette jumps up, bumps into an armchair, and collapses with a loud curse: "Ah, *yes* alors!" (Not that it really matters: but having heard that word so many times in her masters' conversation, she has taken it into her thick skull that *yes* is a pretty strong British swearword, to be used in extreme situations.) But she picks herself up and my mother, with a friendly swat on her behind, sends her off in the direction of the door.

Ginette opens and finds herself in the presence of two bald, merry-faced gentlemen, one not too tall and the other rather short. The taller of the two hands her an old battered gray fedora and pinches her left nipple good-naturedly through the black satin dress, with a deft twist of thumb and index finger. The other, who is his exact replica, only smaller, studies Ginette from head to toe, gives her his hat, and pinches the other tit. From the kitchen door, my mother witnesses the scene and exclaims:

"Good heavens, and Jack isn't even home yet! These characters are an hour early. Go take care of them, children, go meet, Maurice. The bigger one, that's Henry Miller, a writer. I don't know who the other one is. Tell them I'm not quite ready. Go on, do something. Give them a drink."

Henry Miller, my idol! I'm strangled by timidity, but I'd better get with it. I come into the living room, my kid sisters and brother at my heels. As we make our entrance, the expression of amused interest on the two pals' faces gives me the jitters. I never felt so foolish before—and God knows. . . . The searing memory of the *Tropic of Cancer* cover strikes me like a dagger between the shoulder blades. Let's avoid the subject at all cost!

"Ah, is that you, Maurice?" Henry growls at me amiably, holding out his hand. "Do you speak any English? Hmm?"

I answer yes, I speak English. That is . . . I get along. It would be fitting to tell him of my admiration for his book— I must impress on him the fact that I'm not just any gawky kid. But introductions must come first.

"This is my friend, Alf," he declares, pointing to his diminutive companion. "*Mister* Alfred Perlès as he likes to call himself."

"*Enchanté,*" I answer in standard conversational French. "Here are my sisters, Nicole and Sylvie, and my brother Eric."

We shake hands ceremoniously all around. Perlès is delighted to meet my sisters and brother, since they are his own size, and begins chattering away in French, onomatopoetically, because after all his interlocutors are still only children.

"Maurice," says Henry Miller, the great writer, in his most

mellow voice, "Alf and I are *dying* of thirst. What about getting us a nice big glass of red wine, eh? Hmm?"

He darts an anxious glance at the vast buffet that is groaning under scintillating arrays of glassware and plates, but still innocent of food and drink.

"Make it white wine for me," specifies Perlès, with some petulance.

"Ah, wine?" I say. "I don't know. . . . There's whiskey, vodka . . . brandy, punch . . ."

"*Punch!* Okay, let's go for the punch!" they say in chorus.

My sisters rush in the direction of the kitchen with the order.

"And if you could find us a little something to nibble along with it?" adds Henry. He shows me his dust-covered moccasins. "I've been walking around all day and I'm famished. Ready to drop, any minute."

"It's that . . . you're a bit ahead of time; my mother hasn't finished preparing the buffet."

It strikes me that my father's job has some drawbacks. If all authors are like that, a publisher's life must be pretty complicated at times. Miller is not what I expected, but he is certainly amiable, like a wise monkey; behind round eyeglasses his blue eyes are pursed with malice; quite obviously he's not as naïve as he would have you think. The high forehead belongs to a medieval monk, I observe to myself, but without the simian foundation, would that fellow be Henry Miller?

"It's not really my fault," he explains. "I don't carry a watch, and neither does Alf, and we haven't had any lunch," he drawls confidentially. "So, we're too early, hey? Hmm. I'll be damned. Listen, Alf, I guess we goofed, we're early, that's why there isn't anybody else around! You get it, Alf?"

"Yes," says Alf, relieved to be able to explain things intelligibly at last. "When we got here and when we didn't see anybody around," he tells me, "and nothing to drink or eat, Henry began to get nervous. Seriously." His little eyes are awash with uncertainty; he has a lot of trouble explaining his friend to the world at large.

"I personally find her very attractive, that young maid with the big tits," Miller resumes, licking his chops quite audibly. "Mmm, she's quite a dish, really *enormous*. How's she called?"

At this very moment Ginette comes in, summoned by some secret signal, and she is bearing a punch bowl as if it were the blessed sacrament. The two buddies whistle politely, and pour her a glass before serving themselves.

"Oh, monsieur!" says Ginette, totally unsettled by the chivalrous gesture.

However, she decides after all, why not play along with them? Ever since she came up to Paris and went to work for these bizarre people, my parents, things have been happening that constantly defy simple common sense. Nothing to do with the society of pigs and cows in which she was brought up. Her glass is full to the brim and she downs it in one gulp; and immediately begins to teeter on her high heels. My brother and sisters, meanwhile, are taking full advantage of these goings-on; they are seated in a row on the couch and follow the action with great attention and delight. The two guests grasp Ginette around the waist to help her retain her balance; she giggles and wobbles, shrieks and fights, hooting with uncontrollable laughter.

"Ginette!" my mother calls from the kitchen. "Ginette! Children!" The scene breaks; the three kids surround Ginette and, supporting her, leave by one door, while my father enters through another, carrying a jar of anchovies.

"Anchovies!" says Miller. "I would have preferred Russian salad. Hello, Jack!"

"This isn't a restaurant here," says my father, absentmindedly. "These anchovies aren't for you, anyway, they're for Mars who sent me out to get them. If you want some Russian salad, do as I did, and go get some for yourself. Here, take some money. There's an Italian grocer on the corner of avenue de Neuilly. And bring back the change!"

"Oh, Jack," cries Miller, taking the hundred-franc note.

"Oh thanks, Jack!" echoes Alf.

And they leave as one man, after having drained their third glass of punch.

"Those two together! Phew!" says my father, talking more to himself than to me. "Even so, I hope they don't get lost on the way," he adds.

Finally everything falls more or less into place and soon the first guests arrive: the Gilberts who are inevitably punctual. I've always loved that magical moment: the transition between the mounting tension just before the beginning of the party and the arrival of the first couple. Suddenly, out of chaos comes order, the three knocks are struck, the curtain rises and the comedy begins. . . . My father greets the other guests, and the living room rapidly fills up, and then the dining room, the bedrooms, and the hallways. My mother has just had time to change her dress and powder her nose before the on-slaught. I receive kisses and the lipstick of Nadejda de Bra-gança, Susan Booth, her daughter Claudie, Anita de Caro, three good friends of my father's. It's all very aristocrat-ic. Besides Nadejda, whose uncle has claims to the throne of Portugal, there's a Princess Troubetzkoï, also American, of course, and a Count Igniatieff, who is an elegant Bolshevik as well as a genuine count, plus an international assortment of barons and marquises. They are all very curious to meet Henry Miller, this scandalous American who is beginning to be talked about in the salons. Editions Stock will soon publish his book in French and they say it's ten times stronger than Céline. *"But where is he?"* demand the lovely perfumed ladies excitedly. We explain that he has been delayed by some ur-gent business.

Like the apparition of light emerging from the shadows, a tall young woman makes a perfect entrance. Her face is sweet and magnetic, a Holy Virgin with artist's eyes. My father leaves the two sisters—Countess Edith Gauthier-Vignal, high priestess of literature, and the Baronne de Marwicz, high priestess of music—and goes to welcome the newcomer and introduce her around. It's Anaïs Nin. Everybody has heard her name, but no one knows much about her. There is talk of a rich husband who remains hidden, of many strange lov-ers. Who is she exactly? Dancer? Adventuress? Poetess? She lives on the Seine, on Michel Simon's houseboat with a crew of pirates, it is rumored. Others claim that she is Henry Miller's muse, the Brooklyn satyr. Anything goes.

Stuart Gilbert, one of my father's old friends, asks me if I am still a fervent student of theosophy. This elderly English-man has accomplished the feat of beginning his career as a judge in India and ending up as a James Joyce scholar and one of the popes of the Paris avant-garde. Ever since the day he came upon me reading Proust, he has treated me like an adult, to the extent of trying to convince my father that my involvement in theosophy was not so silly. His wife, Moune, is French; her mouth is so small and her voice so tiny that when she speaks everyone around her is forced into silence, as if by magic. The Gilberts belong to the rarefied Ile Saint-

Louis elite, and the literary salon surpasses even that of Jenny Bradley, their neighbor, whose husband, Bill, an American literary agent, had caused Henry Miller and my father to meet for the first time; and sure enough I can hear her thundering laughter piercing through walls of bodies: She's never very far from her Ile Saint-Louis rivals.

Joining the group of which I have become a part is another international couple: Eugene and Mary Jolas whose concentrated energy I find terrifying. A Frenchman is with them, a bespectacled young man, studious-looking and soft-spoken, who lived in Ireland where he married another disciple of James Joyce's: It's Georges Pelorson. While he's talking to me about the literary magazine *Volontés*, that he's just started with a few of his friends from Ecole Normale, my father comes up to us with the Bogouslawskys. Michel's formidable Russian accent rolls and thunders above the surrounding noise like cannon salvos at Waterloo; his ruddy face looks like a huge pumpkin about to burst. My mother suddenly appears from nowhere.

"Jack," she says, "if you're looking for Henry, you'll find your guest of honor in the kitchen."

Everybody troops to the scene. The great writer and his coadjutor, looking somewhat miffed at the sudden invasion, are sitting in front of an enormous bowl of Russian salad and spooning it up. One hundred francs worth of Russian salad! They sneaked in the back door so as to indulge themselves on the sly; now the countesses are pouring in from everywhere, tittering delightedly at the sight: *"Here he is!"* Or rather, here they are! There is not one Henry Miller, but two of them, or so it seems; a bigger one and a smaller one. Oh, wonder of wonders! My my, it must be so good what they are eating out of that bowl! Everybody wants a taste of the Russian salad and they all start dipping into it with soup spoons. Alf now realizes that he has no real existence except as Henry's small-size replica, and he bursts into tears, crocodile tears to be sure; Ginette grabs his little bald head and presses it to her bursting bosom. Meanwhile the evil kids, Eric and Sylvie, pretending that they are reporters, rush all over the place, busily taking notes on imaginary pads. A faint breeze of madness turns all verbal exchanges into absolute nonsense; everybody talks at the same time, nobody listens to anybody, and the only ones to laugh at the jokes are those who crack them.

The decline of the West. As a leftist I could only look upon those blatant contradictions of the capitalist world with virtuous disdain.

Not that my forays into revolutionary circles have been all that conclusive. The Front Populaire meetings I have attended in my capacity as representative of the UJC have shown the militant Socialists and Communists to be, on the whole, just as conformist, and even bigoted in their own way, as the young monarchist agitators I used to know in former years in Neuilly: the Camelots du Roy. Right, Left, it all comes to the same; the truth of the matter was that politics themselves were the enemy—the subservience to clichés. What had started two years before as a new dawn is already ending in confusion, compromise, and disaster; the way is now open to Stalin, Hitler, and the other dictators to take over in Europe, and soon after in the entire world. Even my faith in the anarchist ideology has crumbled in the face of reality: In Barcelona, the anarchists had got mired for good in an escalation of violence.

What could I do? Who could I speak to? Vivian dismissed the circumstances of politics as being unworthy of his time and attention. He didn't see anything wrong in the fact that soon millions would surely perish; these were merely episodes of limited value—the fate of the individual people mattered very little to the cosmic scheme of things. Sitting high on his command cloud Vivian presided over the movement of the worlds, and the rise and fall of human empires were no more than insignificant ripples in the river of endless time. So, why worry about the ethics of Right or Left as long as Vivian reigned supreme from his esoteric throne?

One morning, I went over with Gregor Louchine to watch the departure of a convoy of the International Brigade; as usual the volunteers for Spain assembled in the south of Paris, at the Porte d'Orléans.

Thus it was that we found ourselves in the midst of a fervent, disorderly crowd that surrounded a dozen open trucks. Men and women were embracing one another tightly, children were yelling slogans in shrill, squeaky voices, waving red flags, and human clusters were forming in a great surge of deep-felt communion. The moment was solemn and pathetic; it reached an extraordinary intensity of feeling, which seized all present, when the motors revved up one after another. In the panic of the last kiss, cries of love and distress pierced the racket as the trucks started off in a slow procession. And then the entire crowd, carried away by the finality of the pain, by the taste of hope and death, found its unity at last in a vast, all-encompassing chant. *L'Internationale* arose, a vibrant call from the heart, a last rite of brotherhood between those who were leaving for their last battle and those who were staying behind, fists raised high in a final salute, bodies rigid, faces contorted in a great shout—*no pasarán!*

Tears and dust streaked faces, frozen still in the direction of the last departing truck. Now silent, transfigured, cataleptic, marked secretly by an event some of those present would perhaps forget one day, but which had modified all of them forever. The people had just sent off the best of their own into combat and toward the ultimate, gory adventure. All this young blood was to be spilled in sacrifice for—for the future. For the children of the people. . . . *No pasarán!*

"Holy shit!" Gregor says in awe. "That's the real thing, you know? A bourgeois skunk would give money for his cause; those people just give themselves."

"Yes," I answer. "You couldn't dream of a scene like this in a church in Neuilly, whatever the provocation."

"That's why there's no hope for the proletariat. If Franco doesn't get them, Stalin will. Or Hitler, or their own government. They work all their lives like animals, and on top of that they're supposed to fight wars, and die to protect the banks. Everybody lies to them, including you and me—because we don't help. I'm so disgusted with myself I want to throw up."

"You go too far, old man. You've got your numbers crossed. You sound like Kyrill or Stepan talking," I said, not too honestly.

"Oh shut up," he growled. "That's just what I mean, you idiot. Kyrill's in Barcelona, Stepan and Ouliana are in Moscow. Perhaps they've gone out of their minds, or maybe they're dead . . . and that makes me sick with being alive, can't you understand that?"

One thousand years ago Paris came to life on two narrow strips of land, the Ile de la Cité as flagship with, in its wake, the Ile Saint-Louis, carrying on its deck the precious towers of Notre-Dame. The Ile de la Cité has the appearance of a battleship of stone, cleaving the ancient waters of the river with its keen prow, and that tapering point is known as le Vert-Galant in homage to King Henry IV, and to his amorous disposition. The quays where the fishermen doze at the end of their lines stop upstream at the Pont-Neuf, and the cutwater surges straight into the current, defying winds and storms; in the background huddles the Paris of yesteryear, its spires, tortuous roofs, deep, narrow streets. Facing this past, proud, virile, bristling with fluttering pigeons, rises the equestrian statue of the good monarch, Henri the Lusty-Lover, pilot of the future. His grand design was to make of Europe a peaceful empire of equal nations, and he paid the price of his dream when he fell under an assassin's dagger, like all true visionaries always will. . . . Two steps away, a plaque commemorates the spot where Jacques de Molay, the last Grand Master of the Order of the Knights Templar, was burned at the stake, most memorable victim of the French monarchy.

At the very tip of this point of the Vert-Galant is a public garden, a slender, exiguous triangle frequented by students and bums; few lovers are found there because this unique spot is in full view of a thousand windows. Unique also on account of its location, as the Vert-Galant faces history on two sides: on one side the Louvre, the majestic palace of the kings of France; on the other the great libraries and universities of the Latin Quarter. The State and the People are thus precisely separated by the river.

Such are the reasons that have dictated the choice of this particular spot to enact the ceremony now under way. Kryia has managed to turn this into an official manifestation: the planting of the Tree of Europe, now only a modest oak tree. In a hundred years, however, it will rise majestically above the river to remind the world at large that it is in Paris, in A.D. 1937, that the Etats Généraux de la Jeunesse Européenne met for the first time, and that this was the first step in the foundation of a united Europe.

The thousands of Parisians who surround us on all sides could see from afar that little cluster of people standing at the tip of the Vert-Galant. What is going on there? Some pick up their binoculars, or their telescopes; merchants on rue Dauphine send their kids to find out.

It does look like an official inauguration, because of those grave-faced gentlemen wearing the tricolor sashes of assemblymen, and of municipal dignitaries. But it cannot be an ordinary inauguration because of those other people, who form the majority in the group. Young women wearing unusual kinds of uniforms, and particularly that striking-looking older woman with Beethoven's forehead. Who in heavens can they be?

In the center of the group, the action is as follows: An old city gardener is digging a hole in the ground to plant the Tree of Europe, spitting and cursing like a trooper, while everyone stands at attention all around. In front of the gardener a tall man in a romantic cape is declaiming a long poem, seemingly addressing the awesome verses to the tree itself. It's Robert Vidalin, a well-known actor from la Comédie-Française, our famous classical repertory theater; one hand is placed over his heart while the other weaves dramatically in the turbulent air, in the manner of the old school, to accompany each verse and strophe of Victor Hugo's interminable ode to Europe:

> . . . *We're a nameless handful of seeds*
> *On the future's somber field,*
> *And there we'll sprout, my brothers, have no doubt,*
> *As in this sand, next waters quick to seethe,*
> *Will grow, betwixt the tide's clashed ebb and flow,*
> *This acorn, on which God will breathe.* . . .

In the first row, facing the politicians and her phalanx of followers, Jeanne Canudo appears to all more as a symbol than as a human figure. She has the austere beauty of an allegory, and I can't help picturing her image engraved on the coins that the European Federation will surely someday mint. At her side, Rolande, the heiress to this future throne, radiant and graceful. Somewhat behind them, Laurette is flanked by two uniformed young women who are almost standing at attention, Jackrosen and Rosenode, the two devoted sisters who serve Vivian and Kryia day and night in every possible capacity, and who will always appear in the attitude of human caryatids in all such public occasions.

Vidalin keeps declaiming while the old municipal gardener of the City of Paris does his best to make the Oak of Europe stand up straight. In fact, this oak is a mere sapling with two or three buds—a twig, really, an absurd little stick of wood. The gardener is senile and inept, and he has great trouble forcing this symbol of our future to stand straight, and curses interminably in the wind.

A barge passes slowly in front of the island, its deck level with the ground on which we stand, with multicolored shirts and petticoats hanging from a clothesline, joyously flapping in the wind, while the skipper's mate, impervious to the gravity of our ceremony, plays a fast-moving waltz on his accordion. Against all odds, disdaining all interruptions, Vidalin continues doggedly to declaim the endless poem; a malicious breeze lifts the ladies' skirts and the politicians' gaze begins to stray. We now observe a strange-looking individual approaching the scene. It's Raymond Duncan, Isadora's brother, who lives on rue Dauphine, a stone's throw from the Vert-Galant; he appears dressed as usual in his Homeric poet's toga, his Athenian-style sandals, with lyre in hand. . . . But to Vidalin, who is not familiar with our neighborhood cranks, this is the last straw; he gets rattled and stops. Highly intrigued, the reporters converge on Raymond and start interviewing him; they ask him to strike a pose with his lyre, and they take pictures of him from every angle. But Vidalin shows again his fortitude in the face of adversity, and resumes his tirade. The wind carries off two hats in a spiral movement, and we see them hit the water and slowly drown in the distance. A rickety pleasure boat looking like a floating bus—we call them *bateaux-mouches* in Paris—passes by, three meters from us, loaded with school kids who yell gleefully the obscene verses of a famous, utterly disgusting school song, *Père Dupanloup*. Vidalin stumbles over his text and then, with arms raised, he takes off with a vengeance:

> *. . . an enormous tree,*
> *Moving as today, as powerful as tomorrow,*
> *Its leaf, its form, its size all symbolize*
> *The growth of humanity. . . .*

From his eagle's nest high above the old palace of Cluny, Vivian pursues his meditations on cosmic affairs while at the tip of the Vert-Galant the rituals he has arranged for us, unfold. A spot on the planet that most preoccupies him at this moment is a castle in the forest, not too far from Prague, where Julius Caesar must be seventeen years old today, in his most recent reincarnation. Upon Caesar's shoulders will fall the task of uniting Europe politically; he is used to the job and no doubt this time he will succeed (but without England or Soviet Russia, which we consider as foreign to the European spirit, incapable of cooperation). Czechoslovakia will be the turntable of the new European politics, and when Caesar marries Rolande Canudo, at the end of the forties, then Kryia will be able to direct her grand campaign for European unification by proxy. For this unique and strictly political reason, Rolande is the only one among us who will know fleshly love. And indeed, to a large extent, this is her day; she holds herself with demure grace, as if she were already the most famous bride in our future world history.

Meanwhile the bums who have been dislodged from their benches become restless; they want their seats back. They spread into the crowd, buttonhole the politicos, cadge cigarettes, and add to the general chaos. Vidalin finishes at last, more absurd pictures are being snapped, the meager crowd disperses; it's aperitif time for some, meditation time for others.

The next four months are telescoped in my memory in piebald succession—a single continuous activity. I had got into the habit of sleeping on a chair or curled up in Georges Jenny's tiny car, or even while walking around the streets. G.J. and I, we spent the whole summer season performing such extraordinary feats in the service of The Cause that by the time the Expo-'37 closed its doors, by the end of October, we had earned a fortune for Vivian's ashram.

Our tourist operation was simple. To begin with, it had been directed toward groups of young Europeans who came to Paris for the session of the Etats Généraux. But as that noble enterprise started to disintegrate, so did our commercial ethics. Any group of any description, coming from abroad or from the French provinces to visit the exhibition, were potential customers for us; we went after them with a package deal for lodging, meals, and a few bus excursions, which they just couldn't refuse.

We didn't promise anything fancy. The army quartermaster corps had installed a huge canteen on the Champ-de-Mars, and dormitories at Buttes-Chaumont, five miles to the north, all done up in rather repulsive barracks style. The rule was to get the money in advance for a given number of beds and meals, and then we would reserve the corresponding accommodation from the quartermasters—less two percent for the first day, ten percent for the second, twenty for the third, and so on. The reason for this diminishing reckoning was that the groups melted away after their very first night in Paris. There were too many temptations: Some spent their time with the whores, others got lost in the subway, in the streets, or in a bistro, and at the end of a week, the group was reduced by half. We pocketed the difference; it was extremely simple, a matter of statistics: The profits were immense, while our fee remained absurdly low. The competition didn't stand a chance.

I would never have chosen to engage in an activity of that sort for my own benefit; and the same could be said of G.J. himself. But doing it for The Cause made it morally permissible, and even desirable. We felt all the more justified in doing so as we didn't make a penny for ourselves. We just kept enough money for our own living expenses, which were incredibly small.

And we did not ask ourselves too many questions about the way those masses of cash were spent. But while we were so busy earning it, it seems that everything else was going wrong. The Etats Généraux was to be sponsored, and even subsidized to a large extent, by the government; but at that point Léon Blum's cabinet resigned, and its promises were automatically canceled. The summer sessions of the Etats Généraux were consequently reduced to a few ineffectual meetings, which were duly infiltrated by Communist apparatchiks as well as by rightist shock troops. The Italian and German delegations arrived in large numbers, and began to colonize our movement. The rue Serpente headquarters were ransacked several times running, alternately by Stalinist thugs and by French Fascists.

It was indeed a surprise to find that Vivian didn't really care: He was already dreaming up vastly more ambitious plans for the future. Apparently, to him, the European Federation and the cooperative ideal were already a thing of the past. Everything will fall into perspective, he once said, when Julius Caesar takes over. Meanwhile there was enough money in the coffers for the boulevard Saint-Germain community to prosper through a few more seasons.

One night I managed to drag Laurette away from her psychic duties, and over a modest meal of Chinese vegetables I tried, very cautiously at first, to express my negative impressions to her. Much to my surprise, I soon got the feeling that she wasn't far from agreeing with me, but didn't dare to waver from the official line. That discovery immediately plunged me into a maze of contradictory feelings. She now spent the best part of her time exploring the astral plane with Vivian.

The intimacy between those two was so complete that she had
become the slave of his outsized ego; and she always forgave
him his faults, just as a mother will. How strange. . . . But
what about *me?* Couldn't she feel that my need for herself,
and for her help, was even greater? Why did she distrust me
now, as she had never done before? Was it because of the
sexual content of my love for her, which I couldn't suppress,
or hide, as much as I tried? . . . After dinner I managed to
lure her to a movie. The magic spell of the darkened house,
the acute consciousness of her presence, all that, for two short
hours, stirred the illusion of my lost love.

Our shoulders were touching, and once again the current
coursed between us, as real as blood. Resting on hers, my
hand felt the movement of her irregular breathing, the
warmth of her body. My own skin was burning, my lips were
feverish, impatient, but I knew all too well that the slightest
indiscreet gesture would destroy everything. I had to pretend
that this hand-clasping orgy was of a purely brotherly nature,
and yet on the back of that hand innocently pressing against
her sweater, I could feel a tiny bit of hard flesh protruding
insistently through the wool, sending terrible phosphorescent
lightnings throughout my entire nervous system. The tension
was so unbearable, and yet so delicious, that I felt unable to
control myself. I looked at her face, frowning slightly, concen-
trating, or appearing to do so, on the action now unfolding on
the screen—a love scene, by the way, at that very moment—
in the faint, flickering silver light. In spite of her elaborate
pretense of detachment, when she felt that I was looking
straight at her, she sighed audibly and moved her hand inside
mine, causing it to press harder on her breast. Was she responding to the film—or to the lust in me? Was it—was it
conceivable that she had been playing a double game all
along? Could it be that she was in fact *enjoying* my terrible
state of excitement, and my frustration itself? Of course she
would never admit to it! But the very thought that she was
perhaps secretly responding to my passion for her—that simple thought struck me with such force that I was promptly
carried away in an immense wave of joy. Such a powerful
emotion took over my body, like an earthquake, that I was
unable to control its fatal outcome; I kept shaking like an epi-
leptic while the back of my hand rubbed maniacally against
her chaste, erect nipple. I was too unsettled to find out how
she was taking all this; but when the lights went up she was

still gaping at the closing scene on the screen as if nothing at all were happening to me.

I couldn't escape the glances of our immediate neighbors, looking at us curiously. Bright-eyed and red-cheeked, Laurette was stretching herself prettily.

"Ah, that Humphrey Bogart," she said. "What a wonderful actor, don't you think? I like his looks."

12

*Some suicides are not meant to last. —A trip back
to childhood. —The Obelisk Press moves to posh
new quarters. —I become part of the staff: exactly half of it.
—Place Vendôme. —Bogous on censorship. —Henry and
Anaïs, a meeting of eagles. —In comes Lawrence Durrell,
a beaming and hopeful young man. —The fruits of
constructive diplomacy: the Villa Seurat triangle. —For
my father, it is time to write the* Memoirs of a Booklegger.

After that extraordinary summer, the fall season came as a
doubtful anticlimax. G.J. and I roamed the russet autumnal
countryside in his little Renault in search of ideas, of something to do. He had various schemes; selling tape recorders to
schools in the provinces, for instance. He was good at it, but I
wasn't; forcing oneself on people's attention, and badgering
them to such an extent that they would be forced to sign a
check or an order form so as to get rid of you, well, that was
distinctly beyond my scope. I had done much worse things
during the past summer, to be sure, but I had been carried by
a high enthusiasm for The Cause, then, which was now somewhat deflated. G.J. sensed my reluctance, and we gave up the
effort.

Besides, Laurette's attitude had become very baffling to me.
Whenever we would meet at the boulevard Saint-Germain
ashram she would ignore me completely; I knew her to be a
gentle, generous person and this attitude on her part was
more than I could bear. The memory of our evening at the
movies filled me by turns with shame, lust, and total despair.
The back of my left hand was still burning with the erotic
stigma, and my dreams were filled with allusions of her.

But all I could do was to sulk somberly in my dismal little
room at the Hôtel Princesse, on the corner of rue du Four.
Since I wasn't earning any money, I was surviving on a

debilitating diet of tea and bread. The very idea of taking an ordinary job struck me as unbearable. The hopelessness of my life weighed down on me, and meditation brought only brief moments of relative equilibrium. I no longer got any pleasure out of reading because my attention was immediately sidetracked into obsessive wandering. I hardly saw anyone, and as to the one I would have wanted to see, to touch, to love every single minute of the day and night, she was lost forever in her own mystical reverie. Sometimes, on boulevard Saint-Michel or on rue Cujas, or under the chestnut trees of the Luxembourg, I would catch her silhouette from afar. . . . Her light brown overcoat, the dancing mass of dark curls, the light step I knew so well—it was her. And I started running after her, my heart thirsting after the long-awaited miracle. And as I was catching up with the brown coat, breathless, my heart would sink fast, hard, into despair. . . . It was always a shadow, someone else. . . . Somebody else's obsession.

My room at the Hôtel Princesse gave onto a dingy courtyard. The odor of mildew, the worn-out oilcloth; the damp bed on which I couldn't sleep, and whose springs would punctuate every movement of my body with the sound of chains; and connected to a devilish plumbing system that brought to my room not only the neighbors' gurglings and other unsavory noises, but sometimes even, in the dead of night, a stinking wad of dirty water—how could I live in such a place? How could anyone?

There were days worse than the others, and this is one of them; I have reached rock bottom. Sitting on my only chair, I contemplate this desolation, this misery that is my sole horizon. Every object on which my eyes come to rest makes my skin crawl, and the more I look, the more I'm overwhelmed by the terminal horror of this human life, lost in such heavy shadows, with its hidden games, inaccessible goals, and the incurable weakness, and, above all, the solitude. My attention is caught by one specific detail, strays away from it, only to return to it—this exposed rafter in the ceiling. *It would be perfect for—* Without another thought for what I am doing I grab a long Indian silk necktie my father once gave me, tie it into a slipknot, climb up on a chair, attach the other end to the rafter, stick my head through the loop, and, in a state of dull exaltation, kick the chair away. I immediately lose consciousness, my last impression before fading out being of a

tremendous racket—due to the fact that one foot remained
stuck between the slats of its backrest, sending the chair to
crash repeatedly against the wall as my body keeps jerking
and twitching, like an electrocuted frog. . . .

I come to with a searing pain in my throat. I'm on my
knees, holding my neck with both hands, and I begin crawling
around the room on all fours, grunting like a disconsolate pig,
my windpipe on fire as the oxygen invades my lungs. Little by
little, things fall into place. Clinging to the bed, I raise myself
up painfully. The tie did its job, it's the knot that failed. *So,
I'm still alive!*. . . I hear voices behind the door; someone's
knocking. I stagger over to open it: I can't believe my eyes,
it's Laurette. G.J., grinning widely, is standing right behind
her.

"What are you doing in this dump?" she asks joyously, embracing me hard. "Listen, Maurice, G.J. and I we've decided
to celebrate. We're going to have a musical dinner at the Coq
d'Or, and we're taking you along. Don't say no; what else do
you have to do? G.J. just got some money from his mother.
. . . But, my God, how can you stand living in a place like
this? You know, it's downright awful!"

"That's right, fathead," G.J. chimes in. "Would you believe
it? A money order from my stingy mother! I never knew she
would save any from her gigolo to give to her son! It's the
sign of the gods, no question about it. Come on, and stop
rubbing your neck like an idiot."

The family had gone back to Rozoy, to spend their summer
vacation. The Gervaises had lent them one of their houses,
and I decided to spend some time there with them and revisit
my old haunts.

They are no doubt unchanged, the barns and the busy
farmyards, the open pastures and the opulent vegetable gardens; and yet my vision of them is so different now. The antiquity of this land is what touches me most. Very little has
been altered since medieval times in the life of the fields and
the farms; and the forest is much older still, studded with
rocks smoothed by the erosion of wind and rain, and you
could easily imagine hairy aurochs grazing in its clearings. The
Gergogne waters still flow their capricious course across the
fields, only to immerse themselves into the marshes, and then
to gather together again as a river beyond a wall of thickset,
impenetrable foliage. The fluid realm of my childhood has

evaporated; only a whiff of regret is left of the past, under the vital impact of today's profusion, of the ruddy, mottled colors of autumn. And of my new life. . . .

Yes, I have been that lonely child, living in dreams I can hardly remember. But now I am quite different; or at least I am determined to be. No longer a dreamer! A creator, an inventor, a man of action, starting as of now! My experience with UJC has given me a completely new perspective of life: It is an exciting game to be played to the full, with complete trust in one's chances. . . .

Such were my dispositions when my father approached me, diffidently at first, with the proposal that I go to work for him. I promptly accepted, trying not to show too much enthusiasm; but it did look like the answer to my secret hopes. Publishing had always attracted me in a manner that was nearly physical. The presence of a book counted nearly as much as its contents; the complex phases of its conception and production, the meeting of author and publisher and the details of their diffident association; and then the mystery of fame or failure, of classical perenniality as opposed to modish transience— what more exciting challenges could you dream up for yourself?

So yes, of course, I wanted the experience, what else could I become, if not a publisher? Perhaps I would be the first French publisher without a *baccalauréat* degree? However— let's be realistic: My job will be very humble, to start with. Now that the Obelisk Press was his sole property, my father will have to make a new start on a shoestring. Paradoxically he was about to move to new offices in the most glorified center of business in all of Paris, the place Vendôme; he had been able to rent there, at No. 16, for a remarkably low rent, a suite of offices that had just been vacated by Curtis Brown, the literary agents from London. This was a very auspicious beginning, but the physical problems of getting started were formidable. Quite clearly my father was counting on my help on the eve of this great battle.

The offices on place Vendôme were spacious and quite comfortable: two huge rooms plus a vast, windowless catchall with an immense walk-in safe attached to it—a place that inspired an idea of wealth. Place Vendôme was perfect for my father, absolutely in his style. You would hear more English than French being spoken there, and those who only knew French spoke it with puckered lips and lockjaw inflections

meant to suggest an Oxford accent, leading one to believe
that their own language was foreign to them. . . . We had the
Ritz facing us across the way, the Westminster Bank on our
left and the Morgan Bank on our right, and all around were to
be found the likes of Van Cleef and Arpels, Duveen, Charvet,
Gélot, Jacques Heim, Elizabeth Arden, all of them top-level
symbols of opulence. Two steps away, the Castiglione Bar
and that of the Hôtel Lotti, and not far off, the famous Harry's Bar at No. 5 rue Daunou (pronounced *Sank Rew Doe-
Noo*). And of course, on the place de l'Opéra, the Café de la
Paix. We were sitting at the very epicenter of our marketplace, so to speak; which is to say, the bookshops of Brentano's, Galignani, and W. H. Smith. Also, you were sure to
meet, on the sidewalks, the brightest stars of fashion and society; walking down under the arcades of the rue de Castiglione, it was hard to miss the Duke of Windsor, with or
without the Duchess; or you would encounter Greta Garbo
with Leopold Stokowski, her most recent date, or Gary
Cooper with a load of newly bought neckties; unless it was
the Begum Aga Khan, or maybe only Adolphe Menjou; most
of those priceless people being followed by a uniformed
chauffeur bearing wonderfully wrapped packages, or guiding
toward a lamppost, at the end of a long leash, some diminutive, arrogant doggie, always prompt to bark at the poor and
the downtrodden.

Since my father had only managed with the greatest difficulty to buy his freedom from Servant, there was no money
left to move the stock of books to our new quarters. For that
purpose I hired the services of a friendly bus driver, Paul le
Niçois, and we piled up all the Obelisk Press books into his
rickety vehicle. Within two days five tons of books passed
over my back, and soon I was able to make my father admire
my beautiful arrangement on the shelves where our fine titil-
lating goodies were stacked. I kind of made friends with the
people at Continenta, all of whom were pleasant, and spoke
French or English with a heavy German accent; their offices
were in the back of our building and smelled of tea and
apples. Stern-looking young women of culture with old-
fashioned pince-nez were wrapping the Obelisk Press bomb-
shells, *Daffodil, Mad about Women, Bright Pink Youth*, and
Suzy Falls Off, not to speak of the Frank Harris and Henry
Miller books, into neat-looking brown paper packages. Quite
a little organization there!

As to myself, I worked like a devil, my duties including storage, packing, shipping, billing, proofreading, talking to many strange people, running errands, secretarial work, and typing with two fingers. My father was as flabbergasted as I was myself by the efficiency I revealed, and he presented me to his callers as his general manager, with a restrained pride that agreeably tickled my superego. He gave me an honest wage, which he sometimes borrowed back the next day; and he paid the rent on a little apartment at the top of the rue Gay-Lussac, not far from the Luxembourg. It was a little better than my suicidal hotel room on the rue Princesse, but not much so.

Seated at my big, tottering desk all heaped with proofs to be corrected, letters to be answered, manuscripts to register, I felt like a big executive in front of his worktable, rubbing his hands with relish at the prospect of the mass of things he has to get done during the course of his working day. My interest in the publishing mechanism was building up. The process that consists in giving value to words, images, and ideas simply by transferring them from untidy manuscript to book print was intriguing to watch; ours was an infinitesimal operation, but we had all the problems of publishing to confront, plus a few others. Indeed our small scale made it easier to understand the workings of it. For example, the fact that we dealt with only about twenty retailers in different countries gave me a personalized image of the bookdealer, more true to life than any I could have gathered from the most accurate statistics.

Those of the neighborhood, Camille Bloch, Pierre Trémois, or Antoine Grandmaison, were good examples of that grumpy and passionate tribe whose prodigious memory encompassed whole worlds of paper, and whose eye, with a single glance, sized up, dated, classified, and appraised all that would appear in print form.

True booksellers were rare; they were possessive of their knowledge to the point of obsession. Like an endangered species waging a losing battle in a mutating milieu, they struggled to resist the commercialization that menaced their profession on all sides; but they well knew that they didn't have a chance. Just as the disappearance of swallows in a region causes a chain reaction that ends up afflicting human economy and culture, it can truly be said that the disappearance of old-fashioned, cultured booksellers was badly impoverishing the milieu. They were a link between reader and author, a guide and critic for the publishers. Well, the old codgers my father visited and bought drinks for would indeed complain about that state of things, and about the unsavory commercialization of the printed word, and about big powers such as Hachette, which were controlling book and newspaper distribution nationwide, in addition to their large publishing and printing interests, their paper mills, newsstands, and the rest of it. Very soon every single bookstore in the country would be Hachette property, run by Hachette managers. There was nothing like it in the entire world, not even in America.

Those complaints were amply echoed, and even amplified, by at least one Hachette man I knew, my father's old friend, Michel Bogouslawsky. He was completely outspoken and cynical about it, and loved to hold forth for hours against his employer whenever we visited him and his wife Dillie in their Auteuil apartment.

These visits began with lunch, and five hours later, everyone was still sitting around the table, which was loaded afresh with zakuski. The hours went by like magic while we listened to Michel's hair-raising stories; he was as inexhaustible as his samovar. In the end, without knowing very well how it happened, here we were having supper, and Michel was still talking, all the while uncorking his best bottles in order to cheer on his audience.

"I, a former revolutionary," he said, "I've become an instrument of capitalism, and I don't mean to say that I'm proud of it. But one has to live in one's time; it's no longer possible to exist outside of capitalism. Capitalism requires more people and less culture, so that's what dictates Hachette's policy, and I am paid to serve Hachette's interests. We are here to make people silly, and to make them believe that they are intelligent. They can't read, but they buy books. With mass production the number of people who read books will soon be multiplied by ten."

"And so will Hachette's profits, eh?" said my father.

"Of course. Hachette is already a state within a state. In Russia, there's a state monopoly for printing and publishing; here it's us. Of course it's not quite official, but it really does boil down to the same thing, and it's one of the calamities of the modern world. But at least people are made to buy books, thanks to our thirst for profits, and perhaps someday it will help them learn to think. You never know! That's why I am all in favor of perpetual growth in the book business—it's good for everyone. But of course, when book censorship gets started in France . . ."

"Censorship in France?" my father exclaimed. "But that's impossible!"

"Not at all," insisted Michel. "With types like Daladier, it's almost sure to happen. To fight Hitler, he will find nothing better than to imitate what Hitler does. Mark my word! Censorship can't be avoided in wartime, and we know there's a war in the offing. In fact governments need censorship less to defend themselves against the enemy than to consolidate their own power internally. You must also understand that censorship provides well-paid sinecures for thousands of perfectly useless citizens, who become excellent watchdogs as soon as they are given a bit of power over the others."

He took a sheet of paper and a pencil.

"I'm surprised that you haven't given a thought to the importance of censorship," he went on, "but it's enormous. It's always discussed as something alien from us, as if it were a monstrous invention of Hitler's, but it has existed everywhere for a long time. As a matter of fact, it was invented in the Middle Ages by the Christian Church, with the institution of confession, and later of the Holy Inquisition; it's as simple as that. And then the Industrial Revolution got going in England and in America, and in order to keep the proletariat from thinking, or having a good time, censorship was developed as we know it under its present form."

"You talk about it as if it were an invention of the Western bourgeoisie," said my father. "But what about Russia?"

"Right you are! What happened in Soviet Russia is that a few idealists prepared the ground for a revolution that would guarantee true equality, including the equality of the sexes, and true freedom, including sexual freedom. And that involved the abolition of bourgeois marriage. But as soon as the Bolsheviks got into power, they swept out all that stuff. First, of course, they started by liquidating the anarchists. But they also found out very fast that social discipline can't be imposed in a country whose citizens are intellectually and morally free. It was necessary to restore the sense of guilt in order to enforce punishment and constraint. And so they borrowed all they could from the Catholic church, from Victorian England. In the Soviet Union, marriage is an affair closely monitored and controlled by the party. And so you have a brand-new form of Soviet puritanism throughout Russia, with the result that today's Russian youth is bored to tears, and the revolution is drowning in vodka. To break the spell, everybody will welcome a war: The government has invented enough foreign enemies for the masses to keep fighting wars for centuries! If the Soviet Union doesn't return to capitalism through too much vodka, it will be through war. Or both combined. . . . But let's get back to censorship. On this piece of paper we will try to map out a world budget for censorship, and the tax burden it represents for the taxpayers of all countries. Right? First of all, it must be said that since censorship, at least in theory, doesn't exist, the expenses it entails must be hidden and scattered under all sorts of different headings. This way, its existence can continue to be denied. And yet, if I send twenty tons of school books from Paris to London, my shipment is going to be combed by the specially trained customs officers assigned to that job. Sometimes they will open every single package; at other times they will only pretend that they've done so. Anyway, you can see for yourself: This makes for millions of workdays, plus the retirement pensions and all the rest . . ."

"Very well," said my father. "But don't forget the police."

"I was just getting to that: A very large portion of the salaries paid to the police force, not only in England or in the United States, but in all English-speaking countries, is spent on the tracking down of pornography. You're never told exactly how much that is, of course, but hunting pornography is a useful stunt for the police. Just imagine, for instance, that a copy of *Fanny Hill* is seized in Boston or in Leeds. Well it's easy for the police to raise hell about it, simply by tipping the papers; the press is always hungry for that type of gruesome stories. Then the mayor makes a speech, the law-and-order candidate wins the election, and the budget of the police department is doubled."

"And that doesn't even take into account the lawsuits against the publishers of London or New York," my father added. "Every one of these lawsuits sets in motion a number of judges, lawyers, bailiffs, and in the end, it's the publisher who foots the bill."

"Of course," Michel agreed. "Serves him right. That will teach him not to take chances with public morals: After all he's a businessman, why should he risk money so stupidly?

And there you have it—preventive censorship through intimidation. . . . But censorship of the mails, that remains without doubt the most costly item. In English-speaking countries, they're still hunting for pornography everywhere, it's really a strange kind of mania. What do they expect? To find satyrs hiding under postage stamps? It's incredible, we're in the middle of the twentieth century, or close to that, and that's how retarded we are! And so now, we'll try to find out how much that worldwide activity costs the taxpayer. Let's suppose that these acts of censorship, all added up, represent on the average the full salary of one bureaucrat for each thousand citizens: a very modest estimate. Seeing that this practice takes place in all English-speaking countries, which means one half the world population, for a billion and a half citizens, that means *a million and a half censors!*"

"Great God!" exclaimed my father.

"On the Soviet side, the same reasoning can be applied. If you add to that all the totalitarian countries, plus the clergy, the administration, the judges, and the members of the supreme court, you will find out that the hidden budget for censorship is very probably equal to the military budget of each of those same countries. And you never hear about it! The funniest thing about censorship is that it starts out by censoring the word *censorship.*"

"Good enough," said my father. "Now we have an idea of what's on the debit side of your balance sheet. But what about the credit side?"

"The list would be too long! What are the benefits of censorship? First of all, the preservation of government authority! The citizen reads what he is told to read by the State or by its newspapers. Then you have sexual frustration organized on a national scale: There has yet to be found a better method for keeping the masses in step, the working classes as well as the others. The consolidation of prejudice, and the destruction of authentic culture, of invention, and free will. The spirit of independence is cut down to its lowest common denominator. The State needs censorship to maintain itself alive."

"However," my father observed, "the leftists in France consider censorship as one of the symbols of Nazi Germany. If the French fight Germany to abolish censorship, that will be something, no?"

"Maybe the French will go to war to abolish German censorship, if their government tells them to do so; but, in order to win, that same government will be the first to impose censorship, *here in France!* You'll see."

All that hot talk caused me to believe that I was working in a kind of anticensorship laboratory, which wasn't far from the truth. My job, however, entailed deciphering the letters sent by the private customers, which were often much more than orders. Each one of those poor devils was desperately pining for some sort of liberation, imploring help of any kind, trying to establish a bridge with the outside world. Millions and millions of private dungeons! The idea was overpowering. And the irony of it was biting: *Who was I to counsel Joe Smith as to the secrets of sex?* At least Joe Smith was brave enough to write us letters, to reach out for help, and to admit to his dreams and frustrations. That's something I would never have done myself! And yet it was my function in life to open those pathetic, ink-smudged envelopes and, after counting the bank notes, to read the miserable confession.

> *. . . I am ordering this book from you at the request of my cousin Billy who has sprained his wrist and is unable to write to you himself. I hope I can count on your speedy service. By return mail! Posthaste!!!* Sincerely yours, Joe Smith. P.S. *I beg you that you send me the book in a plain wrapper.* No return address! *By return mail, if you please, if possible.* P.P.S. *Do you sell pictures of beautiful women with no clothes on?*

Joe Smith, my brother, my look-alike, how old are you? Nineteen like myself, or eighty-nine? To unburden myself of Joe's tragedy I showed his letter to my father.

"Poor bastard," he said. "He certainly needs something more than a book, but he won't get it by writing letters like this. I can sympathize with him, I know something of the system that turned him into a retarded idiot. I was there . . ."

And he proceeded to describe the method of bodily punishment he had known as a kid in the Manchester public schools. The beating would be announced in advance, and would take place in a small hall, in front of a hand-picked public of dons and senior students, sometimes even parents. The kid is already frozen with terror, crying his heart out. He is perched on the back of a burly handyman who starts turning methodically around the room; at each turn the meanest schoolmaster of all, an experienced sadist, swats him a terrible blow on the behind, with a truly vicious malacca. The pain is awful, of course, but the terror and the shame of it are even worse. That's the way they train the little boys in England; that's how they turn them all into people like this Joe Smith.

In just a few years, Obelisk Press had acquired an international reputation all out of proportion to its production and to its turnover, which was still close to insignificant.

The reason for that fame was not just the fact that it fulfilled the lurid dreams of so many repressed males (one hardly ever thought of repressed females), but that it offered a small measure of encouragement to some very authentic writers. For anyone who wanted to write freely, outside of any censorship parameters, there was now at least a technical hope of publication: The Obelisk Press, in Paris, had already put out a small number of explosive books of real quality— enough to show that there existed an alternate to the general stodginess and cautious policies of the traditional British and American houses.

The thirties had seen a series of attempts at establishing English-language avant-garde publishing houses in France, but all were definitely noncommercial. For instance, Edward Titus had used some of his wife's money (she was Helena Rubinstein) to set up his little publishing house, The Mannikin Press, and after she threw him out he had promptly declared bankruptcy. As to Harry Crosby, founder with his wife, Caresse, of the Black Sun Press, he had all the money needed to last forever, but he was too committed to drugs and suicide to survive the publishing experience. Sylvia Beach, from her bookshop, Shakespeare and Company, had devoted years of her life to the publication of James Joyce's *Ulysses*, but, having been repaid with black ingratitude, she had decided never to try publishing again. . . . Robert McAlmon was nothing but an elegant memory. Nancy Cunard, the shipping heiress, and Walter Lowenfels had given up the struggle. They had all failed, flashes in the pan, the whims of rich young people, but they had prepared the ground with their cumulative failures for someone else's success. My father had learned the lesson: Publishing must be made to yield a profit. He had learned this first of all at his personal expense, in 1929, when he had gone into business as the silent partner of Henry Babou, and lost a fortune in no time at all. This time he would go after success ruthlessly, with hammer and tongue. To achieve this, all he had to do was to stick to what he had learned much earlier in the velvet and cotton business. He was lucky enough to have received that training at the hard school of Manchester's businessmen, the toughest in the West: Caution and obstinacy was their motto.

Unfortunately, Henry Miller and his friends were enraged by what they mistook for phlegmatic indolence; Henry and my father had tortured each other at every turn during the two years before *Tropic of Cancer* came out. But once this test was passed, Henry calmed down and a permanent truce came into effect between author and publisher. They were too far apart to become real friends but their relationship was based on mutual esteem, and on a sound business instinct as well. For, in his own way, Henry was neither deaf nor blind to the facts of life. It was indeed a well-balanced give-and-take situation: By helping Henry become a famous writer, my father was satisfying his own professional ambitions as a publisher.

Tropic of Cancer was the culmination of a long struggle, and it became the acid test. After years of abortive attempts in America, Miller had invested one year of concentrated effort into it; he had promised himself that if with this book he couldn't prove to himself that he was a genuine writer, he would give up trying. . . .

Obviously the signing of the *Tropic of Cancer* contract, after all those preparations, came as the central event in Henry's life. It was the psychological shock he had needed for so long in order to complete his metamorphosis into a writer. Despite the interminable delay that followed, things being set in motion, Henry went cheerfully back to work. He completed his second book, *Black Spring,* which came out soon after *Cancer,* and then began writing *Tropic of Capricorn,* which was scheduled to appear at the beginning of 1939. He also had a volume of short stories in progress, *Max and the White Phagocytes,* plus an endless, exuberant study on D. H. Lawrence that he didn't manage to finish, an equally interminable dialogue with Michael Frankel on *Hamlet,* and all kinds of other writings.

Anaïs was somewhat overwhelmed by these events. From the minute they met, she had cast herself without hesitation in the role of Henry's muse. Such was her vocation, a midwife to genius. From Antonin Artaud to Otto Rank, with quite a few lesser luminaries in between, she had demonstrated an almost supernatural flair for discovering these very special men just at the moment they were experiencing the major crisis of their lives. She had a predilection for desperate cases, preferably at the higher echelons. She was a proud masochist.

At first glance, Henry had appeared to be one of the world's worst losers; his age, his Brooklyn accent, his shabby clothes, his bald pate: None of that fitted the figure of a young American Rimbaud that he seemed anxious to imper- sonate. And then he had chosen to arrive on the scene as many had already left. And what about his *friends!* The only ones he had were picked right out of the gutter. He was lead- ing an ambiguous, floating existence, half bum, half tourist, spent mostly in the expectation of checks that sometimes ar- rived from his wife, June, whom he had left in New York— and often didn't. His only fortune, in fact, consisted in the manuscript of his first, unpublishable book, *Tropic of Cancer:* This was *truly* a desperate man!

Anaïs immediately decided to devote a good part of her time and overflowing energy to him. Henry accepted her dedication as the homage of a disciple, as something that goes without saying. But she gradually realized that Henry was far from defenseless; it wasn't easy to realize that he was using her, at first, because he was doing so with such good-humored cynicism. He chuckled a lot. Then she would rebel, but only to let herself be seduced once again. Was this really a desper- ate case? Henry was driven by a powerful ambition, which sometimes reached prophetic heights. This was no defeated artist with a sensitive soul who was looking to her for help and protection, like her other protégés: Henry Miller was her pimp. But at least he was a literary pimp, and she believed in his rambunctious genius, having lived through the birth of *Tropic of Cancer.* It was like being a geologist who has been privileged to witness the eruption of a volcano as seen from inside.

A truly exciting experience! But as she was observing the unfolding process in him, she began to feel sorry for herself. She had done ten times more work than he, and where were the published results? She had been writing all her life, and had already filled more than fifty volumes of a diary begun in her childhood, a literary undertaking probably without prece- dent, but also without any practical end in sight: What publisher would be crazy enough to get involved in printing these thousands and thousands of pages? These millions of words devised and arranged with an artistry that was all her own? Perhaps she had subconsciously chosen a form of expression meant to make any kind of publication impossible? As if it weren't enough of a handicap to be a woman writer.

Henry's example had reawakened all those painful feelings of inadequacy and frustration. But there was something else, probably even more important than that sense of personal loss. Henry's seminal powers were just that, seminal, a constant affirmation of malehood. There was a deliberate crudity in his conduct and language whenever he dealt with women, or femininity in any form. If Henry was the great emancipator of modern times, as he himself would have it, all he was liberating was merely the male libido. He could only deal with women as legends or as objects, and this had become totally repugnant to her. Instead of liberating humankind from the great fear of love between the sexes, he was erecting a Great Wall of China between them, a wall of pornography.

He would not listen to her; he was too busy consolidating his phallic monument. Perhaps, at the beginning of their relationship, she had dreamed of contributing to his *oeuvre*, to the refinement of his ideas. Henry, who dreaded women with a mind, had rapidly discouraged her. He was often surprised, of course, at what he came across in Anaïs's diary, and wasn't even beyond letting it inspire him sometimes, all the while treating each of these discoveries as a happy accident due to Anaïs's powers of observation, a minor quality that in no way offered real proof of her ability and judgment as a writer.

The cumulative effect of those skirmishes was such that she finally decided to write her own book: It would be her response to *Tropic of Cancer*. She would do for the world of women what he claimed to have achieved for that of men. And this is how she undertook to write *Winter of Artifice*, her own first novel.

From then on, their relationship took on a different turn and fell into the classical pattern. They were constantly goading each other with a jealousy that was at times quite unconcealed. In a cruel way Henry would challenge Anaïs to burn her diary, and in return, she accused him of being a soulless pornographer. Cut to the quick, he would immerse himself in Lao-tzu, or in the study of astrology.

Upon which Henry's wife, June, who was as seductive as

she was unpredictable, arrived in Paris and fell madly in love with Anaïs—love at first sight, perhaps, but it certainly served Anaïs's strategy in her war against Henry. She was prompt to capitalize on her victory: She made it clear to Henry that he had never understood his own wife, even while making her the symbol of all women. A blow below the belt! But Henry, the old fox, eventually came out on top, having talked her into devoting all her funds to financing the publication of his book. Although it was thanks to her that *Tropic of Cancer* could finally come out, she had not yet been published. Thus she found herself slyly relegated to the rank of muse.

And yet there was no denying her virtuosity as a writer, her book was like a ballet on ice. If she decided to set herself the task, there was no reason why she would not become, if not Henry Miller's equal, at least his equivalent. Between her dedication to the genius of a man she admired, and her own need for self-expression as a writer, she was still torn by a conflict for which there seemed to be no solution in view.

Henry had found happiness in a dead-end street buried in the depths of the fourteenth arrondissement, the Villa Seurat. Day and night, he machine-gunned the surrounding silence on the typewriter Anaïs had bought for herself, and which she had given to him at the beginning of their friendship. A heavy symbol, the gift of that typewriter! It was a brand-new machine that she had bought especially in order to start typing some of her diary. Thanks to her act of renunciation, Henry would transform tons of paper, inflating the sacks of mailmen on five continents with a barrage of proclamations, diatribes, hoaxes, and letters meant to electrify, discombobulate and stun their recipients. He answered all his fan mail—sometimes with five dense pages in response to a mere three lines—and kept up a correspondence with an extraordinary variety of people. It was a way of spreading his presence around the world, perhaps just as efficient as finding readers for the books themselves. He was fast acquiring a vast underground reputation in America and in Europe, even though only one thousand copies of his first book had been sold. My father considered it a miracle to have an author who busied himself so passionately with his own publicity.

Editions Stock had abandoned their project of publishing his books in French, but Denoël et Steele had expressed interest in the French right to *Black Spring*; despite publishers

and censors, Miller's reputation was spreading further everyday, to Paris, to London, Athens, Mexico, Melbourne—in fact
all over the world. Villa Seurat had become a lighthouse in
the night for thousands of budding writers and young rebels,
from California to Japan; and also for supersnobs, aes-
thetes, and collectors of human phenomena. As he was passing
through Paris, Huntington Cairns, who was the special adviser
of the U.S. Customs in matters of literary censorship, and
who bore, as such, a personal responsibility in the blacklisting
of *Tropic of Cancer* in America, came to express his personal
apologies to Miller for what he had been obliged to do in his
official capacity. Cairns took him out for dinner, showered
him with courtesies, and told him repeatedly that he was a
genius. A strange conduct on the part of the oppressor! It
seemed to presage an eventual change of attitude on the part
of the American government; although surely it wouldn't
happen overnight. In 1931, the rehabilitation of *Ulysses* following Judge Woolsey's famous judgment had shown that there
existed a distinct current of liberal opinion in the States and
that certain people there were beginning to feel that in a modern, civilized society, all artists should be allowed to express
themselves freely. But that was still a very distant prospect,
according to Cairns. "It won't happen during our lifetime,
alas! Maybe in three generations it will be possible to publish
Tropic of Cancer in the United States. Certainly not any
sooner."

One day I was hard at work at my desk when the door
opened. I saw a sunny-looking couple standing there, beaming
at me as if I were an old friend whose name they had forgotten. The man was quite young, short and chubby, with pleasant features; she was half a head taller, slim and rather pretty.
Both of them dazzlingly blond.

He introduced himself. So that was Lawrence Durrell! And
his English wife, Nancy. They were both wearing identical be-
rets and camel's-hair coats, and seemed so anxious to please
that one couldn't help finding them both funny and likable.
They had just arrived, all the way from Greece, and they were
anxious to see my father. He was out and I promised that he
would ring them at their hotel later in the day.

Of course I had heard quite a bit about Durrell since he had
started that enormous, coruscating correspondence with
Henry Miller; I knew that he had a civil servant's job with the

British government, being in charge of its information office, or in other words, of its public relations, in Cyprus. A sunny job indeed! But Larry was a poet, and his life's ambition was to become a full-time writer. Two years earlier, when he was twenty-four, he had completed a long epic work, half novel and half diatribe, *The Black Book*, whose purpose was well-defined by the subtitle: *A Chronicle of the English Death.*

It is only after having finished writing *The Black Book* that Larry had understood that no publisher would ever touch it; not just because of its mildly obscene contents, but essentially because of its subtitle. *English Death?* No decent English-speaking person would think of buying, let alone reading, a book denouncing Englishness in this day and age. But such were Larry's contradictions, perhaps due to his Anglo-Irish origins: His mind was British, but his heart was Irish. He was a civil servant, and he wanted to be a poet and a writer. He wanted to start a literary career thanks to which he could make a living, and quit his job; and there you have it, *The Black Book.* That's quite exactly what they call biting the hand that feeds you.

Nevertheless, Larry had felt vindicated when he read *Tropic of Cancer*, which came to him as a multiple revelation: Miller had dealt with American culture in exactly the same manner Larry had wanted to use with respect to English culture. But Miller was more professional, being also much older, more experienced, and therefore more effective. However, for Larry, one impressive fact about Miller's book is that he had managed to get it published. Larry felt that there was no reason why he should not get his chance just as well with the Obelisk Press; he had started writing Miller many long complimentary letters, which were no doubt sincere enough, but which also served to create a favorable climate and to cause Miller to come to his help. He wanted to be introduced to the owner of the Obelisk Press with Henry Miller's warm recommendation, and in this at least he had succeeded. My father wrote to him in order to express his willingness to read the manuscript. But instead of sending it by mail, Larry had decided to make the trip to Paris to bring his book personally to its potential publisher—and not to return to Cyprus without a decision. The ostensible reason for the trip, however, was his desire to meet with Henry Miller face-to-face at last.

That meeting was in itself not very productive but quite

friendly; and its vital side-benefit proved to be Larry's encounter with the remarkable Anaïs Nin. An alliance was immediately formed between those two, who had so much in common besides their devotion to the master and his work.

Their literary affinity became obvious to Larry as he started reading some extracts of Anaïs's diary; the ecstatic compliments he paid her then were quite sincere. But he was also rather puzzled by Henry's condescending ways regarding her work; and this only confirmed what he knew already, about Henry's egotism and intense self-absorption. However—that was the privilege of genius, wasn't it? Larry was a diplomat by nature as well as by profession; he understood the many reasons Anaïs had to resent Henry's attitude, but it wouldn't pay to confront him as she had done, so uselessly, herself. Anaïs and Larry had a very simple objective in common: to get their first books published. As for himself, at least he was quite determined to abandon all hope of a literary career if he failed to get *The Black Book* out in print. And it so happened that there was only one publisher in the world who could bring it out, and this was Jack Kahane; and that there was only one person in the world with enough influence on Kahane to force him into making the right decision, and this was Henry Miller. In short, the professional future of both Anaïs and himself depended on his ability to manipulate Miller.

It wasn't easy. The rather florid and Gothic style of *The Black Book* was just as alien to Miller's taste as was Anaïs Nin's volatile femininity; Larry was well conscious of the fact. It would not pay to start an argument with Henry over the respective qualities of the two books. No, the right approach would be to work at convincing Henry that he was now the head of a new literary school, and that his personal glory would benefit substantially from the success of his disciples' books. And this meant that Henry had to work for his own fame by having them published, by hook or by crook.

To achieve such a plan would take time. Larry had understood Henry's constant need for a male interlocutor in order to stimulate his creative process; usually a nervous, puny person like Alfred Perlès or Michael Frankel, who could serve as a whipping boy and be thrown out, after a couple of years of loyal services, like an old mistress. He undertook to play that role in his own way; he lavished praise on him at every occasion, rendered homage constantly to his creative, revolutionary role, and acted more or less as an overenthusiastic sparring partner. Anaïs was quite overwhelmed by those tactics, all the more as they seemed to be working quite well. And yet it took several months of that feverish activity to produce a concrete result: Henry finally promised that he would talk quite seriously to the publisher about giving their chance to both Larry and Anaïs.

But Henry himself did not believe enough in the quality of their two books to convince my father decisively that he had to publish them: The answer Henry received was that the two books would certainly be given their chance when the time came, but that the press could not afford this at the moment. With such a tiny business, depending on the quick sale of a dozen titles at most, my father was forced to concentrate on novels titled *Love Counts Ten*, *Bright Pink Youth* or *To Beg I Am Ashamed*; his only extravagance had consisted in publishing Miller's own books, *Black Spring*, *Tropic of Capricorn*, precisely because, although they would go much more slowly, Miller's reputation was now sufficiently established to guarantee the sale of a thousand-copy edition in two or three years. There were plans to publish Miller's fourth book, *Max and the White Phagocytes*, and that alone would absorb the press's margin of security, and beyond. To produce one thousand copies of a book of average length, with a retail price of sixty francs, cost fifteen hundred francs, and he had to use every penny that came in to pay the printers' bills and the authors' royalties: It had taken two years to repay the loan made by Anaïs to print *Cancer*, and there was just not enough money coming in to speculate on more than one fancy author at a time.

What is more, the international situation made that project very unwise. At least such was my father's opinion; but neither Henry, nor Larry and Anaïs would agree that this should be taken into consideration. The idea of publication was so deeply implanted in them that they would have done just anything to make it happen. This attitude was particularly surprising in the case of Larry, a man with a wife and child, who depended on a modest job for his livelihood: He was ready to give up everything for the publication of a book that might never get a review, and that had absolutely no chance of selling more than a few hundred copies—if a war did not break out. It was sheer madness, but he would not give up, and Nancy was backing him all the way.

The obstacle was, as always, the publisher himself, that cautious, cold-blooded British hypocrite, Jack Kahane. It was Larry who, remembering the circumstances of *Tropic of Cancer*'s publication, came up with a practical idea: He had enough money put aside to finance the printing of his own book, and he knew that Anaïs herself could do the same for her own; but paying to have your own book published was too much like an admission of defeat, and so Larry, the diplomat, suggested that he pay for Anaïs's book, and she would do the same for his.

And this is how the Villa Seurat series was started; my father agreed to include it as a separate venture within the Obelisk Press production. Henry Miller's projected book, *Max and the White Phagocytes*, would be the first volume, and the publicity it would no doubt generate was to help launch the other two. *Max* would be financed by Obelisk, *Winter of Artifice* by Larry, and *The Black Book* by Anaïs. The three would be released in a special cover and format as soon as possible in the course of the following year, 1939. More books would be added to those three in years to come, the authors to be co-opted by the three founders of the series; perhaps one day the Villa Seurat series would become famous not just because it had launched Anaïs Nin and Lawrence Durrell, but dozens of new authors as well. In any case, Larry and Anaïs were now convinced that they would leave their mark on the world—provided that the said world did not collapse before the books came out.

The First World War had ended hardly more than twenty years before, to the cost of millions of dead. Twenty years: enough time for yesterday's losers to come up on top. The French government had not even tried to contain Franco's rise; how could they possibly hope to deal with Hitler? The invasions of Austria and Czechoslovakia, the Franco-British diplomatic defeat at Munich in 1938, all this pointed to the imminence of a war much more destructive and savage than the first one: It was all written down black on white in *Mein Kampf*. In the face of that very obvious prospect, all that the French government was able to offer was more and more rhetoric.

Talk, speeches, proclamations, statements, debates, caucuses, votes, campaigns, slogans, denunciations, petitions, betrayals—the French republic was defeated by political sickness. The very image of democracy, of which France was supposed to be the guardian and champion, was being ridiculed each day by Hitler's rise, by his crude insolence, by the total ruthlessness of his methods.

The evil absurdity of this tragedy was probably more painful to my father than to most men of his generation because of his fragile situation. It was painful enough to have fought a war and suffered as he had, only to find out that it had all been in vain. But the worst part of it was the racist aspect of it. Having divorced himself as completely as he had from his Jewish origins, he was now forced to consider Hitler's threat not only as a Jew, but as a renegade. This I did not perceive too clearly myself, being situated even further away from my Jewish roots than he himself was; but I was well aware of his state of silent, impotent anger.

There were also the material aspects to consider, of course. A publishing business such as Obelisk Press did not have a chance in a million to survive in a war such as the one coming up, and it seemed desperately important to find some other source of income to continue feeding the family.

Fortunately, my father's conversations with his friend Bogous had led gradually to a rather spiffy project. All the books published in England and America appeared exclusively in hard covers, since they were meant only for the upper classes, for the people fortunate enough to afford the leisure to read, as well as the high price one had to pay for books; a price that was necessarily steep because each printing was small—sometimes only a few hundred copies—and because the quality of the production itself had to be worthy of praise from librarians and collectors.

The prices of the books were generally one-half or two-thirds lower in continental Europe because paper covers were used there instead of the elaborate bindings and jackets typical of Anglo-American publishing. At the beginning of the century an astute German publisher, Bernhardt Tauchnitz of Leipzig, had conceived the idea of buying the continental reprint rights of successful novels from British or American publishers, and printing paperback editions of them. Since those paperback reprints were only sold in continental Europe, they did not compete with the original hard-cover editions. But they sold in large quantities in hotels, resorts, railway stations, everywhere in Europe where tourists would travel for pleasure. And they were cheap enough so that the wealthy buyer would usually throw away a book after reading it, just like a magazine or a newspaper.

In the thirties an adventurous Englishman, Allen Lane, had tried to introduce the paperback formula in Britain proper with his Penguin books; but the conventional houses had strenuously resisted that devilish innovation, which threatened the entire structure of the publishing business. Penguin had managed to survive, but just barely.

Then a third paperback series, called Albatross, had been founded in Europe by a rather flamboyant adventurer, one Holroyd Reece, which was based in Paris and presented itself as a direct rival to Tauchnitz. But the Reece flamboyance did not pay, and his venture was now in a very shaky condition.

It seemed therefore possible, and even highly desirable, to take over the formula and start a new series of continental reprints. Because of his role within the Hachette group Bogous had a sort of monopoly over the distribution of foreign books in France. He could not only block the sale of Tauchnitz books in France, but also help a rival line to come to life by providing Hachette distribution and financing.

This clever project, unfortunately, had failed to materialize, due to the constant worsening of the international situation. The smell of war was in the air, a collective death wish had seized a large segment of the population. . . . It was essential to stop thinking, to let the future take over on its own. . . . Utter passivity was the only defense against the mounting dread.

Whenever they visited Paris, Blanche and Alfred Knopf, the New York publishers, always stayed at the Ritz, right across from the Obelisk Press office on place Vendôme. My father became good friends with Blanche, and the outrageous stories of an outlaw publisher that he told her over lunch appeared so delightfully bizarre to her that she ended up by offering him a contract to write his memoirs. The American public had a strong taste for famous bandits and racketeers, and it would be amusing to capitalize on the image of a latter-day Zorro of the literary world. Title of the book: *Memoirs of a Booklegger*.

The London publisher, Michael Joseph, heard about it and he offered a complementary contract for the British rights. Each publisher had paid a modest advance upon signature of the contract, at the beginning of 1938, and the money had immediately gone to George Hamm of the Castiglione Bar, and to the owners of other drinking establishments where my father used to entertain on credit his many friends and flames. The size of his bar debts would give one a good idea of his popularity in the cosmopolitan Paris scene—which in turn had caused Blanche Knopf to offer him a good contract for his life story.

As the deadline for the delivery of the manuscript drew closer—December 31, 1938—he became increasingly nervous and depressed at the idea of the job he hadn't yet had the courage to undertake. He finally decided to square up with his publishers, asked them for a two-month extension of the deadline, and set to work. Every morning, long before daybreak, he would sit down and write about his past, trying not to think too much about the meaning behind the words he was putting down on paper.

A life that had misfired. . . . A fire spent in vain. . . . Great loves for persons unknown. . . . Money had played a central role in all of that, as a hard symbol for the waste of all true values; indeed, an entire life spent in the search of that thing he disliked and distrusted so deeply: *money*. . . . The chaos and humiliation of it. . . . The four well-dressed children to whom he found himself unable to speak, either as a father or even only as a friendly adult. . . . His perfect French wife, and her moral rectitude so overpowering that, liberated as they both were, he still couldn't look at her without feeling guilty. . . . Guilt, always guilt, a degrading, impoverishing sensation that he was made to feel for being a failed writer, a fickle lover, a frivolous publisher, a turncoat Jew. And he was supposed to write a jolly, dashing, entertaining book about all of that! How could he possibly do it? But he had been paid for it, and as always, the money obligation was to dictate his duty. Pen in hand he would cover page after page in his neat, tiny script, reciting the episodes of his life on paper as accurately as he possibly could.

The British publisher decided to release the book in the early summer; but Knopf's editors decided that the book was just not good enough for their purpose. Blanche wrote him a nice personal letter, telling him not to worry; at least her firm would not ask for its money back. That well-intentioned phrase made Blanche's kindness look like charity, which it was; a hard pill to swallow.

Paris was fast emptying itself of its human contents, first the foreigners and now even the Parisians themselves, who began emigrating to their country houses in droves long before the start of the summer season.

The Delamares were in Brittany, and Laurette was in the Pyrénées, in the small village of Campan near Bagnères, together with Rolande, her sister Jenny and her husband, François, and of course Mona and Lionel, plus a few friends.

My visits to Vivian's ashram left me with a very uncomfortable feeling, and I suspected that Laurette's absence was not unrelated to the crisis one felt looming on the horizon. It seemed so essential that I see her, that I question her about her feelings. . . . So many things had to be explained now that did involve the survival of the group, and Vivian's authority.

At several meetings where I went, I noticed that nobody dared ask any hard questions, including myself, about the course of events, which was running so contrary to what Vivian had announced. The Rome-Berlin axis was growing by the hour, just as fast as the Anglo-French alliance was wasting away; which didn't jibe at all with Vivian's former master plan. And where was Caesar? What was he doing? Was he ever going to come out of his castle near Prague, where his trace had been found by telepathic clairvoyance, and take command of his widely scattered forces, initiates and Kshatriyas lying in wait for his signal in the various countries of Europe?

In a remarkably short space of time everything had gone wrong. The ridiculous miscarriage of the Justin Godard election, the collapse of the Etats Généraux, of the UJC, of everything. In a warm voice, more self-assured than ever, Vivian spoke of mysterious, unidentified enemies, forces of darkness now surrounding the planet. But this, he asserted, was only a passing cloud; it would perhaps delay the manifestation of What Was Written, but it could not prevent it from happening. . . . True faith could not be bogged down by trivial details, dates, and so on. . . . No clairvoyant is ever above making mistakes. . . .

A sly dig! It amounted to making Laurette, who was not with us at the time, responsible for the mistakes that had clearly resulted from Vivian's own interpretation of her images. A pretty sordid attitude on the part of such a smart guru! I wished someone would tell Laurette about it; I wondered how she would have responded. I could not help hoping that she would break away from Vivian one day; but at the same time I hardly dared admit to myself that I was entertaining such thoughts. Like my friends, I wanted to remain a true believer, partly because there was nothing equivalent to Vivian's group in Paris, but chiefly because all I had already invested of my own time and energy, and imagination, in the service of the Cause, would be lost forever if we all left. The compact should not be broken.

As summer approached, and the news about Hitler's plans for the annexation of Danzig began to get more attention, my family left Paris in the first days of July for a village west of Paris, Orvilliers, where they had rented a rustic country house. My father spent only his weekends there, and I saw him the rest of the time at the office. Paris was empty and waiting, and I was left with very little work to do; my last job was to wrap up and send out copies of *Memoirs of a Booklegger*, which we had just received from London, to my father's friends. . . . And so he finally decided to close shop, gave me a month's salary in advance, and told me to get out of the city and improvise some sort of vacation for myself. I looked as if I needed one.

13

Passion on two wheels, and five fateful letters.—At the
birth of Synarchy, an oath with the sacred sword.
—Hitler is already in Prague, and Daladier
gets ready to fight . . . obscenity.—A small review
in a large universe.—Gregor as saber rattler.

All during this strange and floating summer, I had suffered
increasingly of an identity crisis that was tearing me asunder.
As with my father, as for Vivian himself, and for millions of
others, the sudden, catastrophic changes in the social and
political structures had shaken the foundation of my personal mythology, of the life-system I had created for myself.
Here I was, full of my own contradictions—breaking with a
society I despised, and yet I was unable to change it. Talking
bravely of freedom, and becoming the slave of Vivian, of Laurette. Madness! I had dedicated myself to asceticism—and
I earned my very bread in an enterprise that lived off pornography. I had discovered the love of my life—but only at
the price of eternal renunciation. As to the guru I had found,
and whom I once thought could lead me to my liberation—
well! Better not examine that subject too closely; here we
were on slippery ground. . . . The past was passing by at a
high speed, the future was utterly obscure. . . . The only tangible reality in my life was already no more than a memory—
that golden summer, forever vanished, which now appeared
to me like a distant mirage, a fleeting instant I had lived in
such pure and deep communion that it seemed as if my life
had ended with that vacation in Brittany.

Why not face things squarely? It is she who's my only hope of
survival. I'm pining alone in Paris, suffocated by her absence.

And that's when, suddenly, all at once I decide to snap out of this nightmare. With my paycheck I buy a bike, a flashlight, a Swiss knife, a sleeping bag, matches, and three cans of vegetables. The crack of dawn finds my equipment solidly lashed to my baggage rack. Soon my wheels leave the rue Claude-Bernard behind me, my chest feels as if it harbored three full shining suns, I'm pedaling in the clouds, insanely in love. *L'amour, toujours l'amour.* . . . In the afternoon, totally out of my mind, I reach Orléans where the cobblestones shake me back briefly to my senses. . . . That's already 115 kilometers. . . . Twenty-five left to go until Meung, where my trusty wheels bring me into the courtyard of an inn. I collapse face-down, prostrate, on the bed they give me, my butt raw and aflame; I immediately fall asleep and into a dream where my pedals have become the paddle wheels of a steamboat sailing up the Mississippi, in pursuit of a distant beacon reflected in the river's inky waters. The dream dovetails with the reality of the next dawn, with the crunching of gravel under my wheels as I pedal, as I brace myself to face the ordeal of the second day. My behind is bruised by pain, butcher's meat and dead nerves, to such an extent that I end up no longer feeling anything. My vision is strictly limited to the immediate necessities of locomotion: I see no farther than the next turn of the wheel, blinded by sweat and fatigue. *Orléans, Beaugency, Notre-Dame-de-Cléry, Vendôme . . . Vendôme.* . . .

Oh, I'm really out of shape! I'll have to do a lot better than this! *Beaugency, Blois, Amboise.* . . . Royal cities, cities of the poet-kings, whose round cobblestones resound sharply in the back of my head. At Tours, I lose my way and find it again. *Azay-le-Rideau, Poitiers.* A sandwich, some tap water, and my last hotel room, because my money's giving out; tomorrow I'll sleep in the open. But I put two hundred kilometers behind me on this second day—that's real progress. The third day looks a little better. I'm no longer blinded by my own perspiration, I breathe better, my legs have found their cruising rhythm, my body has become a pedaling machine guided from afar by some abstract volition. *Angoulême, Bordeaux, Arcachon.* As far as the salt water lake of Biscarosse, 280 kilometers! I sink down with my bicycle beside the water, too weak to fend off the mosquitoes who instantly attack me. In the middle of the night, I wake up with a scream as I reach the culmination of a dream sequence so erotic and so vigorous that it takes me a full minute to understand what on earth this bicycle is doing between my legs. It's a pitch-black starless night, and my famished gut becomes the sole reality; the flashlight glare attracts all sorts of winged companions that waltz around my head while I open a can from my provisions. Problem: How to eat cold stringbeans with a Swiss knife? This shadowy meal will have proved to be yet another failure in my life. . . . All around me, the nocturnal breeze stirs the rustling world of reeds; stringless fiddle bows whisper dance tunes in the festive hall of the frogs.

Why, you might inquire, why not take a more direct route in order to fly to my beloved, by way of Châteauroux, Périgueux, and Tarbes, which would have saved me a good fifty kilometers? The answer is—*I managed to convince myself that I'm not in search of her at all!* I'm merely doing some tourist-biking in the Pyrénées, that's all, and if it happens that I should stumble on her threshold, well, so much the better! But this would happen only as the result of purely fortuitous circumstances, quite obviously.

I cross the Landes on a boring stretch of road as straight as a plumb line, stupefied by an endless landscape of dunes and pine trees. . . . At Castets, I branch off toward Pau but, as I'm leaving Dax, I feel I just can't go on any longer. With these mountains ahead of me I'll never make it today, that much is certain. I go to sleep in a grove and take off again at sunrise. The road grows steeper, but I hardly feel it; in going up the foothills of the Pyrénées, I see only the sky at the top of the rise. Swarms of fireflies seem to burst forth out of my eyes. *Pau, Lourdes, Bagnères.* . . . And finally the last of the steep hills, and then the descent into the village of Campan, half-buried in the evening shadows from the surrounding mountains. Searching for Laurette's house, I try to ask directions of a peasant, and that's when I discover that I have lost the use of my voice. Once again! I write the address on the back of an envelope and show it to the good man—only to discover that he can't read. A complete breakdown in communications. But not so complete after all; the old fellow must have guessed me out, and he points to a house in the distance. It must surely be hers! As soon as I see her, I tell myself, surely my voice will return.

The door of the villa opens onto a staircase that I climb with great difficulty, like a worn-out centenarian. I come out on a terrace where I suddenly find myself in the midst of an entire extended family just sitting down to dinner. Rolande is the first to spot the ghostly apparition.

"Oh my God! Laurette! Come quick!" she cries. "That's

incredible—but tell me, where have you come from, Maurice? *It is you, isn't it?*"

"Argh . . . !"

"You're not kidding, are you? *You've really lost your voice?* And he must have lost half his weight, he's unrecognizable! Poor devil—"

"*Argargarg . . . !*"

And I fall into a heap on a deck chair, totally exhausted. François brings me a big glass of red wine. Lionel takes it out of his hands, saying that it would surely kill me. Laurette shows up, seems taken aback for a while, and then embraces me somewhat nervously, and starts talking to me. After that difficult beginning, she sits quietly next to me for a long time while the others, speaking in hushed voices, go through their dinner. Night falls on the surrounding mountains; as a falling curtain, just as if I had truly come to the end of my quest. She is there, next to me, hearing my heart beat for her, as no other heart has ever beaten. Tomorrow, when I will have found my voice, I will tell her, yes. . . . But right now my head is spinning, my ears are ringing, and the figures around the table, half-visible in the candlelight, seem to me to belong to another world. I hear far-off voices carried back to me as if by a lunar echo. And then everything vanishes into the night.

The next morning, I wake up in my deck chair; someone had put a blanket over me. To my great surprise, I find Laurette standing over me, smiling and looking very fresh; and the rush of pleasure I feel at her sight is enhanced by the fact that she is holding out a tray laden with food.

"Impossible!" I say, feebly.

"And true nevertheless; you've even got your voice back."

"You know that I'm crazy, don't you?"

"Oh, everybody's got a little screw loose somewhere or other," she says pleasantly.

This breakfast is extremely tasty. Jam is running all down my chin.

"I have to go to Bagnères to get the mail," she adds. "I don't propose that you come along. It's only five kilometers, but you must be pretty sick of riding a bicycle. . . . It won't take me very long."

"Oh no! Just let me take a shower and I'll go with you."

And here I am again on this devilish vehicle, that I haven't even taken time to unload; but this time it's the triumphal lap of the winner! I pedal behind her, the better to see her, the better to assure myself of her physical presence.

She comes out of the post office with a handful of letters. We sit down in the shade of a terrace and order some coffee. She opens her mail and each one of her gestures is a delight; it seems that I never see her with the same eyes, but even the most modest versions of her, unembellished by my imagination, strike me as enchanting. Twisting a lock of her hair as she reads her mail, she has the expression of a preoccupied child—will I still remember this blessed moment fifty years from now?

It soon dawns on me that the five letters that she opens and reads so attentively, one after the other, are all written in the same handwriting, by the same person.

I'm suddenly invaded by a feeling of foreboding. She finishes the last of the letters, sips her coffee, and smiles at me.

"Now that you have found your tongue, can't you tell me a bit more? When did you leave Paris?"

"Five days ago."

"What? You did eight hundred and fifty kilometers in five days?"

"Oh, it's nothing, really . . ."

She examines me with a dreamy eye. Will she finally understand? *Will she remember?*

"Listen, Laurette, I know that I haven't any right to ask you, but those letters, there, can you tell me . . . ?"

"Oh, I'm terribly sorry, Maurice! I shouldn't have spent all that time reading my mail; it really wasn't very nice of me. . . . But I'm worried about him, about my poor fainthearted lover—Robert, you know, who's so sick, it's totally without hope. His sister won't give up, she absolutely insists that I spend a few days with them at their place in Alès. . . . Let's talk about something else. I don't want to depress you with other people's problems. . . . But explain to me . . . last night . . . I mean . . . your arrival, how . . . ?"

"I was just passing through, it was more or less on my way."

"You plan to go farther? Somewhere else in the Pyrénées?"

"Of course. That's why I'm here."

"Well, at least that's a tangible fact: *You're here!* It's a fantastic surprise, you know? Last night, everybody wanted to make a big fuss over your arrival, but you were so tired. . . . How long can you stay?"

"I'm not staying. I can't."

"*What do you mean?* You just got here, and after such an incredible trip—don't be silly, it's absolute madness! Please, Maurice, if you won't stay for me, at least you must spend a little time here for Rolande's sake. You know she has an old weakness for you. . . . It's true, you know."

"Tell her good-bye for me. I'm sorry, I've got to get going."

"Now? Already? *Maurice!*"

Her shout rings in my ears as I'm already straddling my bike, already speeding down the steep incline, my eyes brimming with tears, looking for the way to Tarbes.

There is nothing sadder in the whole world than the Pyrénées when it rains. And in line with the mood of the day, it was pouring as I rode toward Paris, this time by the most direct route. Straining on the pedals under that merciless deluge, I felt as if I were becoming more and more ghostlike, reduced to a few kilos of pedaling substance. This marvelous love, beyond time, beyond the planet—I had dreamed it. This passion that had ravished my soul, it had been conjured by a play of mirrors. I came into Bergerac feeling so wasted, so bewildered—in this little village that seemed so completely unworthy of the great Cyrano—that I sold my bike and with the money I got for it, bought a third-class train ticket for Paris.

Shocked by my skeletal appearance, my father sent me off to recuperate in the country with the rest of the family. Two days later I received a very friendly letter from Laurette that helped me to put my ideas back into order. All right, I had better face the reality of my fate; my destiny wasn't going to be that of Tristan, of Don Juan, Faust, or Tolstoy, not that of Lord Byron, of Shelley, or Havelock Ellis, of Prince Albert, Robinson Crusoe, nor Othello, of Goethe, nor Chopin, of T.E. or D. H. Lawrence, of Rasputin, Saint Anthony, or Nicholas Flamel . . . but that of Abelard, doctor of abstinence. Ascetic by the grace of ritual castration. Such was my future, such was the lesson that my rival and guru Vivian had clobbered me with from the wings, perhaps not so innocently as all that.

In spite of all my doubts and torments, I return to take up again my modest place in the group sessions.

During the summer Vivian had brought forth a definitive monument, *Le Pacte Synarchisque*, in the shape of a mimeographed manuscript with a gilded binding all edged in red. I didn't have time to soak up its contents, which were rather startling, since I had been given a copy to look at only a few moments before the grand inaugural session.

I was being taken into the inner circle for good, despite my youthful acts of misconduct of the past few months, and I was going to participate as such in the foundation of the Synarchist Order. Each one of us was to take an oath and be received as a knight of the order, in due pomp and circumstance. It wasn't clear what was expected of us, except that we should be ready to give our life to The Cause at all times. All of which looked pretty much like the repetition of past experiences—only more so—and I went to look for Laurette, who had just returned from Campan that very morning. She had just dressed herself in her scarlet robes for the ceremony, and I was so happy to see her again that all my doubts were instantly dismissed. Yes, I would embark on this new quest, and I decided to dedicate my life to the Synarchist cause.

What is snyarchy? In his inaugural speech, Vivian defined it in terms clear enough to satisfy the critical mind. Imagine the antonym of anarchy. Anarchy is a powerless utopia inspired by a spirit of revolt that calls for the suppression of any kind of government, an impossibility at this very point of our human history. Synarchy is government in common where, according to his capacities and his particular role, everyone participates in decisions that are of importance to the collectivity. Democracy has exhausted itself in useless struggles—we have ample proof of that today—for the simple reason that the very principle of parliamentary representation is a hoax, a pseudosystem, an oversimplification that cannot be applied to the great diversity of human situations. Thus you have the Soviet Union calling itself a democracy, though it's a bureaucratic dictatorship; or France, with its constant political chaos; or the United States, which is in effect an elective monarchy with its presidential system; and a false democracy since it will not accommodate more than two parties.

Hence synarchy is founded upon four orders that correspond to the Hindu caste system; which itself is inspired by a recognition of the basic psychological differences between four very distinct categories of humans. The first, that of the Brahmins in India, will form the order of philosophers, artists, educators, thinkers, and other creative types; the second, that of the Kshatriya, is equivalent in a synarchic society to the class of administrators; the third, to that of merchants, of business managers; and the fourth, that of working people. Each order has its own hierarchy, and government is exercised in common by their elected delegates. This division of the people into orders is natural and conforms with tradition; the French Revolution had adopted the principle of it until equalitarian Jacobinism, and later communism, created a uniform population of one single class despite the evident realities of social life. Thus synarchy restores a natural order within societies, which befits the spiritual classification of individuals. Synarchy fulfills the aspirations of the esoteric tradition, as transmitted by the Rosicrucians, by great enlightened beings such as the Count of Saint-Germain. In modern times Saint-Yves d'Alveydre has adapted traditional thinking, in his writings, to the needs of the society to come. . . .

I listened to these marvels in a sort of trance, permeated with an ineffable happiness because Laurette was sitting next to me, and the sense of communion between us was so acute that, in a completely natural movement, she had put her hand over mine. Just as Vivian was winding up his discourse, carried away by my enthusiasm, I gently freed my hand and placed it on hers.

Out of nowhere—a smart rap—a ruler struck sharply across my knuckles. Taken aback, I looked at Kryia who was sitting on the other side of Laurette: She was looking straight ahead with a knowing air. This schoolmarmish swat of a ruler had been lightning-swift, as soon as my hand had come within her reach. She spared Laurette, Vivian's protégée, and humbled me, treating me like a naughty schoolboy. I was flabbergasted. Laurette withdrew her hand without saying a word, leaving me seething with silent fury. I was truly fed up with their pretensions, and all those ridiculous mummeries—this was the last straw.

The time had now come to take the oath, and with a sword, if you please! Vivian said no more and sat back with an absent air while Kryia explained that we didn't actually have a sword and that we were going to use the symbol of a sword. She brought out a souvenir letter opener from Mont-Saint-Michel.

"It's silver," she announced, with an air of defiant authority. "Someday soon we will have a real golden sword. My friends, I hope that you will all be able to surmount the feeling of absurdity that some of you might be tempted to give in to at the idea of using a letter opener to take such an important oath. Because this is your first trial, a test of your ability to create. For me, this letter opener is a sword. Synarchy will triumph just because I have in me the power to make a sword out of it. And I also have the strength to confound those who smile when they hear me say that this paper cutter *is* a sword. Faith is our only weapon and our only proof. The details don't matter. Those who are gathered here, those who have been judged worthy of being among the first knights of synarchy, are being admitted into the order because they have the capacity to create myth. I trust that I have made myself clear. *To all of us!*" she added, looking right at me. "And now let's go, who's first?"

We all stared at her, taken aback, petrified with respect and admiration. Vivian seemed to be suppressing a smile. Gauthier-Walter was first to take the oath. Strutting up in his long scarlet robes, he looked a little like a starving newborn bird with its hackles up. He recited his oath in his usual raspy, intense voice.

Next it was Armand Mora's turn, Kryia's political adviser who came from Toulouse, as his accent would tell you. Then came G.J. whose stooped shoulders, foggy glasses, and weak voice didn't do justice to the text. Then Witold, Hélène Anikeef's husband, the two of them recent recruits of Vivian's; Hélène, who was a great Slavic beauty and very aware of her looks, took her oath with a tiny dreamy smile, casting us a sidelong glance of her mysterious blue-gray eyes in order to check on the effect. They were followed by Rolande and the other women. My turn came last, and I had to borrow G.J.'s red robe because I didn't own one. Kryia's speech had roused me to such a pitch that I delivered my vow in a firm voice, without batting an eye, as if I'd been a synarchist all my life. As soon as the swearing-in was duly completed, there was a moment of great collective exhilaration, and Laurette gave me a brotherly accolade, right in front of Kryia. Thus harmony was restored among the soldiers of the future. We were the army of the Great Hierarchy, united behind the one and only leader, Julius Caesar. . . . But, indeed, where was Caesar?

Would Hitler's invasion of Czechoslovakia cause him to flee to the West, to France? The times were ripe, to say the least. And so also was Caesar's fiancée; since Rolande, at sixteen, had attained such a carnal glow that there might be complications for all involved if he didn't hurry up and get here. There were a lot of healthy young men floating around the lovely redhead, and they weren't all sexless theosophists. Meanwhile Rozenode, who hid under her uniform jacket the heart of a romantic spinster, was assembling in secret a precious wardrobe designed expressly for the future heir of the throne, Julius Caesar II, the as-yet unconceived son of our friend Rolande.

Printing the first three titles of the Villa Seurat series gave us a good deal of work, due in part to the printers' failures, but also to the intensive care with which the proofreading was done. This was to be an impeccable production, my father had decreed, a new departure for the Obelisk Press.

He had chosen a slightly larger format for the cover design with an obelisk motif, the colors of which would change for each book; and the retail price was to be seventy-five francs instead of sixty, which was a bit higher than the cost of a hard-cover book in London. It had been finally decided to inaugurate the Villa Seurat program with *The Black Book*, and to find printers for the three titles who could guarantee a fast delivery.

Finding printers wasn't easy, since very few had typesetters who knew any English; and those who had were extremely snotty, and expensive into the bargain. But the others would make so many mistakes that the job of correcting galley proofs became a truly heroic challenge; and the books finally came out full of monstrous bloopers, which had become more or less of a hallmark for the Obelisk Press type of novels. "Not to be sold in the United Kingdom and the U.S.A." We had started to search for printers abroad, in Belgium—and even in Hungary. The quality of their product wasn't bad, but we had to wait for weeks for the delivery to reach us, since they were transported on slow-moving barges along the waterways of Europe.

Proofreading was one of my jobs, for which I had developed a certain talent, although my knowledge of English was still so rudimentary. But I appeared to have a very good visual memory and a knack for guessing out what was wrong about the spelling of a word just by the shape of it, even when the meaning escaped me. Proofreading helped me a lot in amassing a pretty extensive vocabulary in English, and yet I could hardly pronounce most of the words I knew; that particular type of proofreading also served to enrich my knowledge of a variety of erotic situations and sexual depravities, and yet I was still living in strict accordance with my vow of chastity. The tension thus created was sometimes close to unbearable; but that was the job, *n'est-ce pas?*

Thus I was fast becoming a doctor of erotica, and yet, being close to twenty, I was still a diffident virgin. You could call this the pornographer's paradox.

Proofreading is a particularly interesting procedure insofar as it shows you the magic of print at work. On your left you have the author's typescript, with its many blemishes, inky blotches, crossed-out words, additions, copy-editors' markings, erasures, printers' fingerprints, a very humane, approximate document filled with the hesitations inherent to the creative process. But on your right you have a long strip of paper, with neat blocks of text in a column, representing the contents of three or four future book pages. Each time you check back from the galley to the typescript, you are surprised by the difference in meaning, in impact, of a given word in these two different forms. Then, a few days or weeks later, you check the page proofs against the galley proofs, and finally, after another wait, you receive the printed volume itself, fresh from the binders. At each stage you can see how the *value* of each individual word and sentence changes. The title itself, seen in print, comes as a surprise; the definitive nature of the printed word turns it into a cult object. Just as the famous author is frozen into a statue by public opinion, so is his work turned into a classic, sitting like a stuffed bird on the bookshelf. Many writers have difficulty recognizing themselves in printed form; no doubt because their original meaning has been obliterated by the manner in which it has been packaged and received, as printed word, by the collective unconscious of the readers. . . . That's even more true with the newspapers—you could say that any lie made into a headline becomes instant truth—*dead on paper*; yet the same words would be entirely questionable in conversation. The printer's ink has that magic property, which has nothing to do with its chemical components.

And that is certainly what determines the publisher's vocation; for instance, my father might have become rich easily in many other ways, and yet he spent all his energies turning himself into a poor, obscure publisher. And what would you say of the fanatical determination of Henry, Anaïs, and Larry to see their works in print, although there's not one chance in a trillion that they will survive in this dying world?

On March 15, 1939, Hitler occupies Prague. A resounding slap in the face for the Allied governments. Daladier takes advantage of this to have the French parliament give him full powers over the legislative and executive branches.

Thus Hitler's move draws that absurd response: To fight him the French give themselves a dictator, but they choose for that role a turncoat politico of mediocre intelligence, a man whose career has been marked by repeated failures—including the tragic defeat by Hitler himself at Munich, only a few months earlier.

The choice is so absurdly wrong that you might think that it had been contrived by Hitler himself!

Furthermore Hitler, having invaded Czechoslovakia, gives a piece of it to the Poles, and they eat it up like dogs, in complete defiance of the Paris-London axis which supported them up to that time. This is done in contempt of the so-called right of all peoples to dispose of themselves—the very principle the Allies have invoked to protest against prior Nazi aggressions.

And so when, at the beginning of April, the same Hitler turns back to his Polish friends and demands of them the gift of a territorial corridor linking the Reich to the Free State of Danzig—which he intends to take over "at the urgent request of the oppressed population of Danzig"—it's not easy to make the usual speeches in favor of Poland, as were made previously for the Czechs and the Austrians. But the so-called democracies didn't have clean hands to start with, to say the least.

Their only answer is to vote a huge war budget. Hitler is amused by this response. He decides to let the Polish situation rot quietly until the summer months. From his Bavarian retreat he writes a complimentary note to Daladier; he seems to have quite forgotten Chamberlain's existence. Would that be part of his divide-to-conquer diplomacy?

So Daladier, sitting on his imperial throne, assembles the dukes and princes of his court and creates new functions for them, as an exact counterpart to the Nazi power structure.

Baldur von Schirach, a hardcore Nazi, heads all Hitlerian youth movements; on the French side it is former tennis champion Jean Lacoste, an aging playboy, who's made boss of French youth organizations—which are nonexistent apart from small local soccer clubs.

Big Marshal Goering, who's married to an opera singer, is the fearsome boss of the Luftwaffe; Daladier appoints as his minister of aviation another suave playboy, Guy La Chambre, whose current mistress is no other than Josephine Baker her-self. And this doesn't do anything to improve France's air power, still mostly limited to the "flying coffins" from Marcel Bloch's factories.

The reptilian Dr. Goebbels is the chief of Hitlerian propa-ganda. His French counterpart will be Georges Duhamel, a renegade pacifist, whose first job will be to organize censor-ship over all books and newspapers printed in France. . . . As predicted by Bogous, our wise friend, only a few months ago!

Dr. Alfred Rosenberg has given the Nazi regime its racist philosophy. Well, it's a bit too early for French racism, per-haps, but there is an urgent need for a minister of information who will be able to express in clear and elegant fashion the democracies' war aims; Jean Giraudoux's fame in Parisian salons causes him to become France's official ideologue. . . . Meanwhile, his colleague Jean Giono, whose poetic, back-to-nature novels had so deeply influenced the younger genera-tion, proclaims his pacifist faith; off to jail he goes. No one dares fly to his defense!

On April 26, Daladier orders the French newspapers to play down Hitler's speeches. He feels quite unable to com-pete with the Führer's electrifying style.

On April 29, Daladier uses his legislative powers to decree a new law for the protection "of the French Family and Na-tional Birthrate."

What is that? Well, that is, again, the Bogous prediction come true: yes, a censorship law. France's birthrate has been going down quite seriously in recent years, as the conse-quence of the First World War holocaust of a whole genera-tion of Frenchmen at the reproductive age. But the clerical and reactionary circles on the Right have argued for years that the real reason for that alarming drop was the life of pleasure led by the French, and particularly the light or scandalous lit-erature being tolerated by the government. In the House a representative by name of Philippe Farine explains to his cap-tive audience the mechanism of that unpatriotic practice: every year licentious reading diverts precious tons of semen away from the reproductive function it was meant to serve. France's enemy is not Hitler, it is not the Yellow Peril; it is misdirected sexuality. He would like to make masturbation illegal, but that's beyond the capacity of the law-and-order forces, eh? How to enforce such a ruling? And so the next best thing is to suppress whatever temptations there are for young men to jack off behind closed doors. Remember the Holy Scriptures! Haven't you been warned by God himself not to scatter your seed in vain on the ground?

The representatives lap it up. It is true that there was no need for Farine's speech, since the new law only required Daladier's signature, but everyone in the House loves the sheer bravado of it, and the speaker is given a standing ovation. Such was the purpose of Daladier's maneuver: to get the conservatives solidly on his side.

Is sexual censorship going to help in the fight against the dictators? We shall see.

Meanwhile, it is spring again, and my heart is swelling with an overdose of unrequited love. Josephine Baker leaves Guy La Chambre and shacks up with Jo Bouillon, the well-known band leader. André Gide publishes his *Journal intime* and *Tropic of Capricorn* comes out in Paris, the third Henry Miller title, after *Cancer* and *Black Spring*.

What is it that makes Hitler tick, I wonder? To say that he wants a world empire does not do justice to that question. He has the means, he has the power to accomplish that without a war: The Allies would prefer to give him the leadership in Europe if he offered them a peaceful settlement right now; and from there he could impose his will on Russia, Asia, and eventually America. It's all a question of diplomacy.

But that would be too easy—what he wants is to draw blood. His ultimate ambitions are less essential than his desire for revenge, his will to humiliate the enemy; that is, Voltaire, Jean-Paul Sartre, and Maurice Chevalier. He wants to humiliate those snotty British peers, and those good-for-nothing French intellectuals. He wants to fill up Maxim's and Buckingham Palace with his storm troopers. He wants to make those people know that he is the boss, and he wants to make them feel the humiliation of their impending defeat in their very bones.

The French are unable to understand that type of hysterical attitude, so incompatible with Cartesian logic. When I visit my friends in Neuilly I find them doing push-ups, or running around the block. Big deal. One day I met successively Laurette's brother-in-law, François Chérel, and my cousin Mowgli Laforgue, both of them professional soldiers now, very smart in their lieutenant's uniforms, and I was duly impressed by the fact that we were now in opposite camps.

With Mowgli in particular, whom I considered as my brother rather than a cousin, I felt that an explanation was needed. I told him that I was determined not to fight in a war, not even against Hitler.

"That's up to you," he answered gaily. "You understand, I don't have to ask myself questions because I got into the army as a professional. And I'm certainly going to knock out a few of those Nazis if I get half a chance; but that's temperamental. Apart from that, I know it's all a big mess, that French army, and that if there's a war, our chances won't be so good. But I can also understand the pacifist angle. It doesn't have a chance now, but after the war, after a few million poor bastards have been wiped out, it's a thing that should be tried."

Later that same day, at the office, among the letters I opened there was one I read without realizing that it was addressed to my father personally, from the War Office in London. Unwittingly, I had uncovered his secret: He had sent an application to join the army, asking to be reinstated with his rank of captain; and he was being told that he could only be admitted as second lieutenant, and this only subject to a prior medical examination.

I folded the letter and closed the envelope as best I could—he mustn't guess that I found out. In his state of health, he should have known that his chances of being enlisted were nil. Why did he try? What extremity of anger, of confusion and despair had brought him to the point of making that useless gesture? How would he like being told that he was no good?

To all my old friends that I met in Neuilly I repeated my intention: I won't go. Not one of them got angry, not one of them told me that I was wrong. The idea had never dawned in any of those boyish heads that there was any course to follow but to obey. To obey who? *Eh bien, cet imbécile de Daladier, bien sûr. Ce salaud, ce pourri, ce vendu. . . .*

What can you do?

I went to see Georges Pelorson, who ran *Volontés*, that literary magazine to which various interesting and lively people contributed, including Raymond Queneau, Henry Miller, Michel Leiris, Georges Bataille. Politically that group was as open and eclectic as you could wish, but none of the people involved was indifferent to the big issues we were all facing in this fateful year—1939.

Georges told me that he was expecting to be called up soon

and then, well, of course he would go. And we went on to discuss the chances France had of pulling out of the present morass. Who could give the country the fiber, the inspiration, the example it needed, not just to deal with the Hitler situation, but to reverse the country's decadence? But Georges was still looking at France as a live reality, as a manageable concept. And I was beginning to understand that France just didn't exist, except as an arbitrary convention, as the result of a pact among politicians.

After that exchange I started wondering about my position. Could I really call myself an anarchist? Or had I abandoned all that it meant when I had become a synarchist? What was the situation at the boulevard Saint-Germain ashram?

It didn't take long to find out. Vivian was of the opinion that the war wouldn't last very long, and he seemed even to believe that he was about to win it, without any outside help.

At the Sunday meditation, Vivian issued an order for the total destruction of Hitler and Mussolini, the heavy artillery to be directed at the two villains personally: We stuffed pikes, tridents, and halberds down their throats.

In the hushed, darkened room, one could feel the deep breathing swell and fall with the mounting tension, and the great Asuras streaking toward their target like psychic harpoons. The spiritual militia of Vivian the Magician was encircling the two wild beasts—our astral bombardment was hitting them with death rays right to the Adam's apple.

After each session, I must admit that I began to feel a little silly. I noticed that Laurette had nothing to impart as to the result of those otherworldly expeditions. . . . Neither had the newspapers. Our hopes to read a headline announcing that Mussolini had been seized by mysterious tracheal spasms had to be gradually abandoned. Actually the dictators all seemed to be in fine fettle.

Having been born with dual nationality I had to opt between the ages of twenty and twenty-one in favor of one of them, and I took the British nationality as soon as I was able to in order to shed my French citizenship. The immediate consequence was that I did not have to serve two years of military service in the French army, as all my friends had to do. The conscription did not exist in England, at least for the time being, and since I was living outside of England, I would probably never be called up, even in the eventuality of a war.

It was not a very heroic way of disengaging myself from my so-called patriotic duty. But, what the hell, if you fight the system you don't have to be elegant about it! The system certainly isn't.

Gregor seemed to have vanished from my horizon; he had not been heard from in weeks, perhaps months, until one day he rang me up at the office, and we made a date for dinner.

To my utter amazement Gregor appeared wearing the resplendent uniform of a cavalry officer, a fine riding crop in his gloved hand, and resplendent riding boots graced with discreet silver spurs. Strange to say, his extreme ugliness harmonized rather well with the officer's strict collar. Searching for some indication of rank, I finally located, hardly visible on his sleeve, a corporal's woolen stripes. So he was not a colonel after all.

"Gregor," I groaned, "your jokes are getting too heavy for me. Why do you dress that way?"

"Typical civilian approach," he spat disdainfully. "You'll have to change your attitude with me, my man. In the dragoons, we're prompt to horsewhip a cur when we see one. *Harrumph*."

"Are you telling me that you're actually in the army?" I pleaded.

"That's enough of that, fishface, let's eat, do not dally." He snapped his jaws noisily to underline his need for food. We promptly sat down at a table; after he had studied the menu and ordered himself a seven-course dinner from an astonished headwaiter, I repeated my question.

"Now, Gregor, tell me what you're up to."

"What d'you mean, 'Gregor, what are you up to'? It's obvious enough what I'm up to. I offered my services to the French army, my friend, although I do despise those little people."

"And they took you?"

"Of course they took me, what kind of a question is that?" he roared. "If you continue with your insults and insinuations, I will have to ask you to leave this table."

"All right, all right, Gregor, but please don't shout. Don't start a scandal before they bring you food, at least."

"Well then stop picking on me. If you don't respect me,

have some respect for my uniform at least, eh? The reason I am in the army is that, number one, I can ride the general's mare every day, and she's a real beauty. And number two, this spiffy uniform, my man, precisely. Now I can tell the maids and cooks to go to the devil, I make it with the lady of the house! Bourgeois types in their forties, well-stacked, ha ha, and with king-size beds and lots of food in the larder. You know, nice and plump, what. And so I skewer them, and screw them, and sock it to them with my incredible schlong until . . . until . . . say, where's my food?"

"Don't fret, it's coming. But tell me, what about your toe?"

"Oh that wasn't the big toe, you know? Only the little pinkie. And then I just told them that I had changed my mind, you see, as I was standing there in my birthday suit. But when they raised their pince-nez up to my famous poker, they understood what they were dealing with. They declared me fit for service and threw in a corporal's stripes into the bargain, just as a mark of their appreciation. Where's that waiter, god-dammit? No second helpings in this place?"

It was a remarkable story but a sad one. He had wanted suddenly to be like everyone else, and he had got himself into that silly uniform, poor idiot. At least he hadn't betrayed himself all the way: A soiled napkin around his neck, he was putting away an incredible amount of food, burping and hiccuping to his heart's content as he shoveled the stuff. The occupants of the five or six tables closest to us were watching us covertly, trying hard to make some sense out of our mostly one-sided verbal exchange.

"Don't you understand my point, you *misérable couillon?* I am happy as a lord, I have my beautiful horse, and thanks to my uniform I get all the pussy I want. Good rich, juicy, greasy, steaming pussy, from the front and from the back, kiddo! I like it better from the back, mind you, 'cause you've got all those things you can grab with your hands. And then you've got a better view of the landscape, hey, what d'you say? Tell me, killer, which way d'you like it best?"

Uncomfortable silence.

"I see," he went on in a disgusted tone, cracking some animal bones between his molars. "Monsieur is still involved in his mystical love affairs, young vestal virgins and all that tripe, isn't that true, fishface?"

He threw the carcass of a bird onto a pile of bones; gravy was smeared all around his plate.

"Gregor, I realize that that uniform has placed you above the ordinary sensibilities of the human race, but everyone must choose his own destiny. I don't envy the carrion-eater who sells his conscience for a murderer's livery."

"Ho there," he thundered, "ho ho! Ho ho ho!"

He interrupted whatever he was about to say in order to belch roundly, causing a certain amount of panic among our neighbors. Having done, he resumed his diatribe.

"Insulting the uniform of the republic, that's not very wise, my boy! Things could get hot for you. If those good people around us could hear you, you son of a bitch, they would lynch you—if they had the balls, that is. And that's doubtful," he added, glowering suspiciously from left to right. "Come on," he growled, "it's time to go hear la belle Suzy Solidor. Ah! How I like the way she swaggers on stage, that big dyke. A sailor with boobs, wouldn't you say? What a sexy piece of goods! Mmm. . . . Gemütlich . . ."

And so now we are in the audience of Solidor's club, not far from the Théâtre Français, and Gregor sits back, ecstatic, having heard the husky mermaid sing her heart out. This brings him back to his favorite subject.

"The day you finally decide to lose your cherry, my man, you just say the word and I'll arrange things for you, with pleasure. It would be an honor for me, seriously."

"Gregor, go to hell, you stupid freak! Can't you ever talk about something else?"

"Never! Listen, if you don't respect my competence, at least respect my uniform. The price I paid for those rags. . . . But, you know, Hitler's a virgin too, and a vegetarian—he's just like you, same type, you just have to look at him to know that. Repressed types, both of you. Always dangerous. That man Hitler, to prevent him from going completely berserk and killing us all, there's only one way, he must be snowed under pussy, buried in cunt. He must be taught to make it from behind, twelve fat broads at a time, assembly-line style, what? For maniacs like him, and you, that's the only cure. Rake the old furnace clean, kiddo! Get into the action, there are armies of dripping pussy all around, waiting, panting. Just give the word, I tell you!"

"Gregor, please, not so loud!"

"Ah kid, you know, you make me sick. Sometimes, I don't know about you. What's the use of talking to you, you won't even listen, fuck you. . . . Ah, here she is again! Look at those shoulders, willya? A real big healthy platinum blonde, no? Hey, kiddo, d'you picture yourself humping a body like that?"

14

The murshid and his brood. —Ah! To be in love with love!
—The dance of the yogurt. —To a datcha in the Paris
suburbs, with a flaming libido. —Henry Miller
and small change. —She's just sitting there in the dark,
waiting, stark naked! —From the great classics to
the red hot stuff. —Didi and Momo forever.

In spite of Hitler and the world cracking up, I'm involved
with creating a new weekly for kids, would you believe it?
There's nothing more optimistic than that.

This project is the brainchild of Noor, the sister of Vilayat
Inayat Khan, whom I met at the boulevard Saint-Germain
ashram.

These two are the scions of a colorful family. The father,
Hazrat, had been a murshid, a spiritual leader of the Sufis. He
belonged to an old Indian family that claimed to be descended
from Tipu Sultan, one of the last heroes of the fight against
the English invaders. The mother, known as the Begum,
wrapped in her spectacular saris, was a figure of mystery, silent, inaccessible, living in nearly complete retirement; it
was not immediately apparent that she was in fact American,
from a wealthy midwestern family. She had been brutally dis-
inherited after having eloped with "that Hindu preacher," a
circumstance that might well explain her permanent migraine.

And so Hazrat had been obliged to get organized, and draw
an income from his spiritual activities. He had to feed his four
children in addition to his three brothers, pay the expenses of
the family estate in Suresnes, near Paris, and keep the Begum
stocked in saris. All this had spurred him to start Sufi groups
in Europe and in America, from Moscow to California. The
whole family being very musical, he had also put together an

orchestra that had sometimes performed traditional Indian music for the great of this world, including such personalities as Gabriele d'Annunzio, and Mata Hari herself. Mme Mignon Nevada, the well-known diva, had become the friend of the family and personally coached Vilayat in his role as heir to the murshid's spiritual throne.

One day Hazrat left his children for a trip to India, intimating that he might never return. And indeed news of his death reached his family a few months later, leaving everything in a state of suspense. In spite of the training he had received, Vilayat wasn't sure that he wanted to become a murshid. He kept dallying. For one thing, he liked girls too much—being a spiritual leader would cramp his style. He was, indeed, a very seductive young man, with the dusky skin of an Oriental prince and the wardrobe of an English dandy.

Noor was less flashy, more reserved, as behooves the sibling of the heir apparent, but I found her charm very touching. Of course that magazine project of ours served me mostly as a convenient excuse for the visits I paid her, two or three times a week, at her small apartment near the Porte Champerret. I didn't believe too much in the project, quite frankly; but I did my best to help her because I had come to treasure her easy friendship. Of course I was in love with Laurette, but since what I felt for Noor was not supposed to be more than a warm comradeship, there was no conflict. . . . The fact remains, however, that, as we worked side by side and I basked in her graceful presence, stealing glances at her studious expression, at the lowered lids and the exquisite fullness of her cheeks, it sometimes happened that I dropped my pencil.

Here was the clear possibility of another impossible love in my life! But perhaps it would erase my excruciating passion for Laurette? At times, when I realized the absurdity of my situation, I really felt like throwing in the sponge. Just imagine: falling in love not with one but with *two* girls at the same time, whose lives were devoted to the spiritual quest. . . .

But what's the good of dreaming. Nothing will ever cure me of Laurette. Nothing will ever change that situation. And the only remedy I've found is to make myself fall in love with Noor, who is surely just as inaccessible. Fool! Idiot! As I leave Noor, that particular day, I am in such a state of anger with myself that I decide to do something drastic about it. I have to bring the whole absurb situation to an end. And so I invite myself to dinner.

Not that the seedy vegetarian fare of the Foyer Pythagore where I take myself looks that inspiring. Very cheap for sure, the fare is hardly edible; it's a place for old fogies, absolutely devoid of charm—except for those, intensely carnal, of the waitress Didi. In my wildest erotic dreams I have never been able to conjure anything as arousing, as delightfully animal. Nothing spiritual *there*, what a relief! She may earn a living by serving watery vegetables to her customers, but I bet you that she feeds herself on the flesh of stallions. I've never seen anyone to equal that beautiful girl from Provence, with her perfect apricot skin, her flashing eyes, and the word *naughty* written all over her. As she dances toward my table the salacious impudence in her eyes forces me to lower my own ignominiously.

And as I do so I come upon the most provocative pair of legs I have ever seen, enhanced by a short skirt, and they immediately set to dancing on my behalf.

I blush violently, like an idiot, and my eyes go up again, encountering en route a pair of well-rounded, supple hips and a narrow waist dominated by, well, how could I possibly describe those lovely jutting globes? My stupefied eyes are suddenly impaled on her devouring glance, as she studies me intently, her order pad at the ready. She sucks her pencil expectantly between pulpy lips.

"And what will you have, handsome?" she coos, exaggerating her southern accent. "We have freshly grated carrots, turnip cutlets, and that yellow goo you people seem to like, I really don't know why, that you always order when you come here with your friend, you know, the tall fellow with the glasses?"

She improvises an imaginary portrait, drawing big lenses around her eyes for emphasis. And then takes my order with her legs akimbo, toes drawn in, pushing out her tongue and making goggle eyes at her pad like a village idiot.

"And for dessert?" she asks. "A little yogurt, huh?"

"Uh, yes, well perhaps, we'll see about that later, thank you, Didi."

"A little later, thank you Didi," she mimics in a singing voice, bounding toward the kitchen like a latter-day Nijinsky.

Alone, I flip the cover of my book, and pretending to read,

I covertly check the assembly. The book has just been published by Payot, a German study by Weisacker on world economic blocs, if you please. Nothing could be more serious, more austere. I feel the murderous glares of the old codgers around me—they certainly resent my presence! They're all losers, like me, but I am by far the youngest in the crowd and they don't like it. It's the same gang of senile occultists with their grimy tomes, and decrepit anarchists with fractured lenses, a blind accordion player, the painful dregs of the Latin Quarter. In the midst of these gray zombies Didi waltzes as she moves between the tables, exuberant and lovely, holding pyramids of dishes in her pretty round arms as if they were trophies won in a beauty contest. Always the same routine. These old wrecks studying their dog-eared volumes, they don't fool me!—since in fact I am doing the same thing. I keep my head bowed over my book, but from the corner of my eyes I register every passage of that inflammatory skirt with a terrific pang, each time storing up huge quantities of Didi so as to be able to fight, later, the bleakness of my lonely garret where no woman has ever set foot.

Alas, it was all too obvious, at times like this, that my vow of chastity was no more than a fraud, a farce. Was I such a hypocrite that I lied to myself as well as to my colleagues of Vivian's mystic circle? No, the truth is that I was just very weak. I believed in what I professed, including the need for chastity to find God. But in the presence of temptation my will was soon defeated. Later I would be punished by pangs of terrible self-disgust, like any theological student after a bout with his favorite succubus; but right now Didi was about to start her *danse du yaourt*, the yogurt dance, and so. . . . There was a good reason why yogurt was so popular at the Pythagore, and it had nothing to do with longevity. The reason was, quite simply, that the jars of yogurt were piled on a high shelf, inaccessible from the floor, and that when Didi was asked for a yogurt by one in the know, she would obligingly pounce onto a chair and stretch her entire anatomy in the most elaborate and enticing manner, displaying the fulness of her quivering charms, which were just as voluptuous on that side as they were up front. All this in slow motion. One was treated to a lesson in erotic anatomy, and it seemed to give a new lease of life to the moribund audience. Before descending she turned around to face the room with a wily smile, and check the percentage of hypocrites and panting masturbators present: 100 percent. Satisfied, she would leap lightly from her pedestal and place the yogurt before the customer, curtsy, and leave the poor fellow in a state of shock, nostalgically playing with his spoon, trying to remember the times when he was still young, and in love.

To be quite truthful, as I must, let me add that this is the first time I've ever dared come to the Pythagore *all by myself*, without G.J., my usual companion, because that Didi, frankly, she makes me unbearably nervous. For a repressed, oversexed fellow like me, close to twenty and still a virgin, torn between mysticism and desire, she is quite simply the devil dressed up in female flesh. As soon as I saw her I would be overcome by excruciating jealousy: I knew that she made love with men, of course, and my imagination immediately produced devilish images of Didi being stripped and brutally possessed by some horrible bully, and liking it. I can't stand it! As soon as I see her paying attention to a customer, even one of the old types, it makes me so nervous that I lose all control, I rap on the table and call for my bill, urgently.

"Monsieur wants another yogurt?" she asks, ignoring my request. She bends over my table, her questioning face so close to mine that I have to sit back as far as I can, rigid with panic. But I can't avoid the plunging view she offers me from that angle of her ample bosom, velvety, so smooth. . . .

"Oh no, no no," I gasp. "The bill . . ."

"The bill, the bill!" she squeals, imitating my terrified tone. "Tout de suite, voilà, the bill, the bill."

She scribbles away on her pad like a maniac, picks up her tip, and mimes the deepest reverence as I struggle to get up and leave without knocking the table over.

"Good-bye, good-looking," she murmurs caressingly.

"Good-night," I bark, addressing myself not to her but to the grubby cashier, M. Jojo, to whom no one has ever been known to say good-night.

That little bitch! Putting on that act. What did I ever do to deserve that? Nothing! I'll never come back here. I'll bet she is already jumping into bed with her lover, breaking him up with stories of how she tortures all these senile guys, including yours truly, a prematurely senile retarded cretin. Yes, me, a grown-up virgin of twenty years! Absolutely unheard of. And when I think that this expedition to the Pythagore was expressly staged to achieve my sexual liberation! No question about it, here's the result of a whole life of self-imposed chastity: I am afraid of women. Not one, not two—all of them.

Over the following weekend I went to pay a visit to Gregor in his family's villa at Le Vésinet. From a distance what you saw of the house above the high walls seemed banal enough, but once inside you were suddenly transported to some far-off province in old Russia. Chekhov himself might be wandering in that sad and dusty garden, in those rooms piled high with Oriental rugs and filled with heavy, ornamental furniture from every period.

The people inside were all characters from a Russian novel, the lost souls of a past which had been transported by some trick of magic to another time, another place. The grandfather was an imposing figure with an Astrakhan overcoat draped over his pajamas. Never having learned French, he greeted me in Russian.

. . . Amid the general commotion: as it had just dawned on all present that Aunt Sophie was nowhere to be found. She had in fact disappeared the night before, though no one seemed to have been aware of it, not until it was time to come to the table. People grouped into search parties according to affinities, and at last she was found in the depths of the garden, sitting on a swing, softly murmuring childish stories to herself like the good little girl that she was, or had been; although always so dreamy and forgetful. "She lives in the past," they explained to me, smiling to her and shrugging apologetically.

The huge table accommodated a constantly shifting number of guests, ranging from twelve to twenty, who were served in a rain of chatter by busty, red-cheeked women bringing out an endless assortment of victuals from the kitchen. The pungent smell of kasha blended with many other aromas. This table was a delight to the senses, but as I said so to Gregor, he shrugged impatiently.

"If you try and tell me that this family scene resembles the tea party in *Alice in Wonderland*, you skunk, I'll bash in your skull." This said in a threatening growl.

An old aunt close to us, lending credence to the tone of his words if not to their sense, pounded the floor sharply with her cane and cried out "Gregor!", following this with a vehement harangue in Russian.

"You see what I mean," he observed somberly. "Let's get out of here. I've had my fill of these old Muscovites anyway, and it's too nice outside. Let's take a walk on the island."

And so we leave old Russia. Only to wander into a postcard jungle straight from the Douanier Rousseau. In winter that small island on the river was something akin to an empty lot, but now, in the springtime, Mother Nature has changed all that with a vengeance. Now it is time to speak to Gregor. It won't be easy, of course, but he is the only one I can turn to, really, being my friend. He knows all about girls, women, love, sex. I don't. Of course I dread his savage irony, but in a case as solemn, as serious as this, he will listen, he will help me, surely. I am walking ahead on the path along the river, narrowing through some bushes that form a natural alcove, and there, suddenly, I stumble on a totally unforeseen obstacle: two girls preparing to bathe. Their skirts are raised, their naked legs bar the way, their feet already in the water. I jump out of my skin! No time, no space to maneuver, and Gregor just behind me, what—

"Speaking of the devil," Gregor guffaws, and he shoves me forcefully ahead.

This sends me stumbling between the first girl's legs, as the second one swivels backward and lifts hers up in the air like a drawbridge to allow me passage, confronting me clearly with the fact that she wears no panties. Shattered by this sudden close-up, I take off like a stag in flight, running as fast as I can, my head completely lost in fright and shame. As I flee between the trees I can still hear Gregor's deep basso from a long distance, from a world that will never be mine.

"Ho ho, you idiot, come back! Come join the party, you fool!"

His booming, satanical laughter pursues me through the bushes. With head pounding and eyes nearly blind, I run all the way to the railway station at Le Vésinet. The welcome rumbling of the next train to Paris greets me, and at last, swimming in my own sweat, I collapse in my seat, burnt out with defeat. Will I ever come to terms with this merciless timidity? Gregor won't speak to me again, that's for sure. And I let myself sink into a morass of self-pity all the way to the Gare Saint-Lazare.

I awoke the next day with the same old taste of disaster. On my way to the office I was convinced that passengers on the bus tread on my toes on purpose, to let me know that they were aware of my shame. I'd known other days like that, when I felt that everyone and everything was in league against me. How could I regress so? Me, the author of published articles on economics and, in a sense, the co-founder of the Obelisk Press? How could one be so foolish at my age?

The office on place Vendôme was as silent and quiet as ever. My father phoned to say he wouldn't be coming, he wasn't feeling too well. At eleven the door opens and Henry Miller enters, his battered felt slouched over his right eye, in the style of a Pigalle pimp. He smirks at me pleasantly.

"Hello, Maurice. Your old man around?"

"No, he's not coming in today. He didn't feel up to it. I'm not sure what's wrong with him."

"What a lousy break," Henry says, slipping into the secretary's chair. "I'm flat broke, you know? Hmm. . . . Well, I wanted to ask him for an advance, nothing much really, a few francs, eh? Hmm. Came all the way from the Villa Seurat on foot, and that's not just for the exercise, I don't seem to be able to afford the subway these days."

He shows me a pair of dusty, worn-out moccasins. His socks don't match, one blue one green. His corduroy pants must have been new once upon a time.

"You should have phoned first," I tell him. "I'm sorry but . . ."

We're in for the old routine, once again. It's a little ritual between us, and I know very well that I am only one stop on Henry's rounds, when he starts in the early morning from his digs on Villa Seurat, in the south of the fourteenth arrondissement, to conduct his own one-man foraging party so as to secure the next few days' subsistence. He has a map of Paris imprinted in his mind, each mark to be approached in an original, specific manner. So far as I am concerned, Henry knows that I am the guardian of a few francs in petty cash to purchase stamps. I know that he knows, and he knows that I know that he knows. He has to create enough of a pretense to justify my relinquishing my hold on that miserable sum, whatever it may be. Sometimes it's so tiny that he has to laugh at himself. But it is a friendly duel and we get along fine; after all, I've been one of his first readers, his devoted admirer and supporter since I was fourteen, still a mere kid, and I am grateful to Henry for the fact that he never even complained about my designing the first cover for *Tropic of Cancer*; he never even mentions the fact at all. After I have let myself be dispossessed of my francs and centimes in the usual manner, we go on for a little while with the banter. In his rumbling voice Henry asks me if I will be an editor one day—a publisher like my dad, or perhaps a writer? He chuckles but his interest is real, he's not merely being polite, and the exchange is so relaxed, so pleasant that all of a sudden I am tempted to tell him about what happened yesterday, the two girls in a bush by the river. Of course turning the whole episode around, like a saga *à la* Henry Miller: me the sex hero. But something stops me, a glint in his eye; you don't fool that man so easily, that's obvious.

"Well, I'm on my way now," he finally says. "Tell your old man he shouldn't knock himself out like that. He'll only ruin his health, everything will work out fine in the end."

And so I go back to my work of proofreading some more smutty material, and this strikes me more strongly than ever for the sheer absurdity of it. By now I've learned enough to become a professor of erotic technology, and all that really to no avail! My head is crammed with all this lurid information and the net result is to amplify my tortures in an unbearable manner. My old school buddies, when we met again, ask me all kinds of questions, but, honestly, what can I tell them? In theory I know ten times more than they do, but in actual practice, it's the other way around.

The day is spent thus, in angry ruminations. And while I hunt the typos in those endless sex scenes before me, I feel my decision growing back from the ruins of my last defeats. Once again, that same evening I push open the door of the Pythagore, enter the mostly empty room, and take my place at a lonely table. It's very late, the place is due to close soon, and I brace myself as I see Didi advancing in my direction. I take a deep breath.

"Good evening, Didi. I'll have a yogurt if you don't mind. Nothing else."

Just like that. My head spins a bit, but I find myself remarkably calm, considering. I try to smile at her, but I don't quite succeed.

With arms crossed over her solid bosom, she plants herself in front of me, an expression of amusement playing on her lips. Struggling to keep from blushing, I manage to smile back at her. At least I hope it comes out as a smile.

"Ca alors!" she utters, obviously nonplussed, as she looks down at me. "Who would have believed this! All by himself too. *So you want a yogurt, eh?*"

It is like asking a great soprano to sing *La Traviata* in private. But how can she resist the request of such a devoted *aficionado?* Didi goes slowly, meditatively, into the first movements of her yogurt dance, which she builds into a pure marvel of comic grace and abandon. Standing on the chair, she turns toward me, posing with the yogurt pot aloft like a torch, imitating the Statue of Liberty. A strong symbol! M. Jojo rings his cash register three times to remind her that it's getting late, but she pays him no heed.

The yogurt arrives on a plate with a soup spoon and a ceremonial bow. And here she is, seated before me, as casual as you please. The ice is fast breaking. Miracles! I dip the large spoon in the tiny pot and offer it to her. She opens her mouth wide as an oven, clasps the spoon firmly in her teeth, and her rosy lips drip with gobs of yogurt. Delightful sloppiness.

From behind the cash register M. Jojo, very agitated, tries to bring her to order.

"Oh là là, Monsieur Jojo," she laughs at him. "Always the bad temper, eh? Don't worry, we're leaving soon, me and the pretty boyfriend." And with these provocative words she tweaks my nose affectionately. All this to the cost of a simple little pot of yogurt!

It is hard to believe that all this is happening, but indeed it is, and faster than I would have thought possible. I don't even have time to think, which is no doubt all to the good. Joyously humming a song, she grabs her bag on the fly and here we are already out on the street, hand in hand, like young people in love. Didi doesn't really walk, she dances, at times hopscotches, and it is not so easy to keep in step with her. It is not clear to me where we are going, but I hope that she's taking me to her home. Yes, she is! Her house appears to be situated across from the church of Saint-Séverin, whose dark Gothic mass is mysteriously engulfed in the night. The Arab territory begins here, and its main artery is the rue de la Huchette nearby, full of the noises and smells of the Orient at this hour. Didi's house, one of the poorest in that ancient, decrepit area, is surrounded by two cafés filled with sellers of rugs and peanuts and by the nasal, plaintive sound of the belly dancers' music. Humming all the way, Didi leads me into a stairway plunged in total obscurity, and to guide myself I touch the walls, which I find to be repulsive with dampness and slime. She warns me about missing steps along the climb, which seems to go on forever until I start thinking that some awful tragedy is about to begin—when suddenly she pulls open the door of a large room under the roof. The first sight I take in, framed in a wide window, is the jumble of rooftops under the low clouds, which remind me of some old German surrealist movies. There emanates from that mysterious sky a twilight effect that bathes the entire room in a bluish penumbra. A forest of plants surrounds the window, under which I can faintly make out what I identify, with a beating heart, as a large bed. The beams overhead, which must have been hacked from huge trunks by some uncouth carpenter some three centuries ago, are decorated with aromatic tresses of herbs and garlic, and the pungent smells of Provence reach me from all sides, carrying me far from Paris and the wild casbah five floors below.

As I seat myself gingerly on the edge of the bed, out of the dark comes a large glass of wine. Wine! I don't drink wine, you know that! Since my alcoholic childhood, when I used to indulge with my school buddies at Meaux, I haven't touched the stuff. But I can't afford to hesitate, or to refuse; I take the glass, close my eyes, and swallow the whole contents in a gulp. It's so strong I nearly pass out, unconscious of Didi's presence, who proudly awaits my comment.

"You like it? It's the best wine money can buy," she proudly declares. "From Algeria. Sidi Larbi, 14°." Just as if it were a Haut-Brion or Romanée Conti. "I don't think we need any light," she adds. "Wait, I'll put on some music."

She disappears into a corner of the dark room while I try to get up. And that is when I discover that with just this one glass of wine, it seems that I've had it; but of course the positive aspect of that condition is that I have neither the desire nor the physical ability to run away, as I might be tempted to do in my normal condition. The strains of a soft waltz reach me in the muffled universe where I reside, and I become conscious, without really seeing anything, of her body dancing between the irregular walls. All my senses dance in unison with the amorous sounds, as the stars are dancing above my head between clouds, as the dance of dervish lovers rises and sways in its circular rhythms, softly and eternally. Suddenly I realize that she isn't dancing anymore but is indeed sitting next to me, and the heat of her side is burning through my tweeds. Oh my God! I almost let out a shout of anguish—as I suddenly realize that she is sitting there *stark naked*.

It's lucky she can't see my face in that darkness. I realize with growing nervousness, however, that the time has come to act, even if I have to fake it: I *must* do something! Anything, anything is better than sitting there with my arms hanging down. If only I could just recall a couple of those things I've read. . . .

For a start I place my right hand on her left thigh.

This is the first time I touch naked female flesh, at least in such circumstances. After twelve years of thinking about it—let's face it, twelve years of frenetic onanism—the sensation is just unbearable. My fingers skim over the firm round thigh, exploring its tender flesh, and the shock of discovery is so electric it triggers the wrong reflex. Instead of backing out my hand plunges ahead, right into the thick bush, which then opens up by itself at the touch of my fingers.

"*Aiie!*" Didi screams into the enveloping darkness, as her muscular thighs lock into a vise, capturing my wrist in their fleshy mass. "Ah, yes, yes! Right there! *Oh là là!* Oh, you *petit cochon!* Oh, you bastard! *Grand salaud!*"

Is she angry at me? Why is she insulting me so wildly? Such violence too! Is it my fault if . . . if I don't know? I yank back my erring hand, confused, not knowing what to do. She's almost having a nervous breakdown, beating her heels against the floor. With stark clarity I recall the scene of Mellors readying himself to make love to Lady Chatterley. He begins with a scrupulously attentive examination of his mistress's body, as a good British gamekeeper should, all the more to enjoy what he knows so well when he finally takes her. But of course in this darkness I cannot do this, and to Mellors's eyes I have to substitute my hands. This will have to be a manual inventory.

Full of apprehension I turn toward her in the dark and lightly palm the velvety skin of her back, an imperceptible caress, so innocent it actually fascinates her, like a teasing game, a loving torture. She forces herself to remain calm, immobilizing her body for me, sitting silent like a mannequin of flesh, an object without will. She is slightly bent forward, supporting herself on her hands, which claw the sheets, providing the only clue to the furnace blazing inside. My fingertips sketch her eyelids, her thick lashes, eyebrows, the full-

ness of her cheeks, the curled ridge of her lips, and, by slow
degrees, the length of her neck.

Surprised, I weigh breasts filled to bursting; a heavy sigh
escapes from her when I tug at the rubber flowers, which tin-
gle excitedly under my fingers. *Danger!* That's going much
too fast, I can see that, let's leave them for later.

Continuing this tactile examination, I descend to a smooth
and polished stomach, a spine as supple as that of a cat, and
then skip a lap, so to speak, to her rounded knees and her
calves, fashioned by constant dancing, down to nervous ankles
easily grasped between thumb and index finger, and finally to
her feet, supple and strongly arched, whose toes abandon
themselves ecstatically to the manipulation of my fingers.

Kneeling before her I can tell that this manual trip has
brought her to the extreme limits of resistance; I can tell that
because the involuntary trembling of her thighs communicates
itself to the wooden frame of the bed. For my part, I am so
carried away in delight that I've completely forgotten my own
desires. A need more subtle than mine has me captivated. I
ask nothing more than to serve my beautiful Didi, for she and
I are now bound by a common passion, which is for her body.
The desire in my hands penetrates her flesh deeply. She loves
that beautiful skin of hers as it glows with the pleasure of my
caresses. My clumsy admiration arouses in her a narcissistic
voluptuousness, for she takes my beginner's errors for subtle
refinements; and she no longer knows what is happening,
she's deliciously disoriented. I thank my stars, I treasure my
luck, I even congratulate myself on my ignorance.

But I can't very well pass the whole night tickling her spine.
We've got to move on. The clue comes from an image that I
found once in *The Memoirs of Fanny Hill*. I'll just have to
mash those big breasts of hers.

Clearly that was indeed the thing to do, but perhaps I am
going at it a bit hard judging from her extraordinary reaction.
All the same, instead of letting go, my ardor redoubles—and
suddenly, here we are, I've gained the field! Her body
stretches out in a bound, crumples and overturns, shaking in
fantastic leaps. I jump up to safety and stand off to enjoy my
handiwork, somewhat troubled by that excessive reaction, but
rather proud all the same.

Peering down at the somber body writhing against the pale
sheets, I feel a little like the family doctor in the presence of

one possessed. . . . Insults, words of love, threats to kill me, all sorts of incoherent things are issuing from her mouth, uttered in the Provençal tongue. And here again, I feel at a loss. What can I do next? In searching my head, another incongruous image comes up, remembered from a scene in *Tropic of Capricorn*. Something that happened in a boat on a lake—involving a naked girl who was slightly mad. What had struck me at the time was the words Miller used to describe her vigorous bush: *a thick sporran*. What a picture! Just like Didi! And with that I've got my cue. Now I know exactly what to do, and without hesitation I plunge my hand between her thighs. My fingers are immediately imbedded in a hairy mess, erect pistil and gluey lips; all this hungry flesh seems to be endowed with a carnivorous life of its own, swallowing me voraciously up to the wrist. This provokes terrific grunts and shrieks, and with my hand caught in a veritable meat vise, Didi's body goes into another paroxysm. The girl's gone raving mad! Her violence is unbelievable—I'll end up with a broken arm.

When the hurricane is over, I find myself sitting on the floor at the opposite end of the bed, groggy, in a state of stupor. As to herself, she is out like a light on the bed, her breathing like a forge-bellows, which gradually slows down to almost perfect calm. "So, that's what it was all about?" I ask myself dazedly. It's hard to believe that here I am at last, making love to this beautiful girl.

And to think that I can unleash such a storm! I am absolutely stunned, overwhelmed, as I sit there on the floor, massaging the pain out of my wrist. Thank God for this dark room, in full daylight this would never have happened. How very extraordinary!

Didi's foot is dangling before my nose, the rest of her unseen from where I sprawl, and dead to the world. I kiss the foot furtively and then, little by little, I begin to realize that I *too* have some rights. Pride, needs, whatever. I can't let her fall asleep leaving me in such a condition! Am I her lover, yes or no? Of course I ought to let her catch her breath, but this lethargy is troubling; although, strangely enough, I also find it exciting at the same time. In a way the tables have been turned. Let's see what we can do with this foot.

Just as I am about to grab it, the foot vanishes from view, and I hear her sitting up heavily on the creaking bed. Then she gets up, swaying toward the table in the shadow, and I hear her babbling to herself in her funny, rolling accent. "Where are you, little pig? Can't see a thing in here. . . . I can't believe this! I want to have a good look at that boy!"

She lights three candles stuck in colored glasses, and this reveals at last this body that I thought I already knew. Jesus Mary Joseph! It has to be seen to be believed. I'm amazed at my own extreme audacity in even approaching this incomparable beauty! But my pleasure is immediately cut short by another salvo—

"What's this?" she screeches. "How come you're still all dressed up? Making it with your clothes on, are you, dirty little pimp?"

She turns into a fury—something straight out of the Marquis de Sade's sick mind. She leaps on me, socks me out of my jacket, twisting my arms nearly out of their sockets, and, turning me upside down, shakes me out of my pants as if I were a sackful of potatoes, hurling every article at the walls with ultimate violence. And she looks just like one of those demented female executioners in the *One Hundred and Twenty Days*, maddened by lust and drunk with carnage. I'm a mere puppet, quite unable to resist the devilish power of those hands of hers as she rends my shirt, scattering buttons—growling and hissing like a panther as she splits my underpants neatly in two. I know that scene! Help! I let out a shout of terror as I see her wide-open mouth, full of shining fangs, about to snap at my helpless virility.

The Debauched Hospodar! Horror! That terrible picture of emasculation, as dreamed up by crazy Apollinaire, spurs me into action and I plunge down between her legs to escape, thus finding myself on the other side of Didi. Frank Harris to the rescue! Yes—just like that scene from *My Life and Loves*—I grab her from behind, square myself flat against her back, and seizing her arms squeeze with all my might, cutting her breath short. Then grabbing her by her muscular waist, I throw her on the bed topsy-turvy as she screams bloody murder, and her body is hanging there like a hunk of beef, stomach in the air and myself on the gallop *tête-bêche*.

With a good grab on her calves I pull back and upward, bringing her body into a vertical position, resting on her shoulders and her legs spread-eagled in a Y—and this is done so fast that she can't even realize what's happening. Holding the cheeks of her ass in this inverted position, I've got this beautiful carnivorous flower spread out at my nose. Never has forbidden fruit been so violently desired—or so greedily tasted—as the piercing shouts from below mount from rage to ecstasy. She sinks her teeth into my rear as her long legs wriggle crazily, and a sudden spasm convulses her body, changes it into a catapult that hurls me to the floor. . . . Once more, down for the count, gasping for breath and covered with foam. At that very time, three heavy blows resound menacingly from the floor below. A male voice follows, raucous and indignant.

"Stop that racket, will ya? There are working people in this house! You disgusting whore, I'll get the cops to take care of you! *Putain!*"

Didi leaps to her feet and in one bound she's leaning out the window, her skin glistening with sweat, her copious breasts hanging out in space.

"Go to hell, Monsieur Victor, you hear me? We are in France here, and in France everybody's got the right to fuck, eh? Who are you to order us around like this, Adolf Hitler maybe? You old crud!"

Applause breaks out from the other side of the street, loud guffaws and catcalls from the surrounding garrets. Everybody seems to be up in arms, someone plays *la Marseillaise* in a fox-trot tempo; obviously Didi is very popular and her harangues famous. Domestic animals and human couples appear to have been fired by our noisy example, and the entire street is soon turned into an erotic pandemonium. Didi closes the window regretfully.

"Those people have no manners, really," she says in apology. "There's no privacy anymore around here. *N'est-ce pas, mon petit amoureux?*"

Tenderly she throws her beautiful arms around me.

"But who cares as long as you are with your little Didi, eh? Tell me now, what's your name?"

"Huh? Oh yes . . . Maurice."

"*Momo*, eh? Momo and Didi, that sounds nice. Or maybe Didi and Momo. My real name is Désirée. Didi. Oh my, how you bounced her around, your little Didi! You are a real *petit cochon*, d'you know that? Where did you learn all those things, you're amazing! Maybe I should not tell you, but in the beginning I didn't think you knew anything about women. Actually, I thought you were a virgin. Silly, eh?"

"Didi, listen now. I just have to tell you. You—were—

right. I was a virgin. What I mean to say, in fact, is that I *am* a virgin, because after all, huh . . . you know . . ."

"*What?* What's that you're saying?"

"It's true, I swear it. I know it sounds absolutely silly. I always wanted to, in fact it was always on my mind, but I've never, well, slept with a woman. Up until now . . . thanks to you."

"Is that *true?*"

"Yes, it really is true."

"My God!" she said, her eyes wide with wonder, her mouth half-open. "What a day! I've gone and got myself a virgin! How about that! And all the time I thought it was just simply for the yogurt. Honestly."

"Honestly? Didi?"

"Well, not really. Of course I knew you had a thing for me. I can read flies, you know, I'm not dumb."

"Well it's nice to know that I am in good hands."

"Oh, but listen, I also read books! At least, I often read *one* book. Have you read *Devil in the Flesh?* Do you like it?"

"And how! Raymond Radiguet, *Le Diable au Corps?* There are scenes in that book just like what's happening here right now, that's true."

"Right," she giggled. "It's just what I was thinking. Reading that book gave me a real taste for making love. I'd like to be thirty years old, and then I would take care of kids, young ones you know, helping them to dress and, well . . ."

"Well I'm twenty. It's probably too dried out for you, eh Didi?"

"Don't be silly. You're not twenty, six or seven maybe. At most. The right age."

She goes to a corner of the room, kneels with her rich back to me, and I see her fumbling with records. Slowly, gravely, the burning winds of the South invade the room, simoon and sirocco, desire waltzes again between our four walls with the deep tempo of Ravel's *Bolero.*

"Come here," she says again. "We're not finished, you and me, you know that, don't you? Tell me, how d'you like them, my big tits? Come here, right here, nice boy, now show me."

15

On the vineyards of the Left Bank one thousand years ago.
—A Pharaonic love in Normandy.—The macabre
industries in those days.—Excommunication.
—More perversities of the flesh, or the Bolero strikes again.
—The Nazis invade Poland, and my father leaves me
with an enigma. —I won't die for Danzig: I become
a boy publisher instead. —Hélène's eyes of pale sapphire.
—The too-tall cadaver. —Love above the Pyrénées.

Every morning at dawn I leave the beautiful body of my mistress, who's sleeping as passionately as she does everything else, asprawl in disorderly sheets, and I tiptoe out, shoes in hand so as not to wake her.

When did it start? Four nights, five nights ago? Time is different now; it is divided between being with her and waiting to be with her again. Her garret has become my home, and the window above the bed is my world. Side by side we look up at the beyond, satiated, fulfilled, exhausted. We let the drizzle refresh us in the warm night; on the second night we even lived through a great storm, complete with lightning and downpour, without bothering to close the window.

Pleasure makes her sleep; and joy keeps me awake. As soon as the sky becomes light I have to get out in the streets and walk, look around, explore the neighborhood, go down to the banks of the river, sit in the public gardens; and while away two or three hours before I make my way to the office, when I will cross over to the Right Bank by bus. This fragment of the old Paris is where I feel most at home now.

Nearly all of modern Paris was built at the end of the nineteenth century, under the Second Empire, when the notorious Baron Haussmann was given the job of redesigning the entire city in accordance with the strategic master plan of the military command. The fear of popular rebellions caused the creation of large avenues and straight boulevards so as to allow the rapid passage of troops, and to prevent the erection of barricades. Much of the old architecture was destroyed then and replaced by the comfortable but undistinguished apartment buildings of modern Paris, whose only saving grace is that they are hidden, at least during the warm season, by generous rows of trees. Islands of antiquity, however, have been preserved, including the Les Halles and Le Marais areas on the Right Bank, and some even older ones around the Latin Quarter and Saint-Germain-des-Prés on the Left Bank. The church of Saint-Séverin is in the middle of a triangular maze of ancient streets that date back to the Middle Ages, or even earlier, since on one side, the rue de la Harpe was built over what used to be a Roman highway. . . . When Paris was first erected as an island fortress on the river, the Left Bank consisted mostly of marshes crisscrossed by orchards and vineyards; a holy man lived there in solitude, in the twelfth century, who was later canonized as Saint Séverin, and the church was built in several phases over what remained of his hermitage. It became a very important parish as the city grew out of its walls on both banks of the river; it had jurisdiction over all other churches and chapels to the south of it.

Part of its fortune was due to its proximity to what later became the first university of Paris. Students were given their courses in a sort of open courtyard, sitting on bales of straw; they are the ones who gave the whole neighborhood its definitive character and its tradition. One studied theology here with Abélard himself; or one could hear predicators or men of learning, at various times, such as Dante, Saint Thomas Aquinas, Saint Bonaventura, or Albertus Magnus. Deep streets with their whimsical layout and their crooked rooftops—the rues Galande, de la Huchette, de la Grande-Truanderie, Maître-Albert, de la Bûcherie, Boutebrie, de la Parcheminerie, among others—were rebuilt time and again, but many of the houses date back to the sixteenth century. Such as the Hostellerie du Cygne on rue Saint-Séverin, which was a fashionable meeting place four centuries ago, and is still recognizable thanks to a medallion carved in blackened stone over its door.

Being a center for students and monks, it attracted prostitutes as well, jolly persons known as *ribaudes*, and much carousing was taking place in the hovels and the burrows. Daily life in the monastery of the Bernardines, close by, was so scandalous that Pope Innocent VIII had to intervene in person and forbid its access to persons of the fair sex *"except for old women tending to the poultry-yard and to the cows."* Visiting poets and storytellers found there the material of modernity, and gave this center of debauchery and perdition a lasting place in literature. Rabelais used it as one of the principal sources for his gargantuan epic, and François Villon for a poetic invention of lasting value: gallows humor. His *Ballad for a Hangèd Man* gives us a nicely sinister feeling of what one would have come across at place Maubert, where stood seven pillories on which executed criminals groaned their last. The gallows were always garnished with a few out-of-joint human carcasses, left there for the delectation of the crows as well as for the edification of the good people. It is well known, He who loves well punishes well.

And such punishment was not exclusively reserved to thieves and cutthroats. On rue Galande, near the little church of Saint-Julien-le-Pauvre, one found in the old days the town house of the Ravalets, an ancient and noble family whose principal fief was in Tourlaville, near Cherbourg. From there the Ravalets had sown terror throughout the Norman countryside for several centuries. Their crimes were as dismal and horrible as those of Gilles de Rais, Bluebeard's prototype, and each generation turned out to be worse than the previous one. To provide a fitting ending for this demonic lineage, Julien de Ravalet and his sister, the beautiful Marguerite, his dark angel, became enamored of each other with a passion so wild it became the exclusive focus of their lives. Incest certainly wasn't unknown in sixteenth-century Normandy, among the peasantry as well as the nobility, but no one had ever dreamed of avowing it publicly, and still less of making such a spectacle out of it. Julien and Marguerite went about the country, flaunting their Pharaonic love, and carrying their madness to the extreme of proclaiming in church the delights of incest as a holy thing. Isn't love the only rule of sainthood? Such an extravagant proposition took the doctors of the church by surprise. Would it be necessary to denounce incest as a schism? But what about the Holy Scriptures? What about the various popes who had followed the tradition of the Borgias? The ecclesiastical authorities had no wish to engage in such a debate; Julien and Marguerite were seized and delivered to their executioners on December 2, 1603, at the place de Grève.

People came from afar to feast their eyes on the lovers' beauty, and to hear their last cries of love. The tortured bodies were hacked into pieces, the entrails and genitals thrown to stray dogs. But the two heads were carefully preserved and placed face-to-face in an urn, which was then buried in the sanctuary of Saint-Julien; they are said to have remained there to this day. . . .

When the Sorbonne was built in its present form, south of its original location, the parish of Saint-Séverin continued to prosper, but more thanks to the industry of death than to the commerce of love. The original island city, which housed the ecclesiastical and military authorities, could no longer bury its own dead and that is when Saint-Séverin made its fortune as a necropolis. Bodies arrived by the cartload, occupying a considerable work force of priests and gravediggers, and underground galleries had to be excavated in order to absorb their growing numbers. The cemetery itself was built next to the church in the style of a cloister with flagstone paving and sculpted arches, crowned with frenzied gargoyles and richly decorated with tapestries; the last rites were highly paid and the macabre professions flourished. Death was so important that the most destitute were assured of a proper Christian burial; in exchange for the benefits of his office, the chief gravedigger had the duty of performing his services gratis for the mortal remains of paupers and prisoners.

In times of plague the corpses disappeared in black smoke on the pyres, and the soot darkened the surrounding façades.

For a long time, I kept looking for the exact location of the tiny stone cell that could once be found leaning against the portals of the church, and which fulfilled a function that I thought was quite fascinating. In the Middle Ages an uninterrupted succession of recluses had themselves immured in that structure, hardly larger than a dog's kennel, in order to spend their last years in prayer, bestirring themselves only enough to consume the bit of bread and water that kept them alive.

The name of Dame Flora, who was one of those solitaries, has come down to us. It is amazing to contemplate the power that must have emanated from the presence of this being absorbed in prayer, summer and winter alike, in the midst of the processions that brushed past, amid festivals and calamities. The divine madness of these Christian Yogis, repeated and continued on this same spot over the centuries, seemed to fix this place as one of the psychic epicenters of Paris. This self-imposed solitary confinement, needless to say, should be understood neither as punishment nor mortification, but as the means of accomplishing a supernatural task without which all would be chaos. Dame Flora's stone envelope made me think of the meditation pits hollowed out of the stone walls of Montségur, the architemple of the Cathari, which dominates the world from its lofty peak.

That morning I found a postcard addressed to me by Henry Miller; the picture was of a great big hole in the ground, *le Gouffre de Padirac*, one of the most impressive natural curiosities of the Dordogne Valley. Sensing that things were turning once again for the worst, Henry had fled Paris in a panic, just like the year before. From where he was now he could either hide in *le Gouffre*, or he could easily reach Bordeaux and sail from there either to Greece, to stay with the Durrells in Cyprus, or directly to the States. Obviously Henry felt that, in any case, he would not return to Paris for a long time; the gist of his message was to ask me to take good care of the two huge wicker trunks full of manuscripts and books that he had left in the Obelisk Press office—also of his and Hans Reichel's watercolors—until "after the war."

Life is shrinking. Paris is stuffed with Spanish refugees who are being hunted by Daladier's cops, and it's fashionable, in enlightened circles, to hide them in cellars and attics.

On the café terraces of Saint-Germain-des-Prés and Montparnasse, no more idle Americans. To make up for it, vainglorious silver-haired heroes of the First World War, decorations and uniforms of all kinds can be seen in abundance. . . .

And at the office, there's a lot of talk about money. Or the lack of money, to be precise. Kurt Enoch arrives with his accountant and closets himself with my father. I sense that whatever is happening behind that door can hardly be pleasant for the participants. During that time I glance at the headlines. The *Daily Mail* is harassing the French government, and *Paris Midi* is full of Polish news in dubious taste. One article is devoted to the culinary prowess of Smigly-Rydz, Polish commander in chief, another to the elegant Colonel Beck, the head of the government, who collects neckties. An editorial speculates on the consequences of the sensation created a few days earlier by Marcel Déat's statement in *L'Oeuvre* where he declared: *"I won't die for Danzig."* Well, I won't either. Déat is a dirty Fascist, but he's right.

France and England failed to fight Hitler when he invaded Austria and Czechoslovakia, not to speak of Spain, and now they threaten to defend the Polish rights over Danzig. They could not have chosen a worst cause to make their stand against the Nazis, since the Poles disgraced themselves so recently by accepting from them a portion of the Czech territory; but also because Danzig, converted into a semiautonomous state by the Treaty of Versailles, is an old Hanseatic port to which the Germans can establish a much better claim than the Poles.

That fellow Hitler is the most fantastic poker player of all times; he is a genius at using his opponents' contradictions to weaken them, to destroy them from inside. He knows how to play on their bad conscience and to take advantage of their lies. To old-style liberals like my father, Hitler represents the ultimate calamity precisely because his very success shows to what extent the First World War Allies had been fooling themselves. Hitler's tactics always rest on a perfect knowledge of the other side's mistakes or shortcomings: the Treaty of Versailles, Stalin's greed, the quarrelsome smugness of Churchill and of the British conservatives, the bluster and flabbiness of the French politicians, the fragility of their allies in Europe—statesmen such as Benès, Titulescu, or Beck. Not to mention the inner contradictions of the Jewish soul! This mastery in the art of blackmail has a touch of genius; everywhere, between the pulp and the peel, one finds the Führer's ferreting finger. As for instance in the case of my father: Hitler has made a Jew of him, and thus compels him to defend his hide rather than fight for a cause. The blow hits me, myself, by ricochet: Here I am, the son of the renegade Jew and steeped in the disgrace brought on by my refusal to fight for a cause that is even less mine than his! Every family, every individual, every party, group, or community is equally split, divided, and disrupted in one way or the other. That psychological preparation is like an artillery barrage before the assault is given.

It's a lucky thing that I don't care a goddamn about patriotic honor. I'm sorry that my father let himself be caught up in this game so readily, but this is no reason why I should do the same! Yes, I prefer a hundred times being called a coward than to let myself be snapped up like the others by the old machinery that gave us the Treaty of Versailles—which in turn has given us Hitler—and so on and so forth. . . .

If ever this infernal circle is to be broken, it will be thanks to those who still have the courage to be free. At least in their thinking. My first law is not to kill, and from this point of view, just one day spent in uniform would be participation in the butchery. Don't count on me to play into Hitler's hands! As I see it being done all around me by so many noble idiots.

It's been two weeks since I have not set foot in Vivian's domain. You could say that, here again, Hitler has won one of his million teleguided victories simply by giving the lie to Vivian's calculations.

On my first visit after that interruption, however, I find that this moral defeat has not altered Vivian's confidence in the value of his newest enterprise. Close to three thousand copies of the secret document called *Le Pacte Synarchique* have been anonymously placed in the mailboxes of politicians and influential personalities. In normal times very few of them would have taken it seriously, were it only because of the cloak-and-dagger style of its distribution: When you open the first page you are confronted with a warning to the recipient, forbidding him or her to reveal the contents of the volume under penalty of death. Well, that's pretty childish, to be sure, but it works. . . . To counter the mechanism of autodestruction in which everyone is caught, it will take nothing less than a true-blue miracle; the revelation of a powerful underground force, of a mysterious secret society on the side of the democracies that can take on Hitler and beat him thanks to its superior strategy—this is perhaps the only outcome left for the Allies to even up with the dictators.

Those cynical people, the politicos, are so shaken by their own failures that they grab at straws, they go for fairy tales rather than face their impending doom. What's more, each one of them likes to be in the know; each one of them believes that he's being singled out for that secret communication because he is exceptionally qualified to receive it. And then, to allude at such a secret in conversation is a good way to impress one's peers; hearing which, the peer who also received the document believes that he is now being directly contacted by a member of the brotherhood. The Synarchist movement, a political ectoplasm, is fast becoming a hardcore reality.

Take, for instance, Jean Coutrot, an inquisitive spirit who had brought together a powerful group of organization men and high-ranking civil servants, all of them alumni of the Ecole Polytechnique—known as "X-Crise." Because of various indiscretions and of mysterious allusions, he convinces himself that he is surrounded by Synarchists. And he becomes a self-appointed Synarchist himself in order not to be found trailing behind his troops. Among the Freemasons, with whom several members of our group have good connections, synarchy's mysterious air makes it a great success: Nothing comes off better in the bosom of a secret society than an ever more secret society.

The success of Vivian's strategy is indeed so impressive that it sustains the comparison with Hitler's own. Where will all that lead us? Taking over the government? Vivian doesn't seem to have the slightest doubt on that score; and I can't help but think that although he has been so often wrong in the past, this time he may very well bring it off. Everyone around him is bracing for the great leap forward.

Not so Laurette, whom I approach with calculated indifference. Will she ask me what's been happening to me in the past two weeks? She doesn't. She smiles at me fondly as usual, but she doesn't appear to have noticed my absence; what occupies her most these days, it seems, is her current studies, since she started working for a degree in Egyptology. This new fervor seems a bit intriguing to me, but frankly I couldn't care less. What am I supposed to do? Should I start taking the same courses, so as to force my existence on her attention?

Rolande takes pity on me, asking me why I look so unhappy. I answer not at all, everything's fine, why don't we have lunch tomorrow? And that's settled. . . . I have just conceived a secret plan, rather infantile perhaps, but I can't resist: to take her into the confidence of my great passion for a lady of high voltage by the name of Désirée, a sans pareil seductress, a person of great beauty and savoir-vivre. Hah! I will ask her to consider this a secret, which will cause her automatically to run to Laurette and spill the beans. . . . A leaf from my guru's book, what!

Very proud of my scheme, I decided to take Rolande to a reasonably quiet neighborhood restaurant, the next day, and maneuvered her into asking me questions about the present circumstances of my life. Whereupon, with apparent reluctance and a faraway look, I make the damning confession. My vow of chastity lies in pieces, right here between us, on the checkered tablecloth. Rolande's mouth is open in astonishment, pink and lovely, and her eyes are big with excitement and wonder as she looks at me across the table.

As I give her a somewhat embellished account of my great carnal discovery, and warm up so much to my subject that I may have become indiscreet, I see her expression become rather vacant and sullen. Why is she so upset? My God, Rolande— As I am describing to her with fiery eloquence an exquisite Mlle Désirée, I am also contemplating with a growing passion Rolande's own perfect features, so delicate that just to look at her defenseless expression would make the most enduring heart melt—and my heart's melting fast —which causes me, perhaps in order to keep that delicious mouth open a bit longer, to launch into a speech about the group, its conformity, its mistakes, weaknesses. Vivian's errors! Her slightly idiotic look of amazement is altogether charming; under the tablecloth, there's a centaur ready to leap. And she knows it. I also know that she knows. . . . I fall silent, and she seems incapable of speech.

This shared silence in the uproar of the students' conversations all around us assumes the proportion of a deceitful declaration, multiple sacrilege, treason all the way down the line. Suddenly she is the only reality in my life. The intensity of this feeling fills me with a fantastic and bittersweet voluptuousness. For years, she has reigned secretly and subconsciously over the world of desires that inhabits me, and I feel that the accumulated charge is about to blow everything to smithereens.

Then, in a toneless voice, she tells me that she's late, that she must leave right away. I'm simultaneously mortified and relieved. . . . Outside, it's drizzling lightly and the fresh air calms me down a bit. . . . I behold Rolande with a wild and guilty rapture; she's as pretty as a violet in her artist's getup. She studies painting and carries a huge portfolio under her arm, the mark of her calling. A hazel-brown velvet beret that matches her eyes sets off her shimmering wavy hair, which cascades luxuriantly onto the cape she holds tight against her, with a perfect pale hand enhanced with an amethyst. A high collar of white piqué channels the effervescence of its purple silk bow and accentuates the touching delicacy of her little angel's face. Confronting each other in silence, we linger for a moment on the sidewalk of the rue Hautefeuille; her face has an imploring and helpless look that makes me quiver with excitement; but when my mouth finally brushes her lips, she starts, as someone waking up from a coma, slips away, and leaves me standing there, stuck to the ground like a lamppost.

Watching her hurry away, almost running, I can see—as if my eyes were endowed with X-ray property—under the purple cape, the white, graceful body of a child-woman hastening away from me. My God, what can be happening to me? Well of course I've always been extraordinarily sensitive to the advent of spring, my heart is bursting out of its confines, a new plant groping in blind glory for the full blessing of the sun: I love all women!

Yes, all girls, all women, and I assure you that this can turn out to be a true calamity. Blondes, brunettes, redheads, and all the myriad nuances beyond and in between. One hour in the street in May or June is enough to have me committed; my head reels with those millions of swinging short skirts, of luscious young bodies ready for love, and I feel totally helpless to control the mounting tide. My vow of chastity is far away indeed! Only two weeks away, to be precise, and yet. . . .

Well, I stand there in the street alone for a while, under the light drizzle, and I spend the rest of the day by myself. Yes, the maudlin Dr. Jekyll takes over from the uninhibited Mr. Hyde, and, thinking of Didi, I decide that I won't see her today. Thinking of Laurette, I know that I won't see her as long as I'm charged with such vibrations. And yet as my mind dissolves into sleep, it is her image that smiles softly at me, a face of wonderful sadness and beauty, a blessing to my heart of hearts.

That same night I had dinner with my grandparents, and that helped me cool down quite effectively; here were people nearing the end of their course, counting the days with a nostalgic anxiety that I found difficult to comprehend.

They had abandoned their Neuilly apartment, disposed of most of their furniture, and moved into a large studio on avenue Matignon. Which would have made a good setting for a high-class call girl, but, for them, was quite ludicrous; to see my old granny puttering around among the astutely arranged gilded mirrors, under the exuberant chandeliers and the frivolous decorations—it did make one wonder! As to my grandfather, who used to speak so freely and bravely about death only a few years before, he seemed to be studiously avoiding the subject now that he was well into his seventies. I noticed that he would talk only about the future, about new plans, ventures he was studying. Even the war, to him, appeared only as a passing inconvenience, a few months' interruption in the execution of his great new schemes. . . .

Two days later, I decided to go back to the ashram for the usual Sunday session, so as to resolve the crisis that had taken hold of me. It seemed important, at this point, to meet all my friends together and, in particular, to see Laurette and Rolande side by side. I had to let my heart make a mature choice, I had to let my reason take over again. If at all possible! It is time for me to delineate a hierarchy of attachments, needs, friendships. It's been four years now since I've been living with those people, and for them, and despite our frenzies and disasters, I feel that I belong to this cell of human beings in a complete, irrevocable manner.

At the close of the meeting Vivian works his way toward me through the jostling crowd, straight as an I in his fiery robe, and suddenly everything appears to turn inside out. We are standing face-to-face in the midst of a small group; I see Laurette on one side, Rolande on the other, and their faces seem to me frozen and expressionless, as if they didn't hear what Vivian is saying. He is speaking with studied, forceful calm, looking straight at me, but I don't quite catch the meaning of his words. . . . I only receive this general impression: Rolande has repeated to him everything I said to her two days before, and my attitude has prompted him to decide on my immediate exclusion as well as the withdrawal of his spiritual patronage—with no recourse to appeal. Only his last phrase, his malediction, reaches me with clarity, like an obvious fact: *"The sun has set down for you."*

Thunderstruck, speechless, I head for the door and start slowly down the stairs. I vaguely sense that the others are waiting for me to disappear before they descend, so as not to have to speak to me. But what about Laurette? Of course I've lost her as well. . . . Vivian's words continue to echo in my head and little by little their meaning unfurls and takes hold of my consciousness. I feel all the weight, all the bitter taste of this pitiless curse. When I find myself out on the sidewalk the reality of my loss springs back at me with increased force; it's irreversible, irreparable.

Didi is certainly not the one to whom I can explain my situation, but in my confusion, she suddenly seems like the only being left to me in the world, and the only source of warmth and love. What irony! Anyway, my steps are taking me straight to the Foyer Pythagore; I don't even have to make the effort of deciding. Inside, a sullen slut is waiting on tables—*no Didi!*

"Can't you close that door?" yelps the repulsive M. Jojo from behind his cash register. "Come in or go out, young man, but close the door, hear?"

He suddenly recognizes me and begins to bellow all the louder:

"If it's that little tramp you're looking for, you're wasting your time! She doesn't work at the Foyer Pythagore anymore! Go on, get out!"

I close the door, stunned by this unexpected piece of news —I make a dash for Didi's house, and take the stairs four at a time in the darkness, breathless and terrorized. First I knock softly, then louder. I beat with my fists. No light filters out from under the door, but *I know* she's there, on the other side. I know it, I feel it, I divine her presence, the scent of her skin, of her flesh. The fragrance of her pleasure.

"Didi, please open up, it's me!"

Silence.

"Didi, I beg you, I've got to see you, open up!"

I hear her bare feet softly grazing the floor; she has gotten up and is coming to the door, slowly. And there she must be standing, mute behind the rough wood, her full, velvety body leaning against the doorjamb, just two fingers' breadth away from my lips, from my hands. My heart pounds wildly, I'm sick with desire, and yet, she doesn't open. She doesn't say anything; and yet I'm convinced I can hear her rapid, husky breathing, like someone who has been running too fast and is unable to speak.

"Didi . . ."

"Leave me alone, go away, will you? I don't want to see you anymore, Momo, you understand? You're a little bastard, an egoist; you dropped me for somebody else and it didn't work out, and now you've come back here to get your rocks off, just like a disgusting old man!"

"Not at all! I'll explain everything. Open the door! Didi, I must see you! Just one minute. The last time, I promise—"

"You're crazy. I've got a fellow right here in my bed who's well worth ten of you. Fuck off, understand? This is not a hotel. Get out of here and let me ball in peace, will you?"

Once again, I find myself staggering down a staircase, feeling my way along the tacky wall to get through the thick darkness. This staircase is like the thirteenth circle of hell, and the pestilence of this well of misery sharply stings my throat; I'm nauseated, I feel like vomiting, or bursting into tears.

Suddenly, the last straw: She isn't sparing me anything! The first measures of Ravel's *Bolero* invade the stairwell, flaring into furious and sibilant rhythms, rolling and wailing to an insane pitch, and my heart leaps in my chest when, through the waves of sound, I make out piercing cries, long supplications, which aren't addressed to me, and they tear my soul asunder—the raucous calls of Didi who's coming like a lioness, three flights overhead. As if I were there, I see the body of my beautiful mistress contorted in heat, given over to another—a real man, that one! I shudder with horror, picturing to myself this hulking savage who's drawing such terrible cries from her. The atrocious and magnificent image of *my* Didi being pinioned, dominated, crushed, and plundered by this brute, this dangerous mass of muscles, hair, and bristling testicles, gives me such gasps of desire that there, in the fetid shadows, by way of farewell, I leave behind the humble homage of my young man's passion.

Thus the whole night passed by in an orgy of solitary misery while I tried unsuccessfully to exhaust my senses. Impossible to sleep, to forget. The next morning, at dawn, I descended from my attic on the rue Gay-Lussac and by way of the rue Champollion, past Cluny and Vivian's fortress, made my way toward Saint-Séverin and Didi's house. . . . Without knowing clearly why I was going there, or what I would do if I saw her in the street. . . . An unlikely prospect, at best, since she didn't like to get up early. Half-frozen, dazed with anguish, I wandered around for an hour, two hours, between the nooks and crannies and the doorways I had come to know so well. The worm-eaten door of her house, cracked and askew on its hinges, was that of an abandoned ruin; the house, with its broken windows, looked as if it had been left unoccupied for a century. . . .

And then, as I was crossing the street for the hundredth time, perhaps, with the same false air of nonchalance, the

creaky door opens with a sudden crash, propelled by a powerful kick, and I see a boy come out, a curly-blonde athletic kid
with a pretty mug. *A kid!* He darts a rapid glance from left to
right without paying the slightest attention to me, and takes
off for the place Saint-Michel at top speed. He's going to be
late for his Latin class.

It's almost funny. He's how old? Sixteen? Seventeen? But
he fills the bill! He doesn't have any complexes, the little bastard. Swinging his book bag, I see him turn the corner at
rue de la Harpe; but at the same time with my mind's eyes I
visualize Didi helping him put on his knickers, rubbing her
cheek against the cloth, at the right spot, or languorously lac-
ing his shoes. Ah, if one could die of self-disgust, I'd be lying
dead, there, on this sidewalk!

But what is there left to kill? I'm worse than dead.

It rained ceaselessly, the summer had turned to water. What
might prove to be the last vegetables of democracy were rotting underground beneath this overabundant avalanche of water. I read, went to the movies, always alone; I spoke to no
one and avoided as best I could the Saint-Séverin neighborhood and the environs of Cluny. That life was over with. . . .
Solitude was more fruitful, and sometimes I experienced a
somber pleasure when I imagined the ideological rout of Vivian and his church in the face of increasingly irrefutable evidence of his political failure; synarchy was his last chance,
and it was about to be ruined by the war. Sometimes, I tried
to imagine what evolution Laurette herself was going through.
Would she someday come to appreciate the value of my constancy? Hm, well, yes, constancy.

Since my mother was spending the summer in Orvilliers, a
little village of Ile-de-France, my father stayed alone at the
apartment in Neuilly. The last of his friends, the Stuart Gilberts, had just left Paris, indefinitely, for Dax, a small city
in the southwest of the country.

We saw each other every day at the office, which had become silent and deserted and where the only important visitor
was the postman. Among other letters, he brought successive
messages of distress from Henry, from Marseilles, from
Athens, from every one of his stops, begging for someone to
wire him money. Failing which he would be unable to pay his
hotel bill the next morning, etc. My father scraped the bottom
of the drawer, the money order was wired posthaste, and the

next day there would come a telegram: "JACK, YOU ARE A TRUE BRITISH GENTLEMAN. CHEERIO. HENRY." My father examined this text pensively and murmured in his hesitant French: "What's the matter with Henry? Is he putting me on?" Good question.

My father spent the best part of his days shut up in his office. I was unable to find out what he did with his time. As for Nadejda, she had left Paris in the spring, and no longer wrote. . . . Paris was like a besieged city, swept with crazy rumors of a fifth column, of spies, and frantic *coups d'état*. Certain idiots still kept talking about a great conspiracy against Hitler that would take care of everything at the last minute.

Sending out the review copies of Anaïs Nin's *Winter of Artifice*, after those of *Max and the White Phagocytes* and *The Black Book*, gave me the satisfaction of having accomplished a truly useless labor. . . . This mad rush for the publication of a first book that no one would read appeared more and more like the perfect metaphor for the malefic absurdity of our time.

Toward the end of August, the Danzig affair had turned into an acute crisis, painstakingly nourished, step by step, by Hitler; and yet, according to what I could understand of the situation from reading the papers, there were still politicians in France who believed in peace and would fight for it, like Georges Bonnet, the minister of Foreign Affairs, or Gaston Bergery, that strange phenomenon, a thinking politician. The London warmongers, however, had their minds set on war: a war that was to be fought on French soil, and by the French army, since their own didn't exist. And those good old French statesmen, all too happy that Lord Halifax had finally deigned to address them a few words from the pinnacle of his glory, kissed his hand and took his orders gratefully, thrilled at the idea that they had been allowed to serve such a splendid aristocrat. Parisian Anglomania had reached its zenith in the heavens of the ridiculous.

For their part, the lords of the Admiralty were devising their long-range strategy with meticulous deliberation. A winning strategy, no doubt, but it implied as a preliminary condition the reduction of the German military power thanks to the sacrifice of two or three million little French foot soldiers. It was sheer profit all the way. It was difficult to tell who the final winner would be, but the loser was already on stage, cheerfully presenting arms in an oversize uniform, nose proudly turned up in the air: our very own infantryman, the popular hero of so many glorious genocides. The French soldier.

And all this is being done in order "to save Danzig," whose very name was unknown to ninety-nine percent of the Frenchmen only three months earlier. Just thinking of it. . . . But no one thought anymore. The level had been reached of gut emotions, anxiety, blue funk, nervousness, restlessness, and finally, patriotism too. Patriotism, something that warmed your innards, a mixture of solidarity, of pride, reinforced by a new sense of identity. A respectable sentiment for sure, but what was its proportion to the rest?

The pound sterling was in bad shape. On the twenty-fifth of August, the news broke of its devaluation, an event that was going, among other things, to price Obelisk Press books out of the market abroad and reduce our chances of survival still more. But that was small potatoes as compared to the announcement of the Moscow-Berlin Pact! Once again all the rules of the game had been brutally reversed; the stunned reaction of the French Stalinists was certainly comical to behold, but nobody felt like having fun anymore. All this had become serious, even grave, and many people sensed it for the first time. Human life was being played with very offhandedly.

Within a few days, the situation in Poland goes from lukewarm to searing. The English don't do anything to fix things up—to the contrary. On August 31, Mussolini proposes a meeting of the four parties, plus Poland, in order to find a solution not only to the immediate crisis but to all the causes of friction stemming from the Treaty of Versailles.

A put-up job? The newspapers hardly mention it; this, paradoxically, strikes me as a good sign. I continue to believe in the possibility of a last-minute miracle, having succeeded in convincing myself that the British and the Germans are playing their biggest trumps at top speed; they are taking dizzying risks, but all the while, from afar, through secret intermediaries, they are negotiating an agreement for which the French, the Polish, and other small powers will pay the price.

It's a frantic race between these two foxes who are cousins but also perennial rivals; Mussolini, the assistant scarecrow, will have the role of helping his crony pull the chestnuts from

the fire at the last minute. Because there's no doubt about it:
In this chess game between England and Germany, it's Germany that's on the way to winning.

But on the first of September Germany invades Poland, and
Mussolini's overtures are hastily rejected. Georges Bonnet
alone still seems to believe in a celestial intervention, in the
chances of a final rescuing maneuver. Historians will someday
shed light on the secret bargaining that has just broken down
between London and Berlin; for the moment I'm obliged to
admit that I've lost my wager. Peace is done for. From the
office, I telephone my father who's in bed, sick. Impossible
to tell exactly what's the matter, but there's something in the
tone of his voice that stirs my conscience; shame swells up
inside me. It had been a long time since I had to anesthetize
myself to my father's sufferings, for they were one of the constant themes of my childhood. But suddenly I understand
with awful clarity all that he must have had to endure. Is it too
late? How could he be helped? It was absolutely necessary
that I speak with him, enough time had been wasted—twenty
years!—perhaps we could still make up for it?

An hour later I walk through the half-open door of the
apartment in Neuilly. I find him in bed, and I note that there
are no books or newspapers lying around. My first reaction is
to offer to fix him a snack; but that doesn't turn out too well,
I'm not the greatest chef on earth, and he pretends to nibble
at it out of sheer politeness. We exchange a few words and
soon find ourselves at the heart of the matter.

"I never told you," he begins, "but it was a real encouragement for me to see how well you are doing at the office. Kurt
Enoch has noticed it too, and he even told me that if I ever
had to be away, you would be perfectly capable of running the
business yourself. . . . Well, we're going to have to talk about
that seriously . . ."

His face was very red, he seemed to me to be feverish,
apparently on the verge of delirium.

"I'm going to go away," he began again. "And you, you
must stay, for your mother's sake, and the children, you
understand . . ."

"But you're sick, this isn't any time to talk about leaving . . ."

He doesn't know that I'm aware of his attempt to convince
the War Office that he can still serve in the army. But that
goes back to last year, and since then he must have under-

stood that at fifty-one and in his weakened state, no army on earth would want a recruit like him, even out of charity! Why does he persist in talking about that foolish project?

"Listen," I say, "you fought in the other war. I think that's quite enough. This time it's up to me to go. I'm at the age for it, and the family needs you, as you know . . ."

My voice wavers a little. He looks at me, not very certain that he heard me right. I myself am amazed at my own turn-about; I'm not sure I've heard myself right.

"No, no!" he answers. "For me it's of no importance if I come back or not. But you, you're just beginning your life. It's not right to ask you to take on the responsibility of the entire family at your age, I know, but with your mother I'm sure you will be able to pull through. Your grandfather will surely help, somehow. People of my age haven't got much to add to the history of our time . . ."

"But you can't say that!"

I don't know where this unlikely conversation is leading us. It's madness, this insistence of his to want to go and fight. To fight how, with what? I realize that he's out of his right mind, and yet I persist in trying to convince him that all I want is to fight in the coming war despite my pacifism, despite everything I've said and believed up to now. This incoherent quarrel between two overexcited Don Quixotes has something truly perverse about it. But—how come I didn't see it earlier? He's intoxicated, he rambles on in the grandiose manner of drunkards, there's no doubt about it. I have responded to his alcoholic delirium with my own heroic delirium, swearing that I was going to disembowel Hitler, track down the monster to his lair, and generally behave in the virile, decent, dutiful way of a gentleman and soldier, following his own example.

Suddenly I'm struck by the extent of our common misery, of our terrible mutual incomprehension. Twenty years of misunderstandings, botched dialogues, hollow pride, inexcusable timidity, and the perpetual putting off for tomorrow of any intelligent exchange. Twenty years. . . . And it is finally Hitler who forced us to have this exchange, and just look at the result. What a waste! I tell my father how happy I am with our discussion but that he should try to get some rest; I'll come back late tomorrow morning. He seems to be already sleeping when I leave. Out in the street the night is dark blue, warm, dense, moonless and starless, without the faintest glimmer of light. Although the war is still undeclared, a strict blackout is being enforced; the switched-off, shuttered, and masked city is unrecognizable. This absolute, faultless darkness invites sleep; mine is heavy, peopled with confused dreams. The sun is already high over the courtyard of my apartment house when I'm brutally awakened by a fist pounding on my door. It's my concierge. My parents' concierge just called her to tell me I should come immediately to Neuilly because my father is sick. I dress as fast as I can, without thinking, and plunge down the staircase, out onto the street, frantically hailing cabs.

At the top of the freshly sprinkled and still glistening rue Gay-Lussac, there appears a taxi, one of those wobbly, old convertible models such as are no longer made in our time. Seated on the cracked moleskin I try to hold my breath and not think of anything during the drive between the Latin Quarter and Neuilly. I spent the best days of the season getting drenched in sudden showers and drying off my jacket in cafés. It seems that we needed a war to get some sunshine at last; the sensual warmth of this tardy summer, the mossy odors that fill the streets, I find it's all coming a bit late, indeed. But in spite of this I'm captivated by the pervading gaiety, a mood so completely unrelated to the sufferings my father is undergoing.

The door of the apartment is ajar, like yesterday. Upon entering my father's room, I'm shocked to find the concierge standing in a corner and, next to the bed, two unknown men contemplating the long body of my father, naked and dead.

As soon as they see me, they raise the sheet and murmur comments to each other that I don't understand. One of them, apparently a policeman, asks me if I'm indeed the son of the deceased, and announces that the medical expert here at his side has just determined my father's death. The heart. . . . The heart has ceased to beat, it's hopeless. . . . Death certificate. . . . But my father doesn't seem dead; he looks less lost, less mad and desperate than yesterday.

The two officials finish their job and leave quickly, muttering some indistinct words. I find myself alone with the concierge, the good Mme Orgelet, who seems to be truly sorry. A little curious, as well, because she has never been inside my parents' room before and she inventories with great interest the rugs, the paintings, the furniture. She recites her story, step by step, in chronological order, all the while continuing her inspection.

She rang the doorbell when the mail arrived and he didn't answer. Becoming apprehensive and seeing the door half-open, she took the liberty, you understand, of going in, and she found him—

"You know, Monsieur Maurice, he was sitting on the, well . . . what. . . . It embarrasses me to tell you that. . . . Dead on the toilet bowl, that's unusual, your father! Ah, poor Monsieur Maurice! Mon Dieu, mon Dieu . . ."

Was her emotion going to draw tears from me? It would be high time, by the way! In conformance with the ritual, I should at least have shed a tear or two, but the concierge hadn't finished her story yet. She explained about telephoning her husband, the police, and my grandfather, who arrived in record time. It was he who asked Mme Orgelet to call me, and he immediately left in his car to bring my mother back from the country. They should be here in an hour or two. . . . She caught her breath for the final announcement.

"I don't know if I should tell you this, Monsieur Maurice, but you're a man, aren't you? Eh, well, here's what I found under your papa's bed . . ." (She holds out an empty bottle of three-star Martel cognac.) "The medical expert said that's what did it. Your poor papa must have known perfectly well that his heart couldn't hold out. He should never have drunk like that! The doctor said that it's really a suicide, but that he will write it down in his report as a case of cardiac arrest. Ah, poor Monsieur Maurice, what a world we live in!"

In my confusion and bewilderment, I fall to my knees next to my fathers's corpse. I don't feel anything, except for dizziness—certainly no desire to satisfy the concierge, who is waiting; she has recited her story, and now she is counting on a sob or two, she has the right to it, like a well-deserved tip. She wants to see me suffer, to verify human weakness, to plunge her plump hand into this very fresh wound; she is waiting. Furthermore, she's quite right: My insensitivity seems abnormal even to me. Nothing doing, the tears won't come. And yet it's my father who's lying there, reduced to nothing; but my eyes remain vague and dry. She remains planted there like a stern judge, and I end up finding this scene so hateful that, with a distraught air, I ask her to be so kind as to leave me alone with my grief. She puts the bottle carefully back under the bed where she had found it and leaves the room, dabbing at her eyes, with an expression of sullen reproach on her round face.

A little while later, I hear a noise in the hall of the building and head for the entrance to the apartment. The door opens on my mother with my grandfather behind her. She comes in without seeing me, heads straight for the bedroom with her face set, talking to herself. I believe I hear: "Why so soon, my God, why, why?" I leave her in my grandfather's care; as to myself I am momentarily out of action.

The day continues in a fog. Telephones, funeral parlor, everything takes place in bewilderment; the panic of people who go in and out, brandish newspapers, gesturing madly, fainting on the sidewalk, in the stores, under the sun, and those who quarrel over the first gas masks. . . . The mayor of Neuilly, M. de Kérillis, is a scrupulous patriot, and his town hall has been stocked full of gas masks for a long time, for this long-awaited—even hoped-for!—occasion: Everyone will have his or her own. Mme Orgelet harasses us for a good part of the day with her own gas-mask story; it seems that the town hall has refused to issue one to her for my father, although he only died this morning. . . . In vain did she point out to them that his name is still on the register. . . . She snivels; it could have been useful to have an extra mask, one never knows what the future has in store for us. . . . This bungled con irritates her immensely; she is disconsolate.

In the midst of this hullabaloo, the Bogouslawskys arrive. It's a very heavy moment that we spend together, the four of us: Dillie, Michel, my mother, and I, standing in the half-dark of the foyer, without managing to utter a single word. The war—*and now this* . . . it's all too much at once. Michel's furrowed, ruddy face contracts into a spasm that changes into a wild, excessive childish sob, but of such impetuous sincerity that at last I feel the tears welling up in my eyes. At the same time I see my mother's lips tremble with the perception of the irreparable shock, and Dillie's sea-green eyes closing with pain on two huge tears, like two mascara caterpillars on a long mask of pale wax. And here we go, all four of us, sobbing, sputtering, and sniffling, a few yards from the mortal remains of our companion on this round, who has just taken off; friend, lover, husband, father, brother. The Bogouslawskys embrace us while crying all the more, taking us by the shoulders, patting us on the head. It's staggering, heartrending, exhausting. It ends with all of us collapsing on armchairs in the living room, wiped out, in a silence broken by brief relapses and a few topical questions from Michel, who doesn't even listen to the answers.

The Bogouslawskys leave just when my grandfather returns. He tries to convince my mother to come spend the night with him, but she obstinately refuses. He resigns himself to leaving us. Tomorrow, September 3, my father will be buried in a cemetery at Courbevoie.

My mother and I settle down and try to sleep in this apartment where a cadaver is already resting, she in Nicole's room, me in Sylvie's. In the middle of the night, or perhaps toward morning, the wailing of a siren breaks out, then two of them, then ten, all joined in counterpoint, screaming terror. Then a hail of heavenly explosions, a feast for demons: It seems that the antiaircraft batteries can't wait for the war to start, they aim at the clouds, cannonade the stars, which haven't voted for Daladier. . . . Still, there are less vengeful ways to wake the sleeping; I was just floundering in a swampy nightmare and then this concerto of furies pulls me out of it—it's like the musical accompaniment of a *danse macabre*, Hieronymus Bosch style.

Fumbling in the darkness, I try to reach a source of light, and the thought of my father suddenly overwhelms me. I had forgotten. From afar I hear my mother groping around her room; she can't find the light switch either. The night is filled with various tumults; in the street, overshrill, overexcited whistles are blowing, piercing the lowing of the sirens, and from the staircase of our building comes the sound of a herd of buffaloes. The tenants are thundering down the stairs, hurrying to take shelter with their Thermos bottles and their folding chairs, already well disciplined even though the war hasn't yet been declared.

In the hall Mme Orgelet, whose husband is an air-raid warden and owns a helmet and a whistle, harangues her people. She opens the door of our apartment and yells in passing, "Let's go, Monsieur Maurice, you've got to go down! Look after your mama! The jewels, the papers! And especially the mask! *Your masks!* And an emergency kit, too; one never knows . . ."

By the beam of a flashlight, I finally locate my mother, who is getting dressed in the darkness, like an automaton, and we go down into the cellar with the rear guard of the tenants. We are the family of the drama, a small drama within a big one;

everybody looks at us out of the corner of their eyes, whispering things to us, touching our sleeves. It breaks my heart to have to expose my mother to this morbid curiosity that death or its approach always seems to provoke, and thanks to which the evening papers thrive so handsomely. Yet, we have never spoken to a soul in the building. It's quite enough if we have learned from Mme Orgelet that the tenants on the third floor eat carrots with every meal. So the neighbors aren't denying themselves a little pleasure from our sorrow; it's only human. The good Lord has punished us for our haughtiness—this thought can easily be read on their faces.

At least on those faces that can still be seen. For the assembly is divided into two camps, and the majority deems that in the event of the alert, it's suitable to put on one's mask without waiting, without beating around the bush. The spectacle is appalling: an assembly of fat metallic snouts crowning bloated bodies stuffed into their chenille bathrobes, probably expecting a mustard gas attack on their precious lungs.

"You'll have to put your mask on, madame," said the concierge, tapping her finger on the cylindrical case my mother has slung over her shoulder.

And Mme Orgelet slips her head into hers, to set the example. My mother doesn't hear her, or pretends not to. . . . Time goes by and one by one, those who have donned their masks begin to take them off, timorously, as if surprised to find themselves still alive. The sirens that signal the end of this one-act interlude have something joyous about them. The *Boche* airplanes must have been routed by ours! And did you hear the antiaircraft? *Boom-boom?* M. Orgelet will have some famous stories to bring home! And Mme Orgelet too! "Hitler will only get what he deserves, I can tell you that. With the RAF, it'll all be over in three months."

The tenants go back to their beds, but it's already dawn. It will be a magnificent day, like yesterday.

The undertakers arrive early in the morning and go about their business briskly. A funeral without a religious service, without anything at all, that's the kind that should be carried out in a jiffy. All the more so since the war's going to bring plenty of work: just think of it! The suicides, the cardiac arrests, the old people dying of fright, or falling down the stairs during the air raids; *c'est bon pour les croque-morts, tout ça!*

The hearse is followed only by my grandfather's Delahaye on the hood of which a silver Venus springs forth victoriously, and the coachman drives his horses at a rather lively pace. Along the avenue de Neuilly crews of workmen are repairing the asphalt as we pass by; they interrupt their labors and stand, cap in hand, watching our convoy go past, doubtless telling themselves, "That one chose the right time to go." At the cemetery, things are speeding up even more; the people from the funeral parlor are no doubt somewhat embarrassed by our little trio without priest, without mourning veils, without black suits. . . . The widow herself refrains from manifesting the usual signs of sorrow; she gazes straight forward, her bearing almost military. The sun is beating down and my grandfather seems to relish the good warmth and the illusion of countryside created by a few scattered trees in the distance. The burial doesn't make him lose sight of his lunch; there's a little restaurant in Neuilly that he hasn't tried yet and has heard good things about, a new place by the name of Mommaton. . . .

So here we are, moments later, seated before a solid meal. My grandfather opens the debate by insisting upon an immediate retreat of the entire family, as far as possible from Paris; according to his usual tactics. Since 1914, the specter of the bombardment and fall of the capital has stayed with him; he offers to leave tomorrow to personally scout out a place in Provence. My mother suggests Dax, where Stuart Gilbert and his wife have already gone; they will certainly help them to find lodgings. "And you?" she says, turning toward me. "And Maurice?" she asks her father.

It is my turn to speak, and so I explain to them that I can very well take care of the office and continue the business with the support of Kurt Enoch, on whom I know that I can count. . . . Until I leave for the army, that is. . . . What army? It's not sure but the future will tell. . . . I'll have to see what happens. My mother isn't against it; she thinks that Michel Bogouslawsky will be a good adviser. My grandfather doesn't conceal his pleasure at seeing me assert an unexpected intention, an ambition to launch myself in business, something he never really expected. Of course, publishing isn't what he dreamed of for me; it's an intellectual profession and it means continuing in the tracks of my father; but he trusts me. He agrees, therefore, with the provision that I use his accountant for bookkeeping purposes.

In this way, without fully realizing it, I have just taken up my father's professional heritage while at the same time as-

suming the burder of his family. And so it is that I became a
publisher.

Several times during the course of this day one of my father's last words comes back to me. When he kept repeating
that he was going to leave, was he talking about the war or
more simply, of death? When he asked me to take care of the
family . . . and said that one of the two of us should stay. . . . I
continue to ruminate on these thoughts while we drive out of
Paris in my grandfather's car, on the way to Orvilliers.

Announcing their father's death to the kids turns into a
heartrending scene. Each one responds in his or her own way;
Nicole, who always had a special affinity for her father, is all
torn up, lost. Eric, the youngest, a fair-haired boy with a keen
mind and always somewhat frantic, dashes headlong, howling,
toward the bottom of the garden. Sylvie, the tomboy, bears
up best in the face of the catastrophe.

The next day is entirely occupied with the task of answering, from the office, innumerable phone calls; it seems that
my father's death has been reported in one or two papers as a
Parisian event expressive of the mood of the day. After all, he
is the first casualty of the war that has just been declared. But
the death of Jack Kahane, eccentric publisher, is much more
directly connected with the war than any one of them seems
to imagine. They all torture me with their sympathy, their sad
silences, their questions—how, why, and my mother, the children, what were we going to do? Other people called by
chance, without having heard the news, and that's even more
terrible; I have to begin from the beginning, explain, repeat,
leaving them the time to take it all in and to swallow it. The
most depressing thing is that all these people are sincere, their
friendship is real. No doubt they are asking themselves, as I
do myself, moreover, how this invalid could have survived for
so long, so joyously, to the extent that his sudden demise
seems absolutely shocking. Friends, mistresses, acquaintances,
each one of them ends up saying the same thing, that his
death was the first death of the war, that it marked the end of
an era. . . .

Kurt Enoch came by and, in a few simple and practical sen-
tences, assured me of his sympathy. He asked me to come
and see him in two or three days in order to discuss the future. I received two other visits, curiously identical, from
George and Tommy, owners respectively of the bar at the
Castiglione and Tommy's Bar, rue Pierre-Charron, who of-

fered me their condolences with great dignity, derby in hand. Like Tweedledum and Tweedledee they both told me that, though they were very sorry to bother me, they found themselves obliged to let me know the amount due on my father's account with their establishments; and indeed these bills were enormous, staggering. I told them that I didn't have any money. They both gave me the same answer: Of course it could wait, but they were obliged to ask me to sign an IOU, and of course they trusted me. So I signed.

Money. . . . I didn't have any, apart from the few francs in my pocket that were left from my last paycheck. There was almost nothing in my father's account at the Westminster Bank—and almost nothing to expect from the clients. If the war is to last more than six months, how am I going to survive, how am I going to feed that whole little family?

The solution came from my grandfather, who months before the 1929 crash had made an irrevocable donation to us four, his grandchildren. Had I waited until the age of twenty-five, my share would have been a quarter million francs—the same as the other three—which was pretty substantial. But having obtained a court order allowing me to draw my capital immediately, I found that it had dwindled, mostly due to the depressed market, to sixty thousand francs. That was enough, at any rate, to make me feel independent and rich. At least for a few months.

My grandfather was both elated to think that this fragment of his former fortune was arriving into my hands at such an opportune moment; and depressed by the fact that it had shrunk to so little. Depressed also at the idea that he could do nothing to help my mother and me, since he had hardly enough to live on anymore. He was about to give up his newest habitat, which he now found he couldn't afford; and this would be another turn in the diminishing spiral of his fortunes. The portion of his wealth that he had rescued from the great crash had been invested into brilliant ventures that had all turned sour. A gold mine in Indochina vanished in a border dispute; and various creations of well-thought-out industrial projects invariably turned out to be extremely profitable to others, and disastrous to himself. He was a born creator, being at the same time a fertile inventor and a good leader of men, but he didn't have the basic hunger and money instinct that make a good businessman. And since these were the qualities he most envied in others, his dream of becoming a successful entrepreneur would lead him again, year after year, to greater disasters. He took them all with courage and fortitude, like a good gambler. Unfortunately, and unlike a good gambler, what he was gambling with was not money, but himself. Every one of his investments had to be dictated by a passion for an idea, a useful invention, a novelty. He had innovated industrially with new techniques ranging from construction materials to plywood and wire ropes, each time giving his all, and quite forgetting that he was in it primarily in order to make money. He was an easy prey for the vultures roaming the skies.

One thing was bothering me about that money donation he had once made in our favor, which is the fact that it had not been extended to my cousins, Jacques and Mowgli, who were his grandsons just like me. But it had always been a dark area, in the overall family relationship, that distaste my grandfather had developed for the sons of his daughter Hélène, as if they were second-rate, a blemish on his own genetic escutcheon; and this was the stamp of his autocratic, tyrannical nature. And my mother, who suffered much because of the difficult relations between her father and her husband, resented this deeply; despite the profound, admiring love she felt for her father, her innate sense of fairness was revolted by his occasional manifestations of injustice, by his bouts of sanguine brutality, of imperial arrogance. She knew it couldn't be helped; that was the wrong side of the coin; and it so happens that she had developed a great attachment for the two scamps, her nephews, who once gleefully confessed to me that they had always found my mother very sexy.

My cousins kept their cool about the situation; and what made things worse, in a sense, is that they showed no sign of humility, or humiliation, in the old man's presence; they were just as macho, in their own way, as he was in his. But instead of drawing pride from this it caused him considerable irritation; which had become something of an obsession as a result of the following incident.

One day Mowgli, who should have been cramming for his exams at that particular time, was prancing down the grands boulevards instead with a pretty girl friend on his arm, when he finds himself suddenly confronted, nearly nose to nose, with a handsome, white-bearded gentleman, himself guiding a very seductive person by the elbow. The instant of recognition was terrific, said Mowgli; the grandfather's cane nearly took a swing at him—but some survival instinct must have cut the gesture short. Rage in his eye, his hair bristling, the old man had passed him in a state of shock; and the two blondes had smiled to each other as if they knew. Phew! More bones for the family cupboard—and more power to the blondes!

My mother returned to Orvilliers the day after my father was buried. I went to get a few belongings from my lodgings on rue Gay-Lussac, gave the rest to the son of the concierge, and settled back, alone, in the family's apartment.

The following weekend I caught an old overcrowded bus for Orvilliers, and it left me there at exactly the same time at which my father used to arrive for his usual weekend visits. In the pleasant rustic house, at the end of its flowery garden, I found my mother sitting next to an old crackling radio set, trying to get the news on the BBC. We sat close to each other, our attention caught by the nasal accents of some distant speaker, meticulously planting a decor of doom all around Western civilization. It was right that Jack should no longer be here to listen to all this; it was right that he should have died now. She looked at me intently as she was telling me those brave, definitive words.

We walked around the pleasant countryside at sunset, arm-in-arm, trying to contain and filter our emotions, to divine each other's needs, weaknesses, and to establish a frail new bridge between the two of us. The two of us. . . .

A new world had to be created out of what was left of the old one. Her twenty-four-year-old affair with a stranger whose language she had never really understood had come abruptly to an end. The man to whom she had devoted all the power of her love had now abandoned her for the last time. . . . And so she was left with those children, their children; including myself, a semi-grownup, an undecipherable individual who was at the same time a partial replica of Jack, her husband, and the resurgence of Maurice, her brother. The two men of her life, the first love and the last: This had given as a product Maurice, her son. It was of course impossible to understand these things, or even to think about them too hard. Her duty was to serve those she loved, as she had always done, to the best of her ability.

So we were at war. . . . For the time being, it was a war of shadows, of phantoms, in a very literal sense; people in the street kept bumping into one another, breaking their bones on the sidewalk, barely missing getting run over by cars without headlights piloted in slow motion by blind drivers. This sudden change of climate, of situation, struck me as strangely exhilarating, and I made my way with long strides through the darkness toward the Etoile, Porte Maillot, place du Marché. The rue Bertaux-Dumas, in this pea soup, wasn't the same: The monument to the war dead, an absurd obelisk by day, in the night became a murky, enigmatic silhouette in the midst of an inkwell.

Our apartment was in violation of the Civil Defense regulations; it was one of the rare delinquents, in all of Neuilly, Paris, and the Ile-de-France whose windows had not been obscured and camouflaged, painted black, sealed up like the Pharaoh's tomb. Hence, no question of switching on the least glimmer of a light in our place, not even a match, now that the war was officially happening. . . . I felt my way to the room where I had slept the night before, dropped my clothes in a heap on the floor, and slid into my sister's bed. The darkness was so absolute I couldn't tell whether my eyes were open or closed—a deep, powdery, devouring darkness, the humid, glaucous darkness of dead eyes. Six feet under . . . bewildered, lost in a sooty universe. I pressed my eyelids down as hard as I could against the interior shadow until roses of blood burst forth inside this catafalque. Among them lay a long, indistinct larval form, which was my father's body being invaded by the acids of death. The horror of this vision struck me with such violence that I awoke with a cry, only to find that the translucent, luminescent image was still there, floating in front of me, absurdly real.

During the days, the weeks that followed, a force that nothing in the world could deter led me to the same bed, every night, and confronted me with the same horror. Not only was I forced to follow all the phases of this body's putrefaction, but I irresistibly felt myself to be the flesh of this rotting flesh, the child of this cadaver. I floundered about in this vermin, in these juices and gases, in a constant paroxysm of terror, as if this death were mine and not his. This hideous caricature of what had been my father didn't let go of me for a minute all night long; its half-eaten contours were only obliterated with the dawn, and the memory of this punctual nightmare sometimes came to torment me suddenly in broad daylight. This oozing corpse still refused to completely die and return to nothingness; it was attached to its lost life by but a single thread, a far-off echo—and it was me, me, the son of this decomposing larva. . . . Me, the captive of this endlessly dying thing. No longer a being, no longer an object, only this diminishing mass of dirt, still linked to me by a memory. . . .

After a few weeks of this torture, I became aware of a transformation taking place in this caved-in shape, which seemed to gain in phosphorescence what it was losing in materiality. I felt the change, without being able to express it, through the simple fact that the horror was less overwhelming. Little by little I was liberating myself from the gory fascination, and as the nocturnal horror subsided, I became conscious of a dialogue or, at least, of an exchange between living beings. Every night I rejoined my father again, and gradually became accustomed to observing the phenomenon of a progressive rejuvenation taking place in his appearance. And this I did not find strange in the least; neither was I surprised by the fact that the words we exchanged were erased as soon as I woke up; and indeed they may have been sounds and harmonies rather than human words. None of it would have made sense in my waking state; and yet those exchanges had a very strong meaning; and during this entire period, which lasted for three months, or perhaps longer, I felt myself to be accompanied by his presence as if I were the Siamese twin of my dead father. One day, as I was crossing the place Vendôme on my way to the post office on the rue des Capucines, I had a sudden acute sensation of a vibrating point at the level of my head, as if the bird Horus had landed on my right shoulder. And that same night, I witnessed his definitive departure; what had been his life, his passage on this earth, resolved itself into a few curves of light vanishing into a bottomless sky, but leaving in my heart an indelible trace, the imprint of a shared reality, a pure and profound joy that was nothing other than this quintessence of life which is called love.

All this might seem like the lyrical description of a trivial neurosis; yet, during this entire period and often in flashes even later on, I felt myself being firmly guided by my father. It was no doubt thanks to this help from beyond the grave that I started out as a professional publisher, and that I faced the many unpredictable problems of my new existence. It would be hard for me to explain the mechanism of this influence, which may be quite banal, but there is no question that my father's death started me in a direction that was much more his than mine.

This ghostly advice was never wanting in terms of daring, or humor. As to its wisdom, it seemed indisputable to me that the decisions I found myself making required an experience of life and of business much greater than my own.

First of all, I had to acquit myself of the pledge I had made him to go and fight. To tell the truth, I wasn't sure if I was still bound by that absurd commitment, in view of the fact that he had died so soon after our conversation. Didn't I hear him tell me that this death was for both of us, that it was our common contribution to the defense of the Western civilization? But I was still dazed by the bluster of my heroic vows, and I wasn't sure I was hearing his voice very clearly on this point; and so I went to pay a visit to His Majesty's military attaché on the rue Boissy-d'Anglas, in order to enlist in the British army.

Contrary to expectation, the military attaché was a man who exuded serenity. He handed me a form that he found with some difficulty after rummaging through the muddle on his desk, and when I had filled it out, he read it, drawing a puff or two on his briar.

"I see that you have a family to take care of," he said. "When you go, will your mother be able to take charge? There won't be any material problems?"

"Uh. . . . Well, I don't think so. If the war doesn't last too long, I think we have enough to get by."

My French accent seemed to surprise him a bit.

"Your mother is French? You were brought up in France?"

"Yes, sir."

"Ah! . . . Peculiar situation, what! Listen to me, I think it's very good of you to want to enlist in His Majesty's army; the only problem is that for the moment, there isn't any."

(Wow! I told myself, is he one of us? An anarchist in disguise?)

"Well, I exaggerate a bit," he went on, sucking meditatively on his pipe. "But only a little bit, really. The draft in England itself is going to take six months, a year, to organize. So for British subjects living abroad, like you, it will be even slower. It's good of you to have come to see me, I'll record your enlistment, but don't expect to hear anything for quite a while."

He showed me to the door, and let me go with a kindly slap on the back. Well! This seems to have been the alpha and the omega of my military career! And yet I had given it an honest try, it seems to me. . . . Too bad that I won't be able to impress Gregor with my beautiful red-and-black Guard's uniform, and a bearskin cap high as a house—but I'll survive the disappointment!

"Mon cher ami," Bogous declared, peeling himself a pear with great deliberation, "I think the time has come to talk to you seriously. . . . I've got an idea for you."

He explained that since, for the duration of the war, no matter how brief it might be, the activity at Obelisk Press will be reduced to a minimum, I should convert myself to other projects, for instance the idea he had already discussed with my father—the project of publishing in France inexpensive pocket editions, in English, of books that had recently been best sellers in London and New York. To take up only very well-known titles, which would be easy to sell. Hachette would take care of the distribution, and if the sales were slow in the beginning, while awaiting that famous English army, it didn't matter: Hachette could wait. And one day, if the war goes on for a while—who knows?—perhaps the Americans themselves would arrive in France, and then it would be a sure fortune. "Sooner or later it will come, you'll see, pocket editions, cheaply produced paperbacks will make a big splash, especially in the United States. . . . To begin with, you can come out with one book a month. . . . It's easy, the competition has been eliminated, Tauchnitz because it's German, Albatross because that idiot, Holroyd Reece, has run his own business aground."

I listen to all that with keen interest. He hadn't yet come to the problem of financing yet—surely he had thought about it?

"And as for the financing, I would start out by getting all I can from Hachette. And there are still a few remaining accounts to settle in favor of Obelisk Press. For the rest, you will have an exclusive contract for distribution with Hachette, and you'll receive an advance of fifty percent upon delivery, for each book. That will cover the expenses and allow you to live. . . . But of course you'll need a little money at the beginning for advances to authors, to purchase paper, all those things. Now, then, you'll receive the remainder of the Hachette accounts, plus your grandfather's money, that should get you started; and I can assure you that with Hachette's backing, you won't have any problems."

It was incredible! He was constructing a business, financing it, and turning it over to me as a gift. He was treating me like an equal, like an experienced businessman. . . .

"However," he added, peeling himself a second pear, "you're not yet a professional publisher, a man of experience, you understand? So, I think it would be a good idea if you found a partner who has the qualities you don't have yet. . . . I thought of Kurt Enoch, who liked Jack a lot. . . . He's a solid man and he knows how to get things going. . . . What do you think?"

"Oh yes, we're getting along fine. But why would he accept?"

"To make money! You'll go fifty-fifty. He'll put a little money into the business, like you. But he won't hesitate for a second at the idea of a partnership with you as long as the business is financed by Hachette—once he gets over his surprise!"

Keeping this last observation in mind, I put the matter to Enoch the very next day, taking care to observe the effect of my proposals. First of all, I talked about the project without mentioning Hachette and I saw an ironic gleam in his gray-blue eyes behind his rimless glasses. This kid doesn't lack nerve, he seemed to think.

"But listen," he finally said, "that's a great project, but you haven't got the capital it takes for such a business, and neither do I. And as to finding someone who does, anywhere, in wartime—"

It was then that I came out with the solution: I had assurances from Hachette, by way of Bogous. The glimmer of disapproval reflected in his American-style eyeglasses changed quickly. Completely. This cold and severe man was at bottom an enthusiast; there was an impulsive and romantic side to him, and the unlikely idea of this association seemed to enchant him. He had two daughters, both younger than I, and no son; doubtless the idea of helping a deserving young man to get a start in life appealed to him. Little by little, without giving it much thought, I adapted myself to the circumstances; I learned to present the image of a thoughtful, well-organized young man, equal parts idealist and realist, and wise beyond his years. Yeah, well. . . . But after all, since the society I had been able to observe seemed to rest on a convention made of sham and crazy illusions, why not play the game? One is— what one has the nerve to pretend to be.

Now that I had at least the illusion of having money, my first reaction was to go and see my neighbor, the tailor Sazarin, an exquisite man with a yellow face, who received millionaires in his quarters at place Vendôme, and dressed them like billionaires. He gave me a deal, two thousand francs per suit—more money than my father had ever spent on his—and soon I found that the investment was handsomely paying off, and not simply in terms of the strong impression I was now making on the neighborhood secretaries.

It was easy enough to dress up as a rich young man; after all, I didn't even need to leave the place Vendôme for that. My hats, of ultralight nutria, made to order, of course, came from Gélot's; my shirts were custom-made at Charvet's. I scorned the things at Sulka's, which seemed to me too loud and not very harmonious, but there were many other resources awaiting me under the arches of the rue de Castiglione and the rue de Rivoli, from Boivin, which I preferred, to Hilditch & Key, where amusing things were sometimes to be found. As for shoes, I ordered them, for a small fortune, from M. Ghazérian, a conscientious bootmaker who worked alone in a small austere shop on the rue Richepanse, a little beyond my usual territory. Naturally, all this vestiary luxury was in perfect taste. Nothing ostentatious. On this point, my father had exercised the best possible influence on my sartorial education, without ever saying one word on the subject. Or rather yes, one thing he once said to me was, "It's better not to be too well-dressed." A gentleman never mentions these things—that's a golden rule. They must come to him quite naturally, without any effort, without even giving them a thought, like a slightly annoying obligation for which one is forced to sacrifice a little time ("After all, one has to dress!"), but which a person of refinement could never take seriously. These were items of knowlege that could not be communicated, seeing that they were never discussed. One was born with this instinct; it couldn't be acquired, talent that remained forever inaccessible to Americans, traveling salesmen, and, let's face it, to practically all of the male population of France. The fit of a suit, the stripes of a tie, the terrible risks of color; the cut of the hair, the choice of accessories such as

one's eyeglasses, cuff links, and cigarette lighters, the style of
the shoes and their laces, from the design of the suspenders to
the finesse of the undergarments, not to mention the linen of
the handkerchiefs, the monograms, the indispensable sobriety
of the eaux de cologne, as well as the shaping of the nails—
these were choices that a man of taste should be able to make
with eyes closed. Ah, how could I forget the look of bemused
irony on my father's face when confronted, once, with the
heraldic jewelry worn by a certain prince of the blood! These
excesses of bad taste, which can be found at any moment in
Parisian salons, served him as psychological clues that situated
his interlocutor, defining his milieu, origin, and character.
There were only certain men who were meant to wear watch
chains, clocked hose, spats, signet rings, or to carry a knobbed
walking stick. But, after all, as the popular saying goes, *"Tous
les goûts sont dans la nature,"* a moronic cliché but true.

As far as interesting women were concerned, they were always well-dressed; bad taste was really a male privilege, and
that was one of the main reasons why my father was such an
ardent feminist.

Such preoccupations may seen extremely frivolous on the
part of a young man who had spent a third of his life sitting on
his butt, meditating on such subjects as perfect purity.

Well, so they are. With my father's death many of his pet
idiosyncrasies seemed to have been mysteriously transferred
to me. In this as in other things I felt compelled, not just to
imitate his example, but rather to take it over, absorb it, and
then project myself through it, in an attempt to go further, to
do better than him. Freudian references abound; but this was
more like an elder brother setting the rules of a game, and
daring the younger one to play it better. Very good! I would
do everything better, and invent my own way to do it. I would
be a more daring adventurer, a better publisher—and, incidentally, I would discontinue as soon as possible the Obelisk
Press trash—also a more flashy dresser, a more spectacular
lover. And would I be an even more sensational failure? That
would be hard to match.

The publishing company we founded on an equal partnership basis with Kurt Enoch was called the Unicorn Press. The
first title we acquired was *The Grapes of Wrath* and I was busy
negotiating the continental rights to books by Somerset
Maugham, Elizabeth Bowen, and others. Guided by Bogous, I
made my little way through the inner mazes of Hachette's

establishment, where he proudly introduced me to all and sundry as a young publisher prodigy he had discovered; the reception I was accorded as a result of these fanfares sometimes made me forget that in fact I hadn't been discovered at all, but fabricated from head to toe, literally, and by Bogous himself.

To him the life of business was a rich source of comedy. Others see it as the major access to money and power, but to Bogous its main attraction was to reveal people's turpitude to the full. He was, like Gogol's Chichikov, using other people's greed as a means to make them believe in anything he fancied; and the book business did look, according to him, like an inexhaustible source of dead souls, characters puffed and inflated by ridiculous delusions of power.

Witness our visit, Bogous and I, to old man Ledeuf, who headed Hachette's legal department, a very important man to have on one's side.

First, how do you accede to the presence? Bogous showed me how, to start with, you open the door just a crack, just enough to force the fellow to raise his nose from the papers on his desk. Once his attention has been caught, the door suddenly opens wide and Bogous, braying a thundrous "Dearr Frriend," holds the pause for a moment, as if struck by the charm of this divine surprise. His face is jubilant, rutilant with mirth and delight. And then he hurls himself into the room, his hands stretched out toward those of this precious friend of whose company he has been deprived for all too long—the gesturing being meant at the same time to introduce this princely character, myself, not really as a human being but rather as a bouquet of flowers.

Who could resist? Old man Ledeuf was suddenly ravished, torn away from his schemes and his legal briefs, like any Cinderella, and made the star of a *Ballet Russe*. How could he resist? He felt under the obligation to rise, to walk around his desk, to come and meet this longtime admirer, and to play the role of the diffident beauty in a pas-de-deux situation. The next step was to make him laugh, and Bogous showed him how; his own laughter was contagious, enormous, the gasping of a locomotive puffing through the steppes; again it was impossible not to answer in kind, and the head of the legal department would then respond with his own meager chuckles. That was enough! The rest was easy, child's play.

And it wasn't easy to make old man Ledeuf laugh, let alone

smile, let alone smirk. His gray-and-yellow face was be-smudged with nicotine, his scratchy claws deformed by the writing of so many legal papers, with a little finger terminating in a long curved nail, in the old-fashioned Mandarin fashion, to mark his rank as an aristocrat among paper-shufflers. Nice work! Thanks to Bogous's efforts on my behalf, I found I had become the great white hope of French publishing, without even trying. Just think of it, at the age of only twenty! This young man will go far, you'll see! No one else but Bogous could thus have given substance to the rather mad illusions I entertained concerning my future as a publisher.

Hélène Anikeef was probably the only one of the vestal virgins from the ashram who was definitely not a virgin, and certainly the only one who had known how to preserve her independence from Vivian. At first I had found her rather too snobbish and haughty, but shortly before my exclusion from the group, she turned out to be excellent company. And then she was Russian, yet another Slav soul in my life . . . a beautiful Slav on the loose. . . . She was the daughter of a bigwig Bolshevik, one of Lenin's first companions, and of a noblewoman, now a refugee in France, with whom she had been living but whom she could no longer stand. Once, in 1936, as she was studying for a master's in philosophy and living in a little hotel in the Latin Quarter, she had decided to go back to her roots and telephoned her father at his office in Moscow. She hardly remembered him at all, and she was taken by surprise by his reaction: She was to leave Paris the very next day to go to him in Moscow. She would find a ticket and some money in her name within a few hours at the embassy, said her father. . . . He made her promise to leave right away. . . . He would come himself to meet her at the Russian border in his car. . . . He had just remarried, to a remarkable woman who would certainly be a marvelous friend for Hélène. . . . Life in Moscow had nothing in common with the nonsense one read about in the French newspapers, and elsewhere. She would find an excellent atmosphere, a whole new society was being built. . . .

So, there she was, at the crossroads. She took the train from the Gare de l'Est with no more luggage than the coat on her back and a few books of French poetry for her father. At Compiègne, she stepped down from her sleeping car to take advantage of a brief stopover, just to breathe in the air of France for the last time on the platform.

"And just see what happened," she said, bursting with laughter, "I don't know why, you understand, but as I was standing in front of the train station, I was amused to find there one of those old-fashioned horse carriages, and I hired it with my father's money, and asked the coachman to take me to the forest. And there I walked, it was so terribly beautiful. Compiègne, a very sad, very French town. Perfect, forlorn countryside. I had quite forgotten Moscow and my father, who was losing me for the second time. When he was executed on Stalin's order, sometime later, his only memory of me would be of a little girl. Perhaps it is better that way."

For reasons that still escape me, she had married Witold, her gallant knight, in a Masonic ceremony, and she turned him into a disciple of the group, all on Vivian's advice. Soon after the wedding, Witold was called up as a reserve officer in the air force; he had been sent with the French delegation to Poland, in view of his Polish origins, to act as a military adviser, as part of France's aid program.

It was therefore useful to Hélène to have a well-tailored young man at her beck and call in order to keep her company in those places where she wanted to let herself be admired. She was quite conscious of her beauty and used her power of seduction over men with great art and humor, being vastly more intelligent than most of them. She was a philosophical adventuress, just as apt at seducing men's minds as their senses; and of course she knew everything about her friend Jean-Paul Sartre's love life; she was intimate with all the young lions at the Sorbonne. At the same time, something in her—the mystic touch—had caused her to fall for Vivian. Since the autumn of 1936, she had been frequenting the group on the boulevard Saint-Germain and had gradually become part of it; but nothing and no one could have made her give up her personal freedom. If Vivian had tried to impose any kind of rules on her, he would have lost her, and the fact is that she fascinated him.

To fascinate men was Hélène's natural vocation, and it must be said that next to her, Marlene Dietrich or Greta Garbo would have looked like servant girls. Her faraway look, both distant and intimate at the same time, an air of amusing herself with being bored, of waiting for the impossible, all this always produced a magical effect on the masculine population of the public places we frequented. Lost in an inaccessible reverie, her gaze heedlessly scanned the handsome industrialists decked out in their millions, the young officers prancing in their uniforms, the old lions spangled with glory. But her enigmatic smile was meant for no one—or perhaps for some sublime and distant hero next to whom these brilliant suitors thronging our table were as nothing.

We had a good time chatting together and devoted innumerable luncheons to it. We had got into the habit of meeting at the Pâtisserie Danoise at the foot of the avenue de l'Opéra, where fashionable people gathered, with a large contingent of people from the theater and the press; it was a showcase for the prettiest models, the best-cut uniforms, the smartest lovers and the most sophisticated females wearing the craziest hats. We had no secrets from each other and served each other mutually as confidants, a very pragmatic arrangement. This certainly gave me very interesting insights into the feminine nature, which, until then, I had only known through the excesses of my adolescent imagination. Despite her already vast experience and her smiling cynicism, Hélène never derided my incurable passion for her friend Laurette; she seemed to find it very touching, this unrequited and hopeless love, and she listened patiently to my divagations on the subject. Nevertheless, she seemed fairly relieved when someone came over and sat down at our table and thus reduced me to silence. We might never have been such good friends had I not been so completely in love with another.

It was from Hélène that I learned, in the first days of the year 1940, that Laurette's stepfather, Lionel Filipoff, was ill, desperately ill this time. Mona and he were in Lourdes where they had gone to spend the winter, in search of a warmer climate. Lionel was about to reach the stars for good at last, should I feel sorry for him? It afforded a chance to break the ice, and I called Laurette, trying to sound as subdued as I sensed her to be. Yes, she would take the train for the Pyrénées that very evening. "Do you want me to go with you?" I asked her in a quavering voice, which I was quite unable to control. "Oh no, no, really, don't think of it!" But it seemed to me that between my offer and her refusal, there had been a slight moment of hesitation.

Between waking and dreaming, I spent the whole night traveling with her, picturing her in the dismal coach, her eyes lost in sadness, her arms crossed tightly against her chest to fight off the cold. I could even hear the rhythmic clangor of wood and metal, the miserable hymn of the night train rolling through the unseen countryside. I spent the next morning pacing feverishly up and down my office, waiting for the telegram I had begged her to send me upon her arrival. I was unaware of big Helga, my secretary and sole employee, who was killing the time by rolling little paper pellets between her sturdy fingers and throwing them at me, aiming at the nose.

The telegram finally arrived. Lionel had died during the night; he was to be buried the next day. I wired back that I would arrive early in the morning, and rushed to pack a bag in order to catch the night train.

The cavernous railway station at Lourdes is empty but for a few handicapped pilgrims on their way to the miracle shrine. Under the huge clock, at last, I see a girlish figure hurrying toward me. She seems to feel my gaze on her even before she sees me. As we come closer to each other, I perceive the changes in Laurette, the maturity and the melancholy, and she is now both close and familiar, and infinitely distant. Here we are, again, face-to-face, our voices tight with emotion out of a new and unaccustomed shyness. Her chestnut curls escape from a beret of a slightly lighter color; she is wearing a plain single-breasted coat that suits her very well. The grace of her innocence, as always, inundates my heart with a feeling I cannot name, or analyze, or understand. It would be so easy to lose control, to make a fool of myself! Finally, we embrace as friends will, and when my lips brush the perfect skin of her cheek, it's as if I had been electrocuted: sixty thousand volts! We hug briefly, all too briefly. I'm on the verge of tears, and she isn't far from them either.

Poor Lionel! As seen from the second floor of that little house in the center of town, his demise is in the style of a surrealist melodrama. . . . Like a sequence in Buñuel's *Un Chien Andalou*. . . . Observed from above, the steep street displays lines of stores selling religious frippery. Processions of cripples on crutches are seen as foreshortened figures awkwardly climbing up the receding incline, like incomplete crabs reduced to one or two defective claws. Yes, Lourdes, in the mist, wrapped up in humid clouds. . . .

Mona, Laurette tells me, is in a state of shock, lifeless, wordless, withdrawn into herself; she would never have been able to cope on her own with all these sad funeral arrangements. . . . The fact is that because of Lionel's inordinate size, it proved necessary to have a special, extralong coffin manufactured to accommodate the body. This Laurette explains carefully to me as we take a walk, and run a few errands. And sure enough, just as we reach the house, we find the staircase blocked by sweating and toiling undertakers trying to loosen the coffin, which has got stuck in a diagonal position between the walls and the railing; nothing doing, the damned thing won't budge. The undertakers seem to be totally unable to cope with their own ineptitude.

Forced out of her grief by this inexplicable racket, Mona emerges at last from her room and I see her from below, leaning over the second-floor banister. She stares with a nervous expression straight down into the stairwell where there unfolds this second drama, unworthy of the first. She's an artist, a woman of sensibility, and there's an uncontrollable twitch in the right side of her beautiful face.

"Let's go, boys! *Heave ho, heave ho!*" yells a heavy man in shirt-sleeves, his red face glistening with sweat. "Give her a push, that's it, toward the top! Heave ho, boys, *there she goes!*"

As the coffin turns loose, out of its depths there comes a hideous dull thud that resounds like someone angrily shoving with his shoulder against a closed door. The undertakers recoil in horror, the coffin slides back into its eerie diagonal position. The hysteria is now general; the youngest of the gang starts screaming incoherent warnings—"He's not dead yet, I tell you! He's not dead!" The others have to thump him on the head to force him to shut up.

The big man in shirt-sleeves makes a desperate effort to get things under control. There's a widow up there who seems about to faint. He holds out his stubby arms to her, miming the gesture of an accordionist:

"Madame, please, there's nothing to worry about!" he pleads. "It's—it's nothing. It's only your poor deceased just settling into position." And he brings his fat paws together to show her how. "Not to worry, it's normal. Get on with it, boys! *Heave ho* . . ."

Lourdes. Yes, that's where Henry Miller had ended up, two years earlier, after leaving Paris in a blue funk because the war seemed unavoidable. After the Munich peace talks he found himself caught in that little mountain city; and he had taken a savage revenge against the world of sickly Christianity of which Lourdes is the symbol: an entire city devoted to pain, a city on crutches, wrapped up in those thick, heavy clouds creeping overhead, where the melancholy waters of the mountains ooze through every wall. When it manages to pierce the wet fog, the sun itself appears to be in pain.

Thus Mona has lost her latest husband, probably her last, to the dull-witted undertakers of Lourdes. Pity the poor woman! To start with she had married a Spanish violinist, a devout Catholic and a man of strict observance. After giving her two daughters, their marriage had fallen apart, but he had refused to grant her a divorce. Her life after that had been marked by a succession of great artistic passions; she was an accomplished pianist herself and belonged to a family in which all the talents had been assiduously cultivated. How could she have fallen in love with an ordinary rich man? Not her! After a long string of flute players, sunset painters, elegiac poets, somber cellists, not to speak of an assortment of composers, novelists, and philologists, she had met her first sculptor: the handsome, inspired Fernand Buzon, who swept her away to his cluttered atelier on the heights of Montmartre. Buzon made her a mother twice more, first of Jenny and then of Laurette, but he proved to be an irritable loner, obsessed by his own pursuits to the point of ignoring her, and forgetting the little girls' existence.

And so they had separated. Fernand had closed himself up in his den, working furiously and seldom going out, and then only to meet his artist friends in the small cafés of la Butte. Mona had taken to the road with the little girls, sometimes giving concerts to charmed audiences at elegant resorts, and at other times working as a scullery maid or kitchen help. When things became too unbearable, she would send her daughters to Buzon and find herself an artist of her own, sufficiently successful and provident to give her some comfort for a few weeks. The girls' schooling had been wonderfully erratic as a consequence, which they didn't mind; in fact, it did enlarge their range of experience and taste for learning. But they had a distinct preference for their life of high adventure with their mother as against the more steady existence in their father's Montmartre atelier. That studio! It was like living in the Stone Age dwelling of a big-game hunter, encumbered with the dismembered carcasses of wild animals; to make a living, Fernand had been forced to humble his artistic ambitions, and he was now in the business of manufacturing papier-mâché masks, Mardi-Gras monsters, and various other contraptions for the Folies-Bergère shows. The little girls were sleeping in a shaky bed under their own skylight at one end of the loft while Fernand was furiously creating cardboard fantasies at the other end, or ardently fornicating with his mistress, the perky Pinsonnette.

Mona was through with her latest love affair, and she had also lost her latest job in a small health resort in the Pyrénées, when she met Lionel. He was convalescing from a bout with tuberculosis, and immersed in his astronomical study of the Cheops pyramid, on the verge of some mysterious, long-sought discovery. As soon as his sick leave was over, he told her, he would return to Algiers, where he was holding a reasonably good job at the observatory. And then, he added as an afterthought, he would get married. Yes, he explained to Mona, who could hardly hide her dismay, such was his plan; although he had trouble remembering the lady's name, he had promised to marry her immediately upon his return.

That unexpected obstacle only bolstered Mona's decision to get her man. She invented a reason to justify going to Algiers herself, and took her daughters along with her. They were already there when he arrived; what's more, she had been able to identify Lionel's fiancée, and had gathered a full intelligence report on her. She confronted him with the facts: The lady was a common five-francs-a-throw prostitute attached to one of the low-class brothels in the old city. Lionel was surprised to hear the news; his impression of her had been quite different, but one never knows, he added with a puzzled look on his face. In short, Lionel accepted this accident of fate with astronomical equanimity. He invited Mona and the girls to share his tiny apartment, immediately forgetting his earlier commitment. . . . In like manner, he had once sat on the bridge of a warship cruising along the Baltic coast during the war, his mind happily lost among the brilliant constellations rolling in the heavens above, when suddenly the deck had gone up at a strange angle under him and shouts from the second mate had warned him that the ship had just been grounded on a sandbank: Lionel had forgotten that he was the skipper.

Although he was a scientist, and a reputable one, that type of behavior made him look very much like an artist; Mona felt that she had found the final haven, a man who lived in a poetic fantasy called *l'astronomie*, and who was paid a pretty good salary for it. And so she decided to put up with all his strangeness, and for several years they had been leading a reasonably organized life between Algiers and Paris. . . . Until that terrible last illness. . . .

Alone in my darkened room, I stand in front of the window; the clouds have gone away and the night is resplendent with all of Lionel's stars. The coldness of the wooden floor numbs my naked feet, and I wonder if Laurette has been able to go to sleep; and I try to picture her, a few feet away from me, behind a thin wall. It is such a small house, I can feel it around me like a light shell. . . . We are three travelers in that tiny mousetrap, dreaming, aching, hoping against hope, lost in despair, sitting, lying, standing; and the sudden disappearance of a complete stranger has just thrown us into a completely new and unexpected triangular association. My feeling for Laurette has reached a new intensity, a higher level of purity, and to prove it I know that I will have to endorse her own sense of responsibility toward her mother, and make it my own. Can I do that? Mona belongs to a world totally alien to me but. . . . As I look up toward the stars, I see that Lionel is already there. Black on blue-black, I can faintly follow the slow flight of the great clumsy bird between phosphorescent banks; the last ill-designed pterodactyl to escape from the planet's gravity, flying forever after into the eternal beyond. . . .

This is Mona's second tragedy since I met her, not so long ago: One of her daughters, Jenny, Laurette's sister, had died suddenly a few months before. Since Jenny's husband, François, had become my friend, my involvement with that attractive and disastrous family seemed to be growing apace with each new catastrophe.

Indeed it all started a few months before her death, when Jenny had left François for an evil, dissolute older man; and I well remember the day it happened. . . . Because that night I had decided to do my best to keep François's mind away from his troubles, and I had taken him out to dinner. . . . Sitting across from him I tried to talk indifferently about this and that; but it soon proved quite impossible not to use words and images that sounded like allusions to his misfortune. The more irritated I became at my ineptitude, the more I found myself saying the wrong things. It seemed absurd—but how can one avoid at all times any allusion to women, girls, marriage, infidelity, or any of the many such other subjects common to all bachelors' conversations? And on each occasion I was doubly crushed to see my friend's handsome features wince, as if he had been knifed from behind.

After an hour of that reciprocal torture, I suggested that we go see a movie. It occurred to me that there was a new Pagnol film with Raimu playing nearby close to the carrefour de l'Odéon; François was relieved by the prospect, and we bought our tickets. And so we sat there, side by side, mute with horror and disbelief as the story of the unfortunate baker, Raimu, and his aggressively fickle wife, Ginette Leclerc, unfolded before us. *La Femme du Boulanger*, Marcel Pagnol's light *tragédie de moeurs*, was surely the most disastrous choice I could possibly have made. Had it been a bad film, we could have left in a huff! But we did not have that excuse to run away from Ginette's hypnotic thighs, or Raimu's eloquent groans of self-pity: Here was the fine art of cuckoldry interpreted for you by two of the most convincing artists of all time. It was hardly up to me to suggest that we leave; and even less up to François! What a mess.

That silly adventure had made our friendship more solid than before. Perhaps François had felt that my style of blundering was a perverted expression of my ominous desire to help; in any case a great sense of solidarity had developed between us after that painful moment.

The conversion of Mona's attitude was obvious as of the very day following the burial. All of a sudden I found myself in the position of a respected son-in-law who had taken a few days off from his important work in the city to visit his wife and her family. With not a care in the world, Mona suggested an automobile excursion to the famed Gavarnie mountain ridge.

> *J'aime le son du cor, le soir au fond des bois. . . .*

Nature's eloquent procession was unfolding slowly on both sides of our rented car, craggy peaks looming above the melancholy forests where Roland had died, fighting the Saracens in ancient days. Gavarnie opened before us, an imposing council of mountains pressed shoulder to shoulder as far as the eye would reach; the temple of nature dividing the kingdoms of France on my right, Spain on my left, the twin seats of man's iniquity.

In the intemporal afternoon light we are gliding noiselessly, Laurette and I, hands softly clasped under the thick wool blanket; and in front of us our mother and duenna (who had insisted she would be more comfortable on the jump seat), her presence now forgotten. The distant driver himself has become an abstraction, as life starts afresh with the silent union of our hands. Reunited at last, yes; in all but in deed we are now married. In the highest sense of the word, indeed that is: the mystical. But the king's sword is lying between us, dividing our blood. Our vow of chastity to God (or is it to Vivian?) will hold us forever apart, and forever we will love each other.

16

*White-on-white combat in Finland.—As to being
a demi-Jew . . . —Gregor in the hole.—Hitler's nature.
—The Germans' no-contest victory.—I choose to stay in
Occupied France. —A last letter from Henry Miller,
a last journey to the Right Bank.—Buying my first
identity card. —40 million people on the run.
—Learning the hard way.*

In Finland the boreal night is alight with white-on-white combat building up in stages on the frozen lakes, bursts of fire searing the dark. In the forests buried beneath the snow, phantom heroes perish and freeze into instant statues in the ice of the rivers. My sole employee, big Helga, who is blond and Jewish, from Lithuania, and pleasantly horse-faced, has told me about those enigmatic northern lands she had traveled as a child, silver lands lost in their own immensity. She described the thrilling resurgence of nature after the interminable winter, the overnight burst of flowers, the awakening of the woods and prairies. And the indigestion of life, love, and sunshine; one went quite crazy with it all during those endless days of the brief summer.

Helga, who was a towering person and sturdy of build, was madly in love with a depraved dwarf. He was a genius, she claimed, and she loved him even though he was so small. She talked constantly about him, but we never met. What was he exactly? A philosopher, a revolutionary artist? It was not clear. As Helga talked about him, her big teeth sparkled; that's how much she cared for him. But that woman of passion was also rather droll and full of ingenuity. One day, out of a clear blue sky, she asked me if we were not, by any chance, coreligionists?

"Eh? You mean Jewish? Not me, I'm Protestant. Yes ma'am, a French Huguenot."

"Ah," she said, "that's funny. And with a name like Kahane."

"Jewish, non-Jewish," I answered, "what's all that business about? Do I have to belong or not belong to something I don't know or care one hoot about?"

"What you care about is something else," she said. "All I want to point out is that your name is Jewish, and that if ever those Nazis should invade France—God forbid!—then they would hang you by the neck, my pretty little bossie, or by anything else protuberant they might find on you."

"Who cares! If it comes to that, I can always change my name," I said blithely. "Anyway, it's not me who first decided not to be a Jew, it's my father. His family was half religious, and half agnostic anyway. But for him there was no question: He was not for or against being a Jew—he was against religion. And then he married my mother who was nominally a Catholic . . ."

"How come that made you into a French Huguenot, as you say?" Helga asked, imitating me.

"That would look like a logical crossbreed, no? The truth is that at boarding school, when I was about eleven, all the kids were Catholics. They didn't believe in anything of that sort, of course, but they went to mass, heard the sermons, confessed their sins, and went through all that rigamarole. What could I do? I could only adopt the opposite course and state my protest by becoming a Protestant. . . . What better reason?"

"But that's a religion too. Did you practice it?"

"To me it was more an excuse to get out of school, as I was supposed to go to the Protestant service in town twice a week. There were five other Protestants like me, five hoodlums, and we had the time of our lives on those outings. In the red-light district we were known as terrorists."

"Just like you, mon petit Voltaire," said Helga with a smirk, as she aimed at my nose with one of her infernal paper balls, and hit it right on target.

That put a temporary lull to our argument, but all of this had set me to thinking. I had rejected the Jewish thing for so long that it had become a mental habit, as well as a self-protective device, to continue doing so. I didn't even want to admit to myself my curiosity for that half of myself that I had thought I could erase simply by denying it. . . . Once, in the old days, some kids had started asking me questions in school about my Jewish name, and I had in turn asked my father to explain. But he had dismissed the whole issue as pure bunk, declaring that no one owes any debt to the past, that we all start from scratch, and create our fate for ourselves.

Well, I rather subscribed to that view, although you should see it as an ideal rather than as a statistic. . . . My father practically never spoke to me, but I was well aware of his distaste for family traditions, conventional beliefs, and religions. . . . Although it must be said that such an attitude was unexpected on the part of a man who was so keen on good manners, and had the poise of a perfect gentleman. However, to think of him as "a Jew" was indeed preposterous. What did that mean?

But hadn't he died, precisely, because he was a Jew? He had spent his entire life denying his spiritual affiliation, when all of a sudden Hitlerian racism had branded him as an ethnic Jew—just like any other denizen of the ghetto, notwithstanding his perfect taste in neckties and walking sticks. That was surely one infernal gimmick: to make a man ashamed of his own blood. Or rather, and even worse: to make him ashamed of having abjured his own blood! There is no denying that he had tried to run away from it all; and here he was, caught by Hitler's dialectics, forced to admit his betrayal of his own race, and forced to return to it, and embrace it, and fight for it. Or die.

Hitler will never stop winning. The very day after my father's death, my own grandfather, whom I had never dreamed could entertain any racist feelings, blurted angrily to my mother: "Remember: I told you not to marry a Jew!"

Fortunately for her, I don't think she was able to hear or comprehend those insane words; but they did stay with me. If that's how one half of my progenitors feels about the other half, where do I stand? What would Montaigne, Picasso, or Marcel Proust, all of them half-Jews, have to tell me about my predicament? How does one function as an ethnic centaur, when you don't even know which part is Jewish, the front or the rear? Yes, a centaur: four legs to flee with, and a head on top to think with; well, perhaps I'm better off than most as a centaur, when all is said and done. To see noble men so easily reduced to idiotic confusion, as my grandfather had shown himself to be, this can only strengthen my resolve to believe

in no one but myself, and to outmatch the worst cynics I encounter on my way.

Why subscribe to those infantile categories? What does it
mean to be a Catholic, a Communist, a Huguenot, or a good
old Jew? It's only a way to situate yourself above the other
groups if your group is on top, or to suffer like the damned if
your group is at the bottom of the pile.

The Jews had often been on top during their long history,
and they had also been at the bottom, even more often. And
yet they went on as if the only thing that mattered in the
world was to exist as a Jew, even when it meant nothing but
pain and infamy.

You could see a good illustration of that proclivity in the
Jewish section of Paris, around rue des Rosiers, which no one
would have called a ghetto because the word was so terribly
un-French; but also because there were no city ordinances,
no laws, and no walls to force them to stay there. It was simply a point of concentration, a Jewish neighborhood, and the
medieval streets with old French names—rues de la Ville-
l'Evêque, du Temple, or des Blancs-Manteaux—had become
adjusted in the course of time to that nucleus which, small as
it is, was making the city different. There you found the old-
timers, the fellows with the big black hats and the haunted
eyes, the kids in yarmulkes, the busy, nervous old men in tatters, the ragpickers and the ragamuffins. You were deafened
by the haggling around street merchants and sour-smelling
stores, and you wondered about the extraordinary tough-
ness of the feeling, about the extraordinary force of the vibra-
tion that held all those people together, absolutely intent on
doing their thing, although they were plunged in an ambiance
so totally alien to it, being that of Paris, under the silver and
blue skies of Ile-de-France.

The French were not receptive at all to the Jewish problem
simply because that Jewish thing could not be identified in
clear-cut Cartesian terms. The French concept of nation had
become in their minds a legal reality that would always have
precedence over religious duties and affiliations. The Catholics and Protestants had accepted that, and they considered
themselves as French citizens first and foremost. But not so
the Jews: They lived in France in a sort of temporary, tran-
sient fashion, and it was clear that to them being Jewish was
the only reality that mattered.

There were of course some old Jewish families, especially

in the east of the country, that had been there for so long that they had practically forgotten that they were Jewish; they had found acceptance within French society precisely because they were no longer real Jews. They were active and successful as lawyers, doctors, or bankers; but they seldom tried their luck at politics because of an invisible barrier, which they felt by instinct they should never cross. Jews who become cabinet ministers or heads of government in France are a rarity: Léon Blum was only given that job as a compromise between extremes during the innovative days of the Front Populaire, mainly because everyone felt that the man was flawed, that he would crumble under the strain; and indeed, that is exactly what had happened. The choice of Léon Blum may have been dictated, officially, by a desire to stress France's support of racial tolerance at a time when Hitler was abusing the Jews. Whatever the reasons, however, the net result of that experience could be seen in the debacle of the French Left, the fall of the Spanish Republic—due to the French nonintervention—the accelerated rise of the dictators, and a world war for tomorrow. And of course Blum's self-inflicted defeat has fueled the latent anti-Semitism of the French.

Which is nothing new. That deep-seated feeling had already been revealed rather savagely in *l'Affaire Dreyfus*, earlier, when the entire French army, supported by the conservative half of the country, had conspired to dishonor, expel, and condemn a French artillery captain simply because his name was Dreyfus. The scandal turned into a national crisis, but when the republican Left finally won and the conspiracy was crushed, the country had remained divided. Even among the true democrats, many were torn between their principles and their secret belief that the Jews could never integrate themselves completely within the national body, however hard and honestly they might try.

The truth of the matter, when all is said and done, is that "race," "religion," "nation," and "state" exist in different parts of the mind, and are hardly compatible with each other; in fact, each one perpetually seeks to eliminate the other three in an effort to gain control over the individual person. But for a Jew those four notions are four aspects of only one reality, which is *Jewishness*. A Frenchman will never accept that. The separation of the French State from the Roman church has indeed become the very symbol of France's republican democracy, and it took the efforts of many generations to accomplish that historical divorce.

Where does all that leave us? Where does it leave *me?*
Now that I have been forced to become a little more con-
scious of my Hebraic half, I seem to be developing a taste for
Jewish low-life. From time to time I walk down the rue des
Francs-Bourgeois, trying to identify my roots among the
Talmudic students and the street peddlers. I consider Berg-
son, Marx, Freud, the Jewish empire builders of our time.
And indeed, there are flashes of recognition, distant echoes,
both in the streets and in the books: I become more aware of
their soul, of their consanguinity as a vast diversified group.
But to me all this remains dry, and alien, very distant. And
too grasping, too demanding, exclusive. I despise all organized religions; to me religion is an intensely personal matter, which clearly means that it would be even more absurd
for me to turn myself into a Jew than into a true Christian. Or
to become a true French citizen, or a true British subject, for
that matter! Being born of mixed blood and conflicting cul-
tures, I find myself compelled to think for myself, and to generate my own environment.

I firmly believe that human society would not survive five
minutes more, in view of its well-known self-destructive
tendencies, if it were not being held solidly together by a
secret prospect in which everyone shares, although no one
knows about it. And also by a network of superhumanity
comprising good people as well as burnt-out artists, and
Bodhisattvas of all ranks and colors. The banal everyday life
blends easily with the miraculous; there is no event, private or public, that does not have a meaning much finer than
the one so loudly broadcast to ourselves, by ourselves. Society, ethnicity, clan, or family is only a metaphor; a gesture of
immediate, consanguine and neighborly solidarity inspired by
the unseen, unrevealed, but constantly inspiring example of
the Greater Humanity; of that network unified by capillarity
through a flow of blood that is no longer a red liquid, but a
revelation of the Outcome. But I would never call that superior reality the Great Hierarchy, as Vivian would, but the
Great Synarchy, or even the Great Anarchy, since its function
is first and foremost to liberate us from all constraints.

To declare war is all very well; but it is meaningless if it
doesn't create hard news, hair-raising headlines, and heartfelt
indignation. And so the French high command had hurled
some of its elite commandos—of which there were very
few—into the Warndt forest to capture a few acres of land

from the Germans. A useless enterprise, and very costly, since the woods had been meticulously mined by the enemy. The Germans retreated in good order, letting the French blow themselves up in their best heroic style. The cost: four hundred young men killed in that short battle of shadows (at least according to the official reports, which are never known to inflate the size of a defeat), plus hundreds more who lost their legs and balls as they fell running over the booby traps. Few Germans died, if any, but the French communiqués went on and on at a feverish pace about *"la bataille de la Warndt"* for several weeks. Not a peep from the enemy. But on the day Hitler gave the order, his troops just walked back over the territory occupied by the French and took it from them almost without firing a shot.

So there you are. We all knew that war is, by definition, stupid, cruel, and criminal. And already now, in the first days, we get solid proof of that well-established fact, and a perfect demonstration of the high command's total incompetence, of its moronic irresponsibility, and of its sadistic instincts. Those old generals don't risk anything by ordering a select bunch of young heroes to go out and get slaughtered and castrated; indeed, it's a good way to wipe out the competition from the dance floor.

Should the war be allowed to continue, then, after such an illuminating prologue? Can we seriously believe that the old idiots are going to improve in the course of time? That their defeats will make them wiser? Their eventual victories more cautious and more humane? Isn't it already obvious that the French army doesn't have a chance; that the French people are just not interested in fighting another war; and that the French government is so totally corrupt, morally and intellectually, that it will never be able to pursue a coherent policy at any time, in peace or in war?

So why go any further? Why not put the totality of the problem on another level, play the game, give Hitler his hegemony on paper; and then civilize him, treat him like the Greeks treated the Romans, make a snob out of him, dress him up in fancy rags, sit him in a princely carriage and drive him along the Promenade des Anglais, take him out to supper with the whole gang, Cocteau, Sartre, Josephine Baker, etc. Corrupt him to death, give full play to the Nero in him, feed him on a diet of Spanish fly and hangman's rope— But I've let myself be carried away by my subject; and yet certainly irony is not enough of a remedy against war! What I should say here rather is that the root of war is found in politics; politics demonstrate our failure to govern ourselves; and war demonstrates the failure of politics. If we would only consider the causes of each war recorded in history, study its true motivations, as well as the methods of intoxication thanks to which two or more peoples have been duped into destroying each other, it would become obvious to us then that wars are only fought because we are too lazy to think with our own minds. By letting sick old men and cannibal politicians do our mental work for us, we exhibit a weakness that is morally worse than all the war crimes put together.

War doesn't pay. And yet it takes much more true courage to fight against war than to die in battle. Where were the men of real courage in 1939, in 1940? Their voice was never heard. No pope, no spiritual leader, no great thinker ever came forth boldly to denounce the dishonor and folly of this primitive carnage. No effort was ever made to elevate the moral horizon, to propose to all a higher vision of the human destiny. Hitler may have felt himself strong enough to defy any military power, but he would have been reduced to dust by a Gandhi. A full-size prophet was required to shake the German people out of its violent stupor, rather than fleets of flying fortresses.

In March Daladier was swept away from the scene.

The Bull of the Vaucluse, as the newspapers fondly called him, fell from his bronze horse and his own troops trampled him quickly into political pulp, and finished him off. Paul Reynaud, a midget economist with a squeaky voice and a tiny face like an Inca sculpture, was now the new master of the French nation.

The powerful stench of corruption was everywhere; war industries produced for their happy owners more millions than machine guns. The French air force was equipped with warplanes chain-produced in the factories of one Marcel Bloch, and known as *cercueils volants*, or flying coffins. The Bloch fighter planes would be no match for the Luftwaffe's Stukas, everyone knew it; but the general feeling was that this technical handicap would give a chance for the French pilots to show how much brighter, quicker, and bolder they were than their German opponents, simply by virtue of being French. Meanwhile, Marcel Bloch was well on his way to becoming the richest man in France.

There was a lot of political activity all around, as the vultures started wheeling above the scene of the imminent slaughter. The repulsive Pierre Laval, with his white necktie and horse-dealer style, had become a front-page attraction, as well as old Maréchal Pétain, whose doctors had freed him from his mothballs. Pétain's standing as a figure of fatherly authority was mostly due to the fact that he had crushed a mutiny of soldiers who were refusing to go on fighting, during the First World War, and had thousands of them shot in cold blood. Although eighty, he seemed quite able to renew that feat, and such talent might well come in handy: The French army was badly underequipped, untrained, and for the most part quite unwilling to fight.

What was truly sinister about Laval and Pétain's comeback, however, was the constant references to their good relations with the enemy camp. Laval had been an active supporter of Mussolini, and Pétain of Franco. They were, therefore, in a perfect position to serve as Hitler's fifth column.

As to Pétain's favorite disciple, the lanky Colonel de Gaulle, he was also positioning himself as close to the government as he could possibly get. The French public started hearing more and more about that politically minded soldier, but they didn't fancy him much, both because he was too tall and too intellectually arrogant. There was something truly disturbing about a colonel with brains, especially one who was nearly twice as tall as the average Frenchman.

A black and heavy sky hangs over the cemetery like an imprecation. A nasty wind blows from all sides, twisting the skinny poplars, and flattening big drops of lukewarm rain on everyone's face. We are all huddled together, with the big Russian priest in our midst, who's fighting hard to hold on to his high hat and long robes without losing his book. The wind tears at his long beard as he starts his chant in a deep rolling bass, as some human thunder responding to the elements.

The implacable sadness of the clouds above us invites us to bow our heads toward the rectangular pit where, suspended by two ropes, the mortal remains of my friend Gregor are being lowered. Brother, pal, my second self, here's my fistful of earth, make good use of it.

There aren't many people here in this cemetery at Thiais. My friends, Edouard and Claude, and on the other side of the hole, swaying in the wind, the tall black silhouette of Gregor's grandfather. Clinging to him desperately is another silhouette, the shorter one of Gregor's father, a middle-aged man weeping like a small child. I wondered what that strange son of his had meant to him. Had he, had anyone ever understood anything about Gregor? His ugliness made one flee from him as from an incurable, infectious malady. Nobody could stand the intensity of his relentless frustration; when he turned his suffering into comedy, as he often did, it only made things worse. Many will be relieved to learn that he won't be coming around anymore to strike fear in them and ruin their appetite. Speaking in Russian, the orthodox priest eulogizes Corporal Louchine, who died for France of a bad cold on a hard cot in a military hospital. Such an absurd ending is in keeping, somehow, with the life of a misfit. Why, the poor bastard didn't even have the courage to live! All right then, you raving maniac, you've got what you've deserved all along, a hole in the ground. Gregor! Answer me, Gregor! Did they bury you in your smart uniform, you miserable cur? How's the coffin, does it stink enough for your taste? Look above your grave at the vengeful sky hanging over your filthy Thiais cemetery. Look at that sepulchral place—it's all yours for a thousand years. Let your ridiculous body rot away in this black soil; perhaps one day from this compost will spring a twisted tree; your dubious reality will lose shape and consistency, like a statue of Pain, slowly eroded by the elements. A frayed image in my memory. It didn't take long, I'm already about to forget you, old buddy, to bury you once and for all. You should never have been born. You know that, don't you? Why then did you come to haunt me on this dark and humid planet?

Be on your way, *adieu*.

How many Frenchmen have ever read *Mein Kampf*, either before or since the war was declared? How many statesmen have had the curiosity to do so? The newspapers make acid comments on the fact that young German couples are obliged to buy their own copy of *Mein Kampf* as if it were the family Bible—thanks to which the cunning Führer pockets mountains of tax-free royalties. We are therefore advised not to read the book because it would make Hitler earn more. And of course the book is dismissed as pure drivel anyway by journalists who have hardly glanced at it.

That's typical of the French attitude of the time: 1939. Although the country's world influence as an imperial nation has been on the wane for such a long time, and although the upheavals of the thirties further weakened it, to the point where it can no longer govern itself, the French nation still wants to believe that its superiority is eternal. All the signs of national decadence are seen as negligible accidents; and yet one can't seriously worry about Hitler since we have Jean Giraudoux, and the Académie Française, and the Eiffel Tower.

Very few French people speak any foreign languages; more can understand classical Latin than modern English, and then only among the Catholic clergy. A visit to London would be a memorable, once-in-a-lifetime adventure; as to Germany, the less said, the better. One does not even mention the hereditary enemy in polite society.

That's all very trite and absurd, of course. The truth is that France is now a very old nation which fears the brutal impact of life; Hitler is too dangerous, too raucous a reality for the French to confront. And so one prefers to ignore what the man says, to wit: that the ungenerous, humiliating treatment of Germany by the Allies when they dictated the terms of the Versailles treaty is the only cause of the German resurgence, and of his own fanatical dedication to it. When the French decided to occupy the Ruhr shortly after the war so as to prevent the rebirth of Germany's industrial power, they gave to the Nazi movement the impetus it needed. And so we, the French, made Hitler, and he tells us so. Isn't that a piece of information worth thinking about?

We made Hitler, and now that he's in business, who can stop him? Here he is, foaming at the mouth, talking about a Europe pregnant with 250 million Germans, and about the world hegemony of the white Aryan race—of which he is himself such a ludicrous specimen! Of course he is an illiterate maniac; but he is for real. Even when he expresses his deep scorn and distrust for that very German people to which he wants to give the entire world! On the one hand he wants to turn them into demigods; on the other he treats them like a sauerkraut nation, and the entire Aryan race like the scum of the earth.

If we had the courage to confront such insanities and wade through those contradictions, perhaps we would acquire a broader vision of the problem. Hitler's hysteria is caused to a large extent by his jealousy for other peoples' success, Jews,

British, Americans; but essentially by his fascination for the French model. Because it so happens that we did not merely invent Hitler; we created his prototype, Napoleon himself. But to us, Napoleon is our famous emperor, one of the dozen greatest men who ever lived, whereas Hitler is a bandit and a madman.

But let's give it a closer look. Just as Hitler, an Austrian, treated Germans like dirt, so did Napoleon, a Corsican, with the French. For each one of them racism, be it German or French, was therefore merely a vehicle to achieve his own personal conquest of the world.

It is surprising that the literary and philosophical tradition of Germany should have ended up spawning a Hitler—but what about us, the French? It took us two hundred years, and generation after generation of philosophers and utopians, and all kinds of thinkers and talkers, to conceive the social philosophy that found its ultimate expression in the great French Revolution of 1789. Just to figure out that lucid three-pronged motto: *"Liberté, Egalité, Fraternité"*—bringing out with such felicity and concision one of the most innovative social programs ever formulated—that took more than ordinary talent, it took genius.

The early days of the Revolution were happily devoted to the discovery of live democracy. The various populations of which France was comprised were treated as equals, and the laws of the republic were translated into Basque, Breton, Catalan, German, Italian, so as to show that the new principles of freedom and equality would benefit all minorities within the republic and not, as was usually the case, the majority, and the political establishment in Paris. But that initial climate of elation didn't last very long; the centralist tendency soon took the upper hand, and the state was consolidated, in 1790, by means of a war declaration to all "the Kings of Europe."

At that point it became obvious that exporting the Revolution would require a national army, thanks to which formal unity was imposed on the entire country. It became illegal to use any language but Parisian French. The way was now open for Napoleon to take the freedom away from those loud-mouthed liberators of the world. The soldiers of the nation's army, singing the heroic songs of the republic, defeated the kings of Europe one by one—but only to build Napoleon an empire, with one man on top instead of a dozen. Napoleon

killed and mercilessly plundered entire populations, to which
he had announced himself as liberator. Between Napoleon and
Hitler, there is only a time difference: two centuries.

Speaking of time, we could also say that after two thousand
years, we are still living under Roman occupation here in Europe, and everywhere else in the world. Our political system
is a direct imitation of the Roman imperial power structure
based on conquest, exploitation, and on the downgrading of
the individual. The French republic, with its many colonies in
Africa and elsewhere, is a democracy in name only, and it can
only continue as a unified nation thanks to war, power diplomacy, the armaments race, and constant confrontations with
the hereditary enemy—which used to be England in the old
days, and now is Germany. The cost of national pride was one
and a half million young men killed in the First World War,
the flower of France's manhood, plus millions maimed, out of
a total population of 40 million. And here we are, twenty
years later, having pushed Germany into a frenzied desire for
revenge, about to start all over again. Like an aged prize-
fighter too groggy to understand that he must quit, here's
the French champion laboriously putting up his dukes. He
loves his punishment.

At least the British have their own Hitler equivalent in the
person of Winston Churchill. Not only is he as bad a painter
as Hitler himself, but he can also scare people stiff with his
healthy disregard for human lives. Old Winnie will show
those Krauts! A prize bulldog inoculated with the national
rage, his mug spiked with a bazookalike cigar, here is a secret
weapon of whom we have every right to be jealous.

We're bragging a lot about France's superiority, over here,
but it's all on paper. Paul Reynaud has Paris plastered with
immense posters proclaiming, "NOUS VAINCRONS CAR NOUS
SOMMES LES PLUS FORTS—Paul Reynaud," but the taxi drivers and the street merchants shrug at the little man's boast,
commenting, *"Oh là là, il travaille drôlement du chapeau le
petit père Reynaud."* And they snap their fingers in awe. . . .
Meanwhile, almost without firing a shot, the Germans have
overrun Scandinavia, kicking a French expeditionary force out
of Narvik on the Norwegian coast, thus protecting their access to iron ore. The French cabinet had taken a victory in
Narvik for granted, and as France was learning the painful
news, another jumbo poster is making its début on the walls:
"LA ROUTE DU FER EST DEFINITIVEMENT COUPÉE—signed:

Paul Reynaud." Hah! I wonder what Goebbels thinks of the French government's idea of a poster war?

Things were taking a very ominous turn; during the first six months, the war in which France was engaged appeared as an abstraction, spreading around a little fever, the kind of vicarious pleasure one expects to get from a Grand Guignol horror play. Well, the blood and guts was getting much closer. Hasty changes were made. People who had predicted the Allies' victory within one year, not so long ago, were now leaving France in droves. As to Kurt Enoch, he had enlisted in the French army and had left Paris, where his distribution business was being disbanded. The first book of the Unicorn Press, *The Grapes of Wrath*, was in production, with four more to follow, at Imprimerie Darantière in Dijon—and we decided to hold them up as long as a clear decision couldn't be made.

One morning at the office Helga came to me, red-eyed; she hugged me between her plump arms and kissed me on the nose. There was no need to exchange words, promises; she had to leave, although she had no clear idea for what destination. She conveyed to me in so many sobs that I was absolutely mad to stay behind; but she well knew that it was useless to argue with me. I would die soon, she knew it, but as a man in love, and so. . . . All the refugees from Germany and Eastern Europe who had flocked to Paris in the past years were now desperately trying to invent a new temporary future for themselves. Where to go? Everyone had been so slow in deciding to leave that there was much confusion and despair everywhere.

Conversely, my mother had decided to leave the South and come back to Paris in July, as soon as the school year ended. Would she be less safe in the Neuilly apartment than in Dax? At least we would all be regrouped within walking distance from one another, my mother and the kids, my grandparents and myself. I felt as if I were receiving insistent intemporal messages from my father, that I should endeavor to help my mother as best I could throughout the years to come.

My decision to stay was comforted by the fact that, since Vivian had decided not to budge from Paris, Laurette would also stay. Since the sad days in Lourdes, a new level of amorous friendship had been reached between us, and I felt that my very life depended on that current of joyful pain; I felt as if I were bound to her by an umbilical cord through which she was instilling in me an erotic secret, the mysterious fragrance of her own desire. I knew that my boundless love for her had become important to her, that she depended more and more on it as an emotional food necessary to her sustenance, just as I depended on her soft presence to reach a curious form of ecstasy of my own that always left me weak with wonder and frustration.

Mona also had returned to Paris, to be close to Laurette. She was living in a room her daughter had rented for herself, on rue Hautefeuille, not far from Vivian's ashram, but never used. At that point, rumors about German fifth column infiltrations began to circulate. On the ninth of May, German troops invade the Grand Duchy of Luxembourg, an easy prey. General Gamelin, the top French strategist, immediately responds to this provocation by sending troops to Belgium, and as far north as Holland. On the fifteenth, the French are smashed at Sedan by the Wehrmacht, with a display of stunning superiority; the survivors are encircled and captured. So much for General Gamelin.

That defeat was demoralizing in more ways than one: France's defenses on its eastern border with Germany depended on the extensive system called the Maginot line, to which tons of self-congratulatory articles and speeches had been devoted over the years. The only trouble with that line of defense was that it didn't reach the sea and that a wide gap was left open in front of the Belgian border; to this day the reason for this gap has not been explained. The Germans started the First World War by invading Belgium; why wouldn't they do the same this time also? Well, they did; and my cousin Jacques, who was stationed in the glorious Maginot line, was trapped in it together with the entire garrison, and duly encircled by the German paratroopers who were raining from the sky, wave after wave.

Paratroopers—yes! The Germans had made a specialty of that form of warfare and it would have been easy for the French high command to study the enemy's tactical innovation, but they had failed to do so, probably because the War Academy had no text books or lectures to provide on the subject. The same could be said about the devastating effect of the Germans' air support, the extreme mobility of their independent mechanized units, and the extraordinary intelligence and sabotage work which everywhere opened the way for their armies. And yet the French generals remained geared to a war of fortresses. For General Gamelin, whom

Paris-Soir said was a student of philosophy and an admirer of the Stoics, this would have been a fine occasion to swallow a double dose of hemlock. Instead of which, he squabbles with his general staff, mopes around and resigns, much too late, in favor of Weygand, another hero from the ancient times.

As the Allies attempt a desperate getaway at Dunkirk, the highways from the frontiers of the Low Countries to the woodlands of Normandy begin clogging up with people. This irrational fear is provoked by the fifth column, and constantly magnified by the strafing from the fighter planes, paralyzing the army's abortive attempts to move in the opposite direction, and wiping out all hope of tactical counterattack. The French government does nothing to stem this human tide in which they doubtless see a manifestation of democracy on the march. One gets the uneasy feeling that this government is itself larded with saboteurs.

In the voluptuous June weather, Paris is turning into some immense ghost town. Half-hearted preparations are made to contain a German attack; the police are wearing helmets and sporting rifles. One morning, on the Champs-Elysées, I see a column of twelve garbage trucks being fitted with machine guns by a troop of white-haired veterans. Whose bright idea is that? Paul Reynaud himself, I suppose, the little fellow is so resourceful! It seems that only the older generation of concierges, the Paris janitors, is left to guard the city, and those witnesses to the many jolly and ludicrous tragedies of our daily lives have been given helmets and whistles to fulfill their new function. It's no small comfort to see them emerge from their dark and cavernous lodges, smelling of cabbage or lentil soup, and take their stand at the street corners with so resolute an air, broomstick in hand, and ready for just anything.

At her suggestion, I went to visit Kurt Enoch's young wife, one afternoon, in their Ile Saint-Louis apartment overlooking the slow-moving river. It was our first encounter, and a bit of a surprise to me because I had not pictured Kurt's wife as being so young and pretty.

She had two messages for me from Kurt, who had managed to reach her by telephone the day before. First of all, he wanted to persuade me to leave Paris immediately; he was himself trying to find a way to get out of the country with his wife and their two little girls. And he further suggested that I take his car, which had a full tank of gas plus some reserve jerry cans, and drive myself and his own family south, to safety. And then we would all meet near the Spanish border, if everything went well—

She stopped, looked at me, and made a little helpless gesture of the hand. "I can't drive a car," she explained.

"Well," I said, "I don't know if I could manage to drive one myself. . . . But apart from that, I just don't feel that I can leave Paris. It's hard to explain, but I have many personal reasons, you understand?" She looked at me curiously, and I felt myself blushing like an idiot under her gaze.

"But you're Jewish, aren't you?" she asked in a cutting, urgent voice.

And so I had to blurt out the whole ancient story all over again, as fast as I could.

"Listen, with your name and a British passport as your only identity paper, how do you expect to survive? You're out of your mind. Please leave with me. Kurt expects you to. He is a good man and he likes you, you know? You shouldn't disregard that."

Of course she was right; but still I trusted my own madness more than her wisdom. I told her so. She shook my hand at the door; I wished her luck with lame, absurd words. Of course she would find someone to drive her; they'd be only too happy. . . . She looked at me gravely, with a little smile, and said nothing.

I found a small room in Mona's building on rue Hautefeuille, next to her own, which I rented from the concierge for a few francs, and I moved some of my dandy's paraphernalia to my humble *chambre de bonne*. The Neuilly apartment was left unoccupied, awaiting my mother's return.

Each day was a long wait, listening to the radio that kept offering nothing but incoherent information. Mona would offer to brew tea for me at all times of the day or night, and I would sit down and look over the pictures, old photos, and the jumble of fans, knickknacks, and jewelry on display everywhere, while she was running her hands on the piano or playing a game of solitaire. A few elderly musicians would drop in from time to time, and I would settle into my role as secretary to this club of survivors. One can only get around on foot now, and everybody tends to stay close to their own neighborhood. There's nothing to do but wait. The newspapers have been reduced to a single sheet. . . . And then to

nothing. . . . From the skylight of my attic, if I stand on the
bed, I can see both the sky above and the street below where
a few intrepid housewives still venture forth, empty shopping
bags in hand. From my observatory, I can also catch a glimpse
of the boulevard Saint-Germain, almost totally free of traffic.
One begins to hear the silence and to rediscover the presence
of sparrows, and the swift flight of swallows in the late afternoon sky. Nature is warm and benevolent, fecund and very
close. Its roots push up under the sidewalks, its pollen fecun-
dates the statues of famous men; it won't take long, after the
city's destruction, to see virgin forests sprout over the twenty
arrondissements. The last Parisian patriots, one is surprised to
learn, are Sylvia Beach, who plans to reopen her bookshop as
soon as the situation allows, Gertrude Stein, and the faithful
Alice B. Good for them! If there is any justice in this world,
three good streets should be renamed after them, when the
war is over, on the Left Bank. From Henry Miller, there
comes a last letter posted from Greece, and then silence; I assume that he managed to get back to America. English has
again become a foreign language—you could even say an unknown language—inside the cafés and on the terraces where
only a month ago it was heard on all sides.

For some time already, on these balmy days, one could
watch the tide of refugees from the North and the East pro-
ceeding on foot down the shady avenues. They cross the city
from end to end, too hallucinated by their mood of madness
to look around at this metropolis that they had visited only in
their dreams. . . . Paris. . . . But Paris is no longer a city, it's a
place from which life has withdrawn, leaving intact an architecture of grand worldly sediments, but annulling in its retreat
a certain state of grace that characterized this moment of Paris
history as we've known it. Even if the city is not to be destroyed, even if the people come back one day, they will
never again know it as it was.

It's particularly the refugees from the North who have
sown panic in Paris and triggered the departure of the last
wave of Parisians, adding their numbers to this exhausted, silent crowd of broken, resigned people, dumbly pulling carts
and pushing baby carriages heaped with their most precious
belongings. Everyone is so deeply impressed now by the feeling of the war closing in, of this abomination, of this
nightmare, that those citizens who had hitherto stood firm
sleepwalk out of their homes into the streets and min-

gle with the moving tide of humanity, fist closed around the handle of an umbrella, around the hand of a child. If everyone else is leaving, they mutter to themselves, then me too. Why ask questions in a time like this? There must be some reason why everybody's going away, leaving, walking away, and for everything to be on the move, on the roads. So let's go. . . .

A strange emotion grips me from just being in the streets, observing the progress of the war in the abandoned city, trying to get my bearings and to understand where all this is leading. But there isn't anything to understand. Everything is in a state of upheaval; the old, rotten world is beginning to crumble, dissolving before my very eyes; events are snowballing, bringing about change, and I am convinced that even if the next steps are unknown and obscure, they will necessarily open out, somehow, onto a sunny clearing. I dash downstairs, seized with a light delirium welling up inside me, and I find myself in the warmth of a street filled with lights. Splashes of color, pansies, foliage, and clematis luxuriantly embroider the deserted balconies, notes of color resonating to the confines of my aura, receding into a sky of pure oxygen that envelops the city in its brilliant weightless mantle. Between my house, emptied of its occupants, and the nearby boulevard Saint-Germain, which is now teeming with people, I plunge into a strange version of what used to be our reality. That is not at all the street life we knew. Almost everywhere, public transportation has ceased to run, and people from the western suburbs and the nearby countryside started flocking toward the capital on foot when they heard that southbound trains were still leaving from the Paris railroad stations of Lyon, d'Orsay, Austerlitz. Everybody suddenly remembers distant cousins who live in the South, vague acquaintances, uncertain hopes. Entire families had spent days on the road from the plains of la Beauce and the valleys of the Seine, making their way wearily through the dust, slowed down by children, suitcases, old folks. This throng having been set in motion by false reports, the migration has now lost all meaning, since the trains aren't leaving anymore. The word has been passed around. Despite this, the mass exodus flows on, feeding on its own first movement, led simply by the dim hope of an ever-possible miracle.

At the crossing of boulevards Saint-Michel and Saint-Germain, in the heart of the Latin Quarter, this sparse column that is trudging from east to west along boulevard Saint-

Germain crosses the dense, uninterrupted column of refugees coming from the North and from the East, tightly funneled by the boulevard Saint-Michel toward the South. At the intersection, the bystander is submerged in an enormous chaos of population, where the migrating herds cross each other at right angles in a dangerous jostling of bodies, wheels, and disemboweled mattresses, with whining kids held high overhead for safety, seemingly floating on the surface of it all. I see the people from the suburbs momentarily hesitate in front of this teeming swarm, and instead of continuing in the direction of the train stations, toward the East, they mingle with the hordes laboriously making their way up the boulevard Saint-Michel, toward the distant mirage of Provence. Might as well continue on foot. . . . Why spend a whole lifetime waiting for a train that never comes. . . . One doesn't even know where one's going. . . . Here's a column of Flemish monks in their coarse woolen robes, mounted on women's bicycles, toiling hard up the incline. They're heavyset men with red faces, unused to this kind of heat, and some of them, pushing down with all their strength on the pedals, mumble a prayer. Would they still remember why they left their monastery, two weeks ago, at the beginning of the invasion? The icy shadow of the Antichrist hovered over the cloisters of Flanders because this Hitler is truly the Prince of Darkness in every sense of the term; demon, son of a demon, breeder of destruction and perdition. . . .

A little further on, I notice with surprise that Marcusot is still open—the bakery-tearoom on the corner of the rue Racine that had been one of my haunts. There's nothing left on the shelves or in the showcases—all the merchandise evaporated as soon as the shop opened, and the salesgirls, thin middle-aged ladies in black dresses with white lace-trimmed aprons, are watching from the doorway, transfixed, unsure what to think or do in the face of this historical defeat unfolding before their very eyes. . . . Maybe, someday, somebody will make a movie about it? Someday, if things ever get back to normal. . . . Yesterday, and the day before, the flow of fugitives included many small bands of bedraggled soldiers mixed in with the crowd, but today few of them are to be seen; these are the last waves of civilians ebbing through Paris, pushed on their way by the arrival of the enemy troops. As I make that remark to myself, I see a little caterpillar tank inching its way through the crush of old and young alike; beneath a camouflage topping of tangled branches a few dazed soldiers are holding on tightly. Just as the tank rolls, clanging on the pavement, past Marcusot's, one of them falls off with a thud onto the sidewalk, but the shock doesn't even wake him up from his sleep. It's a young peasant lad with a head of curly hair and beautiful blond flesh bursting through his khaki rags. The Marcusot spinsters rush out and fling themselves on this windfall treasure. I watch them, bustling about like black ants, dragging and pulling their quarry toward the shelter of their tearoom lair.

My plan for the day includes an expedition across the river to the Right Bank. Should I try the subway? The Saint-Michel *métro* station is still open. I go down the endless flights of metal stairs that lead to the platform, having heard that the north-south line is the last one left in service. As a matter of fact, a train of subway cars is awaiting departure; but it's blocked, paralyzed in the station by a seething jumble of bodies that prevents the doors from closing; within a few seconds, I see more examples of human savagery than I've ever witnessed during my twenty years on this earth. Arms are being twisted, suffocating old ladies trampled under foot, faces clawed with the nails of both hands—all that for the doubtful privilege of covering a kilometer or two without having to walk. . . . This looks promising for what's to come! But for the moment, my only thought is to get out of there, and with great difficulty, I force my way up the metal stairs, fighting against the frantic crowd that keeps storming down, gesticulating, trying to cram into this line of subway cars that will obviously never leave, since there are now people spilling all over the tracks in front of the train.

I reach the Pont-Neuf, and crossing the Seine, I find myself under the high gray facade of the Louvre, majestically enthroned on the bank of the river. Hitler's conquest will never erase the regal glory of France's past, not as long as the Louvre stands up as its witness. Inside the kings' palace, the Victory of Samothrace continues to triumph in a silent tempest of marble. As I proceed beyond the gates of the palace, I'm stunned to find the Tuileries gardens overgrown with man-size weeds. The attendants have deserted their job, and the lawns, thickets, and bushes have grown into a thick virgin forest in a few weeks, since the last time I was here. Above this strange vegetal exuberance, the statues of naked stone seem to fly off in movement, lunar Dianas hunting the deer, powerful centaurs grasping defenseless nymphs around the waist. As I emerge from that mythological greenery, I find that the arcades of the rue de Rivoli are empty, nothing stirs. On the place Vendôme, not a human being in sight; only a few slate-gray pigeons who have apparently not understood that their city is empty and that they, in turn, should emigrate. All around the majestic square the tall portals are closed, double-locked, and I ask myself how I'm going to be able to get inside my own building, at No. 16. For a long time, and without much hope, I ring the yellow brass night bell, which seems to have been polished that very morning. And indeed—surprise!—the concierge, M. Raphaël, is still at his post. Since the door is much too grand to accommodate a peephole, he has no way of knowing whether or not it's the *Boches* who are summoning him; after a long hesitation he opens up, ready for a quick death, his old heart already pierced by a bouquet of bayonets. But it's only me, not the German army, and he sighs with relief and smiles weakly as he recognizes one of the tenants. Poor old fellow, he can hardly stand on his feet, and that's why Mme Raphaël finally decided to stay. But he went through all the horrors of the First World War, he's seen it all; and those memories aren't easily forgotten. Whatever happens, he'll know how to speak to the enemy; and if there's no time to speak before he dies, he will still find in himself the strength to utter a last feeble *"Vive la France"* in his hoarse voice. But it's only me, *eh bien alors, quelle surprise!* M. Raphaël will perhaps be allowed to live until nightfall. For her part, Mme Raphaël tends stolidly to her stew, the aroma of which perfumes the concierge's lodge.

The office bearing a plate with the words OBELISK PRESS, JACK KAHANE is situated at the bottom of the long courtyard. This sign had better go right away, I tell myself. I hardly recognize the disorder that reigns over my work table. Helga left hers neat and clean; she was a woman who knew how to work. When was that? Two, three weeks ago? Helga on the move, me at a standstill, memories receding into the past. I hardly recognize this place where I used to spend most of my time. I am tempted to push open the door of my father's office, which I had avoided entering since his death, except when absolutely necessary. After skirting the big square fake-Empire table, I sit down in his leather-upholstered swivel chair, which squeaks a bit. His absence manifests itself in a feeling of profound calm that accentuates the visual impact of every object, the letters lying open where he had left them, the scattered books he was the last to touch. Pinned to the gray burlap that covers the walls are the actors of the past, each one looking into the dim, dusty room from his or her place in space and time. The mysterious eyes of Anaïs; a photo of Joyce, the sour-faced magister; Durrell's profile, chubby and pugnacious; the satanic face of Charles Beadle, the author of *Dark Refuge*—who knows, perhaps one of the true prophets of the future? And other, gayer, spots: Miller's watercolors, a large sepia portrait of Nadejda, book jackets, crank letters, Christmas cards. Gone are the passengers of this ship, and few remember the stop they made at this port of call a while ago. The owner of the room is gone, and the faces all around the room appear disconnected from their purpose, like dead zodiac signs.

Sitting in that chair, I feel overwhelmed by a profound fatigue, numbed by the cold air after that long walk in the afternoon heat. The silence is so deep that I feel drawn by it into a semiconscious state. I make a great effort to resist an overpowering desire to sleep, and to get myself out of this tomb. But where should I go from here? I decide to head for the faubourg Saint-Honoré; why not have a look at what's happening at the British Embassy.

Not surprisingly, the gate is locked, the vast building seems absolutely empty, and so I walk from there to the office of the military attaché just around the corner. What am I looking for? I don't know. Perhaps I feel superstitiously compelled to pay a final visit to this place where my fate has been decided, perhaps for my entire life. If I had not signed up to join the British army, which I knew did not want me, then I would now be a soldier in the French army, and who knows what!

It's impossible to tell if it's three o'clock or six; all the clocks have stopped or gone mad, and starving cats are rummaging through the contents of garbage cans. . . . Having pushed my expedition as far east as the Marais, I set off in the direction of the Pont du Châtelet in order to get back to the Rive Gauche. The place des Vosges seemed tinged with a more sustained shade of pink than usual, as if the brick façades were glowing softly from inside. As I come closer to the river I realize that for the last few hours the sky has been filled with huge purple sails, great cylinders of light coming from above, although it is still only midafternoon. Crossing the bridge, a few stray bewildered-looking pedestrians stare at the sky, as if awaiting the first trumpet of the Apocalypse; it casts on the river's water a dazzling metallic reflection. As I'm halfway across the bridge all colors turn to dark, clouds spread out over the roofs, and suddenly a savage rain bursts down on the city and the river. A rain of black ink, like liquid soot falling straight from the heavens and instantly transforming all the pedestrians into silhouettes of night. When I finally reach the rue Hautefeuille, I call through Mona's door that I'm back, but I don't let myself be seen, as the shock would be too great. Blackened by the celestial axlegrease, my clothes are fit for nothing but to be thrown away, which I do. I wash myself as best I can, bandage my aching feet, and fling myself on the bed. The daylight fades slowly and the far-off rhythm of a solemn and circular chant descends on me from the small overhead window, and lulls me into sleep. The breeze invades my dream with faint echoes of the chorus of barbarians who are waiting at the gates of the city, preparing to make their entrance in good order.

The sun itself wakes me up. My first movement is to stand on my bed and look out the skylight. . . . No, I haven't dreamed it after all! Twisting my neck a little, I can make out, a hundred meters below at the corner of the street, the outline of a soldier dressed in a long stone-green leather coat, helmet down to the eyebrows, directing traffic in an efficient, offhand manner. Along the entire length of the boulevard Saint-Germain, there's an uninterrupted procession of military vehicles and trucks neatly filled with silent, rigid soldiers.

That's it, then! I can't complain I haven't been warned that once trapped I would be unable to get out. One by one the doors of Paris are slammed shut and an army settles down inside the city to stay. It is just the right time for me, with my usual acumen, to realize what a fool I've been. It all comes back to me—the Jewish name, the British passport, and how little is left of my grandfather's money. Somehow, up to now, these seemed like remote, abstract details. Not any more now, starting with the simple problem of going out into the street. Assuming that the trains were to be restored, would we be allowed to travel freely outside the city? Perhaps, at this very moment Kurt was preparing to land in New York Harbor.

There were no telephones in our *chambres de bonnes*, and all we could do, Mona and I, was to listen to the continuous rumble of the army trucks, the clanking of caterpillar tanks rolling heavily along the pavement, and it gave us the feeling of being inside an enormous factory. That's the new reality: We have suddenly become a command post of the Third Reich. Where is Daladier? What happened to Paul Reynaud? Did he use his big posters like a magic carpet to fly away to a more peaceful land? "NOUS VAINCRONS CAR NOUS SOMMES LES PLUS FORTS," the poster said. . . .

We had reached our fifteenth cup of tea when we suddenly heard the sound of heavy hobnailed boots on the red-tiled corridor, and the door was forcefully pushed open by two preposterous-looking tourists in mountaineer outfits draped with threadbare raincoats. Mona and I had to adjust our sights in order to recognize Laurette and Rolande.

"It's our antirape uniform," explained Rolande. "Laurette wanted to come at any cost and reassure you, both of you, but Kryia didn't want to let her go out. And so we demonstrated to her that everything is only a matter of appearance, isn't that right . . . ?"

"And anyway," added Laurette, "these people seem to be very disciplined and well-behaved."

"Yes, and they're not too disagreeable to look at, on the whole," specified Rolande. "Big blond fellows . . ."

"Have you seen any Frenchmen on the boulevard?"

"Not a single one," said Laurette. "People are looking through their windows from behind the curtains, but nobody seems to be in a hurry to try the streets."

The conversation that followed was confined to elementary problems: the curfew, how were we going to stay alive, and get around? It was decided to organize an expedition to a bicycle store at the Porte Maillot that, according to public rumor, was still open, and where we could each get a bicycle—notwithstanding my vow never to set my behind on that damned saddle again, which I had made to myself after my expedition to the Pyrénées, two years earlier. But times have changed a lot since then.

My name has also changed. I have decided to adopt that of my mother, Girodias. But it's not enough to just make that decision; it must be backed with a credible set of French identification papers, a problem of which I become increasingly aware as I explore the city, now so strangely transformed. The new population is in gray green or blue gray, but remarkably organized. No saber-rattling, no abuse of civilians, no sign of drunken brawls and brutal behavior. The officers are young and well-dressed. I try to picture in my mind what the reverse situation might look like if the French were to occupy Berlin, for instance: That would make quite a different picture, it seems to me. These Germans don't even seem to have gone on a good old-fashioned drinking-spree to celebrate their victory, as the French military wouldn't have failed to do. They are mostly dazzled by the nonersatz food; I cross paths with two infantrymen coming out of a dairy shop, each one with a stick of butter in his hand, eating it nimbly as if it were an ice cream cone, like the rarest of treats.

Up to now, they had the guns and we ate the butter. They chose to live on reconstituted waste and chemical foods, and to wear uniforms made of synthetic fiber, which gives off this peculiar stench, sour and quite beastly. They live like animals in boxes. They're healthy enough, trim and muscular, but they act and behave like brainwashed, preconditioned robots, even when smiling, even in civvies. The Nazi salute, reduced to a little flip of the hand accompanied by a mumbling that ends in "tler"—for "Heil Hitler"—isn't that rite in itself the mark of a complete alienation of the individual person? And so they won a victory, and the French lost a war, and who knows what is going to happen next?

But let's leave all this aside, as there are more pressing matters to consider. I have decided to consult a man of experience about my problem, a bartender who works in a place near the Opera, and who calls himself Red (a name his French clientele persist in pronouncing *raide*, meaning stiff, which rather angers him). Red, who is really Scandinavian while passing as an American, is an extremely smart operator. He knows all the tricks in the book; in the past few months, I have imbibed many a tomato juice at his bar, absorbing his superior hustler's wisdom, so great is my need for that particular knowledge! And he always responded to my questions with as much good grace as cunning. Having heard that he continues to operate behind closed doors for the benefit of his clientele, I went to see him one afternoon. I explained my urgent need for a French identity card. He kept pouring drinks for his guests, each one with a distinctive flourish that seemed dictated by the nature of the mix, but he was listening to me carefully.

"Don't beat your brains out, kiddo," he answered. "Come

back tomorrow at the same time with a passport photo and a thousand francs in big bills, and you've got your card. The money, it's not for me, you understand—it's for the guy at the police station who's willing to help. No, I don't want nothing, 'cause you're a pal, understand?"

"Really! That's great, Red. I won't forget what you're doing for me."

"Aw, come on, kid, it's nothing," he said modestly.

The next day I had an identity card in my new name, all stamped and everything, very official-looking. That's it: "Maurice Girodias." With a dashing picture.

Red had his finger in a big deal he was counting on to make a quick fortune and get out of France. He was anxious to go back to his native Denmark, and from there to America. . . . One of his friends had a warehouse full of canned goods; because he was Jewish, he couldn't come back to France and had instructed Red to sell the whole lot, at the best price he could get.

"In three months, this stuff will be worth ten times its price. It's a blue-chip investment and I'm keeping it for just a few close friends, people I can trust completely. . . . As long as they have a place where they can store the stuff safely, too. It's only a matter of days, a few weeks at the most, before everything is under some kind of rationing, and after that this sort of quality canned food will be absolutely *priceless*."

These revelations didn't fall on deaf ears. Two weeks earlier, I had withdrawn the rest of my fortune from the bank, and I was keeping the thick wad of bills under my mattress, as did everybody else. It wasn't very much: ten thousand francs. Enough to bring my family back from Dax and to send them on vacation for the summer, not far from Paris. That would leave enough for me to hold out for a few weeks. . . . And after that? Nothing! I had better start thinking seriously about making some money, one way or the other.

Fine, I told myself, here's my chance. And I entrusted my bundle to Red, who did not refuse, and proceeded to count out the ten thousand francs carefully. It was arranged that delivery of the cans was to be made to my office at place Vendôme, but by night, and through the rear door of the building so as not to attract any attention whatsoever, particularly not that of M. Raphaël, the concierge.

"Not that it's illegal," said Red. "But nobody should hear

about it—in your own interest. You get me, kid?" Wise and tough.

And so these five tons of canned goods had to be delivered surreptitiously at night from a truck with no lights on; then they had been noiselessly carried in big bags on a man's back down a long dark corridor and hoisted on tiptoe up the service staircase to the first floor where my office was located. Swearing away in muffled voices, a team of hoodlums under Red's direction unloaded these thousands of cans, working in pitch-black darkness. Meanwhile, I racked my brains trying to find a suitable camouflage for the metallic pyramids that were fast mounting toward the ceiling of my office. I did my best to hide them behind walls of cardboard, leaving a sort of arch in the middle. The result was to emphasize the fact that I was desperately trying to hide something behind the cardboard. Fortunately few people came to visit me at the office.

Dawn was breaking as I completed my labors, long after Red's departure. My office was now reduced to this narrow corridor between two craggy partitions, and I decided that from tomorrow on, I would definitely have to start using my father's room. Dealing in canned food did take a lot of space, and I was beginning to wonder whether I wouldn't have been better off investing my money in a more portable asset, something that would be more easy to conceal. . . . Anybody could find the cans and bring my secret to light. . . . And I began to feel, once again, like a damned fool.

These cans . . . what exactly is in them, anyway? "Prime quality, *guaranteed*," Red had said. But what does that mean, professionally speaking? Prime quality *what?* Guaranteed by *whom?* But of course Red must know. As far as the resale is concerned, he told me not to worry. "Don't beat your brains out, kid. The longer you wait, the more you'll get for the stuff. Just put that through your noodle."

"But in order to sell the stuff, I must at least know what's in the cans! They don't have any labels, how can I guess?"

"Tut, tut," Red replied. "Calm down, kid. *You know me*," he added, pointing with a sausage finger in the direction of his heart where a catsup stain adorned his white jacket. *"You can trust me, no?"* He seemed mildly indignant. And he added comfortably: "For that kind of price, you wouldn't expect *labels* as well, eh? Now, you must be fair to me, kiddo."

Well, all right. And that's when the ten thousand francs had changed hands. . . . My office was now filled with tons of the mysterious canned goods . . . What can I do with it? I suddenly decided to sample a can from one pile, taking one where it seemed least likely to bring the whole lot down, and slit it open with the office scissors. Swimming around in brine, I found a grayish vegetable that appeared to be celery. Hey, that's pretty unexpected, but not bad at all! I repeated the experiment, hoping to find something truly exciting this time, with a can taken from the opposite end of the pile. Celery again! Third try: celery. The fourth: the same. . . . More celery! I had become the proprietor of five tons of limp canned celery.

I began to think. Fresh celery is wonderful, but what do you do with *canned* celery, kid? Serve it with mayonnaise and French cancan?

I dialed Red's telephone number, which rang a long time before he answered.

"What, it's *you?*" he finally growled into my ear. "What is it now? Say, I just spent the night breaking my balls in your service, and now can't you let me sleep in peace? No, really, this takes the cake!"

"Red, it's only celery . . ."

"Ah so, you finally found that you had bought yourself five tons of celery. And for a pretty good price too, eh? Well kid, you're just brilliant. My, what a fast learner!" he laughed. "Tell me, kid, do you like celery?"

"I eat it two, maybe three times a year."

"Well, now you're going to have to get used to eating it. Maybe two, three times a day. Unfortunately for you, canned celery has exactly the same taste as boiled rutabaga, the stuff you feed to cattle, and that's the reason why there were no labels on the cans. Nobody wants to buy that stuff, but of course it's not my fault if you wanted it so bad. I knew all along that you were making a mistake, but that was your decision, eh? Me, I was only trying to help. Anything to help a buddy, that's what I say!"

"*You goddam bastard!*" I shouted.

"Tut tut! No vulgar words into my phone, if you don't mind. You've got your stuff, I've got your money, and everything is hunky-dory and tralala, savvy?"

"You goddamn crook . . ."

"Kid, I assure you, you ought to think a bit before you talk like that. I've done you a damned good turn, believe me. Two good turns, even. One, I made you buy something to eat this winter, you and your family, and that's a real favor because you don't know how to handle your money. Two, I taught you to think a little more before doing something foolish. The world is full of crooks."

"You know that's not funny!" I was screaming desperately into the phone. "Give me back my money! You know very well that's all I've got!"

"Come on, kiddo, listen to you talking! Ha ha! You make me laugh. You sound like the Merry Widow, you know that!" And he made an an ugly noise of the most objectionable variety.

"I'll go to the police . . ."

"Ha ha!"

"Well, all right," I say. "We'll see. I'll be over to talk to you when the bar opens."

"Don't count on it! And please, don't bawl so loudly, you're hurting my ear. It's no use looking for me, I'm on my way out, old man. In one hour, I'll have left my apartment. And don't bother to go to the address I gave you the other day. It's phony."

"I'll catch up with you!"

"Never! Listen to me—*honestly*—I had warned you: As soon as I made my pile, I'd fly the coop. Yesterday, I got rid of my entire inventory of canned celery selling it to three guys like you, plus yourself. You're the fourth, and you got home delivery. The others, poor little creeps, they had to go out to the suburbs to pick up their stuff. Ha, ha, ha! So long! and *bon appétit!*"

17

*1914–1940: the death of a nation.—Raymond Queneau
teaches school.—A monopoly at work: Hachette.
—The humble potato becomes a remote princess; old people
die like flies in winter.—The Baron de Makiavellyckxz
wants all.—Inside the Gestapo.—Birth of
Editions du Chêne. —A fine banker.—Thanks
to all my errors, I become a resounding success.*

News from some of my friends began to trickle in slowly. Hélène had been seen for the last time in a truck with three dozen little Polish refugees, heading for Bordeaux. Vilayat and Noor had made their way to England, where I heard that Vilayat had joined the navy. Him, a Sufi! Vivian and Kryia had made it known that their first impression of the occupation troops was not too unfavorable. In order to ascertain the situation firsthand Kryia had rented a rickety horse-drawn carriage in which Vivian, an invisible shadow behind tinted windows, was able to make his first tour of the capital in five years, and take the pulse of the masses so to speak. As for the rest, Vivian's group lived in a reduced fashion, waiting.

Despite my financial disaster, I was able to bring my family back and send them out again to spend the summer in a little house near Chantilly. Jacques was in Germany, a prisoner of war in a Pomeranian stalag; he was now the father of a son he never had a chance to see. Mowgli, on the other hand, who had spent his younger years dreaming of heroic deeds, hadn't seen any action at all, having been evacuated from Bordeaux before the German victory. He was now somewhere in Africa. As for Lieutenant François Chérel, he had been given a bridge to defend during the German advance, with one antitank gun and a handful of men. He had carried out his orders and loyally given battle to an entire

Panzer division. Of course the others had got the better of things, but they were so surprised to find people that pugnacious on their path that after the skirmish, they went to see what was left of the little group. Not much. Yet François was still alive, with a machine-gun bullet lodged in his lung. He was rushed to a military hospital where he was treated like a staff general. Once healed, he was sent back to the French, who seemed quite flabbergasted by this unexpected gift. The same general staff that had sent him out to get killed couldn't do any less than promote him to the rank of captain, with a few citations. He himself, on the other hand, looked upon those events with quiet irony, serene but disillusioned. His only merit, he assured Mona and Laurette who had gone to see him at the military hospital in Verdun, was that he belonged to the tiny minority of those who hadn't taken to their heels. Not much to brag about! As for Georges Pelorson, who was also in the East, he belonged to the immense majority that didn't have any choice but to take to their heels —because there was no other choice, it was an irresistible, inevitable mass movement. It wasn't in his nature to flee, but there were other battles to be fought as a consequence of the defeat itself; and as soon as the token fighting was over, he had somehow managed to get back to Paris, covering about four hundred kilometers on foot, mostly at night. He finally reached home, exhausted but safe and full of projects.

At last here was someone who was sure to have useful advice and ideas to impart! Our reunion was a very exciting event, and soon developed into a general meeting of *Volontés* contributors and editors. Like all little reviews, this one had gone through a chaotic career, being exclusively financed by Georges's earnings as a journalist; but it had come out with some good things by Georges Bataille, Henry Miller, Michel Leiris, Raymond Queneau. When Georges was called up shortly after the outbreak of the war, I had offered to finance and print the issue then in production, which I did; and that had been my first statement as an independent publisher, although I had not done much more than spend my money on it. The title, *Volontés*, despite its allusion to will power, did not imply a dedication to power politics, since politics were seen as a very inferior sport by the participants, all of them people of a higher intellect. Up to this time, that is, because the German victory over France seemed to have changed their attitude instantly.

The general mood of the meeting was indeed violent and somber. People started quarreling, and it became obvious that those formerly apolitical folks had suddenly become quite obdurate, as well as obstinate, in their extreme political positions: pro-Russian, which meant crypto-Stalinist; or pro-Pétain, which is to say potential collaborators of the Germans; or pro-de Gaulle, which implies that you believe in England's eventual victory over Germany, which as we all know will only happen if Roosevelt manages to get the United States into the war, and that certainly does look like a very far-fetched prospect right now, doesn't it? America is basically isolationist, don't we all know that!

Listening to all those good friends bickering with such ardor and venom was quite a shattering experience. Georges was trying to calm them down while Lucien Combelle, a big loudmouthed fellow whose only claim to fame was that he had been André Gide's secretary, was abusing him and ordering him out of the room.

"Listen, this is *my* apartment, Lucien; you're the one who's going out of his mind! Anyway, what I want to say is simply that we should all remember that since the Hitler-Stalin treaty and the breaking of that treaty, all in the space of one year, we should rather be looking for a purely French solution to solve what is after all a purely French problem—"

"Ha ha, did you hear that jerk giving people lessons in politics? A *French* solution! It's too late for that, you ninny. We are Hitler's pawn, and there's just no time to argue, and no room to maneuver. In a few weeks, he'll be in London and the war will be over, anyhow. Can't you people see that?"

"You're a traitor and a cur," a woman named Violette spat at him. "This fight is the people's fight, and it will be won by the people, by my comrades. Not by half-baked pimps like you! Good luck to you all." Having said her piece, she went out the door and slammed it on us.

Later, we resumed our conversation more quietly, Georges and I, and it was agreed that *Volontés* couldn't possibly continue under the present circumstances. Since Georges was by profession a journalist, he was out of a job, as the only sheets now being sold in Paris were printed under the direct control of the Germans.

And so he was very tempted to accept the Jolases' offer to take over their small, exclusive Bilingual School in Neuilly, as they were about to leave Paris and return to the United States. Georges's wife was Irish and he himself had always been interested in education; and so he was thus prompted to say yes. But what would *bilingual* mean under the German occupation? Would it be possible to teach in English as well as in French? And then—where were the pupils to be found? Eugene and Mary Jolases' school had catered to the sons and daughters of a wealthy, cosmopolitan Neuilly fringe, which seemed to have quite vanished; all his efforts to round up pupils had produced only two candidates so far. Incidentally, what did I plan to do about my young brother and sisters' education? Shouldn't I endeavor to make them bilingual?

We struck a bargain, and my three young siblings were enrolled. That made five students in all, then, with as many professors to teach them whatever fantasy would dictate. It must be said that this was no ordinary faculty and that the kids were always blissfully wondering what the next day would bring. The most colorful and disconcerting of these magisters was undoubtedly Raymond Queneau, who taught geography, algebra, phrenology, climatology, grammar, French, Latin, Greek, and linguistics, among other subjects and always managed to raise a thick halo of chalk dust around himself as soon as he went to the blackboard.

By coughing and puffing, wiping and gesticulating, and overturning the chalk box, he would quickly set the whitish cloud in motion. As he left the classroom, with white elbows and a huge satchel crammed with books, one would observe his fast and uncertain progress along the boulevard, unseeing eyes peering abstractedly through thick lenses. His steps would always catapult him in the way of a tree trunk, which he would cleverly manage to outmaneuver at the last second, marking the near-collision with a mumbled apology. My brother, Eric, then fourteen, was completely absorbed by his teacher, thanks to whom he was fast assimilating a great variety of subjects that had absolutely nothing to do with the curriculum.

"Today we're going to talk about winds," Raymond would propose. "Ah, the winds. . . . And the sound they make—" (Here the teacher interrupts himself for a moment in order to dream about what he has just said.) "Take a look at this chart of wines, eh . . . chart of *winds*, with all those colors. . . . Oh! The sirocco, the simoon, the tarantane—I mean the tarentula—the tarlatan, *no*, the tramontane, well! You know what that is, you people, the tramontane? And the minstrel, you know about it? Uh, I mean the mistrial, no, let's see, the mistal. Let's have a look, such a promising word, now . . ." (Belatedly, he consults the book open in front of him.) "The mis-tral, ha! Mistral! The brave poet. Do you know his work? But of course one has to understand Provençal." And on and on it went.

Unfortunately for the Ecole Bilingue, its central heating system was in pitiful condition, and as there were hardly any students and no money to get the furnace back in working order, Georges finally gave up his enterprise after a very chilly first trimester. This was a relief for him because teaching at that level was really a waste of time. He had other ambitions which were beginning to take shape in the realm of politics. The Vichy government sponsored various projects having to do with education in which Georges thought he could play a role, and steer political currents in the right direction.

The Bogouslawskys had only left Paris shortly before the fall of the city in order to take refuge as comfortably as possible in a hotel at Rambouillet, and to see what was going to happen. France was now partitioned into two sections, the larger one being occupied by the German army in the North with Paris as capital, and the so-called *zone libre* where the Pétain government operated from the small town of Vichy. Most large businesses had moved their headquarters to the south of the new internal border, which was fiercely guarded by German troops. This happened to be the case in particular with Hachette, whose board of directors had emigrated to Auvergne. To rule such a vast empire from there soon proved impossible; if Hachette wanted to survive, they would have to find some accommodation with the Germans. But none of the old directors and members of the board had the least desire to play the difficult diplomatic role this would involve, and finally a complete outsider was chosen for the job, one Henri Filipacchi, who was hastily promoted to secretary general of operations in the occupied zone. This Filipacchi, who was a Jew from Turkey, but claimed to be descended from Corsican pirates, had in his favor the fact of being married to the sister of the wife of Jean Luchaire, founder of the first daily newspaper under the Occupation, *Les Nouveaux Temps*, and thought to have been the great guiding spirit of the fifth column in Paris before the arrival of the Germans. To have a brother-in-law of this sort absolved Filipacchi from the crime of Jewishness, and gave him sufficient qualification for his heavy responsibility—all the heavier as the Germans wanted tight control of the press and its distribution. To this end, they had installed a resident commissioner, a Dr. Conrad, a dour and suspicious character, in their building on the rue Réaumur.

Bogous described Filipacchi to me as supershrewd, a crafty and dangerous being; nevertheless he promised to introduce me to him when the right moment came. While waiting for better days, Bogous had managed to get me a few orders for reprints of English books through Hachette, which helped me a bit to live. He had perfected a stratagem that made it possible to put over the idea of adapting Unicorn Press to a more modest program of school books . . . Somerset Maugham, Elizabeth Berridge, Thomas Hardy, nothing but safe stuff.

This is only one instance of his indefatigable efforts on my behalf, in using the vast resources of that great sprawling enterprise to invent ways for me to make money. He was a model director, a sharp operator, and respected by the hierarchy, but he despised them all. He paid them fat compliments with his broad Russian accent and that funny unctuous smile of his, delicate masterpieces of hypocrisy. Everybody loved ugly, jovial Bogous; but had they only been able to guess what he thought of them, they would have dealt with him as others did once with Rasputin.

To him, the entire Hachette operation, its spatial immensity combined with the pettiness of those on top, the global wastefulness and maniacal obsession with minute details, all of this could be seen as a metaphor of the entire Western world. Just bear in mind that the business of Hachette was *culture*: education, communications, information! That they had a national monopoly on press distribution as well as book distribution; that they were also powerful publishers, printers, paper manufacturers, landowners: one of the richest enterprises in the entire world. And those archcapitalists, with not a thought in their minds but of money and power, were sitting on top of French culture. How very bizarre.

Would Hachette survive the occupation, the take-over of most of their organization by the Germans? But of course, Bogous would exclaim: The leeches are always good survivors!

The winter began with terrible cold spells, which suddenly brought home to the Parisians a keen sense of their distress. As predicted, rutabaga was the only vegetable on open sale in the markets, the humble potato having become a remote princess. Butter was already selling on the black market at twenty times its official price, and the feeding of newborn babies presented serious problems. Not to mention the elderly who were dying off like flies; my grandparents themselves were declining rapidly in health as a result of the food shortage.

When the Germans announced in the city halls that coupons for the purchase of wine would be distributed in exchange for copper objects in French possession, I learned with a heavy heart that my grandfather had gone to yield up his weighty collection of Moroccan trays and other bric-à-brac in order to obtain his little supplementary ration. . . . How unfair! When young, my grandfather used to down his average of three liters a day, which any healthy Frenchman would do in those times; he was a hard-working man then, and certainly not an alcoholic. Then, when he reached sixty, he had cut down to two liters. And now, not only was he forced to starve, but he was reduced to a half liter of wine *per week!*

As for myself, a vegetarian since childhood, this diet was easier to put up with, but for many Frenchmen accustomed to stuffing their bellies voluptuously, this alimentary vacuum led to a rapid weakening, and the cold did the rest: an exceptional cold, universal and implacable, which gnawed away not only at bodies, but at souls and character as well.

The Champs-Elysées stretched out, empty and lugubrious, a steppe plowed by the ceaseless passage of military convoys. Nothing else was rolling. Layers of dirty snow were crusted and encrusted in superimposed layers, frozen and frozen over, and walkers didn't venture forth on this battlefield without recommending their souls to God and their limbs to Saint Christopher. I was to be found walking among them, among these bands of miserable pedestrians, much against my will. But the fact is that very often I didn't even have the fourteen *sous* for the *métro* ticket, proletarian second class, to cover the distance that lay between the place Vendôme and the center of Neuilly. And all that street exercise wrought serious damage to the beautiful shoes fashioned so painstakingly by M. Ghazérian, ages ago.

When I arrived, exhausted, at the end of my journey, and gallantly offered my celery hearts to my mother—because I brought home only one can at a time, so as not to depreciate their value—she always found *le mot juste*, the modest joke that brought back a little laughter into the refrigerated atmosphere of the apartment. We had acquired a new kind of economical tin stove in hopes it would allow us to heat the living room, at least; it was an exemplary product of Parisian resourcefulness which worked only on sawdust. Gathered together around this miracle, we all held out our reddened hands, swollen and cracked from the cold, forcing ourselves to fight against this adversity with good humor. My sister Sylvie, for example, complained about chilblains at the tip of her nose, and was never seen during that winter without her noseholder, a kind of fur bandage she had fashioned in order to protect the threatened appendage. . . . When we sat at the lunch table to contemplate the contents of our plates, we were joined by Miss Allison, an old abandoned Englishwoman who was no longer all there. Finding a home where people would feed her daily hadn't been easy for Miss Allison, as she had that unfortunate habit of removing her false teeth and laying them on the table next to her plate before attacking her pap; nothing would ever cure her of that idiosyncrasy. My mother herself could only look at her and sigh. And finally, with a heavy heart, she resigned herself to making daffy Miss Allison eat in the kitchen.

With the help of a printer I had recently encountered, and of two fellows from Neuilly, the brothers Bariatinsky, I started the publication of a brochure listing all the films showing in Paris, and other entertainments, a modest weekly publication.

Cinema is the only thing that's thriving in Paris these days. "These nights," rather, since we seem to be living in perpetual penumbra, even in full daylight—that time just after sunset when you start thinking that you'd really like to see a good movie, and actually begin to see it rolling on your inner camera! Our dreams are thus given a dimension of absolute need, the need to recapture the world we have just lost. They wear the very specific coloring of the recent past in the form of films by Jean Renoir, Jean Vigo, René Clair, and Marcel Carné. The superimposed images of Raimu, Dalio, Jules Berry, Louis Jouvet, André Luguet, Pierre Fresnay, Jean

Gabin, and Jean Trenet give us the average image of what we've known to be the French male, an astute loser. Claude Dauphin, stepping out forever youthful in *L'Entrée des Artistes*, symbolizes the future; the fake Prussian officer von Stroheim and his French captives in *La Grande Illusion*, the past. When Jean Dasté and the great Michel Simon bring to us in *L'Atalante* an alien wind, a touch of foreign madness on a super-French background, it reaches me just as deeply as Buñuel's surrealistic paranoia of *Un Chien Andalou*. The women are less dazzling, less colorful, because this is really not their moment of glory here in France; no Annabella, Yvonne Printemps, Danielle Darrieux, or Michèle Morgan can hold a candle to the Garbos and the Marlenes, and even less to my own personal goddess, Louise Brooks.

Theater owners, pouncing on the golden opportunity, have reactivated many old films I never had a chance to see before, and we look with a new eye at the lightest Hollywood comedies, at their innocent song-and-dance rituals so alien to us, so far away and mysterious. And yet this vigorous new style of cinema ranging from slapstick to historical melodrama derives directly from European sources, the Folies-Bergères and the Yiddish Theater, Charlie Chaplin and Louis Lumière. And yet it is already worlds apart! Between the fading black-and-white nostalgia of our early flickers and those big glossy full-color Cecil B. DeMille star-studded make-believe cheesecake specials of the giant screen, you can measure the neat distance between past and future, between Europe and America. How obvious it is that the war and the capture of France have descended suddenly like a black curtain, darkening the stage forever! The very emptiness of the American melodramas, the chilling Scarface syndrome, the sizzling peroxide blondes and Cadillacs—what a break with our own exhausted, consumptive world. . . . Nothing happens anymore *sous les toîts de Paris!* Baudelaire, Rimbaud, Mallarmé, and the others have pumped out our last energies, and it's not Jean-Paul Sartre who's going to restore them.

The Vichy government has also understood in its own way the vital importance of cinema in a period like this, and the official help gives birth to a new wave of wartime French cinema but doesn't bring up much that is new, or hopeful. The message of Carné's *Les Enfants du Paradis* or Cocteau's *Les Enfants Terribles* is that this adult world is really made up of retarded children. The never-never land of *Les Visiteurs du*

Soir doesn't deserve all the cardboard employed to build those dungeons of the mind.

Thus *Paris-Programme*, which was started at the end of 1940, happened to be my first full-blooded publishing venture; a dismally utilitarian product, to be sure. The brothers Bariatinsky, whom I had known in Neuilly when they studied at Lycée Pasteur, were to serve as ad salesmen. They did, to a certain extent.

The elder brother, known as Vlad, called himself Prince Bariatinsky. He was tall, handsome, and vacuous, and remarkably lazy; it was difficult for him simply to up and go into the field, as a good salesman does, without being told, because he was forever expecting phone calls concerning a choice part in a major production. Vlad was convinced he was about to become a great film star, but nothing ever happened—since he did nothing to make it happen.

It was the younger brother, Michel, who did all the footwork. A short, plump little fellow, modest, active, and methodical, he went by the simple name of M. Bar. The Russian prince stunt, it must be said, had gone out of fashion ages before; however, while M. Bar was helping me by selling the cans of celery one by one, the Prince, his brother, was spending much of his time in the studios, and it is thanks to his gossiping that I heard about an old acquaintance from Neuilly, Simone Kaminker. She had changed her name to Simone Signoret, and although her father was Jewish, now a speaker of the Free French radio in London, she was trying to launch herself as an actress. This was big news indeed! I didn't doubt that she had the talent to succeed, but she was certainly taking chances, and since I knew all too well how willful and determined she was, I could only admire the quality of her madness. Cheers, Simone! Those dangerous, all-seeing panoramic gray eyes of yours will no doubt benefit the silver screen in a unique fashion.

In a way, my situation was not unlike hers. Every minute of my life was a gamble, since I spent most of it inside the very fulcrum of the German high command in Paris, the big army brass in Western Europe being concentrated in the few acres of the posh Opéra-Concorde-Vendôme area. And I walked around in the midst of it all without any papers to speak of. Sentries would snap to attention and click their heels as the generals came and went, goose-stepped and cavorted around in mechanical-toy fashion in front of the big hotels. Immense red banners stamped with the swastika floated from the balconies, and military proclamations in Gothic script were lending our polished neighborhood the air of a Prussian garrison town.

The military police stopped passersby, checking their papers at every street corner, more or less at random. On the route between my office and the Concorde station, I was therefore constantly exposed to the risk of arrest by a patrol. If need be, I was counting on the fairly authentic appearance of my phony identity card in order to get out of trouble, but that appearance was most fragile, since a telephone call to the prefecture would have been enough to determine that it was false; it was therefore preferable not to show it to anyone. And to bring that off, I developed the technique of disidentification; the art, in other words, of turning oneself into thin air.

This is a talent at once simple and subtle that Parisians acquire in childhood on the terraces of cafés: the art of not seeming to be there, or, better yet, the faculty of passing as someone else.

Sazarin, the tailor, had let me take advantage of a piece of magnificent Scottish tweed that he had left over from better days in order to make me an overcoat of great elegance; a few months earlier, its almond-green shade had made me hesitate. Now, however, the annoying color of this coat turned out to be an extraordinary godsend and doubtless more than once saved my life. When worn with a certain detachment and a touch of military haughtiness, this garment enabled me to project the image of a young officer in civvies, a bit of a dandy—which of course meant high connections—and one who would not tolerate the affront of being asked to show his papers.

After a while, I would slide into the part so effortlessly that it became a delicate and wonderful sport to steal their act, and in fact improve on it. No young Prussian aristocrat walking along the sidewalks of Paris, reciting some verse of Rilke under his breath, would have appeared as natural and gemütlich as I did. When I reached that point, I did actually manage to forget the little problem of my identity card.

The looks of my office had changed. The new secretary was a little Russian *demoiselle* I had hired because of her pretty eyes: Natalie. It didn't take long for me to regret this because she was even sillier than pretty. And then, occupying what had been my father's office, there was the mysterious Baron de Makiavellyckxz.

He was from ancient Baltic lineage, the baron wanted me to know, but his mother was English and lived in Sussex. "I understand that you too have English forebears," the baron had added in a slightly condescending manner. He was rather tall and good-looking in a heavyset manner, with brooding features and a widow's peak that accentuated his diabolical air.

"Here, keep my card, my dear fellow, people often spell my name wrong." Whereupon he handed me a large visiting card beautifully engraved with the words

BARON DE MAKIAVELLYCKXZ.

No Christian name, no address, just those three words, straight out of the Gutenberg Bible.

Faugère, the man who printed *Paris-Programme*, had introduced me to him. The baron was supposed to be very good at public relations, and a keen salesman as well. I had been looking for someone with that sort of talents to become manager of *Paris-Programme*.

Suspecting that in such a business it was necessary to be a bit of a pimp, I forced myself to find him likable, and foisted upon him the directorship of my weekly sheet. He immediately started to throw his weight around by demanding an office, and over my objections, he installed himself in my father's room, which I had just begun to fix up for myself. This caused me to be relegated once again to the company of my canned goods. Next he cast a spell over the innocent Natalie, by riveting her with a sinister eye while dictating his correspondence; he had even gone so far as to ravish her innocence. Now, while tapping his hand impatiently on my father's desk, he was in the process of explaining to me that I was an idiot.

"I don't want to upset you, but in all honesty this weekly sheet is the work of an amateur. You're not registered with the Propagandastaffel, you have no permit for publishing a periodical, anything could happen to you. Anybody who felt like it could publish a rival sheet, and put you out of business. It's Faugère who put you in the saddle, but tomorrow he could change his mind—"

"Listen, I know that my business could stand some improvement, but isn't that what you're here for?"

"Undoubtedly so, but then you must understand, *mon cher*

ami, that if I am to be responsible for this venture, it cannot be, in all fairness, as an employee, but as your associate. I would like to propose to you a simple partnership arrangement, with a distribution of capital in the proportion of three quarters-one quarter. It's only fair, don't you think?"

"You go a bit fast. Give me a day or two to think about it. You want a quarter of the profits on top of your salary?"

"My God, not at all! You haven't understood a thing! It's for you, the quarter, for me it's the three quarters, don't you see? Since I'm in charge! Plus my salary, of course, which I do certainly earn and deserve."

"Listen here, don't you think that you're going too far? That's quite crazy, in fact! Your offer doesn't hold water. Have you forgotten that we've got a year's contract?"

"I remember. That's got absolutely nothing to do with it, and I haven't got any time to waste. Think it over, if you want, and we'll talk about it again in a couple of days."

The next day, when I got to the office, Natalie told me that I had had a call from the Propagandastaffel. A certain von Hoffman, something like that.

"It's not for me, it must be for the baron," I said in a tone that I did not attempt to make pleasant.

"No, no, he insisted that you call him back personally right away."

Strange. . . . Not very comforting, though . . . I figured that perhaps it might be better to make this call before the baron arrived, and I telephoned Hoffman.

"Hauptmann von Hoffman zpeakink," answered a voice out of a melodrama. "*Ach!* Ist to Monzieur Chirodias I haff de hunner off speakink? Dear monzieur, I vould like verry mutts to mague your agvaintance. Coot you come ofer to my ovvice? In von hower?"

"One hour! Well I'm very . . ."

"Gut, In von hower, zen, iss underschtoot."

Might as well get this over with right away, after all, and go see what he wants of me, this Hauptmann von Hauptmann. The worst thing he can do to me is to have me shot, no? So why worry. On the way down the stairs, I glance quickly at my identity card. A few weeks' sojourn in my back pocket has given it at least the beginnings of a dog-eared look. . . . Well, that's something. One grasps at any straw under such circumstances.

The Propagandastaffel, which housed the censorship bureau

of the German army, occupied huge offices at 52, Champs-Elysées. Von Hoffman had spacious quarters all to himself, and he appeared to reign over a little department independent of the rest. He promptly enlightened me as to his position: He was in charge of intelligence, the Gestapo having assigned him to the Propagandastaffel. All told, he wasn't too bad: a tall, elegant man with very blue eyes who spoke French fairly well despite his ridiculous accent. He must have sold eau de cologne in Paris before the war.

"Zo, fairy vell, dear monzieur, I vut lygue to underschtant better vot iss it you are doink, ant who you are."

I explained to him about *Paris-Programme*, certainly a very innocent little enterprise. He remarked right away that, as a weekly publication, it was in an illegal situation, since it was not registered as a periodical. I replied that it was strictly confined to advertising, without any editorial content, and so it should not be subjected to the regulations applying to periodicals. And it was then that he asked to see my identity card. *Jésus Maria!* I fished it out of my pocket and handed it to him as nonchalantly as courtesy would allow.

I was now able to see that there was more to the fellow than met the eye. As soon as he had turned professional on me, all signs of humanity had been erased from his face, and he went into a strange routine of tics and unexpected gesticulations; I guess it was standard Gestapo procedure, to throw off the interlocutor. Right now, he had fallen into a catatonic contemplation in front of my identity card, which he scrutinized with his blue eyes as if he suspected it of harboring the secret of transmuting lead into gold. At the end of a long while, he straightened up and, without even looking at me, pressed a buzzer, whereupon an orderly immediately appeared. Von Hoffman whispered a few words to him in a low voice and handed him the card. The soldier clicked his heels and disappeared. Mercy on me, my poor identity card! It was certainly not worth the thousand francs I had paid for it, but even so. . . . Von Hoffman turned his back on me and shuffled through some dossiers on a side table. . . . And when the orderly returned, after a quarter of an hour, he took my card from him plus a sheet of paper which he read attentively. He then placed it squarely in front of him and turned toward me. He had a particularly weird trick of passing his hand in front of his face and stopping at the level of his eyes. Then his blue gaze would fix on you intently through the tiny slits between his fingers. . . . It may have been grotesque and silly, but it worked! I was beginning to squirm.

"You are gonzealink zumsink vrom me," he said.

He rang another buzzer and soon another door opened admitting a little old man with goatee and pince-nez, dressed in a three-piece suit of synthetic material, a little button bearing the swastika in his lapel.

"Heil Hm," he said, vaguely flapping his right hand as if telling a child to go outside and play.

"Hm'tler," answered von Hoffman, not moving any arms or hands at all, since the other was a menial. He whispered into his ear, the other darted me a quick glance, took the paper, the card, and went away. Without a word, the captain turned back to his work at the neighboring table.

The little old man reappeared and handed him the card and paper plus another sheet, this time of yellow paper, and the officer dismissed him with a gesture, sighed deeply, and turned again to me, passing his hand over his face. Ugh! Again this horrible trick! Looking at me fixedly through his fingers, he said:

"Lizzen to me vell. Iff I haff zummoned you here, iss begause uff an anonymoose ledder. It iss zigned "A Badriot," but off course, zat doez not mean a sink, a badriot. . . . Ha! Dis ledder agguses you off beink Briddiche, Chuish, ant Fvreemazon, bezides. Dot ist a lot, unt I don't believe it, rreally. Aggording to your idendiddy cart, you are rreally Vrench. Dott ist an autentic dogument," he assured me, showing me my card. "Fvreemazon, dot doesn't bozzer me. But Chuish? Dis name, Chirodias, vot iss its orichin?"

I told him it's from the Limousin, like Giraudoux, and explained my origin to him as best I could, shifting around the personas of my father and mother. It wasn't that easy to invent a genealogical tree at top speed with this character staring at me through his fingers.

"Lizzen to me," he said finally. "Effersink you tell me, I don't haff time for verifyink it. Zircumzision, in our days, dot doesn't mean anysink anymore. But aggordink to dhe law, it's zufficient iff you can broove you haff at least von Aryan grandbarent out from four, before you get gonzidered Aryan yourself. Iss diffigult to imachin a more liperal law! Zo, iff you can broof to me you haff a non-Chuish granfadder or a granmutter, I fill let you go in peas. Iff nod . . ."

"Oh, that's easy," I said. "Can I use your phone?"

He pushed a phone over to me, connected to a line which bypassed the switchboard. I dialed my grandfather's number and rapidly explained the situation to him.

"Give me one hour and I will present you with an Aryan grandfather," I said to the man from the Gestapo.

"Fery goot. I vill be fairy habby for you. I am goink to make you vait in der next ovvice."

He locked me in a little room that gave on to his office. In former days, I used to carry around a copy of the *Bhagavad-Gita* in my pocket for such occasions, but I had lost the habit. . . . I began to get seriously worried about my grandfather. . . . Perhaps I had drawn him into a frightful ambush. . . . But when the door opened and Von Hoffman waved at me to come in, I was quickly reassured. Another opened at the same time, and my grandfather made his entrance. I was therefore able to behold him through enemy eyes, so to speak, and what I saw gave me a little thrill of pride. Despite a considerable loss of weight, he was still a handsome old man, a model of dignified bearing, perhaps more Henri IV than François I in style, but a man obviously born to command.

Von Hoffman introduced himself very correctly to my forebear and invited him to sit down, noting the beautiful white beard, the discreet but prestigious decoration in his buttonhole, the well-tailored suit. My grandfather was very relaxed, and briefly summed up his career, saying that of course, he was not of Jewish extraction and that his wife was likewise a Catholic. Von Hoffman didn't even ask him for his papers. The game was won.

A few minutes later, as we were leaving the Propagandastaffel, the old man blew his top. "Really, this Jewish business is a calamity! Come, let's go sit down for a while in a café, I have to drink something. Really, this thing has got to stop, don't we have enough trouble without all that? To imply that I might be Jewish, *me*, right offhand like that, really, it's not in the best of taste, I don't think!" He was red in the face, quite furious.

The next morning when I came into the office, I found Natalie in tears. I had phoned her the night before, after my visit to von Hoffman, to reassure her. Soon afterward the baron had called, apparently to try to find out from her what had happened to me. She hastened to reassure him: I had not been detained by the Germans. The baron then started insulting her, and she couldn't understand why. And then he had told her to empty out his drawers and put all his things in a suitcase, to be left with his concierge. She had done all this without asking for any explanations.

"He didn't even ask to see *me* again," she whimpered. Her sobs went on and on and threatened to develop into hysteria. Finally, the truth came out: Natalie had been to see a doctor the evening before and he had told her she was pregnant. Pregnant by the baron, of course. I ground my teeth in helpless anger, picturing in my mind the ridiculous seduction scene, probably in my father's swivel chair. Well, let's turn that page real fast.

The experience was concluded with a minimum of damage. Thanks to M. Bar, I succeeded in getting rid of *Paris-Programme*; Natalie was taken back to her family's bosom. She was replaced soon afterward by Marie-Paule whom I had met at the time of the Etats-Généraux de la Jeunesse Européenne. She was an enthusiastic backpacker, an activist in the Auberges de la Jeunesse, an avid reader of Giono, and she had walked the roads of France with her guitar; she had a fine voice and a vast repertory of old songs. Thanks to Marie-Paule and Odilon, her Russian-born boyfriend, I became acquainted with an entire social phenomenon of which I had not had any direct knowledge up to that time, since it had developed very far from the bourgeois horizon of Neuilly, among the young leftists and disaffected kids who emerged from every class of society during the days of the Front Populaire. I had known some militants in various leftist movements a few years before, but I hadn't understood then that the apolitical groups on the Left were more numerous and perhaps also more interesting than those which were politically committed. Indeed, their very presence proved the fact that the Front Populaire was, much more than a political adventure, a very real human experience in communication and solidarity.

Too spontaneous to become intellectualized, too modest to express its existence in the form of ideas, it was not meant to leave many traces, or to spread very far. The youth movements in Germany and Italy, during the same years, formed the basis of the Nazi and Fascist régimes thanks to the form of fanatical discipline that was drilled into their subconcious. The French movement was the opposite. Deeply steeped in anarchy and individualism, this made it in fact not a movement at all but, rather, a state of mind, a way of life. It situated itself beyond politics, of which every sensitive or sensible person had an indigestion, and therefore it didn't have a very tangible reality. It concerned itself essentially with nature, authenticity of life and feelings, free love; it despised power, money, war, and most of what a modern industrial society had to offer. But I imagine that before the Russian Revolution, the young nihilists had played the same role of a lost generation: *too good to live*. Politics hates the void; it cannot tolerate anyone who wants to do without it.

And so, to put a lid on that generation of the thirties, the European leaders had found the ideal answer: a war. In that war, who were the real victims? As always, the young, the kids, the future. And who were the winners? What else: the war monuments to be erected when it's all over.

It is at that time, during the winter of 1940, that Raymond Queneau sent me an editor in search of a job, André Lejard, a friendly, lively fellow with an inquiring mind and a worldly experience of the arts and of artists.

It never took long to make friends with André, and it proved all the more easy in our case as our needs were so complementary. I had grown interested in books on art and had noticed how insignificant were the French productions in that field. The Austrians and the Germans did much better, but in France we had only two well-known art magazines, published in Paris, Tériade's *Verve* and the *Cahiers d'Art* produced by Zervos—both Greek, by the way.

There was a third magazine, but it was mainly restricted to the graphic arts, *Arts et Métiers Graphiques* (AMG for short), published by a founder of printing type, Charles Peignot, and they were planning to issue art books as well when the war put a stop to all those projects, and AMG stopped publication. In fact most publishers, big or small, had remained in a state of suspense since the beginning of the occupation. The printing presses were at a standstill, the paper mills had not been reactivated, and no one dared to make the first move.

André Lejard was among the many who had lost their jobs, and he was anxiously looking for an opportunity. He had been AMG's editor, and not only did he have vast experience in a field that was of great personal interest to me, but he intimated that he could bring me two other people, two highly competent women who had been responsible with him for the magazine's publication.

Clearly this was my cue, this was my chance to turn idle dreams into a highly professional reality. But what puzzled me was this simple question—How is it possible that this obviously seasoned fellow should be taking me so seriously? He is trying hard to sell himself to me, but does he know that my whole fortune consists only of a few cans of celery? How could I pay him the high salary he obviously expects? How can I finance art books?

In fact, those questions only passed briefly through my mind. It seemed simpler to trust my luck, and so we made an appointment for the next day, when I would meet the two AMG ladies.

The meeting took place in the faded decor of the Rumpelmeyer tearoom on the rue de Rivoli, and it immediately confirmed my hunch that things were about to happen, and fast. Both women were in their late thirties, strong personalities but very open and friendly, and obviously curious about this bizarre young gentleman's project. Guiton Chabance, a tall, intense, somewhat ravaged woman with large intelligent hands, was a book designer, and Germaine Riedberger was an art historian who had studied with Henri Focillon, knew all about book production, publicity, and was a highy qualified editor as well. Who was I in front of those three people? How much did I know? Why were they talking to me?

One reason had no doubt been Queneau's introduction; another one the address on the place Vendôme, which spelled money; a third one might have been my well-tailored suit. A fourth one was possibly that these were absurd times, and that you could expect anything to happen even if it didn't seem to fit the rules—including a boy of twenty-one deciding to launch into the publishing business in a big way.

Our conversation was surprisingly relaxed and comfortable, and I made no real effort to hide my lack of knowledge. Queneau had probably described me as the son of an old-time British publisher, or something equally misleading, which left some room for both naïveté and eccentricity, plus a youthful lack of experience. And so I conformed myself to that fiction. To compensate for my young age, I had to impress them with my precocity and the evidence of an enterprising mind: All right, I will gladly be a whiz kid if you want me to be one. And I wasn't faking! I was simply learning fast from what they said and from what they were, and returning it to them under my own colors. Indeed that is the nature of any conversation, of any exchange; but since in that particular situation the gulf between their experience and my ignorance was so vast, I had to jump very far ahead of myself in order to be a little bit ahead of them. Thus our association was not really sealed on the basis of a misapprehension, but of a practical program. They needed a leader badly enough to invent one; and so I let them put me in that role, and teach me what I had to know in order to be their boss. I felt especially attracted to Germaine; her neat elegance and sharp features gave an impression of power and efficiency, and yet the essence of her charm was unquestionably female.

The name of the publishing house I wanted to create was already in my eye: *Editions du Chêne*. We were going to begin with easy projects, art books for which there existed a ready market, so that sales would present a minimum of problems. After that, we would really take off; but to start with, why not a general book on the different styles of French furniture, for example? It could be called, simply, *Le Meuble*. And this would be the beginning of a collection that would deal with the artistic aspects of all the other traditional French crafts, from tapestry to jewelry, book designing, and so on—there were plenty of possibilities. Each book would be an inspiration and an illustration of many currents of French art, which had long been neglected because of their utilitarian nature.

Our mutual understanding was perfect. The roles were already well-defined. Right now Germaine would participate only from a distance because with her husband interned as a prisoner of war in a German camp, she had things to do for him, and children to raise. But André and Guiton were going to set to work immediately on the first projects.

Well and good. And now, how was I going to make those wonderful things happen? Everyone had taken it for granted that I had the money, and that I could find the printers, the paper, and the book distribution to make all this happen. However, I had neither the first cent, nor even a precise appreciation of the problem I would have to solve. My only capital was my blissful ignorance.

The idea of *Le Meuble* was good and easy to realize. Guiton improvised a pasted-up dummy of the projected book, and I took it with me to a bookstore on boulevard Saint-Germain that I had heard acted as distributors for some small or specialized publishers. The owner, M. Rombaldi, had died a few months before and I was received by his son, Laurent, who was now running the business. And when I saw Laurent, everything became simple.

He was a kid like me, even perhaps a few weeks younger, and like me he was playing at being what he was not, an experienced businessman. Sitting gravely in his daddy's swivel chair, he was leafing through the dummy, and I caught some surreptitious side glances at my shoes, necktie, and splendid suit. I was much better dressed than he was, but he wasn't jealous, just interested. He smiled at me, easily, and I smiled back. All right! We are in business. We'll show those constipated old publishers and assorted book people that true talent starts early!

We arranged for a contract under which Laurent acquired the exclusive distribution rights of all the future productions of Editions du Chêne, against his commitment to give me a firm order for each book printed, which should be at least sufficient to cover the cost of production. As for money to pay salaries, overhead, and the rest, that was my business, and he seemed to take it for granted that I was as wealthy as I wanted him to believe I was. At least he would pay every reorder immediately upon completion, and that would certainly help build up my cash flow.

As I was concluding that negotiation, I was overtaken by an awful feeling that this was all a waste of time. The selling was easy, but the manufacturing impossible, since there was no paper to be found—especially the high-grade coated paper I needed for the color reproductions; and thus my contract with Rombaldi was so much pie in the sky. This is when another miracle happened, when André Lejard brought me a dignified gent sporting a magnificent silky white handlebar moustache: M. Amelaine. He was a sales representative for a big printer operating south of Paris, Imprimerie Kapp, and he was desperately searching for orders to get his presses rolling again. He was prompt to give me what looked like a reasonable estimate for *Le Meuble*, and when I told him about my paper problem, he immediately came up with a solution.

Kapp had been printing a swish, expensive house organ, before the Occupation, for Les Laines du Pingouin, a large firm of wool manufacturers who were, like everyone else, waiting for better days. They had thirty-five tons of excellent coated paper set aside that they would not use any longer, and he was certain that they would be willing to sell the whole lot at the prewar rate, which was just under two francs a kilo. That looked like the second miracle in less than a week. And getting that paper at the regular rate would be a godsend, since black-market practices had started for many products that were about to be rationed, including, of course, paper.

The Prouvost brothers, owners of Les Laines du Pingouin, were very cordial and receptive, no doubt due to Kapp's recommendation. They agreed to let me have the thirty-five tons for two francs a kilo, and introduced me to their business manager, who would settle the details with me.

It could have been a very simple affair, but it was not.

First of all, I didn't have the money. And so I sent Marie-Paule to place an ad in a financial paper on rue de Richelieu, which ran as follows: "New publisher seeks facilities to finance top quality project. Maurice Girodias—Les Editions du Chêne." No beating around the bush here!

And sure enough, early the next morning, an elderly gentleman arrived at my office and introduced himself with great dignity.

"My name is Hyppolite Léonard," he said. "I am a broker, and I happened to read your advertisement."

M. Léonard took his time to sit down, join his fingertips together in a meditative stance, and observe me with a piercing eye. I realized that he was about to start selling me some insurance, and noted with discomfort that he was wearing beige felt spats over brown suede shoes. My father would have ordered him out of the room immediately, but I am less sanguine than he was about sartorial etiquette including the vocabulary of dress, and so I waited.

"I was curious to meet you. Because of the style of your request for money, as if it were owed to you. You are right, that's the way to get what you want; but so few people know that. . . . Well, anyway, your time is valuable, I shall not waste it. I am here to tell you in so many words: Cher monsieur, I have your man."

"Not yourself?" I asked.

"No no, I am only a broker, it is not my business to lend money. But do you know a banker by the name of Thollot? Marcel Thollot."

"Sorry, I never heard the name before."

"Well Monsieur Thollot, that's your man. An enterprising private banker, a man of considerable affluence and impeccable taste, and a patron of the arts to boot. Marcel Thollot is a connoisseur! I am sure that you two were meant to meet and do profitable business together. Would you be free to meet him tomorrow morning?"

How engaging. I said yes, thanked M. Léonard, and we bid farewell to each other:

"A demain!"

The banker's offices were on rue des Italiens, large and well-appointed, and the banker was a handsome man with a ruddy face and pleasant manner, rather on the pompous side. He wanted very much to be a shrewd banker, a man of the world, a patron of the arts, and even, in fact, an artist. I gathered that he sang *bel canto*, dabbled with the paint brush, and was very sensitive to things beautiful. M. Léonard had been perfectly right: Here is my man!

It was my turn to explain my problem about the paper, and I showed him my contract with Rombaldi. He looked very pleased with all this, his only distress appearing to derive from the fact that I didn't need more.

"Will you have a whiskey? I can offer you very good Scotch, here, bourbon, practically anything you want," he suggested.

The display in the bar must have cost a fortune at current black-market rates. I declined the drink, however, mentioning the fact that I drank no liquor. He looked at me speculatively, noting *en passant* the fine quality of shoes, necktie, and suit. He himself was well dressed, but in an excessively conservative fashion, typical of someone who must constantly restrain his secret taste for the flashy.

"My God! *You don't drink?*"

"I'm afraid not. And you'd be amused to know that I am also a vegetarian."

"A vegetarian! I've never spoken to one face-to-face! Isn't that supposed to be a Hindu sect?"

That was a silly remark I had made, quite out of the blue; this sanguine fellow was pretty antipodal, that was obvious enough, and I had to steer him away from the subject. It proved to be easy enough, as he was anxious to touch all possible bases besides food and drink. And I needed all of M. Léonard's help to put him back on the right track: money. He assured me that as soon as the deal was about to be executed with the Pingouin people, he would have a check ready for them. And he would immediately consider the problem of long-term financing based on the Rombaldi contract. Wow, I told myself as we left the building.

"Splendid!" chimed in M. Léonard. "It went very well, and you acquitted yourself of your task in the most creditable manner. Now you have a banker."

"Monsieur Léonard!" I said, turning to him. "It's all thanks to your intuition, let me shake your hand."

"But that's nothing," the broker said modestly. "Nothing but a little gift I have."

"En . . . ar . . . perhaps we should have discussed the matter earlier, but what is the custom regarding your . . . er . . . fee, expenses, whatnot?" I asked.

"Don't think of it," Léonard said. "Monsieur Thollot will take care of that."

All of this left me perplexed as well as wonderstruck. Why is it that one only has to will a thing forcefully enough for it to happen?

The next day I rang up the Pingouin's manager and told him that I was anxious to conclude the deal quickly. We had the same printer, no need to move the paper, when did he want his check?

"Oh no, not so fast," he said. "We must check the quantities, make an itemized invoice. It will take some time. Besides the Messieurs Prouvost, I regret to say, misinformed you about the price. It is not two francs a kilo, but two ninety-five."

"But it's *impossible!* That's fifty percent more! I'll have to talk to them."

"No you won't," he said. "Neither of them is in Paris, and it would make absolutely no difference in any case."

So I would have to get more money out of Thollot, and I would look very much like a fool.

Having gone successfully through that trying experience, I was ready to call the Pingouin man again, two days later. He told me that I could only have twenty tons out of thirty-five, at two-fifty, and he totally disregarded my outraged protest.

The next day he said that he could only offer me ten tons at four francs net a kilo. I didn't even have time to shout at him; he hung up on me.

Once again my dream of glory was being deflated in front of my very nose! I hardly slept at all that night. And when I called the fellow once again the next morning, I was told that he would be out of town for an indefinite period of time. End of the script.

Stunned by this final blow, I was sitting at a café terrace, trying to console myself with a beer and the benevolent sunshine. And visions of nymphs zipping by on their bikes. . . . Until I realized that someone had sat down at my table, ogling the same thighs.

"Klop!" I exclaimed. "Haven't seen you in ages. . . . So you stayed in Paris, eh?"

"Baris ist az gutt az anywhere elz zeeze days," Klop responded. He was Dutch, with an impossibly long name that started with Klop, and an incurable accent.

"Vhat about yourzelf? Vhat are you doink?"

"Well," I started, "well now, what am I doing? Just like you, sitting in the sun, hoping for the best."

And then a lightning bolt struck me. "Klop, old fellow," I asked the Dutchman, "how would you like to earn one hundred francs for five minutes' work?"

"Ant how! Ist illeakel?"

"Not really. On the contrary, for me it's superlegal. But in any case, you, you don't give a damn, you're just an instrument. If anybody's going to hell, it's me. . . . Good, listen closely. Imagine that you're a German officer, a captain in the Gestapo, and that your name is von Hoffman . . . a shrewd hood—"

In broad outline, I wrote out the scenario on the back of an envelope, gave him some change, and shut him into a phone booth. Through the glass, I could see him really getting into his role and gesticulating with indignation. He was shaking up the manager of the Prouvost brothers—it was a pleasure to watch. . . . He was telling him that he, von Hoffman, had tracked down the existence of this undeclared stock of thirty-five tons of paper. . . . verry illeakel . . . the zituation hat to be put in order widdin vorty-eight howers, or elz. . . .

Through the glass, I signaled him to stop. He had better not go too far, there might be a chance that the other one would offer him money, one never knows, and then he might be tempted to take it, and run: Paranoia was not far! But he emerged from the booth very pleased with himself, and I thanked him for a job well done, paid him off, and rushed to my office. Exactly five minutes after I arrived the Pingouin manager, just as foreseen, called up and asked to speak to me.

"Listen, my dear fellow," he started, "I'm really sorry about all the complications of the past few days, but it couldn't be helped. Now, I've just spoken again about your business to my bosses, and they suggested coming back to the terms of the original agreement. You're quite pleased, eh? Thirty-five tons at two francs per kilo. Total: seventy-thousand francs. Have you got the money?"

"Yes."

"Good. But there's one condition. It's necessary that we carry out the transaction not later than tomorrow night, including payment—for internal reasons that would take too long to explain. Is that possible?"

"Well, that's rather short notice, really. But just to help you out, I'll swing it. You can count on me."

So there it was. I, of whom it was said, in my family and elsewhere, that I had so little talent for business! When I told the story to Bogous, he guffawed heartily as was his wont, and told me that he was proud of his pupil.

As for me, I was proud of my teacher! Without the philosophy he had patiently instilled in me, how would I have become, at twenty-one, the youngest publisher in Paris? Who knows, perhaps in the entire world?

18

Hunger in the night; how the French learn
to be a slave people. —Free spirits take to the woods.
—One glimpse of Marina, and here we go again.
—The mystery of the fetish foot. —Onward to
Mont Saint-Michel.—Slow progress inside enemy territory.
—Dining in splendor.—I wake up
for the first time really a man.

Yes indeed these were hard times. And to call this the Occupation, when no one had anything to do, what kind of black humor was that?

First the defeat, a complete surprise, just like being knocked down in the street by some bully, for no reason at all except his own good pleasure. And then the way they had to make you feel defeated. Everything was being reduced to this shrunken reality, empty, monotonous, stationary. The art of living had been replaced by the art of survival.

Old Hitler had taken really good care of the French, he had settled their goose for them in his own inimitable way, no doubt to punish them for having ignored him for so long and with such pigheaded impertinence. You should hear what popular wisdom had to say about this in any café, around the time of the aperitif: "That fellow Hitler, he eats nothing but vegetables and he drinks only water. No wonder he's so mean."

The French had placed much pride and pleasure in their gastronomy until then, so that being abruptly deprived of food was not just physical torture but a moral one as well. France's cuisine is the Siamese twin of her culture: Kill the one and the other promptly dies.

That feeling of everything slowing down, of nowhere to turn, of nothing to hope for; now you really understood what it is to lose a war. One was living in the dark in every sense of the term, that is to say, power came and went, and during the short time when you could use electricity at home, you were only allowed to do so behind blackened windows, and now it was no longer because of German, but because of British air raids. There is something truly eerie about a big city like Paris being permanently plunged in pitch-darkness year in, year out, without end; the winter nights were deep, stark, and cruel. If you were brave or desperate enough to venture from the cold inside to that blackness outside, you had to inch your way like a blind man who's just lost his dog, feeling the unseen façade of buildings with your hands to avoid crashing into them. Perchance, on your way, you would pass a ground-floor window and discover through a crack in the shutters a group seated in the inside gloom at the dining table, motionless in front of empty plates, with sullen faces and hanging arms. All sitting there, uselessly, by sheer force of habit, and for want of anything better to do until bedtime.

Where was the famous French *joie de vivre?* But how can you clink glasses in friendship if there's only water in them? Drinking songs stuck inside dry throats. Gone was the good cheer, the bellyfuls of suave foods, the three-day-long banquets. And what was there left to talk about? Ration tickets, where to find powdered milk and shoes on the black market for the kiddies, all the awful, miserable, minute survival problems that made up everyday life now. Such was the true sense of the defeat: It had not been enough for Hitler to call the French impotent and degenerate, he had to make them prove to the world that indeed they were, and that Jean-Paul Sartre and Josephine Baker were responsible for that shame. To add insult to injury, besides being taught lessons in austerity by that high-way bandit, the French also had to praise that man Hitler publicly day and night for teaching them how to live. Oh, the bastard!

Not only the traditional chicken-in-every-pot had walked away, but, worse still, on the day of the armistice every citizen of France had been nailed solidly to the ground by the suppression of practically all means of transportation. The trains were rare and their schedule unpredictable, and, besides, traveling made you too highly visible, railway stations and the railways themselves being subjected to constant controls and surveillance. As to the family automobile, still a mark of bourgeois privilege before the war, it had been stashed away in some stable in the country, its wheels removed so as to avoid requisition, its cushions sprouting all varieties of mold and mushrooms, a sign of the times.

And of course France was strictly divided by its internal border, drawn and fiercely guarded by the Germans, the so-called demarcation line. Those who were stuck in the Nazi-controlled northern portion of the country were dreaming of the mellow, balmy south as if it were a distant, exotic land. And those rooted in Auvergne or Provence were full of nostalgia for the glitter of Paris. You started by dreaming about lost friends, until the time when you realized that you had forgotten even what they looked like. And so most people had no choice but to stay at home, leafing through old peacetime magazines, and this resulted in a tremendous amount of nagging, squabbling, and backbiting. Gone were the cozy little business trips, so convenient to enhance the sexual diversification of the families.

The first winter was particularly severe, and without food or heat the old folks gave up the ghost in large numbers. These were hard, terrible times for the destitute: the tramps froze to death in doorways, and even scarecrows were robbed of their coats in the open fields.

Then, as time went on and spring weather came to soothe all that misery, many of those who had survived found that the forced diet had indeed saved their lives. Liver ailments, kidney trouble, gout, obesity, cirrhosis, heart failures, in short, every possible malady caused by the three huge meals a day, the fantastic overindulgence of prewar years in rich food and wines—all that had been miraculously cured. Walking had become a vital necessity; muscle was now the one and only source of energy.

All industries being either totally stopped or considerably slowed down, the air had become clear and healthy; exhaust fumes had disappeared with the cars themselves, and you could count those going up and down the big avenues on the fingers of one hand. They were dull gray German military cars mostly, plus a few decrepit trucks belching their way shakily toward Les Halles—the huge central marketplace of Paris—their engines powered with the gas from wood or sawdust burning in a huge cylindrical furnace attached to the side of the vehicle, and known as *gazogène*.

Paris had become rustic, countryfied, and this became even more evident with the rebirth of the bicycle. The streets gradually filled up with cyclists of every age and description, and you would be amazed to see the Champs-Elysées swarming with businessmen in three-piece suits, zigzagging down the hill on sparkling wheels, or rickety pedicabs in which fat black market *nouveaux riches* luxuriated, with a scrawny fellow pedaling in front, who played the roles of both driver and engine.

Why, I even saw my own banker, Marcel Thollot, arrive for an appointment one day primly perched on a remarkable cycle of ancient British make, a true museum piece. The cuff of his trousers was carefully bound by silver clips, his black Homburg was sitting on his head at precisely the right incline, and the precious malacca handle of his umbrella was sprouting from the frame, to which a special fixture had been added to hold it. You could only stop and gape at such a splendiferous spectacle.

It is true that the man was a social climber who insisted on being the first and the best at anything that happened to be fashionable; but it really took a very special mentality to turn oneself into a bicycle snob. And yet how else could you explain the deployment of deluxe gadgetry affixed to that dazzling, haughty, unique nickel-plated number? It was pleasant to picture M. T. at home with his favorite cycle, the two of them posing in front of a large mirror in search of the best angle, now full-face, now in profile. Just try to imagine a grown-up banker spending his time like that! A good symbol, too, of our national humiliation: It became clear, in these times of trial, that what distinguishes humans from vegetables is, first and foremost, mobility.

It had taken only those three short summer weeks of 1940 to destroy the most ancient and venerable state of them all, France, the political model emulated by every other national community since the Middle Ages. Each one of the heterogeneous populations that had been welded together over the centuries to form the French nation, usually by ruse and by violence, was now free from the central authority, traditionally identified with the city of Paris, where one tenth of the country's population is concentrated. Each province was now living a life of its own, just as if the French state had never existed, and it seemed quite inconceivable for the time being that those pieces would ever be brought together again under a central government.

Here again you find Hitler's hand, his psychological insight, his use of people's vanity to induce them to destroy themselves. Why had the Germans refrained from invading all of France? It would have taken two more days to do it. But by leaving its freedom to one third of the French territory, Hitler had played on the political ambitions of Pétain, Laval, and other right-wing politicos who could not resist the lure of forming their own makeshift government in Vichy, and thereby hang themselves. Certainly for the Nazis that phony government was an ideal device because, although politically impotent, it still had just enough power to levy taxes—thanks to which it was expected to settle the fabulous sums extorted daily by the Germans, under the excuse that they had to be compensated for the expenses incurred in occupying the country. In fact they claimed enough money to finance an army of 18 million soldiers. None of the other occupied countries in Europe, not even Norway with its pro-Nazi dictator, Quisling, had disgraced itself in such a stupid manner.

And so inflation was fast killing the French economy, such as it was. With their trainloads of surplus francs the Germans had also set up discrete trading centers where their agents would buy anything the impoverished French bourgeoisie had to offer, art collections, châteaux, farms, *femmes*, factories, you name it—which was promptly paid to the sellers with their own money. And of course that did not take into account the estates of the Jews, now in exile or in death camps, since the notion that the German government should have to pay anything for *that* was too absurd to bear mentioning. . . . Such perfectly detailed and executed strategy bore the evil mark of Hitler's genius; indeed, who in the whole vast world of politics could possibly equal such formidable statesmanship?

And to make the disgrace of the French even more supreme, Paris had been turned into a sort of vacation camp for Nazi troops and personnel, where they were sent as a very special recompense after all those years of sweating and toiling in Germany. The culture-minded had plenty of museums to visit, plus a wealth of beautiful architecture and noble landscapes to enjoy. But the vast majority was content to get drunk in Montmartre, to paw the *danseuses* and to mob the nightclubs. And where did that leave the French?

For the average French male supremacist in particular, these were not only hard times, it was in fact total bankruptcy. His prestige was down to below zero, he was an all-time loser, his cuffs frayed, the girls sneering at him, and he did not even have enough cash in his pocket to buy the love he could win no more. Total degradation. Famished and sullen, the Paris Don Juan whiled away his time at café terraces in front of a day-long, watery beer. Somberly ogling the cycling beauties with their skirts happily flying to the winds, and tender calves pushing the pedal with athletic determination.

Where to escape? The only place to which one could travel by train within a reasonable distance was Fontainebleau, the pleasure city of Renaissance kings, with its vast surrounding crown of woods and picturesque villages tucked away behind the trees. That forest soon became very familiar to me; I spent many weekends there, sleeping in small inns or more frequently camping out in the open in the company of kindred souls, under the vast rocks for which that forest is famous.

The weekend population in the woods around Fontainebleau could have made a subject for a fascinating sociological study. It might have supplied interesting insights into the reasons why France had lost the war. My new friends presented a perfect cross section of every possible shade of dissidence against the established order.

Many simply came from the movement of the Auberges de la Jeunesse, the vast Youth Hostels movement, which had sent millions of young people on the roads of France in the thirties, equipped with a guitar and a sleeping bag, and inoculated them with the love of nature and the greatest distrust for the deathly contradictions of the bourgeois society. There were those who were simply nature lovers, often ex-mountaineers who trained nostalgically, climbing the steep rocks in the forest dreaming of the Alps; but also many disaffected leftist militants who had fought the political battles of the thirties, including some veterans of the Spanish civil war. Few were still politically active, because if you are a true anarchist you are bound to turn eventually against all forms of classical politics. That lack of any governing principles made that antiestablishment subculture even more impressive by its determination to stay out of everything, particularly after the Soviets' traitorous alliance with the Nazis.

Under the tall trees, crouching around huge campfires in the starry night, that rabble of small-time outlaws became a real society of young people, lively and refreshing. They were good company, and I became used to leading that wandering life for a couple of days every week, and this made a fine contrast with my elegant career as the young founder of an already prestigious publishing firm which was mine the rest of the time. There was only little communication between the two worlds in which I led my double life.

Until, that is, a certain day, when I was walking past a forest inn with two of my hirsute companions, and I saw coming out of the door that remarkable Greek girl. (Now—what's her name?) I had noticed her two or three times, a year before, at meetings of the boulevard Saint-Germain ashram, and I had wondered about her. Nothing very mystical about her! A wonderful-looking female, giving an impression of demure sensuality, with a slight ironic smile, radiant blue eyes, and that fantastic mane of dark blonde hair, this. . . . (What *is* her name? Is it Ma, Ma—.)

"*Marina!* What a surprise!" I blurted out ineptly.

"Oh, Maurice!" she responded, peering at my strange costume. "Just like that, out of the woods! So nice. . . . What are you doing here?"

How long would it take to answer *that* one? I would have to explain my whole life, my double life, and there certainly was no time for that. I was just dazzled by the apparition, remembering with a sudden shock that I must have dreamed several times about her of late, and that although I had never even really spoken to her before, I must have had a fantastic crush on her all along—without being even aware of it, yes. Strange! Being so much in love, excruciatingly and tragically in love with another one, this had just obscured the fact. . . . Can one be genuinely in love with *two* women at the same time? Ah, why ask myself such a question? Don't I know the answer!

Marina was looking at me with that light of friendly amusement in her luminous eyes. The mildest challenge.

"Well," I stammered, "I was just walking by, you see . . ."

"I am Pierre," said one of my buddies, coming up to her with his hand held out wide. The fatuous grin on his face made me wince.

The other one, an inveterate skirt-chasing Armenian, was about to catch up with us when from a second-floor window a deep male voice called her name.

Marina instantly turned on her heels and walked back through the door, ignoring my helpless comment, and vanishing with a last dazzling smile in my direction. Not another word. . . . Leaving me feeling totally dismayed, crushed. . . .

Everything had gone so quickly—she appears—I fall in love like never before—she disappears to fall into the arms of that other man who's waiting for her inside: all of that in the space of twenty-five seconds *flat!*

The story of my life in the tiniest nutshell ever.

But it was already too late to reason about it. Those twenty-five seconds had changed everything—enough to plunge me into that state of high fever, that seizure of delight mixed with anguish that seemed to be my lot. . . . Hope without hope, once again. . . . *Marina*. . . . I did not even know her last name.

And then some minor helpful miracles began to happen. First, I discovered her name, and, second, I found that she was friends with the owner of a posh beauty parlor on rue de Castiglione, and went there often. It was around the corner, a three-minute walk from my office.

After that the slightest excuse was enough to cause me to scurry back to the shops in the rue Castiglione, buying dozens of neckties at Boivin's next door, books at Les Arcades, pipes, roses, ladies' purses, toothpicks, combs. None of this I needed, but I wanted to make myself look as casual as possible in anticipation of the magic occasion of our meeting. I was living only for that moment, dreaming about the first words, the first look, the first, well, touch. . . .

At the end of one week, no magic encounter, alas, not the slightest glimpse of her, no results, except that I was now a millionaire in neckties and the owner of twelve different shades of lipstick. Of course I could have tried to find her address now that I knew her name; but then what? Call her to say *what?* I did not have the nerve, and I was relieved when I saw that she was not listed in the phone book. Nobody I knew seemed to know exactly where she lived; and whether she actually existed became a question. Perhaps I had been in love for so long that the condition itself had become my second nature. A smile had been enough to get me started. A true sickness! How could I fall in love with a woman half-seen, such a long time ago, never approached, and in fact only half-remembered?

The truth of the matter is that I am an idiot, a cretin, an idle dreamer, a nincompoop. And then, in a bout of self-loathing and disgust, I throw the last batch of pipes I just bought into a garbage can and walk to the corner newsstand to buy the evening paper.

A thick throng is scurrying up and down the rue de Casti-glione, the usual mix of *midinettes*, secretaries, old beaux and countesses, interspersed with a medley of German officers, stiff and awkward in their long coats, foreign bodies that the French have taken the healthy habit of ignoring alto-gether as if they just don't exist. Reaching out for my news-paper in that melee, I find myself suddenly thrust bodily face-to-face against somebody, a body that is *her*—and I regis-ter this as a shocking, incongruous fact; why did this have to happen now, when I am least prepared for the encounter? She responds to my look of sinful astonishment with a smile of delighted complicity.

Not only has the dream been made flesh, but that flesh is overwhelmingly present, as she is pushed against me by the throng. At such close quarters I can see the minuscule lines at the corners of her sparkling eyes, that I had never noticed before. She is not in her early or mid-twenties, as I thought, but closer to thirty, then, much older than I; and I love her for it. Hastily, passionately, I drink in everything that makes her so special, so enchanting, so warm and spirited. But it is also necessary to speak, to say something exceptionally clever.

"Marina, what a surprise!" In a strangled voice.

"Maurice!" she answers. "It's so rare to see you! And when I do you always seem to be in such a hurry to be somewhere else." She touches my cheek lightly with her warm fingers, a totally unexpected gesture. "Do I frighten you? Tell me."

"Frighten, oh no, *no*, NO!" I stammer, absolutely undone. Inwardly I kick myself and tear my hair; but at the same time breathing in her fragrance—we are so close—and I know that I am about to pass out. Her pink lips are saying words I can-not hear, so fascinated am I with the delicate curve of her smile, which fills me with a madman's hunger. All this time, indeed no more than a few seconds, I am still being jostled and pushed against her, in a narrow corridor of moving bod-ies. . . . Her last words find their mark—

"That's settled, then? *I can count on you?* Tuesday evening, no later than eight, and here's my address. *Mardi!* It's going to be an all-Greek dinner, just you and me, I know where to find all the good things, you'll see. You won't forget, will you, *Maurice?*"

"Ah yes, Greek dinner. *Mardi prochain*, oh yes, oh yes," I hear myself stupidly babbling away. "Oh, Marina, *I wanted so much to tell you* . . ."

"*Mardi, mardi!*" she sings laughingly, as she is drawn away into the crowd, turning that day of the week into the most voluptuous word in the French language. "*Mardi* we'll tell all . . ."

Mardi, *mardi*, then. Until that fateful Tuesday I hardly slept, ate, or made sense. She lived in a reasonably elegant apartment building on boulevard Suchet, of modern design, tastefully anonymous.

I find it hard to ring her bell without losing my grip on all the presents I am carrying in my arms, and I am still trying to do it with my elbow when the door opens of its own free will.

"Oh, Maurice! What an angel. . . . Is that all for me? Yes? But why *two* bouquets? They're both perfectly lovely, but . . ."

"Ah yes, well, oh, what, that is, I couldn't choose . . ." Red-faced, stammering, deliriously happy. She is gorgeous, so help me God, gorgeous, gor . . .

"Hah, listen to him, he couldn't *choose!*" she cries. "How precious." Laughing like a child she opens the flat package, and exclaims once again: "Oh, how *ex*quisite, how perfectly *lovely*. What a beautiful print, and how *quaint!* Is it very old? Tell me, what *is* it?"

"Hmm, well, it's an artist's rendering of *La Carte du Tendre*, it shows how to travel in the country of love. Well, you know, the French romantics of the seventeeth century, Mademoiselle de Scudéry and all that . . . ," I end lamely.

"You mean, it's three hundred years old? It must be extremely valuable. Really you shouldn't . . ."

"Oh no no," I plead. "It's nothing, nothing at all. Actually the frame is quite old, it's perhaps worth more than the print itself. You can put it in your bathroom, in the kitchen . . ."

"Ah now don't be silly," she sighs. "But tell me more about those wonderful people, Mademoiselle de. . . . How do you call her . . . ?"

"Scu-dé-ry," I answer happily from the vast sofa, heaped with pretty cushions, on which I now sit. "You see it was the literary fashion of the time, a resurgence of courtly love as it had been sung by the troubadours in the Middle Ages. During that second era, however, it sank into excessive mannerism. Very decadent in its excesses: Madeleine de Scudéry had her fiancé wait seventeen years until she consented to . . . hm, er . . ."

"Seventeen *years!*" She turns her attentive gaze away from the flowers she has been arranging in two very tall vases, and looks at me. "What the French have done with *love*, really! Why be so cruel?"

"A lover proves his passion by suffering for it," I utter, quite foolishly.

". . . By suffering down to his last breath! What poppycock," she rejoins heatedly. Which makes her look even more glorious. There is something irresistible in the way she pronounces French with her light Greek accent, rolling her *r*'s dreamily over her tongue, and then letting the words roll out like so many little erotic animals. . . . But she is taking all this quite seriously, I can see that; and I am dismayed by what comes next. Her face suddenly turns serious, even somber.

"Certainly I believe in hope, in patience, even in fidelity, of course I do, but there ought to be a limit to everything, don't you think? I also have been waiting myself more than a year already, and how many more years do I have to wait! The Lord only knows. Kostas, my fiancé you know, although he is Greek like me, fought with the French army, he was captured, and who knows when I will see him again. He is in good health, his spirit is unbroken, he seems to manage; but this degradation, that terrible camp in eastern Prussia, and all those young lives being wasted, when will it end? Oh yes, his letters are very beautiful, he's showing wonderful courage, and that's a constant inspiration for me. . . . We were so happy together . . ."

My fiancé you know . . . She is overwhelmed by her emotion, her features suddenly seem older, but also ennobled by her grief—which is of course immediately being echoed by mine. Tenfold.

My implacable frivolity had distorted my vision of her, I am seized by a wave of intense grief and remorse as I discover my terrible error of judgment. All the time I had been pursuing her she had been hopelessly in love with someone else, just as I had been trying to make myself forget that I was also desperately in love with another. . . . Lie upon lie. . . . Marina, I ask her wordlessly, is it possible that we have been brought together simply to compare the depth of our sufferings, and compound them in this devastating manner? A Greek tragedy in a Greek household? I am speechless with misery.

As I feel the tears welling into my eyes, in spite of all my efforts to suppress them, I see her turn away and leave the room with a pathetic sob. Should I follow her into the kitchen, try to console her? But I just can't bring myself to do that, and I continue to sit there, gasping, savoring my grief, hers, as if it were some evil candy. And much to my surprise, after only a few minutes she reappears, pushing a trolley crammed with silver and white porcelain, and piled high with sumptuously exotic foods. Even more astonishing, her face is once again radiant, youthful, and actually glowing with earthy mirth. How can she . . . ? Well, anyway, ah, women are full of surprises. I am only too glad to take my cue from her, and I feel instantly cheered and refreshed at the vision of her serene beauty.

We are sitting across from each other; over the fine white tablecloth she now appears to me framed between two huge pyramids of flowers, as she earnestly explains each dainty item on display. It dawns on me that authentic Greek cuisine has only little to do with what is sold in the greasy spoons of the Latin Quarter. So many subtle flavors, fresh and tangy, such delicate textures, I am simply amazed by the wealth of sensual experience. Which in turn brings on a dangerous euphoria; other thoughts are again floating into my feverish brain, aiming for other pleasure centers. Well, my eyes can hardly leave Marina's mouth, greedy, mobile, thirsting for sensations. Lips made for love of all kinds, devouring infinitesimal mouthfuls with girlish mimics, and, yes, those perverse and caressing lips of hers, always smiling. How I would enjoy tasting this fabulous repast with her very own lips.

The impulse is so strong, I tell her.

She stares at me with an even gaze, somewhat amused, mildly intrigued.

"Is this your way of telling me that I have a pretty mouth? Then why not simply tell me: *'Marina, my dear, you have a very pretty mouth?'* "

The way she articulates those unexpected words—with that very mouth we are now discussing—does something terrible to me, and I stammer helplessly, "Why, I didn't mean, ah you know . . . ?"

"But certainly there are others who have pretty mouths," she goes on cruelly. "Your Laurette for instance. If I were a man I know very well what I would do to that girl of yours. But *you*, you wouldn't dare. Ah, Maurice, poor sweet lover; I've never seen a lover as smitten as you, I swear to God, my poor dear friend. Not on my account, of course dear heart, that much I know; it's *her*, she's the only one for you. You will always return to her, as the saying goes in my country, like the sea goes back to the sandy cove. You ought to take her away; be bold, marry her if such is your destiny."

"You know very well that it's out of the question," I say mournfully.

Why is Marina torturing me so? Her moods are so unstable, you never know if she's playing games, or what. . . . And now she is quietly contemplating me from her smart sophisticated vantage point, her hands primly crossed in her lap, ensconced in a vast straw armchair that forms around her white silhouette an icon's halo of old gold. Indeed the color of her own hair is a very similar shade; not your pale, silvery Scandinavian blondness, but darker and richer, like vintage honey, the type of blondness one finds sometimes on the northern shores of the Mediterranean. Like her skin itself, whose sunny color is emphasized by the snowy linen of her long gown. As I drink in every detail, still feeling like a man about to die, I become gradually aware of a fluttering sensation, something alive and frolicsome, invisible under the tablecloth, now wandering along the length of my leg. When I entered the apartment I had noticed no cat or dog, but. . . .

"Ah yes, Vivian and his ideas on asceticism," Marina is saying in a tone of scorn. She is luxuriously reclining in her chair, in an attitude of quiet repose. However—*there's no mistaking it any longer!* It has to be her foot, her own well-shaped little foot that is conducting that indecent campaign under the table, unseen and diabolical, now reaching boldly right under my napkin, teasing, retreating. Wild-eyed, I keep staring at her, at that very picture of innocence and peacefulness, and I know it can't be true, it's not her, she has nothing to do with this . . . this. . . . It could be some strange phenomenon. . . . The occult? Perhaps some teasing materialization of my secret thoughts? Perhaps I am being punished by the spirits.

"As for me, all that business about asceticism, you know; well it may be very good for certain people"—she is calmly holding forth, very rational and convincing—"but I still suspect that Saint Paul's famous epistle to the Corinthians has been misread all this time, misunderstood by everybody. . . . Such hypocrisy, I assure you, it's not for me. And as for your Laurette, you know I love her, she is my friend, but I am convinced that, deep down, she is not exactly the saintly person

you see in her. She is not a nun, even if she believes herself to
be one."

Her expression is demure, a touch severe, as she speaks of
nuns in that detached voice, nearly solemn. I am gazing at her,
caught in a sort of catatonic trance, in a delightful humiliation,
as the small warm ghost goes expertly about its business
under the table. Yes, beneath the snowy tablecloth lives a methodical houri, versed in every nuance of the erotic arts. What
is happening is something that my weak intelligence cannot grasp, but the fact is, I just can't resist anymore the flow
of exquisite, tingling sensations mounting in me, wave after
wave of sensual delight. . . . This foot, assuming that it is a
mere foot, must have instead of toes the fingers of a great
pianist. This foot is a doctor in erotic lore, nimble, imaginative, capricious, roué, impudent, implacable, devastating,
strong as a bull, although its caresses evoke the wings of a
butterfly, so light and subtle they are.

She is still studying me, gaily chattering, smiling, the very
image of candor, of sweet benevolence. *Is she truly aware of
what I feel?* Of what is presently happening to me? Could it
be that she is *really* unaware of what her foot is doing to me?
By now I have become so confused that the only thought in
my poor head is to hide from her knowledge that terribly
indecent traffic going on under the tablecloth. *Ouch!*

"But don't you have anything to say about it? Come now,
young man, get it out of your system. But you are blushing! Did I say anything to offend your sensibilities?" she asks
with an air of friendly concern, staring at me questioningly,
drinking in my emotions.

"Ah, oh-ho, Marina, *listen!* —"

The foot has apparently decided to call it a day, and the
crude vigor of the agile toes *(ouch!)* is irresistible. I jump in
the air like an electrocuted puppet, and then start a slow fall,
like an accordion being dropped from the fifth floor, shaken
with incoherent spasms, cries, implorations, down, down,
dragging down with me the tablecloth as if it were a shroud
for my shame, and along with it a fortune in crystal, delicious
Greek pastry, silver, and fine porcelain. Down at her feet,
ahhh.

That dinner left me in a very pensive and amorous mood.
Having played with my, er, feelings, in that interesting man-

ner she gently escorted me to the door, ignoring all pleas. It dawned on me that her life was constructed as a great game composed of diverse minor games, and for each one of them I imagined that she had a carefully selected partner. Not just games of the flesh; I soon discovered the extent and versatility of her interests. Clearly I should consider myself lucky to have been recruited to serve in the Erotic Suspense Department; she made good use of my masochistic tendencies, but so help me God, the wench was going too far! She had challenged my virility, whatever the meaning of that silly word: I would show *her* a thing or two, then! Yes I would.

And then I went a little further with my thinking. Perhaps she was in fact trying me, to find out how much I could understand and endure. To win the hand of the princess I must first of all confront and slay the evil dragon lurking inside the very heart of the princess. She was too clever, too complex and demanding; perhaps youthful passion and boyish naïveté like mine were the only remedies she had not yet tried to restore her rapport with common humanity. A boy was what she needed. But what a task for a boy! Particularly with that diabolical foot, feet even, which seemed always to materialize from nowhere each time I tried to speak to her seriously, or at least with some minimal coherence.

There was a memorable promenade in an open horse-drawn carriage (the kind you could rent now in lieu of taxis), all the way from the Champs-Elysées to the Bois de Boulogne, one fine day in the early spring, when I was once more subjected to the exquisite torture, but in full sight of the public, this time. To take advantage of my weakness in such a blatant manner—that was too much. I decided that I could stand no more, I must deal with her, or I would have to renounce her.

But the routine between us was already much too solidly established. The only way to break it, I decided, would be to take her on a trip, somewhere, as far away from Paris as possible. Slyly, I made the suggestion to her, and her response was instant. She was all for it, but when she asked, "Where do we go?" I felt like a fool because the fact is that, of course, traveling was virtually impossible, except once more to Fontainebleau. But we were both familiar with these woods, there was no true romantic novelty there, and I knew that the place was teeming with loudmouthed buddies of mine, and one of them would be sure to find us at some crucial moment.

"To Mont-Saint-Michel!" I said without thinking. More

as a joke than a serious suggestion—which I immediately regretted.

She was jumping up and down with glee, her dark blue eyes scintillating; and she wouldn't even listen to what I said from then on to explain that it was a rotten idea after all. Of course, I insisted, it was much too far, transportation being what it was, and the place itself was situated in a restricted coastal region, at the very border of Normandy and Brittany, which was being fortified by the Germans. Did she know that its access was strictly *verboten* to anyone who was not a resident? Even if we reached the Mont, which would take nothing short of a major miracle, we were sure to land in prison as soon as we got there.

"But don't you *believe* in miracles?" she asked in a tone of intense surprise. "Listen, Saint Michel happens to be one of my big favorites! The dragon slayer. When do we go? I'm dying to see that place, I've heard that it is so stunning, so majestic, so wild and beautiful. . . ."

Wild and beautiful, then, that's my baby. How can I reason with her? The lack of a German permit, the indispensable *ausweis*, did not phase her in the least. Plus, there were no trains from Paris; we would have to change maybe five or six times from one little old ricketyboop local railway to the next, and their schedules were known to be hopelessly erratic. . . . But none of that seemed to impress her in the least. I was also very acutely aware of the fact that my only official papers consisted of a phony identity card, purchased once upon a time from a crooked bartender. But I was careful not to bring up that particular point since she would have been sure to accuse me of rank cowardice.

What the hell, then, *let's go!* Perhaps she's right and Saint Michel will take care of us; at least no one else will. And taking a good look at her radiant face, I swore to myself that before the end of that desperate adventure, I would triumph—well, one way or another. If you don't give yourself to me of your own free will, I will take *you!* I threatened her—inwardly. Just like that! Rape, so to speak. If that is the only way. . . . Well, hmm . . . I would have to think about it. I had never raped anyone as yet.

On the appointed day I rose early, before daybreak in fact, and arrived at boulevard Suchet to pick her up, in a fever of anticipation; and this did not diminish in the least when she opened her door, offering herself coyly to my admiration, all dressed up in her own version of a traveling outfit. Breathtaking, oh yes.

Her shorts, to start with the most obvious item: There is enough right there to make any real man lose his mind instantly. Her blouse is made of wide-meshed silk net, the same warm tint as her skin, leaving the aureolae perfectly visible, the color of burnt roses. Thank heavens, those uncanny legs of hers now stand in sturdy walking boots with thick studded soles, which is reassuring, especially insofar as it offers protection against those predatory feet. On her back, a haute couture version of a knapsack is affixed to her lovely rounded shoulders with straps of black velvet; and one assumes that this so-called knapsack is filled with ribbons and perfumes, and not one single useful object. . . . On her pretty blond head a spectacular ragamuffin's hat, also made of black velvet, is posed at a jaunty angle so that one eye is hidden. With the other she is contemplating my gaping face with some amusement.

"You like it?" she asks pleasantly, rotating in a model's pirouette to make sure that I won't miss anything.

I catch my breath, torn between desire and terror. "Listen, Marina, it's . . . it's absolutely *stupendous!* But you know, we have to take the subway to go to the railway station . . . and . . . and it's a bit chilly outside at this ungodly hour, you know, really. Don't you have a pair of *warm pants* in your lovely knapsack? And perhaps *a sweater*, ah hem . . . ," I finish lamely.

She gives me a terrific blast from her blue eyes.

"My friend! I have spent an entire day getting ready for this excursion, sewing, trimming, ironing, and traveling to the other end of the city to get what I didn't have. And now *you* want me to put on some old trousers? Do I have to hide my legs, am I knock-kneed, or something?"

"Oh no, no!" I exclaim in despair. "Your legs are in fact too good to be true. . . . But it's just that a war is going on, don't you understand? . . ."

"*What does that have to do with my clothes?*" she hisses. "Oh, you make me *so* mad. You've just ruined my pleasure, you idiot. Look at yourself in your baggy pants, you think you look smart, eh? Listen, what I am wearing now I designed especially to wear to Mont-Saint-Michel. It's obvious that you know *nothing at all* about fashion. This is the way *I* intend to travel, and *you* can stay behind and knit me a pullover if you want."

What can a fellow do? Sheepishly I amble after her out in the open boulevard, all too conscious of what is bound to follow. I know the Parisians, the French, rabid sex maniacs all; a band of rapists will attack us at the next street corner, and that will be the end of it.

Fortunately, it is so early the streets are empty, and there's hardly a soul in the *métro*. Even rapists need their beauty sleep, it seems. . . . What I feared most was the Saint-Lazare station, and indeed it is heavily populated with the working class, and crisscrossed by various types of police. To my amazement nothing happens. A lot of ogling, for sure, and some whistles are heard, but there is such an air to that half-nude traveler that none of the early morning Casanovas dares try his hand at seduction. She is just magnificent. Even the train conductor gasps when he sees her marching up to him; he helps her find a seat for the two of us, and even brings up her knapsack, which no train conductor has ever been known to do in the entire history of French railroad transportation.

After that auspicious start, the trip proved to be just as awful as I had anticipated. In fact, much worse. You should have seen the once superb Marina, now encrusted with grime, groggy with fatigue, and dressed in a moldy sweater and an old pair of dungarees she had finally grudgingly accepted from me. We tried to snatch bits of sleep in waiting rooms, as the unpredictable schedules made it impossible to seek hotel rooms. In Dôle, where we arrived at three in the morning, we were allowed to sit in the decrepit old train that was due to start off at seven, if everything went well, to bring us as close as we would ever get to our goal by rail; that is, to Avranches. And so we settled down on the hard wooden board that served as a seat, in pitch-darkness, vaguely aware of someone deeply asleep on the bench across from ours. We were starving, freezing, dizzy with exhaustion, utterly spent. But under my right arm, against my side, I was holding Marina tightly against me, and I could count the beats of her heart, and the powerful mixture of bliss and misery filled my head with fiery hallucinations. Did she sleep, did I, or were we daydreaming our way through the night? Whatever would happen to us later, jointly or separately, I knew that those four hours would remain as a time of truce, a time when the duel over sex and other metaphors had been brought to a draw. A very fragile moment. I sit in the dark, counting minutes, counting her heartbeats, having quite forgotten everything else, waiting for dawn, for shattering happiness; and, yes (where is it we are supposed to be traveling to?) for Mont-Saint-Michel as well.

When dawn comes, it reveals to us the facts of life, alas, once again. Out of the penumbra slowly emerges the gray sadness common to all French railway stations, the regulation signs and posters, all the built-in mediocrity typical of the Third Republic, now deceased, and of its dull bureaucratic architecture.

Daylight also reveals a pair of white socks on the seat opposite ours, which belong to what proves to be a hunchback. He sits up, stretches himself, yawns, looks at us, blinks his eyes, breaks up with laughter like a true maniac; gets up and leaves. Very unsettling. Whereupon the train makes its chaotic and noisy start, and proceeds along a happy-go-lucky route through a series of fulsome, rich verdant Normand landscapes to Avranches.

We are heading for the forbidden zone, and from now on we are on our own. Since Avranches is situated on one side of a large bay across from our goal, we will have to walk some twenty-five kilometers to reach it, and we will run the risk of being intercepted by the German military police at every step of the way.

The station itself was teeming with German troops. Marina, as usual, glides over those contingencies, breezy and magnificent, with such assurance that the herd moves out of her way, opening a passage for us as if she were the queen of Prussia accompanied by her valet. All I have to do is to follow closely as we walk out of the station, out of the city.

In spite of the intense fatigue it's a wonderful feeling to be back in the open, joyfully treading the country road and filling our lungs with the light tangy breeze coming from the sea. We are equals now at last, two tramps on the road.

"So far so good," I declare. "But what do we do when we meet a patrol?"

"Nothing," Marina answers. "If they ask questions, just pretend that you don't speak the language. *'Me no understand.'* That's simple. Stare at them stupidly; you know how to do that, eh? But listen, why do you have to worry so much about everything *all the time?*"

What can one do except grit one's teeth until it hurts? The witch, the bitch! But the fact is, just looking at her *sideways* is enough to make me tremble. Those grotesque old pants she is wearing are mine, and so is the discolored sweater; and this gives me, somehow, the ludicrous feeling that I actually *own* the person who dwells inside these rags of mine. Here is the hobo with the smoothest skin and the roundest behind one has ever seen in these pants, for sure. Sweet hobo! Soon to be mine.

This is one of the reasons why I try so hard to keep our pace brisk. But with *her*, such male attitudes will never prevail. Hers are dictated by the mood of the moment: What's the big hurry? Let's enjoy the rolling countryside, the hedgerows and the meadows, all studded with spring daisies, buttercups, and forget-me-nots. And there she goes, running after butterflies, chewing the cud with a cow in a field, saluting the birds wide and large with her velvet sombrero. How am I supposed to keep her on the road, walking in a straight line? After complaining of the heat, she disappears to show up again in her former scandalous outfit. My protest is blissfully ignored; I am told to shut up, that I am disturbing the peace of the day.

As the air becomes heavier and more sultry, we reach a point from which we can discover, across a wide expanse of reed-laden marshes and open waters, the legendary profile of the Mont, the enigmatic figure remembered so clearly from the old engravings, the old memories, embossed in dark silver on a light gray background. The sky is low, heavy banks of clouds are forming an immense, tumultuous backdrop over the flat maritime horizon. By contrast with the stormy spectacle in the heavens, everything lies still in the world below, there's hardly any breeze at all anymore, all is quiet and silent in the stifling midafternoon torpor. Standing side by side we stare in wonder, in silent awe. Here is our goal, the symbol of victory, where winner takes all in the very human game we've been playing with each other. Yes, when eventually we reach that mysterious rock across the bay, she will give herself to me; although this was never said in so many words, it is our secret understanding. . . . I feel weak with expectation. . . . But it is so far, still, will we ever get there? Saint Michel, knight of the deep sapphire, lend me your star and your sword, this victory will indeed be yours.

But, rather than such fairy-tale equipment, it is crutches that we really need, in fact, so great is our fatigue. I still manage to struggle on, but my companion threatens to stop for a nap each time we pass a convenient bush. We haven't had any real food for I don't know how long, apart from some bread and cheese bought in Avranches, but it is thirst that tortures us most. In the end we decide to throw caution to the winds, and bravely knock on the door of a farmhouse to ask for a drink.

The woman who opens the door stifles a gasp when she sees us, looking wide-eyed at Marina's legs.

"My, my, you young people must be out of your minds, going on the roads dressed like that. . . . I mean the lady. . . . If my husband were here he would have a fit. . . . But please come in, I have some good cider for you. . . . You live around here?" she asks incredulously.

"No, we come from Paris."

I know I shouldn't have said that, but how else can I explain Marina's special Mont-Saint-Michel attire?

"Oh my, my, *Paris* . . ." says the woman. "My cousin Eugene was there once, before the war, for the Exhibition, in '37. . . . How's my cider? Cool, eh?"

"In fact, I love it so much," Marina answers, "I'd like some more. Could we take a bottle for the road?"

The cider is wonderfully refreshing, but very strong. As we get up to go the lady of the house opens the door for us, and I am about to zigzag past her when I see from the corner of my eye a half-track turning onto the road silently from behind a neighboring farmhouse, loaded with Germans, some with the breastplate of the feldgendarmerie, their rifles at the ready, peering right and left from under the rim of their helmets. Turning around I close the door briskly, as if struck by an afterthought, and ask the woman if we could have a *second* bottle of cider to take with us?

"Oh yes," says Marina. "You're getting to be *so smart* since you started traveling with me, aren't you?"

She may joke all she wants, but this was too close a close shave for my comfort. Perhaps we *really* are under Saint Michel's personal protection? Let him take care of those evil men in green, then! The poetic cider has improved things considerably; a few yards ahead of me Marina in her black velvet hat and heavy boots is dancing her version of *Swan Lake*, showing off her pretty legs for the benefit of some sheep and a donkey in a field. And perhaps for me as well?

After a period of alcoholic elation, we both start feeling

very low once again. That was predictable. Marina complains that her knapsack is too heavy; I take it from her, and pile it up on top of mine.

"You're really such a sweet beast," she tells me with a weak smile, and a tap on the cheek.

"Oink, oink, honk-honk, glop," I happily respond.

"And now help me walk straight. I am drunk, dead and done. Hold me, I know I can trust you. Tell me, will we ever get there?"

Arm-in-arm we struggle on, led by our blind determination. Why we must try so hard to reach that particular destination, what it is that draws us there so strongly, and why did we ever decide to go there in the first place—all that is part and parcel of our past. Our present is nothing but hard, sweaty work. But our future is beckoning; our nuptial chamber awaits us at the top of that rock. Three more kilometers to go . . . two . . . one. . . .

And then we arrive; that is, alas, we arrive not at the Mont itself, only at the entrance to the interminable jetty that leads to it. We have been misled by the signposts. Marina lets out a loud incoherent yelp in Greek, collapses, and sprawls out on the roadside, feigning death. Right in front of me the wide jetty recedes far into the distance, narrowing to an invisible point, as in a diagram meant to teach perspective to school children. It must be three hundred kilometers long; or at least three. I feel weak and dizzy. What am I going to do? How am I going to get her started again? It seems to take me hours to shake her up from her lethargy, to pull her back on her feet, until we resume our step-by-step approach.

As we come closer, dazedly limping along, the fortified shrine appears slowly to rise in a cluster of prodigious verticals, an entanglement of sheer walls and buttresses, with a network of steep staircases that serve as streets. The immense rock, surging from the shallow sea, stands glorious and alone in the midst of quicksands and low waters; the medieval builders have patiently sculpted it, century after century, into a monolithic prayer. Above the heavy towers and the narrow dwellings of the old city rises the castle serving as a foundation to the cloisters and, as a crowning jewel, Saint Michel's Gothic basilica, known as La Merveille. And in turn, we know that at the summit of its delicate spire stands a gold effigy of the archangel, his sword uplifted, whose point aims at the very heart of the heavens.

As we walk under the deep vaulted archway past the outer walls, I grasp her hand, and she turns to smile at me; her face may be caked with dirt, but she has already quite forgotten her ordeal. We are now in the heart of the enemy fortress, and also back in the Middle Ages, just as if we had landed in a painting from a book of hours; those soldiers swarming around us, wearing steel and leather like warriors of old, one feels certain that they were here already during the Hundred Years' War. In fact we find only very few civilians inside the Mont, which is part of the German coastal defense system, apart from a few residents who have been allowed to stay and who all seem to serve the military in some capacity or other. But tourists and pilgrims are denied access, no one who doesn't belong is allowed to spend the night here; the two or three small hotels have been requisitioned by the German brass. As in Avranches we are finding ourselves in the thick of the German military; and it seems that we owe our safety simply to the fact that our presence in their midst defies the rules of common sense to such an extent that, once again, they prefer to ignore us rather than ask us to account for ourselves.

But Saint Michel's protection is truly working in our favor, and here's another proof of it. After climbing the endless steps to the very top, we find a small hotel there, whose proprietor has saved a room for himself that he seems willing to rent, for a hefty price. "My very best one," says that wily Normand with the red nose; and has us pay in advance. Ominous. I have a suspicion that we've been had.

Since we expect the worst, our surprise is all the more pleasant when we discover to what extent he has refrained from cheating us. The room is very large, with a low ceiling, beams everywhere and all sorts of windows opening onto a rambling balcony. From there we discover a vast horizon of sky and sea, and steep slated roofs far beneath us, which give us the feeling of being in flight, far above the surface of the earth, like those sea gulls we see floating and weaving in the air currents, above and below us.

But what appears to me as the most immediately attractive item in this wonderful room is the huge, heavy four-poster in dark polished cherrywood. So inviting that I lie down to try it and—quite forgetting what I had come for—immediately fall deeply asleep.

Much later, upon waking up, I find that all is dark inside the room as well as outside, except for a small pocket of soft light, the dressing table where Marina is sitting between the twin halos of two candles, meditatively gazing at her perfect face in a large, cracked mirror. She has her back to me and she is in the last steps of some subtle grooming operation, certainly a delicate affair; from under half-closed lids I savor the scene at leisure. Her magnificent chignon forms an interesting contrast with the simplicity of her white dress, and three strings of pearls enhance the perfect curve of her shoulders. Her feet are free again, naked and alive in high-heeled silver sandals. She is perfectly groomed and dressed for a peacetime outing, cocktails at the Ritz and perhaps a play, before supper at our little table at Chez Maxim's. . . . But here, in the midst of this enemy garrison, her perfect Parisian elegance looks like pure provocation; something like Pierre Fresnay washing his white linen gloves in *La Grande Illusion*.

"Marina," I breathe helplessly from the shadows, "how perfectly exquisite. So, you had an evening gown in your knapsack? I should have known."

"Oh, you're awake at last, lazy bones," she chides me. "Listen, I am just simply famished, we have to go and get ourselves some dinner. Get up and let's try La Mère Poulard. It seemed to be open when we passed it on the way up."

"But it's too late now, I'm sure," I answer. "Besides all the customers there are bound to be Germans . . ."

"So what?" says Marina. "Hurry up, I'm on my way."

She hardly gives me time to wash up and slip into a clean shirt, and already she is heard running down the stairs in a clatter of spikes. We are back in the street of stairs, the high walls now lost in powdery blackness. Muffled German voices are heard in the dark, and the red glow of cigarettes pinpoints presences all around us. Shadowy men in uniforms bow respectfully as they make way for the lovely apparition in white, no doubt a guest of the general. Why should I ever worry anymore about identity cards and such trifles? All I need is to have Marina with me.

When we reach La Mère Poulard it is just closing; but as the owner sees Marina entering his establishment, he switches on his chandeliers precipitously, and welcomes us to the dining room as if we were royalty.

"And what does Madame wish to drink? Champagne? But

certainly. Our best? That would surely be the Veuve Cliquot 1934, *tête de cuvée*. Right away, madame, monsieur, at your service."

"All this thanks to you," I tell Marina as the man leaves us at last to ourselves. "It's quite wonderful here, except that I can't tell you that you are the most beautiful woman in the room, since you have no rivals. I will have to say it in some other way."

She gracefully acknowledges my strenuous compliment with a wan smile, the very image of a jaded socialite.

"You could also try the direct approach," she remarks in an offhand, conversational tone.

Those words immediately trigger in me a rush of mad hope, anger, and dismay, in equal proportions; but before I can think of a response the conversation is being brought back mercilessly to the subject of Laurette, who she always professes to admire, and of Vivian, my erstwhile guru. Marina wants me to describe in detail the scene of my excommunication from the group. My story seems to make her quite angry.

"That man is trying *so hard* to make us believe that he's a true-blue guru! That Vivian, I assure you that he's no more than a common pimp. All gurus are pimps anyway. Guru is not a man, it's a function, it is like a powder spread out in the atmosphere. You catch it like spring fever, it's not something anyone ever owns, or can use on others as a special gift . . ."

She looks at me dreamily.

"*Right*, Maurice?" she asks.

With that question the diabolical foot attacks me so suddenly, and frontally, so to speak, under the tablecloth that I send the ice bucket flying off the table.

"*Ouch!* Yes, Marina!" I implore her. "Anything you say! But can't you tell your guru, er, I mean, your *foot* to leave me alone? Just this once?"

"My *what?*" she asks, with the distant air of someone who has just heard something distasteful and proposes to sweep it back under the rug.

"You know what I mean," I say bravely, blushing a bit, but determined to confront her.

"Well, I see you've grown pretty audacious since you travel around with me," she says in a low voice, very smooth. And then she looks at me with a level glance. Dangerous. "Very well, young man," she adds in a businesslike manner. "We'll see what we can do about it. Why don't you ask for the bill?"

So that's it then. That's the wedding bells I hear chiming. Of course I would prefer her to be a bit less, well, less *crusty*, shall we say. But I know that behind this surface Marina there is another creature of a very different quality.

As I follow her out of the restaurant, I proudly admire her regal bearing, the superb, practiced manner in which she effects her *sortie*, just as if each one of those white, empty tables were occupied by droves of ogling monocled gentlemen.

The moon is now up, and although as yet unseen, it brings out of the night fragments of roofs and gables detached from any logical design. Security measures are enforced even more strictly here on the coast than in the cities, and not the smallest light is allowed to filter through. From our balcony high under the stars we can hardly guess which way Avranches lies. Between our arrival this morning in that city and the present moment there is a distance as between two worlds. All signs of human presence have been erased from this pure lunar landscape before us, made of quicksands and shallow silver waters. The wandering river, the Couesnon, is said to pursue its course right under the distant sea; and at the time of the equinox the tides are known to rush over this immense no-man's-land at the speed of a galloping horse. Other worlds are faintly perceived behind the burnished surface; many levels of half-seen underwater reflections mirror our world of thinkers, of stone carvers, in dark, disincarnate perspectives.

"Don't turn around," she calls suddenly from inside. "I did not bring a nightie with me, I'll tell you when you can look."

What did she say? *A nightie?* What use would she have for such a garment? With a surge of helpless despair I realize that I've been cheated, again. . . . That woman is simply bent on destroying me, I don't know why, but I can see it now, so clearly. She only gave me hope in order to laugh at me; she is pure evil, an incurable sadist. I should have known better— ever since the first time. . . . But here I am, always the fool, absolutely hopeless. As I gaze at the vast romantic landscape at my feet, without seeing it, I begin to feel very sorry for myself. Quite desperate in fact.

"Slowly now," comes her voice again, quite low, and so soft, hardly audible from that distance. "Very, *very* slowly. You may turn around now."

Thereafter no more words will be used by either of us, not for a long time. As none are necessary, and none could ever prove adequate. Right now total silence reigns in the room, and as I turn away in slow motion from the balcony, a wonderful female nude comes into view, smoothly rounded and velvety in the dim candlelight, as if posing elegantly for spectators gaping at a fashionable erotic show window.

There is sauciness too in the display, a certain seductive tartness in the way she wears those three rings of pearls, and the high-heeled sandals of shining silver, and nothing else. With proud detachment she exhibits the remarkable body she is about to deliver to my care. Motionless, with the distant, staring expression of a wax beauty. Is this a real person? My fingers begin to itch, but I know that they must be held in check. *She* is the one in command of the ritual, which must be slow and respectful. I realize that I am not to question her will: She knows best, now is the time to simply look, admire, desire.

The eyes strain to absorb all of this exciting spectacle, the opulent honey-colored woman-body emphasized by its still adolescent waist. As I circle around her perfectly motionless form, like a wonderstruck student, I try to guess what thoughts she can be hiding right now behind that fixed, vacuous expression: but the haughty mannequin look painted on her face is clearly contradicted by certain signs, in particular by the taughtness of her round breasts, her quickened breathing, quite audible now. . . . Perhaps also by a little dampness I seem to detect, upon close inspection, on her upper lip. . . .

It seems that the best position for me to play the wily game she has invented for the two of us will be right there, behind her flawless back, where she cannot see me or read my thoughts. From there I can breathe in her strong musky fragrance; it is exhilarating to be able at last to pay her in kind, even if it's only a waiting game. I can sense the great hunger invading her flesh, a hunger that's clearly about to overcome that famous iron will of hers. . . . But of course there had to be a time when, finally, my hands themselves can stand the suspense no more, and my fingers sink deep, convulsively, into her flesh, which is rigid and vibrant below its downy surface. Under the urgent work of my hands I feel all of a sudden her body beginning to collapse.

Joyfully I acknowledge to myself that hard-won victory, and when she crashes heavily into my arms, at long last, I gather all of her against me, my thing, my baby, and I stagger toward the bed, half-crazed by fatigue and by desire, by her low, continuous keening, and by the irresistible love perfume coming from our two bodies. We fall into a sweaty heap into the white softness, but I still find enough will power somewhere in me to carefully untie her silver shoes, and to kiss her feet gently, fondly, gratefully, admiringly.

And then all paradise breaks loose; in a raging embrace we fall right out of this world. The night devours us, a night full of helpless whimperings, of half-words vainly attempting to translate ecstasy. Each act of sex becomes an act of concrete love, each caress leads to a climax of adoration. The night is restless, heavy with passion, fiery, inexhaustible.

Opening one eye at daybreak, I realize that we must have eventually fallen asleep; and thus I awake for the first time really a man. What happiness it is to be the friend of a woman such as the one who lies in a profusion of pearls on the great rustic bed by my side, deeply asleep, naked and peaceful, with the traces of a smile of gentle irony still caressing her pretty pink mouth.